(147)

(886)

The
Fred
Chappell
Reader

Books by Fred Chappell

NOVELS

It Is Time, Lord
The Inkling
Dagon
The Gaudy Place
I Am One of You Forever

SHORT STORIES

Moments of Light

POETRY

The World Between the Eyes
River
The Man Twice Married to Fire
Bloodfire
Awakening to Music
Wind Mountain
Earthsleep
Driftlake: A Lieder Cycle
Midquest
Castle Tzingal
Source

THE FRED CHAPPELL READER

FRED CHAPPELL

Introduction by
DABNEY STUART

St. Martin's Press/*New York*

"Humility" and "Child in the Fog" were first published in the *Sewanee Review* 85 (summer 1977). Copyright © 1977 by the University of the South. Reprinted by permission of the editor.

The essay "A Pact with Faustus" first appeared in *Mississippi Quarterly*, Volume XXXVII (1984). Reprinted by permission of the editor.

"Linneaus Forgets" is copyright © 1977 by Fred Chappell; originally appeared in *American Review* #26, published by Bantam Books, Inc.

"Notes Toward a Theory of Flight" is copyright © 1987 by Fred Chappell.

It is Time, Lord © 1963 by Fred Chappell; *The Inkling* © 1965 by Fred Chappell; *Dagon* © 1968 by Fred Chappell; *The Gaudy Place* © 1972 by Fred Chappell. Reprinted by permission of the author.

"Mrs. Franklin Ascends," "Thatch Retaliates," "Moments of Light," "The Thousand Ways," "Children of Strikers," and "Blue Dive" originally appeared in *Moments of Light*, © 1980 by The New South Company. Reprinted by permission of The New South Company.

The World Between the Eyes © 1971 by Fred Chappell; *Midquest* © 1981 by Fred Chappell; *Castle Tzingal* © 1984 by Fred Chappell; *I Am One of You Forever* © 1985 by Fred Chappell; *Source* © 1985 by Fred Chappell. Reprinted by permission of Louisiana State University Press.

Design by Manuela Paul

Library of Congress Cataloging-in-Publication Data

Chappell, Fred, 1936–
    The Fred Chappell reader.

    I. Title.
PS3553.H298A6   1987   818'.5409   86-26236
ISBN 0-312-00012-X

First Edition
10   9   8   7   6   5   4   3   2   1

I love, Susan, you.

CONTENTS

III. Poetry

Contents

"WHAT'S ARTICHOKES?":
An Introduction to the Work of Fred Chappell

> *The child is father to the man, we say. Let me then praise my father, even salute him: for he stood there without any ulterior motive, furtively gazing into heaven: he didn't make a song about it, didn't dream of writing it up as a poem to be praised and admired—just stood there and gaped!*
>
> —*John Stewart Collis*

*I*n *Poison Pen*, his recent compendium of cultural and literary satire, novelist and poet George Garrett, faintly disguised, calls Fred Chappell the John-Boy Walton of American poetry. It's a facetious remark, of course, but there's enough truth in it to afford an unexpected entrance to Fred Chappell's work. Chappell was born May 28, 1936, and grew up on a farm in Canton, near Asheville, North Carolina, but his family poems in *Midquest* give a tougher, less whimsical access to the kind of hardscrabble farm life popularized in Earl Hamner's television series.

Midquest's narrator, "Ole Fred"—composed of Chappell's attitudes, memories, and experiences, but not identical with the author—celebrates his thirty-fifth birthday in four groups of poems, one series each for the elements once believed to have been the components of all matter—earth, air, fire, and water. He begins the second poem of the volume by quoting Dante—"Midway in this life I came to a darksome wood"—establishing another classical basis for what follows. I will come back to this, but the focus for now is Ole Fred's family, which populates the volume via monologue and dialogue (with Fred as a boy), centering its down-home humor, grit, and independence.

His grandparents and parents are the principals, sharply individualized, economically rendered, living at harmonious odds with each other in hard times, honoring each other's idiosyncrasies, complementing strength with weakness, weakness with strength. The mother's account of her unique courtship—J.T., who taught at the same schoolhouse, borrowed her slip to use in his class experiments with electricity, flying it past her window like Ben Franklin's kite—acts as a screen memory that helps her not dwell too closely on how difficult life actually was. Her real code word is "hard." Fred's father, for whom money is scarce and a burden simultaneously ("Thinking of nothing but money makes me sick") burns a dollar bill to assert his freedom, and in another instance makes up for his son a beguiling tale in which he itemizes the contents of the layers of a hurricane. For the grandmother it's the disintegration of the family that is worrisome. Noting Fred's "bookishness," she fears he'll grow up to be a lawyer, becoming "second-generation-respectable." She also believes he can never cut loose from his roots altogether; she says to him,

> "Not all the money in this world can wash true-poor
> True rich. Fatback just won't change to artichokes."
>
> "What's artichokes?"
>
>   "Pray Jesus you'll never know.
> For if you do it'll be a sign you've grown
> Away from what you are. . . ."

Another central character, though not family, is Virgil Campbell, who runs a general store and generally keeps the community from hunkering too morosely on its problems. His first name echoes his literary predecessor, but one of the pitfalls Chappell successfully skirts is solemnity, and his guide through the difficulties of daily life navigates by means of humor. "Campbell," he writes in the introduction to *Midquest*, "is supposed to give to the whole its specifically regional, its Appalachian, context." In "Dead Soldiers," instead of recalling disaster and loss, the focus is on Campbell's shooting his emptied jars of whiskey as they float from the basement of his store on floodwater. Eventually the bridge just upriver starts to sway and groan, so he takes a shot at it as it falls, bcoming known as the man who killed the bridge.

There is, of course, more to such procedures than fun. Humor's relationship to survival and sanity is a matter for celebration on any account. To this Chappell adds, as a premise on which his "character" poems rest, the understanding of the psyche's way of turning its attention aside from events of disaster and grief to scenes and activities obliquely attached to them. Too direct a memory numbs; the indirect route makes us able to continue the trip. It's a compromise struck between facing reality head on and trying to evade it altogether, and is one reason this aspect of Chappell's work, though affectionate and open, is bracingly unsentimental (which helps, incidentally, to distinguish him further as a storyteller from John-Boy Walton).

The focus on rural character and situation I have approached through *Midquest* extends, unsurprisingly, into Chappell's prose as well. A cluster of four stories in *Moments of Light* could be considered as stages in the declension of the life of Mark Vance from the coherencies of rural experience to the debilitation of the city. Though he is not uniformly happy as a boy on the farm—indeed, one observes in his inattention and lack of will the seeds of later problems—he is nonetheless in an environment that requires certain contributions from him necessary to survival. If he doesn't get water to his father at work in the long sun, for instance, the man's labor will be more tortuous; if he's not responsible with his ignorance about items such as blasting caps, his life is at risk. He is also surrounded by people who care about him, and who seek to help him grow into a productive place among the family and its traditions.

In the university town where we later see him, however, he is cut off from such people and the land with which they share a covenant of nurture and increase. The result is a harrowing rootlessness. To feel how sharply Chappell suggests the disparity of the two environments one could compare the good-humored, brightly surprising introduction to sex Rosemary gives Mark (in "The Weather") with the dissolute, hollow visit he has with Norma in "The Thousand Ways."

One of the few black characters in Chappell's fiction, Stovebolt Johnson in "Blue Dive," acts as a central instance of civility, decorum, and balanced regard for both himself and other people. The dramatic structure again involves the paradigmatic polarization of rural and urban. This time, however, Chappell puts the big city dude—Locklear Hawkins, who runs the dive where Johnson seeks a job as a guitarist —in farm country, an inversion that enables him to have Johnson play with the homefield advantage. His ability to restrain his anger under considerable pressure is in part due to his being surrounded by people whose pace and habits he is familiar with and can therefore draw succor and support from. Chappell's phrase for a central quality of farmers is "inspired patience," an attribute that Johnson, though not a farmer, embodies.

Although over half of *Moments of Light* deals with other subjects, Chappell sets all of *I Am One of You Forever* on a farm. It is a series of stories, too, but they are loosely connected through form and characters to approximate a novel. Chappell's use of humorous exaggeration in many of the chapters is an obvious indication of the book's genial tone. *I Am One of You Forever* is also his most extensive dramatization of the values of a farm family's cohesion and support, which foster the mutual independence and growth of its members.

The various eccentric uncles who visit young Jess and his parents become involved in situations whose familiar American hyperbole (à la Paul Bunyan, Epaminondas, and Mark Twain) is, first of all, entertaining. It is also, I think, suggestive of one of the necessities in a kind of life whose intimacy and death-defying routine are always simmering tensions that might eventually erupt in strife and disharmony. That necessity is the acceptance of idiosyncrasy and outright craziness. A farm family has to make room for its loonies, much as certain tribes of native Americans once did. Again, the issue is survival, and comic inventiveness plays a basic role.

One of the uncles out–Don Juans his namesake until his life is bogusly threatened; another's beard grows to incredible lengths; another, when he comes to visit, brings his coffin and sleeps in it. The pleasure of observing young Jess watch these men includes seeing him become alternately curious about and afraid of them, and, eventually, with his father's help, learning to incorporate them into his sense of life and its possibilities. Chappell complicates those possibilities by interpolating other considerations through occasional non-uncle chapters. The audience he desires, whatever else it may be, is not naive. Humor isn't escape, but accommodation; Chappell romanticizes neither it nor country life. Jess must confront, among other things, the loss of a close friend, the challenge of competition with other men, and the eternal need on a farm to rebuild what nature destroys and will destroy again. The following paragraph concludes "Overspill," a story about just such a destruction. Jess's mother has come home to find that the bridge built for her has been brought to nothing by a flood.

> *The tear on my mother's cheek got larger and larger. It detached from her face and became a shiny globe, widening outward like an inflating balloon. At first the tear floated in air between them, but as it expanded it took my mother and father into itself. I saw them suspended, separate but beginning to drift slowly toward one another. Then my mother looked past my father's shoulder, looked through the bright skin of the tear, at me. The tear enlarged until at last it took me in too. It was warm and salt. As soon as I got used to the strange light inside the tear, I began to swim clumsily toward my parents.*

Jess's vision here reveals better than any commentary the complex centrality of family life as I have been discussing it in Fred Chappell's work. But if he was born and raised in rural western North Carolina, he went east to a fancy college, "deserting," he says, "manual for intellectual labor," and has made his living as a teacher of literature and writing for twenty-two years. It would be a shock similar to encountering a black hole in space if his fiction and poetry didn't reflect the part humane letters has played in his life, too.

Chappell has been around long enough, in fact, for apocryphal rumors to have sprouted. He is alleged to have started writing before he could talk, and in his early teens to have printed reams of science fiction stories under an undivulged pseudonym. Fortunately, more dependable information is available about him as a poet in high school, and later during his checkered undergraduate career at Duke University.

His "Rimbaud Fire Letter to Jim Applewhite" (in the *Bloodfire* section of *Midquest*) reveals, from an affectionately amused adult perspective, something of the intensity with which he immersed himself in his image of the feverish young *auteur*.

> Four things I knew: Rimbaud was genius pure;
> The colors of the vowels and verb tenses;
> That civilization was going up in fire;
> And how to derange every last one of my senses:
> Kind of a handbook on how to be weird and silly.

I don't want to veer toward biography here so much as to point at the fierce allegiance, however adolescent, to literature the poem recounts. It is one of three such letters in *Midquest*, written to other authors, that focus this allegiance, as well as a few of its particular objects: Rimbaud, Dante, and science fiction authors, especially Poe, H. P. Lovecraft, and H. G. Wells.

A cursory skimming of *Midquest* will show how pervasive Dante is, for instance. The conception of the book, as well as much of its overall structure, derives from *The Divine Comedy*. I've already mentioned the "darksome wood" beginnings of both poems, and Virgil Campbell's kinship to the Roman epic poet who guides Dante through hell to heaven. That *Midquest* lacks the inclusive theological system of Dante's trilogy is part of its meaning. It is, after all, written three-quarters of the way through an exhaustingly secular century, determined, it sometimes appears, to exceed past human horrors without the hope the church afforded in previous times. Chappell's poem, however, is no less serious in its scope and intention than *The Divine Comedy*; God and the Bible suffuse it. There are descents into hell ("Cleaning the Well"), rebirths ("Bloodfire," "Fire Now Wakening on the River"), frequent ponderings on flesh and spirit ("Firewood"), and no embarrassment accompanies the evocation of the spirits of the dead.

From this perspective even the discussion of literature in the playlet "Hallowind" (whose title, too, has religious implications) assumes an added spiritual dimension. Note this exchange between Ole Fred, Reynolds Price, and the personified rain:

FRED: The most symbolic line there is,
And fullest of hard realities,
Is Shakespearean: "Exeunt omnes."

REYNOLDS: Your poet's a foe to love and laughter.
Here's the line one gives one's life for:
"They all lived happily ever after."

THE RAIN: What say we work us up some brio
And drown this silly wayward trio?
My favorite line is "Ex Nihilo."

From "Ex Nihilo," with its suggestion of the creation, to "exeunt omnes" covers much of the ground human beings travel. When the narrator prays at the close of the opening poem in *Earthsleep*, "Hello Destiny, I'm harmless Fred,/ Treat me sweet Please," he isn't asking for a favorable literary reputation.

The Divine Comedy is to *Midquest* as Vergil to Dante, I think. This is the most important antecedent evident in the poem, though Chaucer's *Canterbury Tales*, Byron's two comic epics, Browning's monologists, and Chekhov's tender, clear-eyed stories exert their acknowledged influences as well. Chappell cites others in his preface, adding that "some of the grand idols of my admiration—Baudelaire, Rimbaud, Rilke, Pound—did not show up, or appeared only in order to be made fun of."

It is in Chappell's early novels that those grand idols exert their power without the filter of distance and humor, more by their example of intoxicated, romantic sacrifice of everything for literature ("Be drunk with something," Baudelaire urged) than by any specific borrowing Chappell does. Thomas Mann and William Faulkner are among the more accessible pantries he raids for particular goodies, using shifting time perspectives and narration within narration in *It Is Time, Lord*, and, in *The Inkling* and *Dagon*, a sweaty determinism reminiscent of *The Sound and the Fury*. *The Gaudy Place*, a sprightlier, less hermetic book, has the multiple narrators of *As I Lay Dying*, as well as something of its mordant humor.

Still, taken together, Chappell's first four novels are very much his own; they receive a fine extended discussion by R. H. W. Dillard in *The Hollins Critic* (Volume X, Number 2). From the wider perspective of his later work, the first three of them constitute a little package of experiment and exorcism, a descent into the maelstrom it appears now to have been necessary to hazard and survive. They honor, as does all Chappell's output, the darker, inarticulate regions of human nature, the ineffable dreamwork done in those depths and the actual dreams that issue from them. They embody, however, as the work that follows them does not, the horrible possibility that the animal in us might indeed be severed from the articulation of mind and soul, and that human life might be reduced again to the mute, destructive servitude of the will. In these books the vision is unremittingly demonic, lacking the modest openness and broad curiosity, and the resulting humor, of the poetry and fiction that have followed them.

I began this focus on education and influence by using the phrase "humane letters" instead of "literature" because Chappell's reading includes an abundance of stuff from a variety of areas. Beyond Vergil, whose *Georgics* are relevant to a farm boy turned author, his classical interests include Lucretius, Horace, Pliny, and Ovid. His historical fiction, much of it uncollected, reveals more than a nodding acquaintance with an astronomer, Sir William Herschel, a botanist, Carl Linnaeus, a vain geographer, Maupertuis, and composers such as Haydn, Offenbach, and Mozart. Apparently minor figures from American cultural and theological history turn up, too, as witness Thomas Morton, whose experiences with his Merrymounters underpin the Puritan explorations (kin also to Hawthorne) in *Dagon*.

This is a partial list, indicative of the breadth of Chappell's interests, but not of the ease with which he carries his erudition. It is not paraded, but subsumed into appropriate situation, event, and character, alluded to quietly enough to alert an informed reader without putting off a less informed one. *Castle Tzingal* and *Source*, his two most recent collections of poems, are further cases in point.

In the former, a verse novel in voices—almost, indeed, a play without stage directions—Chappell plies together, amidst a diversity of forms similar to *Midquest*, a number of allusive threads. The context and plot are medieval, as is enough of the vocabulary ("grutch," "frore") to suggest the period: a deranged king murders and decapitates a traveling minstrel whose isolated head continues to sing, haunting the surviving members of the court. The consequent societal- and self-destruction is Biblical in its visitation of sin upon the sinner, and assumes that humankind has an operative conscience despite the modern overlays of this or that theoretical utopian salve. A background twine is the legend of Orpheus, to which Chappell gives a science-fiction twist. Instead of being borne down the river Hebrus, the singer's "comely head," hidden in "a grotesque undercellar," is "suspended in fluids beside a gurgling retort."

Source shows Chappell moving through various image clusters in the book's earlier sections to a culminating vision that is atomic, explicitly based in Lucretius' depiction of the universe in *De Rerum Natura*. Chappell's use of Lucretius' atomism ranges from the minute—frost seen as "emery," a fog dissolving solid objects "into spirit"—to the intergalactic: the stars, in a representative instance, are a "bright fishnet lifting from darkness those broken/ many heroes we read the mind with." Between these extremes the volume's individual poems show the illusorily solid human species carrying out its daily heroism, its sweet music, its longing for rest, as well as its potentially sudden joining up with the eternal smithereens.

Though from the outset of his career Chappell has published poems in which he observes particular details in nature, he has not, to my mind, ever been a "Nature" poet. The poems in *Source* offer a fresh illustration of this point. They refer consistently to such items as Queen Anne's lace, the milking of cows, the slow spread of evening, and much else we associate with the term *nature*. All these details, however, are perceived as parts of an inclusive vision of human experience, current and historical. Of all theories of matter, atomism by definition dwells most insistently on the discrete, but it also views its particulars from a unifying perspective.

Which brings me to the basic oversimplification of this introduction. Fred Chappell's work is not as sharply bifurcated between the rural and the intellectual as the convenient shape of my remarks has so far implied. It is also significantly more varied in its subject matter than

I've had space to suggest. The second of these deficiencies will be easily remedied by dipping into the deliciously thick right-hand side of the volume you are holding. As for the misleading division itself let me conclude with a couple of observations.

John Stewart Collis' words at the head of this essay suggest the first one. Fred Chappell the author who thinks is Fred Chappell the farm boy grown up, and what he thinks about is partly unified by that process. His grandmother's warning that he might grow away from himself wasn't an old woman's ignorant fear, but it appears equally true that Ole Fred has grown toward himself as well, as any plant grows away from its necessary root to flower. The fifty years this has taken (so far) is misleading if one conceives of it spatially—a "long" time. It is more helpful to say it is *one* time. Fred Chappell is one person, though unfinished; in *Midquest* Ole Fred refers to himself as "halfway halved and halfway blent." Similarly, his thought is rooted in that gaping child, who, as we all do, took everything in without thought. Chappell's tireless, wide-ranging intellectual curiosity, and the poetry and fiction that issue from it, are the attempt to understand wholly that "ulterior motive," however complex, that comes with consciousness. Intellect is vapid if it doesn't proceed from feeling; the feeling intellect in search of ecstasy keeps the twin hopes of recovery and synthesis alive, the future positive.

Finally, Fred Chappell concludes a recent essay about Vergil's idealized vision of the farmer in his bucolic poetry with a paragraph that could as well be, and I suspect is, about himself.

> Most poets would make better lutenists than farmers. But even the most inept of us still feel close kinship with the man in the fields, with his life of ordered observation and inspired patience. That is the one life besides poetry and natural philosophy that still touches an essential harmony of things, and when a civilization discards that way of life, it breaks the most fundamental covenant mankind can remember.

—DABNEY STUART

I

Novels

It Is Time, Lord

ONE

I was born May 23, 1931, in the house of my grandmother. No doctor could be found to attend, only a midwife from three miles away in the country. My birth was loud and troublesome; the midwife, who was but a young girl, fainted away and my father, who was assisting, had to force her again to consciousness. I lived in the room later for a long while with my grandmother. It was in this room that we took our meals and every night kept a watch until midnight, she reading the Bible, I myself reading a queer story of adventure. On the mantel above the iron stove there was a large clock, which was wound with a key stuck into two holes in its face. A brass pendulum swung inside the glass front, uttering a solidly satisfying click at each foot of its arc. My mother in the labor cried for the clicking to stop. My father opened the face and clutched the pendulum, but his hands so shook that he succeeded only in making the clicking faster. He was forced to take up a pair of scissors and a pencil and hold them on each side of the pendulum in order to halt its motion.

I was born in Gemini, which is the sign of the arms and denotes balance. We born in Gemini are fond of mathematics and science, or, perhaps, acting and oratory. We have a middling talent for commerce, are of a saving disposition, are moderate in all things. In short a fine sense of balance marks our undertakings.—Not so my sister, who is four years my junior. She was born in Leo, August 2, and they born in the sign of the heart have lofty minds and moral seriousness, dignity and firm will. Ptolemy of Pelusa hazards that one of the sign of the heart will achieve positions of honor and trust: thus, my sister has two children, and they are obedient. She never bends to them, and merely laughs at their egotistical whimsies.—She and I are temperamentally opposite. She is confident and graceful in her certainty that she always has the right in things, while I attribute my indecisiveness to my habit of weighing all particles of a problem. My two children obey me but tolerably, for I take their reasons seriously. The world my children see is very different from the world I see, but I discover in it a substance, and it is not less broad than my world. Leo, too, is a masculine sign, dry and barren, a fire sign; and so my sister has really the soul of a man, perhaps the soul of a prince. Gemini is also a masculine sign, but it is an air sign. An air sign has the disadvantage of inconstancy, as of the winds, but air is the temple of space, of infinity. Nothing so pours through me as the blueness of the sky in a cold, clear day; no eyes trouble me so much as the peculiarly flat blue eyes of babies or of ruthless blond women.

That room in which I was born had blue walls, too. They were plaster walls with tiny pimples everywhere, like a coat painted on. The ceiling was fairly high—it was rather an old house—and the single illumination was from a bulb suspended by a gilt chain from the center of the ceiling. When I was very young I liked to mount a chair and bat the bulb with a newspaper in order to watch the shadows of the furniture stagger on the floor, dart in and out beneath each object like animals frightened and bold by turns. The room always smelled of camphor, oil of wintergreen, and tonic: medicines my grandmother absorbed continually for her varied complaints.

The house was brick and there were fourteen other rooms. It was set on a hill in the center of the farm. Three barns stood together two hundred yards east of the house; behind them pasture stretched over a hundred acres of hills, below them lay the grain and tobacco fields, and a crooked creek, gradually chewing away the edges, the course being twisted and spring floods coming annually. The stream was well populated with muskrats, too, and their burrows ran sometimes into the middle of fields. The bottom fields were the best evidence of the present fortune of the farm: my grandparents could neither afford to have the creek straightened nor to leave it crooked. The buildings were all in good condition and the land well cared for, but the fence rows

were grown with ragweed and locust and sassafras bushes, a sign that
tenantry was unwillingly employed.

The fourteen other rooms of the house I remember as being always
cold and dark. My grandmother was unwilling to give a room heat or
light except when it was absolutely necessary. When I was older I lived
in an upstairs room with two gable windows facing west. The room was
paneled with notched pine slatting, and in the stream of the grain I
would find rivers with islands, flames, tongues, heads of dogs, men,
and bears. A long ridge fenced away the town from the farm and when
I darkened my room for the night the gray aureole of the town lights
lay along the top.

But I did not live in this room until I was fifteen, when I had
already felt the first vague desires of sexual life: to sleep all night in a
muddy ditch, to hang dead by the toes like Mussolini, to eat hashish
—I fancied that one ate it from a bowl with a spoon, that it was of the
consistency of jelly and black and bitter. And too—unfortunately—
these upstairs bedrooms were furnished with dressing tables with large
mirrors. For the vulgar saying that one cannot live on love is true only
of romantic love, and certain persons there are who can live fatly on
self-love, can devour themselves to the last gut and toenail, Narcissuses
who play with themselves the game of Zeus and Selene.

And this is not on my part self-castigation for adolescent guilt. The
chances are good that the remembrance is false. Pray God that it is.
For the rich money of dream is generally debased by the counterfeiting
of memory, and in the same manner certain reminiscences gain especial
value by the significance of subsequent events. To illustrate, if a stranger
approached you with a handful of diamonds, you would not attempt
to judge his character by admiring his jewels. We can form no idea of
the history or mind of a past century by reading its best poems, nor can
we discover ourselves by the single remembrances that fasten to us.

I choose a single memory which has gathered such patina of usage
that it seems much further distant than it is. My sister was three years
old and she was following me to the barn. It was very cold. When the
wind blew it hurt, but there was not very much wind. It hurt too when
I walked fast, the cold air cutting my lungs as I breathed more deeply,
and so I walked slowly.

Step for step behind, my sister whimpered. She wore only a little dress with puffy sleeves smothered in a thin blue sweater. She had long blond curls and I thought they were brittle because it was so cold and that they might splinter on her shoulders like golden icicles. It was late dusk and the moon was yellow, bulgy and low over the hills of the pasture, a soft handful of butter.

There were men in the barn I had never seen. They sat on sacks of crushed corn and cottonseed meal in the dimness. They looked mute and solid. Someone said, "That's a little girl behind him."

One of the men rose and approached slowly. He was tall and his gray eyes came toward me in the dusk. His hair was blond, but not as yellow as my sister's. "Where you from, boy?" he asked.

"Home."

"Is that your sister?"

"Yes. She's Julia. My name is James."

"Don't she have something more than that to wear?"

"I told her not to come out with me."

"You better strike out," he said. "She'll freeze to death out here."

"Strike out?"

"You better light out for home." He rubbed his big wrists. "Hurry up and go on before she freezes to death."

"Come on," I told her. She was still whimpering. Her hands were scarlet, smaller and fatter than mine. I touched her hand with my finger and it felt like paper. There were small tears in her eyes, but her face was scared, not crying.

I started back. The rocks in the road were cold. Once I didn't hear her whimpering and I looked and she was sitting in the road. I went to her and took her elbows and made her stand up. "Come on," I said reproachfully, "you'll freeze to death."

We went on, but then she saw a great log beside the road, and went to it and sat. She had stopped whimpering, but her eyes had become larger. They seemed as large as eggs. "Please, come on," I said. "You'll freeze to death out here."

She looked up at me. I pulled at her. Her wrists felt glassy under my fingers. "What are you doing?" I cried. "Why won't you come on?

You'll freeze to death." I couldn't move her. It terrified me because I thought she had frozen to the log.

It had got much darker and the moon was larger.

I jerked her again and again, but she didn't get up. Nothing moved in her face. Two small tears were yet at the corner of each eye. She looked queer, stonelike, under the moonlight, and I thought something terrible had happened to her.

"What are you doing to her? Why don't you leave her alone?"

My father suddenly appeared behind me, huge and black in the moonlight. He too had a small tear in each eye. He was breathing heavily in a big jacket. White plumes of breath bannered in the air.

"What makes you hurt her? What gets into you?"

She raised her arms, and he gathered her to his jacket, holding her in both his arms as in a nest. She knotted herself against his chest, curling spontaneously.

He turned his back toward the moon and strode. Sometimes I had to trot to keep up, and I continued in the limplike pace until we got home.

"Open the door," my father said hoarsely. He knocked the door with his foot.

My mother stood waiting inside and looked through my head at my sister, red in my father's arms. "What happened?" she asked. Her mouth thinned.

I went to the brown stove and put my hand flat against its side, and it seemed a long time before its heat burned me. My face began to tickle.

"What were they doing?"

I walked to the window and looked at the moon huge and yellow behind the skinny maple branches. A dim spot emerged from the window pane as I breathed, and as I stood there it got larger and larger, like a gray flower unfolding, until it obscured the total moon.

This was winter, specifically January; spring is another matter entirely. April is even now chartreuse for me, a color which retains the dizziness and inspiring sickness of the liqueur. The new grass of April is chartreuse, and the new leaves on the long withes of weeping willows.

It seems my father kept an ape, a tall, ginger-colored beast which wore a red collar about its neck, but was otherwise entirely free. The nameplate on the collar read: Modred. He had given me a long reap hook and told me to cut the lawn. The pale new grass was very short and limp. The hook would not cut it; the grass blades bent under it, and seemed to squirm away from it. Finally I threw the tool down in exasperation. My father came out upon the porch with the ape—he was quite as horrid as Poe's ape of the Rue Morgue—and said to it, "You'd better get him before he gets any worse." The ape felt the back of its neck under the collar and put some lice in its mouth. Then it came down into the yard for me. I ran to a willow tree and climbed to the shuddering top before stopping, but when I looked down I looked into the face of the ape directly beneath me. It seized me by the ankles and pulled me down against its chest. I could hardly breathe. It clutched my left arm and bit away my hand. I could see the bare silver bones of my wrist. The ape looked down, and my father, who was standing at the foot of the tree, tossed it a salt shaker. It began to sprinkle salt upon my wrist.

So this is probably a dream, though perhaps it is injured by things which have since occurred or by dreams I have since received. But it is more tangible than many things encountered in the flesh. For instance, among our linens now is a washcloth with the print of a rose; nothing is more unreal than to see it floating alone, half-submerged, in the white bathwater. Or I would play chess or Chinese checkers with my grandfather and suddenly there would appear upon the squares of the board the hump and tail of Ursa Minor or the long spine of Draco. What is less real than this? We played on a marble chessboard which my grandfather had himself set in a heavy oak table he had made. To see these constellations emerge from the aggregate of pawns and knights was like seeing Atlantis raise its head out of the cold ocean, or, perhaps, like seeing in the marigold faces of human men the sudden roses of divinity: Dionysus before Acetes; Christ:

> *Lo, how a rose e'er blooming*
> *From tender stem hath sprung!*

My grandfather and I would befuddle the eternal summer afternoons with games: chess, checkers, poker. He sat in a leather rocking chair on the open porch. By him a small table held a pitcher of water, a glass, a pint of whiskey. He drank slowly and thoughtfully. Flies strutted on his knuckles. He had a very bald head, deep green eyes, the face of Sibelius with the identical veins distent on the temples. It was a face such as the Emperor Augustus must have had: and this was how he sat, the melancholy emperor of the afternoon. He was a builder of houses and a good carpenter, but now for nearly forty years he had been able to walk only with the support of a crutch and a cane. Sometime in his twenties his legs had been completely shattered in a sawmill accident, and, because medicine in that time and place had been so very bad, he had never recovered. In the afternoons he did not like to walk. Besides games his other amusement was swatting flies. He wore out any number of fly swatters before he fashioned himself a leather one from the tongue of an old shoe. Like my sister, he was born in Leo.

Leo is summer, a lion with a hide of shaggy gold. Its haunches are sunlight, its flesh the logos of God.

> *Strong is the lion: like a coal*
> *His eyeball, a bastion's mole*
> *His chest against the foe.*

My grandfather and my sister are searched into by this majesty, kneaded in the glory of it. But are we merely masks of the stars and seasons? Apple trees are of summer, too, but they remain in winter, and not entirely asleep. For my grandfather lived through many winters and died in a summer. Once, I remember, he and I walked together in a December morning. We walked through the orchard in the first heavy frost of the season—or at least it now seems that it was the first heavy frost. Suddenly he said, "Look out, boy. Reach me that apple." Above my head hung a great yellow apple, which somehow had escaped apple picking and autumn. I leaped as high as I could and felt it thud heavily in my hand. I gave it to him, and he, resting lopsided on his crutch, inserted both thumbs in the blossom end and tore the fruit into irregular halves. The meat was white as linen. The sunlight glittered on the moist flesh as on dew. Two black seeds glared from its heart. It was so cold it hurt my teeth.

Leo endures. There is summer in winter. My grandfather spent most of the winter before the cast-iron stove in the warm blue room. The stove was wood-burning; the top slipped sidewise on a socket hinge and chunks of wood were thrust in. Ashes and coals fell into a long, narrow trough beneath the grates. I used to lie on my belly on the floor and gaze through a small window into this trough. Everything grew small and the dropped cinders were great boulders and mountains. The scene was illuminated by the red-orange glare of the fire above. It was as arid as sand, and live coals dropped through the grates, splashing the walls with sparks. This is the best notion of hell. When I would dream or daydream of going to hell I always wound up in the bottom of that stove.

"Don't look into the fire so long, boy," he said.

"Why not?"

"It's bad for your eyes."

"How come?"

"You'll go blind if you keep that up long enough."

"Is it bad to be blind?"

"You can't see nothin when you're blind. Man that's blind is in bad shape. I used to know a feller in Fletcher Forks that was blind. He was sworped across the eyes with a sharp chestnut limb when they felled the tree."

"What did he do?"

"Well, he used to log a little. Had a good matched team, used to bring hardwood about halfway down Turkey Knob and J-hook it off the mountain."

"What's J-hook?"

"Look here." He held out his left arm, his hand bent toward the inside. His fingernails looked tough and oily, like cow horn. "This here's your hook, and this here's your bar." He put his right forearm against his left elbow to show me. Then he picked up his crutch from

the floor. "Now, this is the log, and your J-hook goes like this and the
bar this way." He held the handle of the crutch in his half-open hand
and laid his arm on one of the stocks. "You start going down with your
mules pulling the log, but pretty soon the log gets to goin faster and
faster down the mountain. See how it goes? It's heavier than your mules
are, put together. Pretty soon it's goin faster than your mules can trot,
but see, you've already got you a chute built on top of some cleft that's
handy to where you're haulin out, so you run on into the chute and
kick your bar. When you do that it flips your hook out and the log's
free from your riggin. The log slides down to the foot of the holler."

"What did the man do after he was blind?"

"Well, he couldn't do nothin much. He sort of got along doin a
little cobblin, although he was never any great account at it. He couldn't
make no shoes nor boots nor nothin; he could just fix em when they
was tore up or wore out in the soles."

"If you can't cobble, what can you do when you're blind?"

"What I was goin to tell you about this feller bein blind was he
was a chinchy sort of eater. He was about like you like that, I reckon.
When I worked with him, he used to take me in home to eat with him.
He ate out of a wood plate he'd made for hisself. He'd cut out little
dips in it for all the kinds of food. He couldn't stand for his food to get
all run together when he was eatin. He just wanted to eat one bite of
one thing at a time and he figured out what he wanted to eat before
time and if he didn't want to eat one certain thing right then he'd wait
till he did. He was the same way after he got blind, too, but he couldn't
tell nothin about what he was doin. He'd say, 'Sary, what's this I've
got?' And she'd say, 'That's beans, John.' In a minute he'd say, ' What's
this, Sary?' She'd say, 'That's grits.' In a minute, he'd say, 'God gast
it, Sary, where's the applesauce?' "

He threw back his head and laughed loudly. The walls seemed to
creak with the laugh. His nose was bushy with black hairs and his cheeks
had blue-red veins.

This was the summer which was in winter, but winter itself was
never nearly so warm or humane. It was ominous and icy, like the first
sentence of Wells' novel:

No one would have believed in the last years of the
nineteenth century that this world was being watched keenly
and closely by intelligences greater than man's and yet as
mortal as his own, that as men busied themselves about their
various concerns they were scrutinized and studied, perhaps
almost as narrowly as a man with a microscope might scru-
tinize the transient creatures that swarm and multiply in a
drop of water.

All the days were overcast or brightly cold. At night the stars shone
like frost on steel. Everything seemed constricted in winter, locked.
The cold allowed me little freedom of movement; it wasn't pleasant to
stray too long from the stove. Ice sealed the puddles in the road, and
the new ice which in the early morning had begun to form in the milk
cans looked like broken panes of glass. I hated to leave the room at
night to mount the dark stairs, to undress and lie in the freezing sheets.
    Curiously, in winter I was not nostalgic for summer but for fall.
As I feverishly shelled corn for the chickens, I would look at the great
heaps of corn about me in the crib, remembering when we had gathered
it. Most of it came from the field across the winding creek. It was
gathered into the wagon drawn by the patient team. But before the
wagon came it was pulled from the stalk and thrown into small piles,
aligned as nearly straight as we could manage. Then the wagon came,
knocking awry the stiff, dead stalks—I thought of chessmen swept from
the board—and the corn was thrown in, and the wagon went creaking
to the barn. We rode back. The horses paused at the edge of the creek.
Uncle George, who was the tenant and not really an uncle, shouted
them in. "Whoo. Whoohaw. Goddamn you, get your feet wet here.
I'll lay onto you proper. Whoohaw."
    His son, Jarvis, rode beside him on the wagon seat. "What if old
Miz Albert was to hear you talk like that in front of honeybunch?"
    I lay behind on the piled corn.
    "He aint hearin nothin to scare him, I guess."
    The wagon squeaked and descended through the water. The water
seemed darker now than in summer; it crawled and wavered around
the wheels. Behind, on the sandy bank, were dark sliced wheel tracks.

This was the sort of thing I would remember in winter: coming from the fields itchy with beggar's lice and Spanish needles, or tired and dusty, but not hot, from the final urgencies of the hayfields. Blackbirds and starlings knotted the telephone wires; the mockingbirds had already gone, and the bluejays. For after supper there would be pie from new pumpkins, sweet and coarse and stringy.

After I had shelled the corn I would feed it to the chickens, imitating my grandmother in calling them: "Here, chickchickchick chickee. Here, chickchickchickchick chickee." They would come running and when a good number was gathered, I would toss the corn in bright handfuls, pretending that it was money I scattered. A red hen would pick up a grain, drop it, pick it up again, bite it, drop it, lose it to another red hen, peck her, be pecked fiercely in return, peck another hen, search for another grain of corn. Then I shucked corn for the horses and the mule and fed them shorts and brought them water. Then I tossed hay down into the lot feed rack for the cows.

The cows never looked to see whence their feed came. They stuck their heads into the rack and the tossed hay fell over their horns and tangled on their broad brows. Occasionally they would shake it off. In the twilight they seemed warm and dim and eternal. If a lantern was lighted in the barn, it threw oblongs and blades of orange light into the lot.

The barns were on a hill, and I could stand in the road by them and see time itself stretching and breathing below in the bright days. In winter we pastured steers and yearlings in the bottom fields, where they grazed on the tough rye grass we had sown in midsummer. The cattle, "calves" they were called, all faced in the same direction, north-northwest, as they cropped in the mornings. About noon they all rested, lying among the broken cornstalks or on the bald spot where tobacco had grown. In the afternoon they began retracing their journey, grazing southeast toward the barns. Again, I was reminded of the black and red counters of the chess game. The steers in the fields were red-and-white or black-and-white. Or I could see the indeterminate masses of shadow laid down by clouds which flew slowly across the sky. In a flat country, the shadows of clouds upon the land are not seen: one is either in the shadow or on a level with it. But these cloud shadows are the best idea of time, for it is only islands of time which touch us, and the vehement deeps of time—think of an ocean or a wheatfield—are alien to us, even though we have floated them or sported within them from the time of our birth. Chambers Mountain, which stopped up like a cork the northern neck of the valley, gathered clouds about its high shoulders like mantles of state.

"Did you ever use to cobble for a living?" I asked him.

He turned his graven head upon me. The green eyes rested, as if he saw me reborn. "I thought I told you once to get up off of your stomach."

"Yes sir."

"No."

"Don't you know how to, though?"

The stove was equipped with an iron footrail and he laid his swollen right foot upon it. "I've had to make my own shoes to do right since I was hurt," he said. "I can do a little. I always knock down the tacks in your shoes when they cut your heels, don't I?"

"Yes." I thought of the queer iron foot in the milkhouse. It was about three feet high, and, set in a block of wood, it pointed toward the sky. The foot was flat and really was only an iron sole, neither right nor left. When my grandfather worked on a shoe, he fitted it over this iron foot and hammered it. A shoe tack looked small, smaller than the hour hand of a wrist watch, in his great hand. His fingers were square and hard; they seemed mostly bone.

On the mantel above the stove the pendulum clock clicked. On both sides of it sat mayonnaise jars full of pencil stubs, broken fountain pens which were used as dip pens, glass gimcracks full of bank statements, i.o.u.'s, financial notes, and there were Bible commentaries and two or three odd volumes of an encyclopedia. I had once begun to read one of these volumes; I read about the aardvark, the aardwolf, and the Aarn River, and then I stopped. I knew all about Aaron from my grandmother.

She would sit under the single bulb reading the Bible. She rocked in a small rocking chair and flat globules of light rose and set like miniature moons in her spectacles. She licked her noded thumb when she turned pages.

"Son," she would ask, "the dogs licked the blood of what great king?"

"Ahab," I answered.

"Ahab, did you say?" my grandfather asked. His voice said, I don't believe you.

"No . . . McNabb," said the redhaired man. "Charles."

"I thought I must not of heard right. Ahab was a Bible king."

The redhaired man nodded quickly. He seemed in a great hurry. He had blue eyes, as flat as glass, the color of oceans on maps. The hair began so suddenly and tightly on his forehead it seemed like a wig. He was smoking a cigarette. He stood just over the threshold of the warm room and seemed to want to enter. "You say you don't mind my using your phone?" he asked.

"How about the woman with you?" my grandfather asked. "Has she got a coat or something heavy on?"

"She's got a coat," he said. "How did you know she was with me?"

"I know your tracks," said my grandfather. "Or somebody's like yours. They're behind the big barn. That's where you pull your car in."

The man stared at him. "What's wrong?" he asked.

"No, I don't want you to call anybody on the telephone. I don't want nobody comin to fix your car with a no-count woman in it behind my barn."

"Wait a minute. I didn't know you objected to my parking there or I wouldn't have done it."

"You couldn't of asked me to let you, either. Not for lettin you lollygag with the town whores. Trouble is, I've found burnt-out cigarettes not more'n a foot away from the hay, where you've throwed em out. That barn would go up like gunpowder."

"You mean to tell me you really won't have the decency just to let me borrow your phone?" He seemed unbelieving.

. . . *L'empereur a l'oeuil mort.*

"I'll tell you 'decent,' " my grandfather said. "I don't see no decent feller around here. You can walk for a telephone."

"It must be two miles, at least."

"That ain't far for a young feller."

"Wait a minute . . ."

"Don't tell me to wait. You're a ragged-ass son of a bitch."

He slammed the door. It was as if he had been snuffed out like a candle flame. We listened to his hard footsteps, and then the outer door closed. The fire in the stove hummed. Outside, the November wind blew.

"I never did like a redheaded feller," my grandfather said.

When I answered her questions about the Bible correctly, my grandmother would smile and nod to herself in approval. "That's right," she said. "Now, can you tell who Abishag was?"

"No. I don't know."

Then she would tell me—but not just who Abishag was. She told the whole story of King David from the beginning. When she got to her question, she would stop and say, "Now *that's* who Abishag was." Then she would tell the story to the end, down to Absalom and his long yellow hair.

These nights seemed eternal. Nothing moved in the room but the hand on the pendulum of the clock until my grandfather decided he wanted water. He rose painfully out of his chair and went to the kitchen. The sound was: *bup, swiss, thum*: first his cane forward, then his right foot dragged across the worn linoleum, then his crutch and left foot forward together. His hands were bald and white as metal on the sticks.

The fire in the stove hummed and belched.

In the kitchen, the water waited in a chipped porcelain pail in the sink. The rectangle of the window, patched with a black angle of the roof and a few stars or the moon, floated on the water like a piece of cheesecloth. But, when I bent over it to pull the dipper up, a great black head rose from the bottom of the pail. Disturbing the dipper made the whole fabric quake and waver. I thought of how a pattern in the slatted pine paneling of my bedroom would change from the head of a snake to the head of a bear to a pathetic ghost. I would shiver because it was very cold. I could not understand how everything changed and yet was always the same in the end.

"It bucks me up," said my grandfather in a July. "But it's just for old men like me; it ain't for young fellers."

"Maybe it will buck me up, too," I said. I wanted some of the whiskey he drank during the chess game.

"I've told you no," he said, "and you know better than to keep whinin. When I know you're old enough, I'll give you some."

"When will I be old enough?"

"When I've decided you are."

"How does it buck you up?"

"Changes a feller's outlook a little. Changes things, swaps em around a little better."

"I don't see anything changed."

"You don't know what to look for, yet, do you?"

"I don't see how it changes and don't change at the same time."

"Well, that's one of the things you don't know. Check."

His knight and rook menaced my king. I moved the wrong pawn.

"Keep your eyes open, boy," he said. "Watch what you're about."

"Are you goin to buy me that Canadian Mountie suit?"

"What do you want to look like your pants are full of corncobs for?"

But the patterns in the pine wall changed and the wall didn't change. And shadows changed, but the objects which created the shadows didn't change.

In a December my grandmother asked me not to bat that light bulb with a folded newspaper. "It makes it hard for me to see the words," she said, licking her knotty thumb.

"Yes mam," I said.

The bulb still swung slowly. I had been watching the shadow of the hanging edge of a tablecloth. It ran on the floor in and out from beneath the table, and it was shaped like a small black rat. I watched the straight shadow of a chair seat go back and forth like a windshield wiper. I looked under the door to watch the bar of shadow squeezed down by the swaying light. There was no shadow beneath the door. There was a pink glow as thick as a finger. I watched it a long time, and my eyes began to ache.

"What was that last chunk you put in the stove?" my grandfather asked. "It don't smell right, someway."

"It was just green red oak," I said. I could smell nothing but the medicines which always odored the room. I rubbed my eyes. The pink bar under the door had turned orange.

My grandmother had stopped reading. Both she and my grandfather sat silent.

I went to the door. "I don't know why this door's so hot," I said. The knob was slippery in my hand.

"Don't you open that door. You get everybody's coats out of that closet. Hurry up." He held both his walking sticks in one hand, and raised himself very suddenly. "Mamaw," he said, "put the papers on the mantel in my coat pocket." He hobbled to the telephone. "Come here," he told me, "and call this here number." He pointed to a number penciled on the wall.

My arms were full of coats. "The house is on fire," I said.

"Hurry up," he said.

Outside, a dry snow covered the ground. The trees looked pink, and it was very cold. We walked only about a hundred yards. Through the windows, the flames looked like fine ladies and gentlemen dancing at a great ball. I had never seen so much light. Chambers Mountain blotted out the last star in the Big Dipper, and, as I watched, light suddenly filled the windows of the tenant house.

There were silent tears on my grandmother's cheek, and a knot pulsed in my grandfather's jaw. "Them redheaded fellers is all no-count," he said.

"I'm going to kill that son of a bitch," I said. I was nine years old.

TWO

My grandmother was very tall, taller than my grandfather, who had been bent by stooping to his walking sticks. She was five feet eleven inches. She was as straight and firm as the edge of a door, and her carriage was perfectly balanced and easy. Tall as she was, she was yet graceful. Her shoulders were wide and her body of a middling slender build, so that her dresses—which she generally fashioned for herself—fell in straight lines from her shoulders. These dresses were all of solid colors: dark green and dark blue predominated among them. She was never without an apron, and in the deep pocket of this garment carried string, a paring knife, some spools of thread with a needle, a thimble, apple peelings, perhaps, a pencil stub grimy with use, a scrap or two of paper, and mail. She carried a handbag only when going to church or to market. These aprons were almost always entirely plain, the edges hemmed merely, and only occasionally had she sewn on red or yellow bias binding. Her dresses, too, were always very severely cut, though she would sometimes allow large pleats under the shoulders so that the cloth fell in large folds, heightening my impression of her dresses as judicial gowns or choir robes. She wore thick cotton hose, the color of creamed coffee. Her shoes were always black, the toes squared away, the leather decorated with perforated swirls. Going to market or to church she wore black store-bought dresses, throwing a light silver- or gold-threaded shawl over her shoulders. These were long shawls; the tasseled fringes brushed her wrist as she walked. Her hats too were black, with frowsy little dotted veils which covered none of the face. Working at home or in the fields she wore the kind of sun-bonnet you find in the hillbilly comic strips.

I remember that her hair was first the vague gray of a cobweb or a glass curtain, and that it later turned stark white like bone china. Her forehead was high; her complexion good, though neither entirely fair nor entirely dark. Her face was wrinkled, especially about the eyes. Her cheeks were wrinkled, but not about her high cheekbones, where the flesh was firm and the color still pink. Her eyes were brown, with flecks of a darker brown; they were not striking eyes. She always wore bifocals with tiny, very delicate gold rims. Her teeth were of course not natural; I used often to find them lying on the windowsill over the kitchen sink. Here she scrubbed them with salt or baking soda. Lying out, they seemed frightening, a dead animal. Her mouth was firm, her lips somewhat thin; her upper lip was short and slightly downy, like the lip of the princess in War and Peace. Her chin was round and smooth, her jaw line strong and straight.

Her wrists were large, the tarsal bones enlarged and prominent. The veins were enlarged, too. They were blue, very noticeable. On her hands, the skin was dry and weathered. When she twisted her hand, each pore made a tiny wrinkle, and when I touched her wrist it seemed as hard and bare as furniture. Her hands were knobby and calloused and she had great ugly knuckles. The fingernails were short, broad, square, with minuscule ridges. The fingernail of her left second finger was black and curled inward from some former accident. When her hands were cold she would hold one in the other, like a ball. And when they were wet, she would dry them by rubbing them once on the apron, flat against her thighs. This is how a man dries his hands.

She had large bones, and her frame was large. Like Sherlock Holmes, she had strength without apparent muscularity. I have often thought that her tendons and ligaments must have been extremely powerful. Her fingers, which seemed clumsy and forgetting, adapted themselves to any tool, pitchfork or paring knife. She peeled an apple by putting her thumb on the base of the sharp edge, with the dull edge against her knuckles, and the handle resting lightly in her palm. She whittled the peeling away, stroking toward her body. The chips of peeling fell in her aproned lap.

With her Sunday dresses she wore rather large brooches of intricate design, made of brass and green glass. Lying on her dressing table, they looked like exotic insects. Also on her dressing table were a brush, a comb, a bottle of hair oil, a box of powder, a tinted picture of Franklin Roosevelt, wearing a deadly sincere expression. She was very likely to use too much face powder when she dressed, perhaps because she was careless, or maybe the mirror was too dark for her to see her reflection well. Grainy patches of powder often were on her cheeks and were noticeable when she smiled.

She had a very silent smile, which drew becomingly from the gravure of her face: it did not wrinkle her face the more, but hid advantageously among the other creases. When she grinned she hid her mouth with her dry hand. The gesture seemed immoderately coy, considering her age, but she hid a gap in her teeth: she had once dropped her dental plate in the sink. She never frowned, but instead drew the corners of her mouth down, elongating the short upper lip, until her mouth was a straight line. Like most elderly persons, her face exhibited little range of expression. When she read, she raised her eyebrows.

Her movements were as graceful as the nature of farmwork permits. Gentleness moved her body. She was wholly feminine, having been born on the last day of June in the sign of Cancer, a watery, fruitful, feminine sign. She had the virtues of women: keenness of mind, moral austerity, quickness and cleverness in business matters. Cancer is the sign of the breast, and the time of Cancer is a fruitful time for all things, even noxious growths. Her proper element was autumn, the harvest season, the rainy season.

She was then taller than I now am, for I stand only five feet eight inches. I weigh about one hundred fifty pounds, have gray eyes, muddy blond hair. My hair has slight waves which my parents nursed for me from infancy and which have begun now in my thirtieth year to straighten. My face is oval and fair and forgettable. My mouth is handsome in its way, but colorless; my eyes placid. My build is rather slight; the bones are small. My hands seem feminine, almost delicate: they are very white.

My disposition is not amiable, but, rather, amenable. I am willing for any interesting undertaking, but rarely enthusiastic. I rarely anger, but can withstand a great amount of vexation: in short, I am easily put upon. But I am not often treated so, for I am retiring, if not really shy. Like Hazlitt's Hamlet, I am more interested in my own thoughts than in the world around me, but

I am not Prince Hamlet, nor was meant to be—

I have no great personal problems, because my thoughts are only accidentally concerned with myself. For me an abstract system is worth a hundred disparate data. I do not read the newspapers, I do not worry about money.

Even so, I am a very prudent person, and do not make decisions easily. To decide which necktie to wear is a source of the greatest confusion. I cannot make up my mind what I might like for dinner. I am introversive rather than extroversive, but I find myself per se uninteresting, and it seems that my self is but a key to some more important matter. Unfortunately, I am unacquainted with this other matter. What is paramount here is that I am by nature blind to a greater part of the world about; I am sealed away from the most of my life. This is an invaginate existence: much too dull to think about for its own value.

The things that interest me are faces, books, flowers, images, sports. I find no more durable pleasure than reading early Christian history, but I am excited by the imaginings of my children and the dreams of my wife and myself. I remain fascinated by my profession: I am a Methodist minister.

Among the questions one is asked before ordination in the ministry is: Do you expect to achieve perfection, with the grace of God? At least, this is the essence of the question; I have forgotten the exact words. One must answer, Yes. Again: Do you expect to achieve perfection in your lifetime? Again: Yes. And, I have often wondered how seriously one is expected to take these two questions. In truth, I believe that perfection will work itself out—on the rare occasions when it is going to—despite anyone's efforts and quite regardless of the grace of God. It depends on where you stand to look at the time of your life.

For instance, I once attended the hospital deathbed of an old man who belonged to my congregation. He was a very old man, a farmer, a faithful church attendant. He had been involved in a highway accident. His hair was white and his face, too, was white, drained. He spoke slowly and thickly and regarded his imminent death calmly.

"Do you have a special burden you would like to pray to God to absolve you of?" I asked.

He was silent a long time. "Yes," he said finally.

"Would you like to tell me, or would you like to offer silent prayer?"

Long silence. "No . . . no," he said. "I can't pray. . . . I don't regret it . . ."

This is the kind of perfection that flowers despite God's grace; it is essentially the same perfection one feels in the first breathing of spring or the first spreading of a new linen tablecloth.

My grandmother lived to see me made a minister and to hear some few of my sermons, and this fulfilled perhaps her fondest hopes. My grandfather did not survive so long. I don't know how he would have felt about my profession. My memory vaguely hints that his attitude toward the ministry was equivocal, although his respect for the Bible was thorough and literal.

"You hear sayin now that the world's round like a orange," he once told me. "But it don't say nothin about it in the Bible, and the Bible mentions about everything else, I reckon: the radio, and television, and the airplane. But it don't say nothin about the world bein round."

"Do you think it's round?" I asked.

"Well, them science fellers generally know what they're talkin about, but I don't know. I passed a lot of flat country on my way to Oregon—miles and miles of it, farther'n I could see, but it didn't look round to me."

"Does the Bible say anything about whiskey?" I asked.

"It says, 'Do not look upon the wine when it is red.' "

"I'll take two," I said. He dealt me a five and a jack of diamonds. The jack had blue eyes and a stiff yellow mustache.

"How will you open?" he asked.

"Three," I said. I laid three finishing nails in the center of the table. I sang,

"Jack of diamonds, jack of diamonds,
Jack of diamonds, I cry,
If I don't get rye whiskey,
I'll live till I die."

"Hold up," he said. "Who's been learnin you that?"

"Hurl," I said. Hurl was Uncle George's boy.

"What's he know about it?"

"I don't know."

Uncle George was about thirty-five years old, hardly old enough to be called "uncle" as a term of respect: it was merely a nickname. He was rather short, had sandy hair, gray eyes. He was as tough and warped as first-growth hickory. He usually wore overalls, a sweatshirt, and Army boots, for he had fought in the Second World War.

I remember once—I was older then—we were painting the barn roof. We were painting it a dull red, the color of a rank chicken. We bent over in the sun. A bursting sun filled the sky. *Pitch, pish:* amorphous areas of gray zinc, created like Asias, wobbly cats, things any shape. I thought of the pine slatting in my old bedroom, before it had been rebuilt and painted white. Sweat dripped off our faces into the swathes of paint. I was dizzy from bending and from the odor of paint and turpentine, and when I stood the emerald landscape oozed and wavered like steam from a kettle. It was far down because the barn sat on the edge of a hill on one side. Below, the fields, where I could watch the shadows of clouds, lay squared or catty-cornered, green candy in a box. To the north, the heavy blue-green triangle of Chambers Mountain like a smoky ghost.

Uncle George said, "It's time for me to get some air."

We went slowly to the corner of the roof and sat. The tin burned my hams. I had been working all summer, from the time school was out until now, dead August, to buy shares on a car with a friend.

"Look at that," said Uncle George. "My crazy old hound's moving them pups again." The spotted dog came out of the barn on the other side of the road. A pup dangled blindly in her jaws. "I bet a pretty she takes him back out to the house. She's moved them pups eight times in the past two weeks. She had em in that barn, and then she moved em down in the weeds next to the cow lot, and then she moved em out to my basement, and then she moved back out to this here barn." The dog padded in the dusty road, headed for Uncle's house.

I stuck my belly out. My back was tired from bending. I looked toward the tenant house where Uncle lived. Two lines of washing winked in the sun. "Look," I said, "look how those sheets are flapping. But there's not the first sign of a breeze up here."

"I know it," said Uncle. "Look how that tobacco's yellowin up. Won't be long before I have to start cuttin it."

I knew I'd be in school by then. "I don't care," I said. "While I'm sitting there taking my ease, I'll think about you cutting that tobacco. And loading it, and hanging it on those wobbly tier poles."

He spat over the edge of the roof. "It's all one to me," he said.

I laughed. "Yes, I'll think about you laying those heavy sticks on the wagon, and dragging them off, and climbing up under the roof with them."

"Don't worry, honey. Your time's comin."

"No sir," I said. "I can't see it. You won't ever catch me dirt farming. It doesn't get you anywhere. You can turn up these same rocky hills here for the next fifty years, and still never have money to stuff a sock full of nickels."

"It's a living."

"That's not what I'm looking for."

"It's plenty, though. By God, I was in Saint Lô, France, durin the war. They wasn't a leaf left on the trees. It was the middle of the summer, too. And you know what happened? Them Frenchmens had cooked em and eat em all up, in salats and things."

"That doesn't hurt my conscience," I said. "I'm not going to start a war. I just want to get me a good job somewhere, to make enough money to live decently."

Uncle shrugged.

"How are we going to paint the other side?" I asked. "It's too steep to stand on."

"That's why I brung the rope," said Uncle. "I reckon it'll just about fit you, while I stay up on the ridgepole and hang on. As long as I hold on, you aint got nothin to be worried about."

"I'm not worried."

The sun broke, an angry chrysanthemum molting. We painted a long while, and then he fixed the rope about my waist. We stood splay-footed on the apex.

"There goes them McNeal girls through the cornfield," said Uncle. "I wonder what they've lost in the cornpatch."

"Nothing they can find," I said. "They're going down to splash their feet in the water. That's hot work, loafing around the house."

We watched the slow progress of the girls, the tall corn shaking as they threaded their way through it toward the creek. The summer shimmered.

"Here I go," I said. Taking up brush and bucket, I inched down the side. "I hope you've got a strong grip."

"You be careful there, boy." My grandfather stood in the road above the barn.

"Well," I said.

Uncle was looking back over his shoulder. "Here comes old Sheba with another pup," he said.

"You better keep your eyes peeled," said my grandfather. "The boy's in a dangerous place."

I looked up at Uncle. He had given the rope two turns about his waist, and twisted it over both forearms. "I'm all right," I said. "Don't worry about me."

I painted a long while, sweat soaking the back of my shirt. My wrists were shiny.

"Whoo," said Uncle, "naked as a jaybird!"

"Who?" I asked.

"Them McNeal girls have took off every stitch. They're dobblin about in the creek without a stitch."

When I stood up, I stepped in the patch I had just painted. I fell on the sticky tin, and rolled off the edge. The hard rope took away my breath. Back and forth beneath me the ground ebbed as I swung from the roof, and I could smell the weeds in the sun, and see in the grasses a glitter of mica or glass.

"Are you all right, honey?" asked Uncle.

"I told you to watch what you were about," said my grandfather.

"Goddamnit," I said, "goddamnit, you old hopping Jesus."

That night my mother went round and round me, painting with an alcohol-soaked patch of cotton at the broad raw red streak the rope had rubbed on my waist. The alcohol smelled fresh and cold, and the long smart of it felt refreshing. Short and slender—she was but a tiny woman—she did not have to bend far over to doctor me. Smiling placidly as she worked, she was poking gentle fun, the only kind she knew, at me.

"I would think a young man on the roof of a barn would remember to be careful," she said. "If I were high up in the air I believe I wouldn't have but one thing on my mind."

"It was just an accident," I said.

"If you found yourself a girl friend, some nice young lady, you wouldn't have accidents like that," she said. She passed her cool hand across the back of my head. "Curiosity doesn't always have to kill the cat." She stepped away from me and looked at me carefully, her head cocked to one side like a catbird. She looked merry, but not unnecessarily or unjustly so. She held the bottle of alcohol in one hand, the blob of cotton in the other.—I have often remembered her like that. I was old enough to think, If it wasn't for her and grandmother, the men in this family would have killed themselves off long ago.

"Does it burn much?" she asked.

"It hurts good," I said.

THREE

_H_imself, the Emperor Augustus, was born September 23, 63 B.C. This day is under the sign of Libra, the Scales, but Sextilis was the month of his greatest triumphs, and the Senate voted that Sextilis be renamed Augustus. And this was the month in which my grandfather was born. One of the favorite maxims of Augustus was: "He who goes a-fishing with a golden hook will catch nothing nearly so valuable as that which he chances." To this my grandfather would subscribe, and so must I, although I recognize that it is in a way sacrilegious. This ministry of the Gospel is not for the timorous.

But, on the other hand, prudence is its own reward, and it is for this heresy that I condemn myself. Let it be. I can face hell, I think, with more composure than I could face any single day of my past come back to accost me, through which I would have once more to survive. Nietzsche remarked that to want an instant of one's past returned is to want it all returned—not just the enjoyment of the moment, but also one's regrets and fears which are coexistent with this enjoyment—but even this does not state the whole case: for to wish a past instant returned is to wish for death. The past is an eternally current danger, in effect, a suicide. We desire the past, we call to it just as men who have fallen overboard an ocean liner call, because we must predict the future. But this prediction, which is most necessitous, we cannot achieve. We back into the future, and are blind to what happens until it has already occurred. Then we only see it receding, metamorphosing with distance and distorted with memory's impure Doppler effect. As far as event is concerned, the mind is an isolated citadel standing in a desert. Miles of sand surround it. A starry sky stretches overhead. The face of God never leans toward it, and in the desert nothing moves. The citadel itself is peopled only with thin ghosts.

An acquaintance once told me that he read a translation of the *Iliad* when he was about ten years old, and that his mother died when he was nine. He can remember Achilles better than he can remember his mother. He has never read the book since, and I am almost certain he is afraid to. This is the kind of thing the past is: it is not unchanging. It grows up soon with weeds and underbrush like a dangerous trail. It sours and rots like old meat in the mind. It is a huge sea with titanic currents—like any sea. And he who fishes it must use a golden hook, he must plunge himself as bait into its depths, and if his past does not devour and destroy him wholly, his luck is insuperable. The self is the golden hook which is too valuable to cast into former days; no line is strong enough to hold it to the present and to the hope of futurity once the cast is made. The self is very precious, too; it is only with the self, open-eyed and sober, that we can accept Christ and the salvation of God. I do not trust another; I do not trust a book, a rock, a stream; I do not trust my friendly Doppelgänger who ranges my dreams and daydreams: these are all traitors, and they will murder me with the Judas kiss of the unconscious. Sleep, the night, belong to the unconscious, but one must take care to cut it off, like an electric light, at dawn. The day has no business with the belly of the mind. For when the mind dies, it goes belly up, a poisoned fish, the sickly white of the unconscious nakedly displayed.

Put it this way: you don't plow with a tiger; you don't hide your money in a furnace. Blake said, "The tigers of wrath are wiser than the horses of instruction," but if what he said is true, it is better that we remain stupid. One hears that he must be sensitive and empathic to the conditions of others. But one can be so sensitive that he is helpless, a mere pincushion, a professional victim. Mark the difference between pity and compassion. Do not love your neighbor as yourself; love him as your brother. One loves oneself too dangerously. Pity is hypochondria, narcissism, one must love men as one loves brothers: with the fine edge of a love, a razor dividing affections and hate.

Take yourself up.

. . . My sermon clanks shut.

The Inkling

CHAPTERS 1–3

<u>ONE</u>

A young man, sixteen years old, was sitting hunkered on his heels in a stretch of tall yellow sagegrass. His hair was yellow like the sagegrass and the slight down sprinkled on his jaws and down his neck was yellow. And his tan windbreaker had faded from foul weather until it too was almost the color of sagegrass, just slightly darker. The wind moved in the sage and worried it over, and the young man did not move except now and then to tip back his head when he drank from the dark bottle. The liquor was yellow and flamed in his throat. The fellow was hunkered in the field, fiercely self-willed; he was like a belligerent voice.

The sun was high and hot, the color of the sagegrass, but the breeze had a cold edge on it. It was early October. The maple leaves were ruby-colored, the beech trees jerked in the wind like giant candle flames, yellow and transitory. In the clear sharp air the mountains seemed to have drifted forward, nearer now without the summer haze. The mountains were spattered with red, yellow, and blue over green. The premonitory wind had polished the sky clear as a lens.

He was drunk. In the yellowed windbreaker his chest swam in sweat and the hair on the back of his neck was damp. In his steel-rimmed spectacles (the lenses of which did not magnify), the reflected sagegrass moved restlessly and in the corner of each glass square the sun was a tiny yellow dot, the size of the pupils of his eyes. His mind was filled with yellow light and with his own presence. So weightily he existed in the field that he might have created it. When he tipped his head back the muscles in his neck distended to the size of fingers. He drank again; again.

Across a trickling ditch about thirty yards before him there was no sagegrass, but a cool smooth lawn in the deep shadow of an oak tree. A swing made of an old automobile tire went back and forth, and the female child swinging uttered mindless whoops. Her pink dress was no longer stiff with starch and it fluttered in the wind. Her legs were skinny and dirty. She swung wildly, shrieking, and already there was much in her voice that was unchildlike.

Near the swing stood the child's brother, a year younger than she, six years old. He too was blond, his hair brighter than the sagegrass, almost silvery. His movements were slow and deliberate as he tossed a baseball gently into the air and lashed at it with a dull-colored bat. When he knocked it some yards away he walked to pick it up; he went slowly and then carried it back to his position under the tree to hit it again.

At last he fouled the ball behind him. It went spinning, arcing up over the ditch and over a pond of the shadowy sagegrass. It fell and rolled forward a few feet and came to rest a yard or so before the yellow-haired fellow. He stared at it. It lay solid and self-contained, disputing his supremacy of existence in the field. He stared at it malevolently.

The boy watched the ball, and when it fell the young man could see from where he sat hunkered that the boy uttered a huge sigh. His thin shoulders rose; fell. With much difficulty he stopped the swing and helped his sister squeeze through the tire. Grasping her hand he led her to the gurgling ditch and they went down. In a moment they bobbed up again like swimmers and came forward. The girl was whimpering and the boy was reassuring her and he told her quietly to hush, keeping his voice low and steady as if he was calming a skittish mare. Still leading her, the boy began making wide steady arcs, watching his feet closely. The yellow-haired fellow watched the ball lying stubborn before him, stiffly resisting being found. He held the bottle in his left hand and did not drink; his right hand was red, wound about with a blood-soaked crude bandage. He did not move as they came closer, and it was clear that they were going to find the ball at last, although they had not yet seen him.

He stood, rising quickly from his hunkered position, as quickly as a knife blade flicked open. He towered over them, looking yellow and wild. He bent and scooped up the ball and held it aloft, and it was almost hidden in his white hand. He had shifted the liquor bottle to his wounded right hand. They retreated a few steps, the boy dragging the girl back, getting her behind himself. They both were white and so fearful they might have trembled out of existence like match flames.

"Hanh, you goddam kids!" he cried. He shook the ball in his hand. "What if you was to die? What if you was to die one day?" he cried.

The boy looked so fierce from fear that he looked like a trapped fox. He snatched a glance behind him into the cool smooth lawn; no one was there.

"One day; what if you was to die one day?" he cried. "Hanh! Hanh!" He threw the ball away into the air. It landed in the lawn, rolling forward fast to bounce against the oak tree. "Hanh! Hanh!" The yellow-haired man was laughing and shouting. *Hanh!* He strode toward them, whipping through the sagegrass, and went past them. He shifted the bottle back into his unwounded left hand. He had to clamber on his hands and knees up the bank to the roadbed because he was afraid of dropping the bottle. As soon as he had begun to walk he felt cooler.

The boy held tightly to his sister's arms above her elbows. She was trying to strike him, to scratch him, and she was gulping air in great murderous sobs. He kept trying to soothe her, to lead her back into the green lawn.

Then a year later almost the same thing happened. The mother and the uncle had gone off to town on some necessary errand. It was later in the season, November or December, and a silent disquieting snow lay everywhere. The smooth lawn was smoother still and it looked like a huge linen tablecloth. A smear of snow was on the bottom rim of the tire swing like a smudge of beard on a round face. They were playing in the living room around the chocolate-colored oil heater which boomed like an uncertain drum when the boy spanked it with an open hand. His sister's eyes were always on him, fearfully trusting. Now she was taller and stronger than he. They were playing together with unaccustomed noise so that at the beginning they did not hear the terrifying voice.

She heard it first. "Jan, Ja-an," she said.

He gazed at her, baffled, silent.

"It's *them*," she said. "I can hear them talking."

"No," he said. "It's not them. You can't hear them."

But then in a moment it really was as if it were the dead people talking. The low terrifying note, wordlessly questioning, sounded in the room, thrilling through the very walls of the house.

"Yes it is," she breathed. She began to cry silently, tears welling and remaining bright in her eyes.

The low cold note sounded twice again.

"No," he whispered, "it's not the dead ones talking." He tore himself from a momentary trance and ran to the door and slammed it open. White coldness flooded his whole body instantly and he shuddered. *Croo, croo.* From the bare oak tree, on a branch above the still O of the swing, the little gray owl looked at him with mean yellow eyes. "It's an owl," he said.

She was behind him in the doorway. The tears were streaking down her feverish cheeks. "Who is it, Jan? What are they saying?"

Croo, crrrooo.

"It's just a squinch owl. He can't hurt you."

The owl blinked as suddenly as a man would snap his fingers. It cocked its head to one side and Timmie thought that it was trying to get a better look at her. "I see it," she said. "Won't it go away? Make it go away, Jan."

"Shoo!" he cried, waggling his thin arms up and down.

Croo.

He ran out into the yard and scooped up snow and packed it, slapping it tight with both hands. The first snowball he threw went far away, not even touching the tree; the second ball splashed on the black tree trunk, making a shape like he and Timmie made when they squeezed a drop of ink in a creased paper. Looking slow, the little owl toppled forward, the long wings outspread. It came swooping low toward him over the smooth snow.

"Jan, watch out! Jan, don't let it get you!" She ran shrieking into the house, through the dark living room.

He ducked, crossing his thin forearms over his head and the back of his neck. The owl passed far overhead, wheeling up suddenly at the corner of the roof, and then beating its wings stoutly as it flew away through the gelid air. He watched it until it was a mere dot and lost among the spiny branches of the woods toward the east. He went into the house and closed the door, leaning the back of his head against it for a moment while his chest palpitated with jagged breathing. Through two closed doors he could hear a dim moaning. At the door to the hall he paused; the moaning had grown louder, and he was scared he might frighten her to death. "It's me," he said loudly. "It's Jan, Timmie; it's me." He went in and found her in their own small bedroom, lying on the floor behind the bed on the other side of the room. She was clutching a giant stuffed giraffe to her. She pressed the dumb head to her belly and had thrown her skinny legs over the soiled neck of the toy. The whole top of her dress front was wet from her crying.

"Hush, Timmie," he said. "Don't keep on crying and crying."

She would not stop; she couldn't stop until much later, when the mother and the uncle returned.

TWO

"Hush, just hush," said Uncle Hake. "I don't want to hear any more about it."

Jan scooted over the worn wool rug; he had designed something important to build with the Tinkertoys.

Uncle Hake had once told the mother: "I ain't no daddy, I ain't no family man. You better stick to your guns and find some guy that will take care of you, some guy that wants a ready-made family." He rattled the newspaper with a great deal of useless verve. Uncle Hake was glum, uninterested, rather stupid. Hard to imagine how he and the mother were of the same family.

He was short, slightly slouched always, his shoulders rounded, his hair gone now; large-jointed all over: he was a funny-looking knobby little man. His nose too was rounded like a ball of dough, and beneath it he wore a dark little bristly mustache. He would sit in the flowery easy chair near the oil heater and rattle the newspaper and if Jan or Timmie came near enough he would very quickly take off his slipper —it was his one deft move—and slap the children across the arms or legs or chest. Every evening and all day Saturday and Sunday he would make quick nervous trips to the bathroom, and each time he returned his breath smelled ever more sweetly and fiery. Once or twice a week the mother forgot and asked him to carry out the garbage; and then he would scrooch his eyebrows down until his whole face was a squeezed lump like an angry fist and he would say, "Why don't you get these

36

damn trifling kids learned to do a little something?" And he would hunt through the house, his greasy bedroom slipper in his hand, until he found them. Swat, swat. "You kids better learn to do a little something to earn your keep around here."

He labored at the crossword puzzles in the newspaper, mumbling and chewing at the frayed corners of the mustache.

Summer mornings he would sit out in the cool smooth lawn in the crooked rocking chair, rocking away. He was barefoot and wore old greasy gray trousers and a yellowed undershirt with thin straps that kept slipping off his round shoulders. Then he was drunk plainly enough; on hot summer nights he couldn't sleep and all night he bumbled about in his dingy little room, mumbling and drinking and gnawing at the bristly corners of the mustache. Wouldn't he at last eat it all away? If he could be zipped open down the front, it was certain there would be a great ball of hair in his stomach, as in a cow's.

Everyone got along with Uncle Hake without respecting or loving him. This was because for everyone he knew he existed only as a sort of chip in a tooth which the tongue is always unconsciously seeking: embarrassingly familiar, faintly annoying, but always reassuring. As long as Uncle Hake was around you knew the universe was still identical with the one you had always known: it had not suddenly been cleansed overnight.

Timmie treated Uncle Hake with a half-fearful reverence, the way she treated all inanimate objects. Jan, who spent all his time training his will, found it easiest to ignore his uncle, not wasting his energy on what was after all an unusable lump. Anyway, what if Uncle Hake had no real will to exercise against?

He had a number of cronies who were all as lugubriously out of kilter as he. They were either short and pudgy and greasy or long and scrawny and sallow, and they had names like Pete or Johnny or Jake. They didn't come to the house very often, but Jan learned to despise the sight and smell of them; Timmie of course ran quickly away to hide, peering out unexpectedly. They wore red or bright blue neckties, these old men, and the knot was never correct but hard and tight, and their breaths reeked with alcohol like painted sores. Uncle Hake sometimes played poker with them, going stubbornly off Friday evenings as the mother watched tight-mouthed, and returning in the deepest hours of the morning. He was extraordinarily unlucky, but now and again he won, and then the two children would find him strutting about the lawn in the morning, without a shirt and barefoot in the iron-colored dew, the ash of his fumy cigar growing always longer and droopier.

On the wall in his dingy room was a picture of a big blond lady in one of the new very small bathing suits. The photograph Jan peeked at fearfully at first, and then later on, belligerently. There were on his dresser three greasy combs and a box of the rank cigars. On a small table by the door were a fountain pen and a pencil stub and a stack of bills, of which Uncle Hake paid a single one every day until the stack was gone. Then the new bills came in. It was merely that he somehow felt that in writing only one check each day he was spending less money than if he paid all the bills at once. He kept all receipts, binding them in thick packets with rubber bands. Trying as hard as she could, the mother could do nothing toward making the room cheery. And Uncle Hake would have possessed a Spartan existence except that he lived in the languorous luxury of blind ignorance, irritatedly unknowing. He did not even really keep up with the war news. In this dim room the lady in the bikini began by being explosively present, but with the months her picture got darker and darker; she too was being ignominiously stained by Uncle Hake, like one of his undershirts.

And he would lounge about for weeks—or months or years if it had been possible—in the same greasy yellowish clothes without changing. The mother would say, "Hake, let me have those clothes and I'll put them in the wash I've got to do today." Uncle Hake would say, "Aw, leave me alone and quit pestering me. I guess I can change my own clothes. You're always pestering me about something, you won't never give me any peace." It turned out finally that she always had to wake up early and sneak into his room and steal his clothes off the bedpost to get them washed. He complained about that too—he was continually complaining about everything, of course, but no one paid him any mind. It was like the noise of traffic at night when you were trying to sleep: you finally got so accustomed to it you didn't hear it anymore.

And it was a silly accident that kept him out of the war: when he was seventeen years old he had dropped a sledgehammer on his left foot. (He had never again picked one up.)

And he worked in a laboratory in the paper mill, testing for the chemical qualities of paper, and he hated the job with a dull and constant hate.

THREE

*J*an had begun when he was very young—perhaps when he was five
years old—to test his will, to flex it. He had begun merely by trying
to outstare Buddha, the gray-and-black-striped mongrel cat. Every day
he spent long hours looking into those feline sardonic slitted eyes, and
his will grew equally in heat as it grew in strength and intensity until
finally he acquired a hateful contempt for this particular object. The
cat was bored in the beginning but gradually became afraid, and then
one day after some weeks of this staring it looked away. Jan was ma-
liciously joyful. He rose from his squat and reached and gathered the
cat into his arms. Across the trickling ditch he took it, into the sagegrass
which swirled about his waist, pecking at his warmly laden wrists. By
a largish rock he set the cat on the ground and placed his foot lightly
upon it, and he raised the stone and flung it down upon the cat's head.
Buddha screeched, a horrid loud babylike shrieking, but there was no
one in the house except Timmie, who was asleep. No one stopped Jan
or called to him. Again; again; again, he flung the stone down and the
cat fought desperately beneath his foot, taking a long time to die. But
at last he had killed it and he grasped the dead Buddha by the tail and
swung it away into a squirmy bank of honeysuckle. The stone he took
up and carried back from the field to the house and put down near the
back door. It was smeared on one awkward side with blood and there

were other, whitish, stains here and there upon it. It was to be a new obstacle for him to vanquish; and in time he came to know every mark, the contour of every stain, each minuscule protuberance, the vague course of every vein, every tiny pit in the texture of the surface. He squatted before it, gazing hotly, and it looked as if he might be worshiping a god in the stone. This time he managed the exercise without gathering rancor and he and the stone in the end became brothers, and Jan was satisfied that he had overcome the will of the stone without having to displace it. Yet despite this truce Jan was a fiery wild being. Under the very blond hair which fell over his forehead his eyes were always scarily direct, as blunt as two fingers. It seemed that all that willed puissance had lodged in the eyes.

Thus, even at a young age, he had made a great part of the world he knew embarrassedly aware of him—and more. With those eyes he could catch things in the off-balance moment, or force things off balance himself. Over and over Uncle Hake said to him, "Stop cuttin them old eyes at me, boy." Swat, with the slipper. Jan shrugged him off as if he were a horsefly. But the uncle's discomfiture about the boy was inescapable, and he found himself avoiding Jan as much as possible; but Uncle Hake avoided everyone, such a dim dingy life he led anyway. The mother watched Jan going bored and purposeful through the house and she kept wondering, wondering.

He kept long hours to himself in the dusty garret or in the disused barn. He sat thinking, watching cool yellow slats of light creep slowly off the floor and higher across the walls. He watched insects crawl along in the dust, and mice would play over his feet sometimes, so long he sat still. From three or four window screens and odd pieces of wood he built a cage—he was seven or eight years old then—and caught the mice, desperate and feverish, in his hands and dropped them in. He fed them on what he could steal from the pantry or the garbage can, and one day he brought Timmie out to the barn to have a look. There were a dozen or so of the gray mice, roiling together in the little rusty cage. In the slant yellow light their eyes were iridescent little red circles.

Timmie advanced; scuttled back. She clutched his arm.

"I'm going to keep on saving them up," he told her seriously, "and

one night after they're good and hungry I'm going to take them into
Uncle Hake's room and turn them loose on him. When we wake up
that morning there won't be nothing left of Uncle Hake but a big pile
of old bones." From his pocket he produced half a soda cracker and
held it dramatically between thumb and forefinger. Quickly he opened
the top of the cage and dropped the cracker crumb among them. They
rushed to it instantly. *Keerk, keerk, keek, keek.*

She watched with great round eyes and dug her fingers into his
arm. "Don't do it, Jan," she said. "That's bad. Don't do that."

"Nothin but just a pile of old bones," he said.

"Don't do it, Jan. Please." Now she didn't cry, but she watched
wide-eyed until the cracker disappeared.

And then that night she had a nightmare and she was racked with
shuddery convulsive vomiting. She shrieked again and again as the
mother bent over her, holding her wet forehead gently and patting her
hands. "There there," she said, "there now, there there. It's all right,
baby; it's all right, honey." She cleaned the girl's neck and pajama
blouse with different washcloths. Jan thought that she would crazily let
it out about his mice, but all the mother could get from her was
something about "a long bony man."

"It was a big long bones," said Timmie, choking. Her face was
white as salt.

"A man?" asked the mother.

"Yes," cried Timmie. "A big long bones man."

"A long bony man," the mother said. She sighed. "There now,
honey, it's all right. You're going to be all right."

Jan moved his legs luxuriously under the sheet. It was so late and
dark outside that the overhead light in the room seemed brighter than
he'd ever seen it. The big stuffed giraffe had tumbled off her bed, foully
spattered.

After a long while the mother was satisfied and went away, en-
joining them to keep quiet and go to sleep. She clicked out the light,
leaving them darkling in the separate beds.

Jan waited until he heard her enter her own room down the hall.
"Timmie?" he asked.

At first she wouldn't answer.

"Timmie," he said, "don't be afraid about it. I was just teasing you. I was just kidding."

"Are you going to put them on him?" Her voice was throaty, rich with dread.

"No, I'm not going to. I was just fooling."

"I'm glad then," she said simply. "Because it would be bad."

"Yes." He realized at that moment that he would have to look out for Timmie, to take care of her. Though she was larger and taller than he, and a year older, he was much stronger in a way that seemed to be important. It was strange to think about in the dark late night with her beside him still lying awake, afraid. In the window eight or nine pale stars glittered relentlessly.

Next day he hid the mice in a different corner in the barn, covering the cage over with some old straw and some rotten burlap, so that Timmie wouldn't run across it accidentally. Later on he would go about the house collecting sharp pointed instruments, pencils, paring knives, and he would throw them away. He would break the points off scissors that were left lying about. He never wondered why the mother or the uncle—well, Uncle Hake; what could be expected?—showed so little wisdom about Timmie. He saw that even the mother was blind on one whole side, gentle and knowing as she was.

He shrugged. His bony shoulders rose; fell. He stood at the window, gazing out into the yard. In the big oak tree an oriole's nest, pear-shaped, bobbed free in the breeze. In an orange ray of light that got through the branches a gang of midges danced brightly, golden atoms. Something twinkled on the lawn, and when he looked closer he saw that it was a snake. "It's a big chunkhead," he said solemnly. He went to check on Timmie. She was in their bedroom, trying to stuff the soiled giraffe into a dresser drawer. Then he went out to look. Sure enough, it was a big copperhead, which drew back into a taut trembling S when it felt him coming. He looked about for something to kill it with, but then thought of Uncle Hake. On a deliberated impulse he decided to tell the uncle about the snake.

He went straight in. Uncle Hake was lying on the bed in his dim room, wearing dark greasy trousers and a yellowed undershirt. "Damn it, boy," he said, "ain't you learned no better than to bust in without knocking? If it was mine to do, I'd whack some goddam sense in your head."

"There's a big snake out in the yard."

"A big snake, huh?" His eyes were dull and his breath was hot with liquor. "What kind?"

"It's a big chunkhead," Jan said.

"Chunkhead, huh? Has it got a spot like a penny on the back of the head?"

"Yes."

"I guess it's a chunkhead then." He raised himself painfully to a sitting position. "You go out and keep it there," he said. "I'll be there in a minute." With his bare soiled feet he felt about on the floor for his shoes. "Don't let it get away."

"All right."

Surprisingly, the snake had not got much farther. Jan stood about five feet away and stamped hard on the ground. The snake hissed, flexed into a coil. He looked at it uncaring: it was merely a big snake.

Uncle Hake came around the corner of the house. He slouched along, one thin strap of the undershirt flopping on his arm as he walked. In his right hand, held loosely at his shambling thigh, he carried a big nickel-plated revolver. Jan's attention fastened significantly on the pistol. It was something he hadn't known about, hadn't actually expected. He determined on the spot to make a close examination of Uncle Hake's room as soon as possible. The uncle raised the pistol and aimed it shakily at the dully glowing head of the snake. He missed with the first shot, spraying the ground to the left of the snake up into a little jet. The snake hissed again and spread out of the coil like oil oozing over a hard surface, and then drew back again into the tense quivering S. Uncle Hake fired again; he shot away the copper-colored head. Then he breathed unevenly and lowered the gun and dropped the cylinder open and shook the bullets into his left hand. The bullets he put into his left pocket, stuffing the gun into the other. "Get rid of that goddam thing, boy," he told Jan.

"All right." Unconsciously Jan kept looking at the lumpy bulge of the uncle's trousers pocket.

"And stop cuttin them old eyes around at me, damn you."

"All right."

Uncle Hake turned his back on Jan and walked away, trying to square back his round shoulders, pulling up the slipped strap of the undershirt with a greasy thumb.

Jan picked up the crazy wriggling headless snake and took it over to the ditch, dropped it into the little oily stream that trickled at the bottom. The body thrashed wildly in the water, turning up the sickening white underbelly again and again. The brackish water began to tinge pink. . . . And he had found out about the gun. He had also discovered that Uncle Hake had been scared of the snake and—maybe—of the gun too. He mulled the thought, scratching his armpit. Yes, it was true: the uncle was frightened of his own pistol.

Two days later he found the opportunity and he searched the room, going through all the drawers and the closet and even looking under the bed. He found the pistol right enough and only one other thing he hadn't counted on, a fairly large tan-colored book of photographs of men and women doing silly things among each other, all of them hairy and huge between the legs. The book smelled musky and queer. It took him a good while to figure out how to get the cylinder of the gun open, but finally he managed, and shook three bullets from the chambers onto the bedspread. He examined them closely, looking at them over and over. They were heavier than he had thought, and this was a distinct disadvantage. He shrugged; it was just something he would have to chance. Taking fine care he replaced everything. He surveyed the room. Had he obliterated his tracks? He was satisfied. He had left no trace.

And then it took about three weeks to whittle out the phony bullets properly. He carved them from hard splintery locust wood, kneading them in a bag of fine sand to make them smooth. The blunt noses of them he colored with pencil lead. He colored with white crayon the jackets; they didn't shine as they ought, but this was another chance he had counted on taking. The brass-colored caps in the butts of the jackets were fashioned of clay mixed with a drop of red fingernail polish.

He hefted the finished fakes; they were crude. They would have to do. He shrugged. The first chance he got he made the substitution, poking the wooden bullets into the same chambers he had taken the real ones from. Wrapping the actual bullets in a scrap of brown paper, he hid them behind a loose board in a stall in the abandoned barn. He strode from the barn into the cold sunlight, grinning. Now Uncle Hake didn't have to be scared of his pistol anymore.

Dagon

Ph'nglui mglw'nafh Cthulhu R'lyeh
wgah'nagl fhtagn.

Part I

ONE

*A*bout 9:30 the next morning he entered the downstairs room which faced the almost painfully blue west and the tall ridge across the little valley, the room which his grandparents had used to call the "sun parlor." He advanced into the room a way and halted, seeming to feel the whole fabric of the house tremulous with his footsteps. And he had paused to consider, well, to think about how much there actually *was* to consider. The onus of inheritance was already beginning to rub a bit.—The room was familiarly musty and the two windows, eyed and wavy, were decent in their gray gauzy curtains. Over the bisected window in the door which opened to the outside, the glass curtain was stretched tight with rods at top and bottom so that the cloth was pulled into stiff ribs, stiff as fingers of the dead. He took another step and again hesitated, hearing the quiet wary rattle of glassware somewhere. Meditating, he shifted his weight forward and back, rocking on the balls of his feet. Had all the floor timbers melted away with dry rot? He couldn't quite bring himself to doubt, staring down frowning at the regular lines of dark oak flooring, board laid solid by board. Even the layer of dust which was spread like cheesecloth about his feet didn't entirely dull the hard polish of the wood. He disliked thinking of these careful rows ripped up, exposing the broad rough subflooring; and then that too taken away to get at the flaking bones of the house. But there was

47

probably no preventing it. He sighed, and as he inhaled, agitated atoms of dust pierced his nostrils brightly. Twice he sneezed, and rubbed his nose roundly with his wrist, squeezed his eyebrows in his palm. Had he really heard an echo to his sneeze? The room hardly seemed large enough to give up echoes—it was about twenty feet square with a high ceiling—but it was a room truly made for secondary presences, for reverberations. This wasn't the whole room. Opposite him, double doors, divided into small glass rectangles, closed off what was actually the remainder of this room. In the left door his image stood, hand still over his face, and he was all cut into pieces in the panes. He dropped his pale hand to his side, and in the glass the movement coruscated.

He moved toward the west wall and once again his image, larger now and darker, accosted him. His head and torso stood before him, sliced now into the pattern of an oval enclosed in roundish triangles and seemingly stacked in the shelves of the dark old writing cabinet. He shrugged, turned away. The low sofa, piled with fancy pillows and cushions, sat stolid against the opposite wall. The obese horror was draped over with a picture rug, but it was easy enough to guess how it was: covered with a vinous prickly nap and with three huge cushions laid on the springs. The wool picture rug had two fringes of red tassel and displayed a Levantine scene: in the market place the wine seller sits comfortably beneath his awning while the dark and turbaned stranger looms above him on his camel, and behind in the dusty street the woman returns from the well, her water jug shouldered. This tableau splotched with a profusion of pillows and cushions, green, red, yellow, gaudy flowers, knowing birds, birds darkly wise. In the center of the sofa were two oblong companion pillows, shouldered so closely together that they looked like the Decalogue tablets. They were white, or had been white, and painfully stitched upon them with blue thread were companion mottoes, companion pictures. In the left pillow lies a girl, her long blue hair asprawl about her face, her eyes innocently shut, asleep. The motto: I SLEPT AND DREAMED THAT LIFE WAS BEAUTY. But the story continued, and on the next pillow her innocence is all torn away: there she stands, gripping a round broom; her hair now is pinned up severely and behind her sits a disheartening barrel churn. I WOKE AND FOUND THAT LIFE WAS DUTY. The pillows sat, stuffed and stiff as disapproving bishops; they could, he thought, serve as twin tombstones for whole gray generations. It was in no way difficult to imagine the fingers of his grandmother, tough and knobbly, wearily working upon these wearying legends, these most speaking epitaphs. It was more discouraging still to wonder if perhaps this task hadn't been performed by his grandmother's mother. Even without thinking he doubted that there was anything in his blood which could now fight back to that bitter use of mind; he just wasn't so tough. . . . No; no, that wasn't true, either. Slow, wet, easy living hadn't got to his Puritan core, not *really*. He *could* hump logs together to make a house; *he* could plow the long furrow as straight as a killing arrow. It was simply that he didn't have to: the world had got easier, even the sky. All that temper was still in him and not really very hidden, and it was no strange matter that these two pillows could cause to rise in his mind narrow visions of those stringent decades. He could see his male ancestry as grainy and rough as if they had all been hacked from stone. They didn't drink, didn't smoke; they didn't read, and all books other than the great black one were efficient instruments of Sathanas. The only fun they had was what he was living evidence of.—And very probably not.—He could imagine them, his whiskery forefathers, stalking wifeward to beget, stolid, unmoved as men readying themselves to slaughter hogs. And some hint of that too. The women were no better. Their hands were pained knots, like blighted unopenable buds. Their eyes were stuffed with the opaque ice which had clenched over the fear of their hearts. . . . And yet, and yet there was always something faintly comforting in thinking upon the gelid principles with which his grandfathers had shored up themselves for duty, military or familial, or for the rich farming business.

He was vaguely bothered, nettled, and he turned away from contemplating the pillows. Across from him was the wide entry to a dark formal dining room, and in the near corner a complacent fat club chair. He turned round and round, feeling the windows slide over his sight and the serrated glitter of the glass doors, and found himself, in a momentary accident, face to face with the wall. It was plaster, and he could discern in its grain the sweep of the maker's trowel and swirled signs of the hair. In the morning silence the wall seemed as vocal as everything else in the room. Illumination, a gilt tin contraption which sported naked light bulbs, hung suspended from the ceiling by a gilt chain, and a thick webby electric cord sidled through the links. Before the piled sofa sat a low table, the wood mahogany-stained, with a glass top which displayed photographs that could dim, but not curl, with age: four rows of gray-and-black squares, instants of frozen miming that he would not examine. More gilt, on the wall above the sofa: a rectangular frame which enclosed a photograph in anemic—"tinted"— colors, the faces of his grandfather and grandmother. Both the progenitors seemed masked for the picture, as severe as if they had plotted beforehand to judge the photographer, to sentence him to a life of hard labor. The eyes of the grandfather were frigid blue, the color of the windwashed March sky reflected in the ice of a puddle. Somehow the tinting process, whatever it was, had made those eyes inviting targets for wishful darts. Set jaws, assured noses, ears which would admit only acquiescent sounds. The eyes of the grandmother were gray and, though doubtless resolute, the gaze was not so personally stationed. In her clear forehead and in the rather distant aiming of her eyes there was not so much of her husband's belligerent certainty; there was a hint of troubled—but still (he had to admit it)—unshaken humanity. But it was an unyielding countenance, and he found himself brushing his hand over his face as if he had just walked through a cobweb. Awkwardly he stepped back, as though he could retreat from his unrealized action or, rather, from whatever vague thought had inspired it. Nor was he delighted to see his mind so often turning upon himself.

He pawed a mass of pillows heavily aside and sat down on the sofa; fumbled in his shirt pocket for a cigarette. The odor of the sofa submerged him; it wasn't sour exactly, but rather sweet-and-sour, palpable; musty, of course, but with an aura of times past so striking as almost to give an impression of freshness. The smell betokened what? Voluminous clothes kept with a sachet too old, so that its power had disappeared into the cloth. Or long dutiful Sunday afternoons spent with the Methodist preacher over a box of stale chocolate candies. Or dripping afternoon funerals set up in this room and garnished with flowers which had very recently given up their sickly ghosts. His spirit seemed drowning in the smell of the sofa, in the swift flood of pastness it poured out. He lit the cigarette and sucked the smoke deep, as if protecting himself, almost in fact as if smoking was an act of defiance toward the past. The smoke rose slowly, the lax strands of it parting and hanging almost motionless in the air, seemingly very solid. It was himself, in fact, who seemed flimsy; even his body, whose weight the hard sofa barely accepted, felt vaporous, tenuous: there was not enough real event attached to it to force it to existence. The room was so silent that he could hear his chest rasp against the cloth of his shirt as he breathed, and for one scary moment he imagined that this sound became increasingly faint, was dying away. He dropped the blackened paper match into a silly little ashtray, a tiny china circle with—again—gilt lines and in the center an ugly pink rose. The dead match lay across the face of the rose like a disastrous scar, and he noted it with a twinge of guilty triumph; so that almost reflexively he mashed the new cigarette into the flower, leaving there a raw streak of black ash. The small coals died immediately.

He rose and crossed the room. As he had suspected, the desk section of the dark secretary was locked, but through the glass cabinet doors he saw the small brass key lying on the middle shelf. The lock was reluctant, but the section did at last let down, exposing an interior less musty than he had imagined. There were half a dozen tight-ranked drawers and a number of bulging pigeonholes. Letters, photographs, books of check stubs, a bottle in which the ink had dried to a circular black scab, a Waterman pen with a discolored yellow nib. He pulled from one of the pigeonholes a resisting envelope and shook the letter from it. The cheap paper had darkened with dust and the recalcitrant words had been formed with blunt pencil strokes, gray on gray. He held the sheet above his head and turned his back to the window. The words came dimly to his eyes: . . . *guess Jasper's note will be alright anyway for this yr and can renew with confidance, I guess in the neighborhood of 1500.* It would of course be concerned with money. He let it drop unfluttering and wiped his fingers on his trousers leg. From a closed drawer peeped the shiny corner of a snapshot, which he slipped out without opening the drawer. At first he couldn't comprehend what object was pictured, but it was, after all, merely an automobile, a Dodge or a Plymouth of the late thirties, black, hardly at repose before the immaculately vertical lines of a walnut tree. Why this photograph? He stared at it as if it were an urgent but indecipherable message, intently personal. The car was not new, had not been photographed on that account. It was perhaps no more than the thoughtless effort to finish up a roll of film so that a brother with his arm about the shoulders of an aunt or a wide-eyed distressed baby cousin might sooner see the light of day in their own white-edged squares. Yet here it was, the car, as bluntly and totally itself as if it had been invented for the purpose of perplexing. He tried to slide the snapshot back through the crack in the top of the drawer, but it encountered a hidden tightness and folded up, the brittle surface suddenly webbed with fine lines like a cracked china plate. He desisted, and let the picture loll out of the front of the desk like an idiot untasting tongue. When he once more glimpsed his darkly reflected face in the cabinet doors, his eyes looked fearful.

He turned again to the panes of glass in the double doors, this time erasing his features by bringing his face directly against one of the panes. He cupped his hands, extending them from his temples as if he were trying to see for a long distance through blinding sunlight. The interior of this room swam forward to meet him. Although there was a row of windows in the opposite wall, they were darkened by a shaggy row of fir bushes growing by the outside wall, so that this room was even dimmer than the one in which he was standing.

When he tried the knob the lock uttered an unnerving scrape, but the right-hand door swung inward easily enough. Here was real mustiness, an odor so stuffed with unmoving time that it seemed strange the pressure of it hadn't burst the doors and windows. Entering, he left unclear tracks in the dust behind him, and the dust muted his footsteps, seemed to adhere like cobweb to his shoes. The dust seemed a huge powdery cobweb. A long low comfortless-looking lounge was pushed against the wall, and the tough ornate wood of the back of it jammed into the windowsill. This sofa was undraped, but the upholstery was decorated with looping broad arabesques which suggested a badly stylized jungle. There were four identical knickknack tables on thin legs; they were cluttered with more of the tiny uninviting ashtrays and with a number of small pale wooden boxes. Against the east wall sat a black upright piano which somehow seemed sagging. He crossed to it and opened it. The keys were discolored, yellowish, cracked, and in some cases the ivory was missing almost completely. He punched gingerly at middle A, then experimented with a simple triad. Middle C sounded merely a dull thump; the E and A keys produced a dissonance. No doubt the strings had rusted, the whole guts of the instrument diseased and disordered. Again he wiped his fingers on his trousers, trying to wipe away that dust which seemed to seep into the pores of his skin. With his cold hand he brushed his face too, and the back of his neck. Over the top of the piano drooped a big elaborately embroidered doily; it looked like a fishnet, a fantastic net to catch—what? Oh, whatever inhabited the surcharged air of this room. Even after he backed away from the instrument, that acrid chord seemed to hang still in his hearing; it was as if he had written indelible curse words upon something which was supposed to remain sacredly blank. He raised and dropped his shoulders in a sigh; he felt almost as if he had been working away in hard physical labor; he had never before felt his will to be so ringed about, so much at bay. Never before had he realized so acutely the invalidity of his desires, how they could be so easily canceled, simply marked out, by the impersonal presence of something, a place, an object, anything vehemently and uncaringly itself. . . . But the pastness which these two rooms (really, one room divided) enclosed was not simply the impersonal weight of dead personality but a willful belligerence, active hostility. Standing still in the center of the first room, he felt the floor stirring faintly beneath his feet, and he was convinced that the house was gathering its muscles to do him harm; it was going to spring. But then he heard the sharp-heeled footsteps which caused the quivering, and then Sheila, his blond pale pretty wife, stuck her head through the hall door.

"Come on outside, Peter," she said. "Come away."

TWO

"I didn't have the faintest idea it was even near lunchtime," he said. Standing out here under the shiny June sky, he felt perfectly at ease to stretch his arms and shoulder muscles, as if he had just awakened from a dreary, unrefreshing sleep. He opened his mouth, tasting the bright air. It was warm; he hadn't realized how cold he had become in the house. Not far away he could hear a bird singing unstintingly, pure filigree of sound. "Here," he said. "Let me take that." He lifted the big wicker basket from his wife's strained hand. "Where are we going?"

Her voice was clear and easy as water. "It's your farm; you tell me. Where is the best place on this magnificent estate to have a picnic?"

"I don't know any more about the place than you do. But maybe we'd better not go too far. They're liable to deliver our stuff today."

Sheila looked at Peter with a secret eye: her tall gangly husband, all bones and corners his body was, had already begun worrying himself. The "stuff" which was to come was mostly books and notebooks and cryptic files of index cards. Already he was concerned about finishing his book—he called it his "study"—in time. They still had about twenty-five hundred dollars left of the amount they had allowed themselves and now this nice quiet place to work, this farm willed to him by his grandparents, had dropped into their laps, and still he was worrying himself. In this warmly glowing landscape his eyes were turned inward. As they went through the sparse front lawn of the house she broke a tall stalk of plaintain off at the top and put the oozy stem end into her mouth.

He swung the basket unrhythmically as he walked. His height and boniness made him seem loping. When they came to the reddish-yellow dirt road which ran northward past the house, he hesitated. "Now which way?" he said. "We can go either way here and still be in our own domain."

It was true. The big ugly house sat almost in the center of the wide farm, the four hundred acres shaped vaguely like an open hand. It sat among smooth hills, so that if they went very far in any direction they would have to climb.

"Your wish is my command," she said.

"Well . . ." He gave her a look. Lightness and irony more or less sweet, that was Sheila. He shrugged a shoulder and started toward their car, the old blue Buick parked in the sloping driveway behind the house.

"But let's *do* walk," she said. "It's a warm lovely day, and walking won't take so terribly much time. It'll be soon enough you're back to your nasty old books and note cards. Surely we're not here just for you to work."

"Still, that's mostly why we're here. At least, I hope it is." But he gave over anyway, and turning suddenly to her took her hand.

As quickly, involuntarily, she almost drew away. His hand on hers was dry and cool, actually cold, and startling in the warm sunlight. "You'll have to get used to walking," she said. "Now that you're in the country, you'll have to do all sorts of rustic things. You'll have to drink fresh milk and rob the honeybees and eat wild flowers. You're going to become a happy child of nature. I'm sure you'll make a great success of it."

"Oh, that's me. A happy child of nature."

In a hundred yards or so the road had climbed, cutting along the side of the hill. A slow dark stream ran in the narrow bottom field below; serpentine, sluggish, it reflected no light through the tall weeds and bushes that crowded to its edges. Sheila pointed toward it. "Maybe we could spread our blanket by the creek down there," she said. "It looks so nice and cool."

"Do you really want to go crawling through those weeds? I bet the whole field is full of snakes and spiders. And the ground down there'll be wet, so close to the stream."

"Weeds won't hurt you," she said. She patted the smooth leg of her pink cotton slacks. "Come on, chicken heart, it'll be very nice, bet you a pretty." She tugged at his hand, drew him to the side of the road.

"Hold on a minute." He shifted the basket to his other hand, and his body tilted perceptibly with the weight. "What in the world did you put in here, anyway? Heavy as lead."

"All kinds of surprises," she said. "Lead hamburgers, lead rolls, lead mustard . . ."

They got through the field without much difficulty and she was right, here by the stream it was cool. They found a circle of long cool grass, almost free of weeds, and shadowed by a stand of scrubby willow bushes. Sheila wafted a blue tablecloth over the ground and crawled over it on hands and knees to smooth it out. Then she stood and fingered her fine blond hair back from her temples. "Oh, this is lovely." She looked at him, an anxious inquiry. "Isn't it lovely?" The stream lapped intermittently at the banks, the dark water moved slow and dreamy through the shadows; now and again it splashed up a wink of reflected sunlight. Her face gleamed momentarily in a pure reflection of the sun. "We ought to take all our meals down here."

"Not me," he said. "I'm not getting out of bed and wallow through weeds and mud for breakfast."

"No, not breakfast. You don't have to be silly about it." She laughed. She began taking paper plates from the basket: held one up and flourished it ruefully. "These really ought to be very fine china," she said. "I've decided that we're celebrating."

"If those had been china, I'd never have got here with the basket."

She produced a large brown paper bag and drew a pretty baked hen from it. "Voilà!" And there was wine too, a California white wine in a green bottle with a red foil wrapping over the top. And a mixed salad tied up in a little plastic bag. "The plates are just for the salad, anyway. You'll have to be a child of nature and eat the chicken with your own crude hands. And look: I bought some ready-made dressing." She held up a small bottle and began shaking it furiously.

He had been staring at her, awestruck. "Where did you get all this stuff? The chicken and everything . . . What is it we're supposed to be celebrating?"

"There's a little old restaurant in the town. They were just delighted to sell me a nice baked chicken. See—while you were mooning around the house all morning I kept myself busy, planning and preparing these nice things for us. Everything just to make you happy."

He sighed. "And what is it we're celebrating?"

"Our vacation . . . Or just being here in this good cool spot by the water. Or anything. Why not?"

"Mmnh." Descending tone of regret. He felt that he had so much yet to do that even to be happy for the opportunity would be in some way to harm it, to jinx the chance for finishing.

"Anything, we're celebrating anything you like. *Remnant Pagan Forces in American Puritanism.*"

"A bit prematurely, perhaps." He cut his words short, isolated each of them with brief pauses. He couldn't help it.

She pouted. "Now please don't be a grouch. If you begin now, you'll just be a grouch all summer and neither of us will have a good time, and you won't get any more work done than if you'd been cheerful."

"Sorry," he said. But still the word was clipped.

"Look now . . ." She leaned carefully from her kneeling position, carefully across the spread tablecloth and pulled his ear lobe. "Eat. Drink. Enjoy. Relax. Nothing bad has happened, and nothing bad is going to happen. . . . And look what I got for you for after lunch." She fumbled in the basket for a moment and took out a fat masculine cigar. "If you don't like it, I'll strangle you," she said. "It was the most expensive one they had."

Finally he relented, or at least his body did; he threw himself back on the grass and laughed. Sunlight spotted his chest and face, spots like shiny yellow eyes.

She was laughing too, a liquid twittering, but suddenly stopped. "I hope you're not laughing at me," she said. She blinked her eyes wide.

He only laughed the harder, laughing at both of them, laughing most of all at the hard core of stodginess in himself that he was afraid of. Unresting shadows poured down his throat, leaf shadows twinkled on his face.

"Oh, you *are*." She was going to become angry. She looked about for something to throw at his convulsed thin chest.

"I'm not laughing at you." He lifted his hand, smiled at her. "No, really, I'm not. . . . But you're too much for me. You're simply too much."

"Yes, that's right. You're a happy child of nature. Simple. Pure. You can't understand my sophisticated complexity." She dumped salad from the moist plastic bag onto a paper plate. "Here, nature boy, eat. . . . You're an animal."

"In a lot of ways, that's true," he said, his voice taking an unconsciously serious edge. "I am simple, and you are pretty sophisticated. Anyway, you understand both of us better than I understand myself."

She took the wine bottle, peeled away the foil, unscrewed the top and poured. "Here," she said. "Drink this down and shut up. You'll give me a headache with all that psychological talk."

He hushed and they ate in silence. He kept looking at her, at her cool blond hair so spattered with light and shadow, at the way she moved her hands so freely, at the whiteness of her throat. So pretty she was, small and womanly, clear-eyed; it was a catch in his breathing. Her emotions were so mobile—she felt and responded to the slightest movement of things about her immediately and without hindrance— that he often forgot the chromium-bright hard mind which shone in the center. She was, after all, possessed of a nice intellect, superior perhaps to his own. In the core of his throat he breathed a wistful sigh, still looking. She colored slightly under his fixed gaze, she had misinterpreted it. Ho-ho-ho: so that was the drift of the breeze, was it? Her careful picnic was really a praeludium to the unaccustomed joy of making love in the open air. "In sight of God and everybody." He leaned back and got out his handkerchief and wiped at his fingers all runny with the juices of the bird. He smiled a slight dark smile.

She moved again, looked away; grew fretful under his stare. "Well, what is it then?" she said. "Do you see something you haven't seen before?"

He grinned, picked up the waxed paper cup and held it toward her. "Let's have another drink."

She mimed drawing away. "I don't know," she said. "Maybe you've had enough already. Maybe too much. You've already got staring drunk." She poured the cup full.

"That's the way, baby," he said. "Lay it on me."

She put down the bottle and flung a chicken bone at him. He sprang at her—the motion exaggerated, sudden—caught her shoulder and tumbled her over. She almost wiggled loose, but he caught her forearm and held her. She tugged as hard as she could; her face was hot and scarlet. They rolled wildly over and over in the grasses and tablecloth. Finally she got his shoulder under a pink-clad knee and held him pinned fast on one side. Her voice took a hoarse false edge. "You idiot."

"Who, me?" He lay still. He touched her breast gently with his forefinger; held it cupped. "Yes, yes indeed," he said.

"You idiot," she said. The hard edge had melted off her voice.

He felt soft and lazy, murmuring, "Yes, yes indeed."

Her hair had come undone; a twig and a few blades of grass were caught in the bright net of it. She loomed above him, as eminent as if she leaned out of the sky. She seemed yielding and fiercely happy. Caught in the top limbs of the undergrowth behind her was a red round flicker he at first took to be a balloon. It bobbed, disappeared.

"Stop a minute," he said. He clasped the back of her hand, squeezed it firmly. "Wait . . . Let me up."

She got off and sat, clasping her knees with her forearms. He rose and the little fat man stepped out of the alder thicket. His face *was* like a balloon, red as catsup from wind and sun, and his grimy grin was so fixed it might have been painted. Yellowish whisker stubble was smeared on his chin and neck. He came forward in a sort of rolling slouch, his hands balled, stuffed into the pockets of his overalls. Under the overalls he wore no shirt and the fat on his chest moved with a greasy undulation as he breathed; one nipple was not covered by the bib of the overalls and it shone, obese; it was like the breast of a girl just come to puberty. Though he wore no shirt he wore a hat, a misshapen black felt object which looked as if it had been kicked a countless number of times. He must have been in his late fifties.

"Who are you?" Peter asked. Thin and ragged query.

"Well," he said. "I'm Ed Morgan. I live a little ways back over yonder." He jerked his thumb over his shoulder pointing north. "I was just kind of follerin' along the creek here. I've got me some mushrat traps strung out along the creek, and I was just checking up on them. Course it's a little late in the day, but I been busy all morning."

He didn't ask the question he wanted to, but the first one that came to his mind. "Why is it late in the day?"

The fat man gave him a wide ingenuous stare. "Why," he said, "a man ought to get down to his traps first thing in the morning. A mushrat'll just chew off his foot and get away. Or even if he is good and drownded might be an old mongrel dog'll come along and carry him off. I ought to got down here real early, but like I said I been busy this morning."

"Who gave you permission to trap along here?" In the fat man's manner there was a careless oily geniality, an attitude of unmovable self-possession, which irked Peter, made the muscles along his shoulder blades feel as if they might begin to twitch. He gave his question a flat tone.

"Well now, I guess nobody did," he said. "I never have thought about that. I just always have set out my traps here. My daddy did, and I reckon his daddy before him. Tell the truth, I was just getting ready to ask you folks what you was doing here. And then I thought maybe I better not." The dingy grin never left his face, not even when he jerked his head aside to loose a spate of tobacco.

Without moving his body he drew himself up stiffly. "I'm Peter Leland," he said. "I own this farm."

For what seemed a long time the old man just looked at him. "Well, I declare," he said finally. "You must be Miz Annie's grandbaby. I don't know how many times I've heard her tell all about you. She set a lot of store by you, you being a preacher and all. Law, she was just as proud of you as a peacock. I don't believe there was ever what you'd call a whole lot of preachers in the Leland family."

He felt the fat man's eyes gauging him, measuring his weight, his probable worth. He would probably look at his caught muskrats in the same way. Peter felt nettled to the point of exasperation. "Am I to understand that you live on this farm?"

"Well, honey, I reckon so. Unless you was to take a notion to put me off. As far as I ever heard tell of, us Morgans has always lived right here on the Leland farm, and even before that, back when it was the old Jimson place. And no telling how long before that, no telling how long we might've been here."

His grin broadened slightly, and Peter had the impression that in the measuring of himself he had been found lacking. Not a pleasant impression. He let the muscles of his forearms relax and found, surprised, that since the little man had come he had been stifling the impulse to strike him in the face. This fat old man's assurance bordered upon, without trespassing into, cockiness. Peter sharply resented being called honey.

"No one told me there was a tenant family on the farm. Mr. Phelps didn't say a word about it." Mr. Phelps was the lawyer who had made the title arrangements, had done all the legal work.

Morgan lifted his hat, scratched the back of his head. Atop his head was a perfectly circular bald spot, the size and color of the crown of a large toadstool. "Well, I declare I don't know," he said. "I guess maybe we been here so long now that folks just takes us for granted. All I know's we been here a long time." His gaze shifted momentarily. "Is that your pretty little wife?"

Sheila still sat on the grass, her knees caught to her chest. Again her face reddened slightly. She gave Morgan a short jerky nod.

"Yes, this is Mrs. Leland," Peter said. He was unwilling to say it; he felt somehow as if he were giving away an advantage.

"She sure is a pretty little thing," he said. "I reckon she's about the prettiest Leland woman I ever seen."

She pulled a weed, flung it down again, a gesture of overt annoyance.

He sharpened his tone, cut through the thread of this subject. "Where do you live then? I suppose you have a house on the farm." He felt that the brunt of her annoyance fell upon him rather than upon Morgan, and this exasperated him; it was unfair.

Again the old man jerked his thumb over his flaccid shoulder. "Just right up yonder, across the creek. You could see it from here if it wasn't for this here thicket. You want to come on over, I'll take you around. It ain't much, but it's what we're used to, what we've always had."

"I think maybe I'd better," Peter said. "I'd better see what I've got into." He turned to her. "Do you want to come along, sweetheart?"

She let drop another weed stem from her fingers. "Not this time," she said. She rose and brushed off her slacks with ostentatious care. "I'll go on back to the house. There's so much work I have to do."

"I'll be along shortly," he said, turning from her regretfully. Morgan had already started through the underbrush, parting the branches carelessly before him, letting them slap back.

Sheila began to gather the debris of the meal, piling everything into the basket. There was still a quarter bottle of wine. She screwed the cap more tightly, looking at the bottle with an almost sorrowful expression.

He followed along clumsily in Morgan's wake. The grass was strident with insects and an occasional saw brier clawed at his trousers legs. Once he almost tripped because the earth around the mouth of a muskrat hole crumbled under his foot. A very narrow footlog lay across the stream; the top of it was chipped flat, bore the marks of the hatchet, but worn smooth. Morgan crossed before him, his hands nonchalantly in his pockets, but Peter had to go gingerly, holding out his arms to balance himself. Once through the thicket on the other side of the creek, they could see Morgan's house. It was a low weather-stained cabin, nudged into the side of the hill so that while the east end of the house sat on the ground, the wall and the little porch on the west side were stilted up by six long crooked locust logs. There was a tin roof which didn't shine but seemed to waver, to metamorphose slightly, in the sunny heat. Few windows and dark, and a stringy wisp of smoke from the squat chimney. In a corner of the yard of hard-packed dirt below the house sat a darkened outhouse.

"There it is yonder," Morgan said. "I reckon you can tell it ain't much, but it's what we're used to. It'll do for us, I guess."

Before them lay what must once have been a fairly rich field of alfalfa; now it was spotted with big patches of Queen Anne's lace and ragweed, and the alfalfa looked yellow and sickly, its life eaten away at by the dodder parasite. Morgan waded through it cheerfully, obviously complacent about the condition of the crop, and Peter kept as much as possible in the fat man's footsteps. He felt that he didn't know what he might step into in that diseased field.

They went over the slack rusty barbed wire that enclosed the yard and went around the house to the low back stoop. There was a familiar kitchen clatter inside, but when Morgan stepped up on the wide slick boards all noise from inside ceased suddenly. He turned around, grinning still and even more broadly than before. "Come on in," he said. "We're just folks here."

He entered. At first he couldn't breathe. The air was hot and viscous; it seemed to cling to his hair and his skin. The black wood range was fired and three or four kettles and pans sat on it, steaming away industriously. The ceiling was low, spotted with grease, and all the heat lay like a blanket about his head. The floor was bare, laid with cracked boards, and through the spaces between them he could see the ground beneath the house. There was a small uncertain-looking table before the window on his right, and from the oilcloth which covered it large patches of the red-and-white pattern were rubbed away, showing a dull clay color. From the ceiling hung two streamers of brown flypaper which seemed to be perfectly useless; the snot-sized creatures crawled about everywhere; in an instant his hands and arms were covered with them. And through the steamy smell of whatever unimaginable sort of meal was cooking, the real odor of the house came: not sharp but heavy, a heated odor, oily, distinctly bearing in it something fishlike, sweetly bad-smelling; he had the quick impression of dark vegetation of immense luxuriance blooming up and momentarily rotting away; it was the smell of rank incredibly rich semen.

By the black range stood a woman who looked older than Morgan, her hair yellowish white, raddled here and there with gray streaks. She was huge, fatter even than Morgan, her breadth was at least half the length of the stove. She bulged impossibly in her old printed cotton dress and he shuddered inwardly at the thought of her finally bulging out of it, standing before him naked. In proportion to her great torso her arms and legs were very short and in tending her cooking she made slow short motions, she used her limbs no more than she had to, as if these were more or less irrelevant appendages. What was obviously important was the great fatness of her breasts, her belly, her thighs. She gave Peter a slow but only cursory look, turned her unmoved, unmoving gaze to Morgan. When Morgan introduced Peter she didn't acknowledge him by so much as a nod.

"This here's my wife Ina," Morgan said. "And this here's my daughter Mina. She's the only one of our young'uns that's left with us now. The rest has all gone off different places, they couldn't find nothing to stay around here for, I guess. But Mina's stayed on with the old folks."

She sat at the weak-looking table. He couldn't guess her age, maybe fourteen or fifteen or sixteen. She sat playing with a couple of sticky strands of hair as black as onyx. She leaned back in a little creaky wooden chair and gave him a bald stark gaze. He felt enveloped in the stare, which was not a stare but simply an act of the eyes remaining still, those eyes which seemed as large as eggs, so gray they were almost white, reflecting, almost absolutely still. His skin had prickled at first, he had thought she had no nose, it was so small and flat, stretched on her face as smooth as wax. Leaned back in the chair that way, her body, flat and square, seemed as complacent as stone, all filled with calm waiting; this was her whole attitude. She played listlessly with her hair, looking at him. It was impossible. That body so stubby and that face so flatly ugly—something undeniably fishlike about it—and still, still it exercised upon him immediately an attraction, the fascination he might have in watching a snake uncoil itself lazily and curl along the ground. He couldn't believe it; maybe it was the crazy musky odor of the house, confusing all his impressions, his senses. He had to use his whole will to take his eyes off her.

"This here's Pete Leland," Morgan said. "He's the one that owns the place now, the whole farm. He's Miz Annie's grandson, and he's a preacher. He's the only Leland I ever heard of that was a preacher."

Mina gave a soft slow nod, still looking at him, and it was directly to him that she spoke. "You're awful good-looking," she said. "You're so good-looking I could eat you up. I bet I could just eat you up." Her voice was soft and thick as cotton.

Morgan sniggered. "Don't pay her no mind," he said. "If you pay her any mind she'll drive you crazy, I swear she will."

But it had started and the whole while he walked back to the big brick house—going not the way he came, but following the winding red dirt road along the hillsides—her flat dark face hung like a warning lantern in his mind. He couldn't unthink her image.

THREE

*P*eter Leland would have admitted himself that his choice of the ministry as profession had risen hazy from his soiled smoky imagination. He would have admitted that he saw the Christian religion as a singularly uncheerful endeavor, and this he would have admitted as a fault in himself, one he felt powerless to remedy. It was simply that his black imagination forced him to take everything all too seriously, and exercised a partially debilitating influence on his work. He had, for instance, no very consoling bedside manner, and his hospital visits with members of his congregation turned out invariably to be extremely awkward affairs. And a few of his sermons might vie with some of Jonathan Edwards' for gloominess, though Peter lacked that zealous fire. One symptom of his racked fancy showed itself in his fantasies about his father, who had died when Peter was so young that he could not at all remember him. His father had died when the family lived here on the farm, and Peter's mother had taken him away then to live with her and her parents in the eastern part of the state. Her family was pretty well off financially—her father owned an important electrical appliance distributorship—and they were able to send Peter to the single large privately endowed university in the state. During his freshman year there his mother had died. Peter was shocked, grieved deeply, but he was not surprised. His mother had been long waning; she had always been a pale silent little woman, and this white quietude he had only half-consciously attributed to her grieving for his dead father. This was

66

the one subject, at any rate, upon which she was completely reticent. The remarks of her family, that before her marriage she had been very gay and lively, he hardly credited; his observation wouldn't bear them out. When he had asked her how his father had died she had absolutely refused to speak of it, had only hinted that there was a terrifying disease of some sort. So that in his dark mid-adolescence he had begun to imagine that this disease was probably hereditary, had begun to wonder when it might overtake him also. He would imagine it as sudden and painlessly fatal, a black stifling area of wool dropped over him abruptly; or he would think of it as gradual and excruciating, a blob of soft metal dissolving in acid. And even when his adolescence was gratefully behind him he had never lost completely a secret vague conviction that his days were limited, that a deep bitter end awaited him at some random juncture of his life. This notion accounted in part for his mordant turn of mind, but still it was mainly a symptom: his whole nature was self-minatory.

And it was mostly because of this that he had become an active minister, for he would have enjoyed much more, and would have been more at ease in, a purely scholarly life. He would have much preferred the examination of Greek manuscripts and of his own looming conscience to the responsibility—he felt it a heavy responsibility—for the welfare of the souls of his little congregation of the First Methodist Church of Afton, North Carolina. His mind wouldn't let him rest in the leather-bound study. When he considered this inviting possibility a voice warning him that he was choosing a career of self-indulgence spoke in his head, and this voice he heeded without too regretful a delay. In his senior year and then during his years in the seminary he had armed himself the best he knew how to meet the world as an active, even a militant, Christian minister. That he had strange ideas about how to prepare himself to encounter the world was a consequence of his sheltered life. His mother had been understandably protective of him, and her family, curiously, had maintained her attitude. It was as if they shared some of his own premonition about his fate. They had been content somehow—they had seemed relieved—with his choice of profession and had willingly seen him through the seminary.

And despite the unworldliness of his younger life he had made a

competent though hardly a thunderously successful minister. Perhaps
it was the continued awareness of his own frailty which made him
tolerant of the frailties of others, but his admonishment of the peccadilloes of his congregation—and in the town of Afton they were only
peccadilloes—was couched in gentle terms gravely humorous. But the
scholar in him *would* come out. A lecture concerning a historical
problem of theology was sometimes offered them for a sermon; and
they on their side were tolerant also. Perhaps they were pleased finally
at having a preacher with brains, for their tolerance actually came to
something more than that. Perhaps they even interpreted the intent of
these scholarly discourses correctly, as gestures he wanted to make to
indicate that even on the other side, out of the competitive fight which
comprised the world they knew, it wasn't easy; that a faith doesn't drop
as the gentle rain from heaven but is formed in continual intellectual
and spiritual agony. Also it was simple enough to give a conventional
sermonizing point to such discourse, for every genuine moral problem
does ultimately impinge on a man's daily life.

It was from one of his sermons, in fact, that his present project
had emerged. Although the problem had at first been no more than a
pretext for a sermon, when he had later pondered his own words the
subject had seized him, and as much time as he could in conscience
squeeze from his duties he devoted to a sketchy research. In time he
decided to write a monograph, perhaps a book. He allowed himself a
couple of months' vacation—the sudden inheriting of the farm was an
almost unbelievable slice of luck—and from their inconsiderable savings
account he had allowed himself three thousand dollars, even though
he wasn't quite certain how all that money was to be utilized. "Three
thousand is an outside figure," he told Sheila. For the sermon he had
taken his texts from the First Book of Samuel, "And when they arose
early on the morrow morning, behold, Dagon was fallen upon his face
to the ground before the ark of the Lord; and the head of Dagon and
both the palms of his hands were cut off upon the threshold; only the
stump of Dagon was left to him. Therefore neither the priests of Dagon,
nor any that come into Dagon's house, tread on the threshold of Dagon
in Ashdod unto this day." Then he reminded them of Samson, delivered
into the hands of the Philistines by the bitch Delilah. "Then the lords

of the Philistines gathered them together for to offer a great sacrifice unto Dagon their god, and to rejoice: for they said, Our god hath delivered Samson our enemy into our hand." It was that temple of Dagon, he said, which Samson had destroyed with his hands, pulling it down with its pillars. Peter, seeming even taller in his perpendicular robe, pale and angular leaning forward in the pulpit, had informed his not very attentive audience that Dagon was simply one more of the pagan fertility deities; in Phoenicia his name was connected with the word *dagan*, meaning "corn," though this name finally derived from a Semitic root meaning "fish." He recalled the description by Milton in the catalogue of fallen angels:

> Next came one
> Who mourn'd in earnest, when the Captive Ark
> Maim'd his brute Image, head and hands lopt off
> In his own Temple, on the grunsel edge,
> Where he fell flat, and sham'd his Worshipers:
> *Dagon* his Name, Sea Monster, upward Man
> And downward Fish.

He had noted how the figure of Dagon had attached to the sensibilities of Renaissance historians, his story being told by Selden, Sandys, Purchas, Ross, and by Sir Walter Raleigh in his history of the world. The congregation shifted from ham to ham, resentfully itchy under this barrage of verse and unfamiliar names. But Peter had continued to read from his notes, saying that the human imagination had been hard put to it to let go this crippled fertility figure. The worship of Dagon had even traveled to America. He read to them from William Bradford's history of the Plymouth colony the story of Mount Wollaston:

> *After this they fell to great licentiousness and led a dissolute life, pouring out themselves into all profaneness. And Morton became Lord of Misrule, and maintained (as it were) a School of Atheism. And after they had got some goods into their hands, and got much by trading with the Indians, they spent it as vainly in quaffing and drinking, both wine and strong waters*

in great excess. . . . They also set up a maypole, drinking and
dancing about it many days together, inviting the Indian
women for their consorts, dancing and frisking together like so
many fairies, or furies, rather; and worse practices. As if they
had anew revived and celebrated the feasts of the Roman god-
dess Flora, or the beastly practices of the mad Bacchanalians.
Morton likewise, to show his poetry composed sundry rhymes
and verses, some tending to lasciviousness, and others to the
detraction and scandal of some persons, which he affixed to
this idle or idol maypole. They changed also the name of their
place, and instead of calling it Mount Wollaston they call it
Merry-mount, as if this jollity would have lasted ever. But
this continued not long, for after Morton was sent for England
. . . shortly after came over that worthy gentleman Mr. John
Endecott, who brought over a patent under the broad seal for
the government of Massachusetts. Who, visiting those parts,
caused that maypole to be cut down and rebuked them for
their profaneness and admonished them to look there should
be better walking. So they or others now changed the name of
their place again and called it Mount Dagon.

Here he had closed his notes and in the few minutes remaining
he preached in earnest. The worship of Dagon, he said, still persisted
in America. The characteristics which had made this god attractive to
men were clearly evident in the society that encircled them. Didn't the
Dagon notion of fertility dominate? Frenzied, incessant, unreasoning
sexual activity was invited on all sides; every entertainment, even the
serious entertainments, the arts, seemed to suppose this activity as basis.
This blind sexual Bacchanalia was inevitably linked to money—one
had only to think of the omnipresent advertisements, with all those girls
who alarmed the eye. A mere single example. And wasn't the power
of money finally dependent upon the continued proliferation of product
after product, dead objects produced without any thought given to their
uses? Weren't these mostly objects without any truly justifiable need?
Didn't the whole of American commercial culture exhibit this endless
irrational productivity, clear analogue to sexual orgy? And yet produc-

tivity without regard to eventual need was, Peter maintained, actually unproductivity, it was really a kind of impotence. This was the paradox which the figure of Dagon contained. To worship Dagon was to worship a maimed, a mutilated god, a god to whom "only the stump" remained. Dagon had lost both head and hands, only his loins remained; and below the waist he was fish, most unthinking of animals. Dagon was symbol both of fertility and infertility; he represented the fault in mankind to act without reflecting, to *do* without knowing why, to go, without knowing where. Was it simply coincidence that Merrymount had changed its name to Mount Dagon after Endecott had chopped down the maypole? Or might it not be a continuation of the worship of crippled sexuality? The ruined Dagon and the chopped maypole mirrored each other too clearly, didn't they? It couldn't be coincidence. But even if these manifestations were independent they still emerged from that human sickness, the worship of uncaring physical discharge, onanism, impotence, nihilism hurtling at a superspeed. It was this unconscious regard that he wished them to root from their hearts. He insisted that a Christian life was of necessity a reflective life, that useless movement, unresting expenditure of substance and spirit, was alien to it. He exhorted them to continual vigilance. He admitted that it wasn't an easy thing he asked.

Here he ended, and was aware for the first time of the weighty boredom his words had created.

His congregation sat before him listless as sun-bleached stones. He looked at them tiredly, then looked at Sheila sitting before him in her encouraging front pew. Her yellow hair shone bright, falling over the shoulders of her dark blue dress. She grinned. Her torso rose and fell with the burden of a heavy mock sigh. With the back of her hand she wiped away imaginary sweat from her forehead. . . . Anger flooded him momentarily. If it was a dull sermon for her, tough luck. It had been for him an earnest try, he had said something that he honestly cared about. His wife, for God's sake, ought to stand with him. . . . But the effort was too much after the long sermon and his anger evaporated. He was merely annoyed and tired. He answered her with a resigned shrug and announced the final hymn. "Let us sing number 124, 'Thou hidden love of God,' " he said. "Let us please sing only the first and

last verses." He reckoned on a long afternoon of relentless teasing—
half-serious—from his bright pretty wife.

And in some ways he dreaded it. As an intellectual opponent she
was formidable, and once she had caught him in an awkward position
she wouldn't let up. This was an attitude of hers he couldn't help
resenting at times, even though he recognized that it was an attitude
which his own nature needed for any kind of wholesome balance. If
he had been deliberately shopping for temperaments, he couldn't have
got better than Sheila's—wry, tough, at times baldly sarcastic—as an
antidote for his own pessimistic nature, which was too often unwillingly
pompous. Marriage with a gloomier, less sceptical nature would surely
have been consummated in a suicide pact. Sheila simply refused to
take him as seriously as he took himself. "All that nonsense . . ." He
couldn't help, in a way, envying her her full generosity of movement
and feeling; but he was simply not like that, he was too knotted, ponderous. She would twit him then, he took it as one takes a too-acid
medicine: *it tastes so bitter, it must do some good.* He would like to
have the barrier broken, that wall between him and the ordinariness of
life. This he genuinely wanted, to prank and disport in the tepid waters
of dailiness, of pettiness, of the trivia which comprise existences. He
would like to spend hours dawdling over his morning coffee, or choosing
which socks to buy or which greeting card to send. But he was as he
was, not even Sheila could break that down. An enervating sense of
guilt drove him to study, to learn, to preach, to visit, to harass, to
perform good works. He could not answer the question whether works
properly good could proceed from an exaggerated feeling of guilt; neither
could he suppress the question.

But there was Sheila. She had married him as soon as he was out
of seminary, though their contact in those four years had been through
letters almost entirely. The courtship and actual wooing had gone on
before, when he was at the university where she was a student. She
had lasted out the four-year wait easily enough, rather gaily; and he
couldn't help wondering if her nature didn't demand his as much as
his demanded hers. His faults were the faults of solidity, and perhaps
the solidity was what she needed to attach to. It might be all too easy
for her free humor to fog away into frivolity. A comforting thought,

her need for him; made him feel less parasitic. . . . She was a fine girl, would be a fine mother, but though they had been married four years—he was now thirty-two—there were no children. The childlessness bothered Peter; he felt it almost as a debt he owed and which he might be called upon to pay at any time, any moment when he would be unprepared. Simply one more instance of the way his impending fate would catch him up helpless.

"Why didn't you just read us the whole encyclopedia?" she asked. She dished out pertly the cool Sunday luncheon salad. "That really would have been entertaining."

"I'm not so sure you ought to come to church to be entertained," he said.

"Wow. You can say that again."

"Maybe you should come with a reasonable hope for edification."

She peeped at him tartly. "Do you know what hell is? It's edification without entertainment. Big mountains of boredom."

His anger wouldn't come back, he felt empty. "Oh, come on. It wasn't that bad, was it?"

"I don't know. How bad did you want it to be?"

"I didn't want it to be bad at all. Matter of fact, I thought it was pretty interesting myself. Sort of sexy."

"That's because it's an idea you found. That's the reason you like it. I doubt if any of it applies much to people now. It all seemed so . . . historical. So distant."

"But that's the point. I don't think it is. Didn't you listen to the last part? I was trying to show the pertinence . . ."

"Yes, yes. I heard. But I don't like it."

She got up abruptly and left the table. He felt morose and dissatisfied. But she came back in a few minutes and poured the coffee.

"Hurry up and drink that down. I want to find out firsthand all this crazy wild endless American sex you keep talking about."

FOUR

*T*he work wasn't coming along so easily. The idea still held him, it still seemed a valid and terrifying notion, but so far he hadn't unpacked his notes and books and papers. He would sleep late in the mornings, a habit alien to him, would lie tossing in the tall dark bed in the upstairs bedroom they had chosen. Dreams tortured him, jerking him awake sweating and with a dusty acrid taste in his mouth, but he was unable to remember these dreams; he could recall only dark queer impressions, odors. Then when he rose and had eaten—for some reason his appetite had increased; he who had never really cared for food seemed now always hungry—he wandered about the house, not speaking much; and in the afternoons he would take long walks over the farm, usually alone. Now and then, with nothing he could perceive to trigger it, the queer face of Mina would pop into his mind, and always at her image his stomach felt queasy, his skin prickly. He complained a great deal.

"Sure enough," Sheila said, "I've never seen you so restless."

"I just can't get started."

"I wouldn't worry about it so much. I've always heard that people who write things have to go a long time sometimes when they can't write. Professional writers and people, I mean."

"This isn't like that." He wished that he didn't sound so abrupt.

She shrugged. "I wouldn't worry about it too much. You deserve a nice vacation, anyway."

"Not till I've really done something."

74

The house managed to occupy much of his attention. It was large enough to explore: sixteen rooms in all, not counting the many closets and areaways and the tall attic. Standing in a room on another floor and at the opposite end of the building he could sense Sheila's movements; that was how alive the house was for him. The pleasure he took in poking about was rather a morose pleasure—like so many of his pleasures. He opened trunks and drawers and stood contemplating the masses of stiff gauzy dresses and dark woolen shirts and trousers. Uncomfortable as the clothing looked he had sometimes to suppress the impulse to dress himself in it, to try to find out, like a child, exactly how his grandparents had felt in it. Now it seemed to him, as he became more closely acquainted with the house, that all his surmises about his grandparents had been only partially correct, that he had missed something central, something essential about them that he could discover in himself if only he looked hard enough. It was not all just soured Puritanism, it was something even darker, if that were possible. One trunk was almost filled with correspondence and received Christmas cards and beneath these, lying loose, about three dozen shotgun shells of varying gauges; but there was no gun in the house. In one drawer was a small tin box half filled with dynamite caps. The correspondence was impossible. Very few of the letters were signed and the writing was always illegible, always bordering upon illiteracy. "Our if i ca'nt pay that much Why then i will exspect just what You had oferd the 1st time . . . my legel rites ech time . . . the religiun you clame to profess." There were words so entirely illegible they looked almost like transliterations from some exotic tongue, ancient Pnakotic perhaps: "Nephreu," "Yogg Sothoth," "Ka nai Hadoth," "Cthulhu." The effort he spent in trying to decipher these letters tired him, and he sometimes got headaches staring at the dimmed writing in bad light. He felt that the letters were obscurely responsible for the bad dreams that came on him late in the mornings. The letters coated his hands with a dust that he had almost to scrape off.

Sheila regarded his explorations with her usual amused tolerance, but this attitude of hers which he had always so needed now rankled him. He felt childish enough on his own without her rubbing it in. She found things enough to do. She kept herself busy with the house;

keeping clean just the four or five rooms that they used was almost a daylong task. And she was making a dress, using the old foot-treadle sewing machine which sat in a downstairs hall. The awkward intermittent clacking of it sang through the house with a sound like a hive of bees. When Peter passed by her as she worked, just wandering through, she looked up and grinned at him in what she had to begin to hope was a friendly manner, but he didn't grin back. He laid a tactless absentminded hand on her shoulder and wandered away, just passing by.

The attic was the worst. It was narrow but tall, and admitted light through a single small round window, like a porthole, high, just under the arch of the roof. But the light that entered, acrid yellow light, filled the whole space. The light locked with the dust—tons of dust up here—and the atmosphere of the place stuffed his head like a fever. The yellow light was blinding and hot; he breathed slowly and deliberately. It seemed that he perceived this light with every nerve in his body. The attic was mostly empty. On the left side the naked rafters ran down, and here and there nails had been driven into them to hold up a couple of wool coats, which looked almost steamy in the heat, and a couple of long plaited tobacco bed canvases. Piled on the floor were thick sheaves of newspapers, brittle and yellow like the light, and in the light the printed words were withering into unintelligibility. When he nudged a thick folded paper with his toe, it slid forward silently in the thick dust.

In his head the sight of Mina's face bobbed backward and forward like an empty floating bottle.

Against the right wall—which was simply ranked joists and nude lathes through which hardened plaster seemed to be oozing—sat a broken sausage grinder and a small empty keg over the mouth of which generations of spiders had stretched webs. Toward the south, the wall where the light entered, there was a queer arrangement of chains. At the angle where the attic floor and two joists met, two thick spikes were driven through two chain links, pinching each chain tightly into the wood. The chains, large chains, ran up each joist to a height of about eight feet, secured at intervals by big hasps, and then from this height they dangled down about a foot. Attached to the ends of the chains were broad iron bands which looked something like colters for plow tongues except that they were hinged on one side so that they could open and shut. Snap. The lock for each chain was some sort of internal affair—the bands were at least a half-inch thick. There was a fairly flexible tongue, notched on one side only, which slipped into the band itself, and on the top of the band was a tiny lever which could be wiggled back and forth. Obviously this lever released the ratchet inside the band so that it could be opened. The chains looked red in the yellow light; he had spent a long time looking at them. He held one of the bands with his index finger and swung it gently. A soft unnerving creak as the chain rubbed against the top hasp. He estimated that the empty oval the band enclosed was about four inches in diameter the long way. He stroked his finger along the inside of the band and it came away reddish. Rust, he thought; but it didn't flake, it wasn't gritty like rust. He stood on tiptoe and examined the opening where the band was hinged, where it would pinch. Small hairs gleamed yellow on the red iron, hairs like the down on arms, or eyelashes. His eyes were wide. He sucked his lips. He put the band about his wrist and snapped it shut. It fit exactly; he nodded. And if his other wrist was in the other cuff he wouldn't be able to reach the little lever to free himself. Standing flat he had a sensation of lightness, of dizzy buoyancy, his arm dangling upward like that. The iron was at first cool, then warm; his wrist began to sweat a little in it. Immediately he felt thirsty.

I could just eat you all up, she had said. *I could just throw you down and jerk all your clothes off,* she said.

He swung his arm idly; it wasn't so uncomfortable after all. Iron rasped on iron. He turned his wrist round in the cuff and, yes, it did pinch and pull at the hinge opening. He thumbed the release lever and it went over quite easily, too easily, and the cuff didn't open. He flipped the lever back and forth and jerked his wrist hard again and again. Then he stood quite still. Plumes of dust rose and settled reluctantly, the yellow motes spiraling down. It was clear that he wasn't going to get himself loose. He tried to remember where in the house he had run across the large old file. Could he signal Sheila? She was on the first floor, busy at something. He shouted twice, and his voice seemed muffled even to himself. The sound locked with the dust and lay silent on the floor. His feet were shuffling, and he sneezed twice, three times. Up here it was simply lifeless; the house which was so alive everywhere else was dead at the top. Or perhaps Sheila was insensitive to the liveliness of the house. He reached to the other cuff and grasped the margin of chain above it and swung the cuff against the joist. He banged it again and again and he could see that the joist was throbbing quite soundly, he could feel the floor reverberating beneath his feet, but when he stopped banging he heard no footsteps. She wasn't coming; she hadn't heard. And then he did hear footsteps, but they didn't come closer, didn't go anywhere at all. It was just his imagination; no one was walking.

She had no nose, Mina, any more than a fish. She deeped in oceans of semen.

The dust rose to his waist, not so violently yellow now. Time was passing, the light was growing less virulent. He leaned against the wall, trying not to breathe too deeply, but it was no good; he kept sneezing and sneezing, and his eyes filled with water, which made the light go all bright again. How could she not feel the house quiver when he hammered? It shuddered all over, the whole fabric of it was shaken. He banged with the chain for a while and then stopped again. His legs ached, it was unbearable. The guts had rusted in the cuff lock, he must have known. Not rust but blood his finger had searched out on the iron cuff; it was old caked blood, it didn't flake like rust. It had got later and later. His mind and his eyes had got full of fear and the house was full of sounds, all the wrong kind, scraping and slithering. It was as though iron were freezing on his legs. He was trying to take shallow breaths, for when he breathed deeply he had to choke and sneeze; but thinking about it made it impossible and he would finally have to take a long deep breath, and the coughing would turn into retching.

The thought came to him, as immediate as the binding iron, that this was where his father had died. There wasn't evidence, his mind didn't need evidence, the whole house was full of the fact. His mind was full of the house. The cuff fitted exactly. The image in his head was an event he had already experienced; had stood here with both arms chained, fallen against the hot wall and sweating furiously in the clothes he had fouled all over. He didn't think he could manage to live through it again. But then he realized that the man he knew, both arms locked in the chains, was too short and he carried too much flesh. . . . They had told him his father had died when he was four. He was a shorter man than his son, the chains wouldn't reach down so far for him; his arms he must have wrenched from their sockets almost. And why had they brought him, Peter, up here to see? His father, not mad, but furiously raging in inhuman anger, with the sweat all over him like yellow paint. His shattered eyes. What was it they had wanted him to see?

He could not see. There was only a round whitish glow in the top of the wall, noseless, unreadable as Mina. In the darkness objects, the broken sausage mill, the hanging coats, had seeped over their edges, occupied space where they had no mass. Now it was night; the house multiplied its imagined noises which would advance and advance certainly and never arrive. But under the narrow door a soft thick pane of light appeared, arced and disappeared; appeared again.

He heard her. "Peter? Peter? Are you up here?"

"Here," he said. He didn't say it. His throat was clogged. He croaked, his mouth was thick and helpless.

When she opened the door the draught blew up the dust, invisible now in the darkness. And he coughed and then gagged; wiped his caked mouth on his hanging arm. He imagined how he would look to her, he would frighten her to death; he turned his head to face the light and made his black lips smile. She was holding a kerosene lamp she had found somewhere in the house. He tried to hold his breath again, but drew it in hard and shuddering. It was Mina, it was not Sheila. He was almost weeping and he turned his face away, then turned to look again. . . . No. It was Sheila, with the darkness gathered on her blond hair, and with the lamp held before her and low like that so that her nose had no outlines, looked gone.

"A fuse must have blown, I think," she said. "This is all the light I could find. What are you doing up here, anyway?" She held the light close; she could just make him out as yet.

He got the smile back, tried to fix it.

"My God." She saw him.

He kept hoping she wouldn't drop the lamp. The attic would burn, go up like a box of matches.

"My God, Peter . . ."

His speech was like bitter black syrup. "There's a big file in the top drawer of the chest in the downstairs hall, if you could . . ."

She came to him. The warmth of the lamp spread on his face and neck. "What is . . ."

"If you could get the file, Sheila." He couldn't be franker in begging.

She stared at his face and then stared away, looking into the glow of the lamp. She had turned the wick too high; sooty threads of smoke rose from the lamp and the bulbous chimney was still blackening. "Yes," she said. When she turned from him her shadow was huge, fell like thick musty cloth on the whole room, on him. Gathered around the light her shape was bunched and dark and it was licked up softly by the dust and fear of the room. He felt relieved when she went out the door, but then she would have to come back again. He feared for her. It was as bad, the way she found him, as he had imagined. He felt a terrifying pity for her.

His legs felt as if they would topple any moment; trembled, trembled. He heard her going down the stairs, and then after that a complete unexpected silence. There were no noises now to imagine. He hawked up sticky spittle, rolled his tongue in it, licked his lips. They tasted acrid, felt puffy.

When she came back she seemed to have regained herself. She came quickly and confidently toward him, holding the file in her left hand. "I declare," she said, "just like a child. I don't see how you could get yourself into such a predicament. Just like a child, can't stay out of trouble."

He took the file she held out. "I need water," he said. "I don't think I can do it without water." He began rubbing immediately at the bottom of a chain link.

"I declare," she said. She went away again.

In the darkness he rubbed hastily at the chain and then his arm would tire and he would have to stop. He had begun sweating again, and as he worked he was panting. He thought about how silly he must look and he felt very clearly that someone was watching him, noted amusedly his every motion, even his thoughts: Mina.

She came back with the water. "I brought a whole bunch of water," she said. "You seemed to want it pretty badly." She set down a galvanized pail half-filled. Inside, a metal cup rolled about slowly. "Here," she said, giving him the cup.

The first gulps turned the thickness in his mouth into a slick coagulant film and he spat the water out. It dropped in the dust with a sound like rope dropping. He began to swallow hard; he wanted it so much he felt he could almost bite it. He squatted dizzily and dipped his hand into the water and smeared it on his face. Immediately the dust was in it, his face darkening. He went back to his filing.

Sheila was all right, better than he had expected. "Do you know how they catch monkeys for zoos, monkeys out in the jungle? They make a hole in the coconut shell—they have the shell tied tight first, of course—and inside they put some kind of small nuts a monkey likes. The hole is just large enough for him to get his hand in, but when he clenches his hand to hold the nuts, then the hole is too small and he can't get loose. He's too stingy or too stupid to let go the nuts. That's how they do it. But you know, I never really believed that they could capture monkeys that way until I saw you standing here with your hand caught like that. And not even having the excuse of nuts or whatever to get you to stick your hand in. Did you ever stick your hand in the fire because it looked so nice and hot? I don't mean now, I know you're too smart to do something like that now; but when you were younger, maybe. Maybe when you were in college?"

He shook his head, keeping the grimness of his face away from her. He had got the link through in one place now and had begun to make a new cut. He thought that she was talking in order to quell her nervousness. He sweated heavily, wishing that he hadn't dirtied the water in the pail; the thirst was on him again.

"But you know, when I couldn't find you, I honestly just knew it was something like this, I honestly did. The way you've been poking about into every nook and cranny in this house a person would think you were expecting to find a fortune, a pot of gold. Behind a secret panel or something like that. Really. I've never seen anyone so dopey about something before. Of course, that's your way—I know it—if there's anything at all around you can take as seriously as cancer, you'll do it. Know what? Watching you wander around all mopey like that, I've just wanted to tell you that if the house bothered you all that much we could get a tent and set up in the fields. Or if you were really bothered we could go home. But you wouldn't let loose of the house, not for anything. Just like those monkeys they catch."

He was almost free now, but he had to stop. The muscles in his forearm were jerking from the fiery exertion. She went on talking and now he wished she would be quiet, just hush up. He stroked his forearm against his thigh and wiped the sweat from his face on his left shoulder where his shirt was already wet and filthy from the reflex. He went back to work.

". . . And if you think I'm giving you a hard time, you're right," she said. "And don't think you don't deserve it, every bit."

The longer length of chain slapped against the wall, rebounded. His arm plummeted, the cuff banged against his thigh; there would be a bruise there. He was free. He sat down, hugging his knees, pain rushing to them. He put his head on his knees. His seeing was contracting and expanding in circles. He was almost weeping.

At last he stood up, Sheila helping him. "Let's go down," he said. He took the lamp from her, turned down the wick, and they went down together. He had retained the file; the four links dangled from the cuff, touched his leg. Stranger than ever, the house in the moving lamplight; shadows deeper and alive, shifting upon themselves. The varnished furniture reflected the dull glow in spots like dull eyes. They were enclosed in the lamp's burning, he leaning slightly against her, dirty, tired, musing, the chain flopping; she took his weight on her shoulder, her arm thrown over his shoulders, her hand gripping his shirt.

In the kitchen they let go. He set the lamp on the drainboard of the sink, ran cold water on his face and hair, shaking his head. When he straightened the water streaked his shirt. "Okay," he said. "I'll take a look at the fuse box." Now she took the lamp and followed him to the short hallway by the kitchen. He didn't open the box. "The switch is thrown," he said. His foot encountered something soft and warm, and he bent and picked up a heavy woolen overcoat; blue this one was. The house was cluttered with them. "This coat," he said, "it must have got hung on the switch here. The weight of it pulled the power off."

She put her fingers on her open mouth, all embarrassed. "I was just straightening up," she said. "I didn't know that it . . . I'm sorry." She brushed her chin lightly, a gesture of disbelief. "I'm sorry."

He threw the switch. All the lights went on. Everything looked naked now, the walls, the furniture; and they seemed naked too and turned away from each other as if in shame. Only for a moment. He took the lamp from her and screwed the wick down almost out of sight; a fragile bloom of black smoke rose from the chimney where the flame went out. "Here." He handed her the heavy coat and she took it, not quite meeting his gaze yet, and hugged it to her. The tail of it fell, hiding her body. She stared at him. "I really am sorry," she said. "Really."

He tapped the cuff on his wrist with the big file. "I'm going to get this off," he said, "and then I'm going to take a bath. Hot water and six bars of soap."

"All right," she said. "Good enough. And I'll fix us some supper. It must be nine o'clock."

He considered. "None for me, though. I really don't feel like eating."

"Well . . . How about coffee then?"

"Coffee, fine."

FIVE

*H*e had found a little straight chair with a sagging cane bottom and he sat there in the short hallway slowly and steadily rasping at the cuff. The grainy powder dripped on his shoes. He figured he could cut through on one edge where the cuff snapped shut and then cut through the tongue. Then he would be free. There was no hurry now, but fear wouldn't leave him. He had seen his father like that, a short man with huge terrifying eyes. Inheriting the farm he had inherited Mina, inheriting the house he had inherited chains. There was more to come, something was catching up with him. He had never considered that fright could have such dimensions as when Sheila had brought in the lamp, he taking her for Mina. He ought to see the girl again; of course, she was only poor and ordinary. It was the house and the isolation working in his head. Incongruous images falling together all silly. But he could not convince himself; all his thoughts, and even his body, lacked conviction.

How well, really, was he remembering?

He has lost the way, his grandmother said. But her voice couldn't have sounded the way it did in his mind, like metal creaking on metal; no one had ever sounded like that—it was the way her image in the tinted photograph in the sun parlor would speak. *He has lost the way, now see what he has come to. You will too if you ever get lost like your father.* He was squirming to get away from her, struggling not to see, but her fingers, complacently strong as iron, held his wrists. He would

84

not look at the attic wall, but he could not help looking. Now he felt that he had been called upon to judge his father, but now he did not know the standards by which judgment was to be made. He stopped the filing and rubbed his nose. Perhaps in his first encounter with the house he had been correct: those standards had disappeared from the earth forever. . . . No . . . .

What was certain was that he couldn't quench the image of Mina; it came to his mind ever more insistently. The confusion between Mina and his wife seemed incredible, even with the crouched darkness and the bad light. It could be explained only by expectancy; he had been convinced that it was Mina who would come through that door. And her face remembered was intractable entirely; it wouldn't respond to any maneuver of his imagination, it offered no similes, as totally itself as the taste of garlic. But what did it mean? Why did it drift in his thought unattached, coming and going like a light winking an indecipherable code?

The cuff dropped to the cool tile floor and he let the file drop too, his right hand hot from the pressure of it. The weight of the iron he still felt on his wrist. He leaned forward to rest, his elbows on his knees. Then he straightened in his chair and kicked the gaping iron ring as hard as he could. It slid across the floor, struck the wall and rebounded, came slithering back and touched against his foot. He rose and went down the hall to the bathroom, rubbing his wrist.

He leaned over the ugly yellowing tub which sat high on four legs with claw feet, and pushed in the plug. He breathed gratefully the steam that rose when he drew the hot water; he had been afraid that the power had been off so long the water would be cold in the tank. When he saw his face in the little streaked cabinet mirror he wasn't shocked, but regretfully assured instead. His eyes and mouth seemed holes poked in stiff gray paper. His eyes were pink-edged, his hair stiff and spiky with the clotted dust. While the water was drawing he washed his face at the little chipped lavatory. The water made his wrist itch and burn and he saw there the broad raw ichorous streak the iron had put on him. Then he stripped; his shirt and undershirt came off reluctantly, plastered to his skin with sweat and grime. He held them at arm's length, they were almost unrecognizable. He let them drop, he had decided to burn them. He climbed into the tub and lolled back, just letting the water lap into the dust. After a while he began to scrub earnestly and the water became almost inky. He had to let it out and draw a new tub.

He lay there, eyes closed, resting in the new water. He heard the door open and looked to see Sheila entering, her full arms cradled. He watched her face, pink and oval but with the sharp chin, a face like a brightly buffed fingernail. "Well," she said, "you seem well out of danger now."

"I think I'll live." He spoke very slowly, his throat still feeling dense. "I hope to God."

"I brought you some clean clothes and things. You think maybe that will help?"

"It'll be fine. How about the coffee?"

"You want it now—in the bathtub?" Then, seeing his expression: "Oh. Okay. I'll go get it. It ought to be about ready now."

In a while she came back, carrying cup and saucer, balancing them with exaggerated care in her left hand. He sat up and reached for it, but she stepped back sharply. The coffee slopped into the saucer. "My God," she said. "Look at your wrist. It looks horrible. Just look at your poor wrist."

He was totally ashamed; dropped his injured hand into the water, hid it behind his naked left thigh. "It's nothing," he said.

"It's *not* nothing. It's all torn up. Here, let me see it. We're going to have to do something about that. It looks just awful."

"It's all right, it's nothing."

She searched his face with the cool gray gaze. It felt like a spray of cold water on him. He discovered that he wanted to cower away from her stare; now she had the goods on him, now she knew his whole guilt. She stepped carefully away from him and around and set the cup and saucer atop the cistern of the toilet. Then she came back, sat on the tub edge. "It's not all right. How can you say that? It's raw and bleeding. . . . Here." She reached for the wrist, but he jerked it away, behind his back.

"No," he said.

She straightened herself, shook water from her gleaming plump hand. She began to talk slowly, in a quiet voice. "Peter, what is it?

What's been wrong with you lately? What happened up there in that attic?"

He shook his head. "Nothing; nothing happened. I was just being silly, messing around with those chains."

"That's not right." She too shook her head, setting the blond strands atwitch. "I've never seen you like that. I've never seen anyone like that." She rubbed her eyes with her forearm. "I hope I never see anybody in such a state again."

She was merciless. He waited, but finally had to speak. "There's nothing wrong. I just got too curious about the chains. Like the monkeys you were talking about. There's not much that can happen to a fellow alone in an attic, after all." And now he felt that he was betraying her, betraying both of them. But, really, wasn't it merely a harmless lie designed to shelter her feelings?

"Oh, that's not right, that's not right at all." Verge of exasperation. "You know it's not like that. . . . Because it's been going on too long. There's been something wrong with you ever since we got to the farm."

"What's that? What are you talking about?" A question meant to embarrass her, to force her to describe behavior for which there was no good description; thus, to draw from her an accusation because of the lack of concreteness. Perhaps an accusation was what he most wanted. . . .

She skirted the trap as easily as a plump dowager, lifting her hem demurely, would avoid a puddle. She looked at his dampening forehead. "I don't think this place is healthy for you, I know it's not. I don't think we ever should have come here."

Now he knew he was on safer ground, but he didn't feel any more confident. "That's pretty silly, don't you think? I mean, really; it sounds like something out of a horror story or a Bela Lugosi movie or something. . . . It doesn't really mean anything, does it?"

She rose slowly (but she was angry) and began walking up and down, taking precise military strides like a man. How often it had seemed to Peter that she was a man, maybe more male in the way it counted than he. . . ."Don't you do that," she said. Baldly warning tone. "Don't you patronize me. Don't say to me, *I mean, really*. You're not the kind to patronize, you don't have the weight. And you know me too well. You know I don't talk just to be talking."

"I didn't mean it that way. Of course I didn't. But you'll have to admit, the way you put it, it does seem sort of silly and made-up."

"No, it doesn't." She was behind him now, standing still. Her voice was tight and even. "But you've made up your mind not to talk to me about it. You don't even know whether you ever will talk to me again. You're as transparent as a child. Fuck you, just fuck you, Peter Leland."

He turned amazed, his torso jerked round, and she flung at him the cup of coffee. Her face was hot and white, pale as her eyes. She threw it at him with the awkward grace of a ten-year-old boy.—The fierce coffee splashed on his shoulder and side. The cup smashed on one of the tub faucets. Coffee, the dark stain, spread in the water like a storm filling the sky. He could not speak, could not think; could never have guessed her violence. She did not relent. She marched out, again tightly military, not glancing at him. Going away, she held her back and shoulders stiff. She didn't slam the door, didn't close it. The cold air of the hall poured in on him.

He could not speak, he could not smile at her rage. He had never felt less humorous. He got up very slowly and carefully. It was hard to see the chips of the broken cup in the darkened water. He sat poised on the edge of the tub, searching the floor. There lay the slim curved handle of the cup, retaining its identity in a surprising manner. He picked his way tiptoe over the floor and put on his underwear and his socks and shoes. Then he felt safer, but no better. He picked up the shards from the floor and dropped them into the toilet; he drained the tub, but let the broken china remain.

Then he felt that he had nothing to do, he was at a loss. Had it really been so bad, trapped in the chains? He went through, sensing the whole presence of the house about him, and in the kitchen took down cup and saucer and poured coffee. A package of Sheila's menthol-flavored cigarettes lay on the table and he got one out and lit it. He hadn't smoked one of this sort since he was twenty years old. The sensation was surprising, but not unpleasant. He puffed assiduously and felt gratified. He drank the coffee slowly. Then he rose; he felt, rather than heard, Sheila's movements in the upstairs bedroom. She was readying for bed.

He went back through the house again, turning out the lights, and he mounted the stairs in the dark, sliding his hand along the solid cool banister. As he went up, it came to him how the things in the house, the furniture, even the stairs and the walls, seemed important to him, seemed to mean intelligible puzzling comments, while things not connected with the house, with his new knowledge—whatever sort it was—did not touch and were unimportant. Even alien, perhaps. What real connection did Sheila have with the house, with his past? With *him?* The thought felt true, that she was an intruder, nettlesome.

She lay in the bed with her face turned away from him toward the wall. The bed had a high solid headboard, about six feet tall, and was dark, like almost all the furniture in the house. Her pale head looked small, settled at the bottom of the headboard, not larger than a thumbnail. It would be best not to speak to her. She had left only the lamp on the big dark vanity burning, and by this light he undressed. His body was reflected in the three mirrors. He looked extremely pallid—the lamp was very small and had a clear white shade—but he looked dark too somehow. It was as if his body gathered some of the darkness of the furnishings, or as if it had been tinged by the thick obscurity of the attic. Especially about his eyes the shadows stayed, and the eyes too looked dark and liquescent, reflecting only in pinpoints the light of the lamp. He was extremely thin and ribby, as if there were just barely enough skin to cover him. But it all seemed natural.

He turned off the lamp, went cautiously through the dark to the bed and clambered awkwardly in. The sheets were of coarse cotton, but they felt soothing. He stretched his thin legs and then let them relax, and it seemed he could feel strength draining into them again. He hadn't quite realized how exhausted he had become. He spoke softly, "Sheila." But she wouldn't answer; her body didn't respond to his voice even by a movement of aversion. It was no good trying to talk to her now. Wearily he began to wonder exactly what there was between them that he had to patch up; he honestly couldn't say what the quarrel was about. And he abruptly put it out of his mind, just shrugged it away, and fell asleep.

A bitter sleep, immediately shot through with yellow sick dreaming. He was still himself, but somehow impersonally so, huge, monolithic.

There was no one else, but there were momentary impressions of great deserted cities which flashed through his consciousness, gleaming white cities with geometries so queer and dizzying as to cause nausea. And when the cities remained stationary they were immediately engulfed by a milky-white odorous ocean. This same smelly chalky sea water was attacking him also and he began to dissolve away; he was becoming transparent, he was a mere threadlike wraith, merely a long nerve, excruciatingly alive. Somehow he perceived a voice in the milky substance, talking clearly and with immense resonance. "Iä, iä. Yogg Sothoth. Nephreu. Cthulhu."

. . . And all that, flashing away. Still dreaming, but now the next dream came to him lucid and so immediate he could taste its pattern. Sheila lay by him, still, absolute, still as rock. His limbs had gathered a terrible energy, felt too light, moved too easily and quickly under his great dry hunger for her. He murdered her. He was confused, the whole time he was killing her he imagined he was making love. And she never spoke, never uttered a sound. . . . The night had increased, it was much later; a shred of moon had driven into the gabled window. The moon looked thin and cheap, like something made of plastic. He was talking, kept murmuring monotonously, his voice thick and deep and full of words he could not distinguish, could not hear. Light poured into the room webby and grimy. It clung to all objects like a gritty gray ash. He kept speaking to her and she would not answer, but in the bed lay a tangle of blood, dark, bluish, in the cheap moonlight. It was streaked, blue, on his forearm and shoulder and chest. It lay tangled with his sperm in the bed; and his body was trembling, evanescent as steam from coffee. He wanted to rise but he kept floundering back; it was like bathing or drowning. The tall headboard stood over him, a black threshold. Every fiber of him was sinuous, but frenzied and impotent. His body suffered agony in the detestable light.

He opened his eyes. Cold with sweat, he stared above him at the black threshold of the headboard. Sheila lay by him unmoving but breathing easily and deeply; sighed once in her warm sleep. He lay for a while thinking, then turned on his side and went back to sleep, to dream even more bitterly and heavily.

SIX

*T*he succeeding days widened the strangeness between them. Sheila would hardly speak to him, even averting her eyes as he passed. And he merely passed, going by thoughtlessly, caught up in himself once more, preoccupied with the house. His books and the notes for the monograph on Puritanism lay unused, asprawl after a halfhearted opening of boxes. The house had claimed him, he examined the corners and the walls, finding or seeming to find that the geometry was awry, windows and doors slightly misplaced. He went back to the letters. Peering intently at faint markings under their coatings of dust.

> . . . *that pece of Land wch boarders on the Mackintosh prop. and probable worth about 500 dols. more or less . . . shamefull incidents talked . . . all the time they talk, one would not think so many idel tonges . . . and even if his religiun is as you clame, no resoun to believe that he wo'nt break down and come under . . . Sothoth, Nephreu, mabe . . . all in whispers . . .*

> *This day I walked the seven miles to Madison switchback and made good going of it and found myself in good health, much better than the dr. had intimated to me. Of course took pains to keep well away from Ransom's grove where body of xxxxx was found dead, and torn in the most awful fashion. Weather*

*delightful even for May, already some of the summer heat is
into it. Observed no interesting birds: crows mostly, cardinals,
a barn swallow wch I hope will take up residence among us.*

Cthulhu [?]. Nyarlath—[?] . . . and will have my SATISFAC-
TON *as i have before this told you . . . will make no differ-
ence, he can craul and beg, he can lick my shoes . . .*
SATISFACTON—

*. . . what rites best employed to bring this about, I do'nt know
& must consult. It may be that Stoddard [?] is better informed,
certainly the Morgans hold the key to any endeavour of this
sort, but are close-mouthed, being the most high adepts. Anyway, it ought to be performed, and although I find myself truly
unsuitable, I can only say that, at the least, I am willing and
that no one else has come forward. Recognize that it demands
a discipline almost intolerable for anyone with a sign of weakness and that considerable bodily pain is involved. I hope
mightily that I am equal to the task and that I may live to
see it accomplished. If not, there is, of course, no great loss
when one weighs what is lost against what may be gained.*

. . . this night evermore the darkness Cthu—

He rubbed the dust between his fingers, like a film of oil or sweat,
and sneezed. He let the brittle papers fall to the open leaf of the secretary
and regarded the loose pile with absentminded distaste. Not a line of
them did he understand, hardly a word; and yet he could not stop
himself from whittling away hours and days looking at them. "All that
nonsense," Sheila would say, had indeed said. He pushed himself away
regretfully and went outside.

A clear day, early afternoon. Sheila sat in a kitchen chair at the
untended edge of the yard, reading a novel. For a moment he was
tempted to go to her, to try to make up to her and trample this silly
barrier between them. But pride was still in him, stiff and gloomy, and

he would not move. He turned instead to the hill behind the house, going between the house and the woodshed, seeking the open fields.

But he came running back quickly when he heard her shout, shriek.

"Peter! Peter!"

Her book lay tumbled open on the ground. She was standing behind her chair, gripping the back of it, and staring at the ground before her. There a snake was poised, not coiled, not menacing to strike, simply waiting, with round head alift and trembling tongue. It was a dull brown color, about three feet long. Peter found a broken rake handle in the litter at the front of the woodshed and walked, not hurrying, to the edge of the yard. The snake oozed smoothly round— not a ripple in that movement—to meet him. It was harmless, just an errant ground snake.

"It won't hurt you," he said. "Perfectly harmless." He felt unaccountably cheerful.

"Kill it," she said. "I don't care about that. Kill it."

He poked the rake handle at it and it recoiled suddenly. Sheila squealed and gave a little jump backward. "I'm not going to kill it," he said. "There's no reason to. It can't hurt you, and anyway they're good to have around. They eat mice and things." He was unsure of this last notion.

"Will you hush up and kill that thing? I can't stand it. I can't bear to look at it."

"No. I won't. Let me get another stick and I'll carry it . . ."

She tried to lift the chair to strike the snake, but it was too heavy. She pushed it aside and strode forward and snatched the rake handle from his hand. He stepped back automatically, bewildered. She was awkward and frightened; beat the snake behind the head and down the length of it, hitting blindly. It writhed, hissed, twisted, trying to get away but injured now. She dropped the handle and ran away, out to the middle of the yard. Tears rolled on her cheeks, and she was sobbing. "Peter, damn you . . ."

Enraged, he picked up the handle. He was burning angry, regretting that now he had to kill the snake. Two sharp blows precisely on its head he gave it, and it rolled over and over. He got the end of the handle under the twisting body and pitched it down into the weeds. As he came back through the yard toward Sheila he could hear it thrashing about in a drift of dead leaves.

"Why wouldn't . . . You wouldn't kill it because you hate me. You really do. And I hate you too. I hate the sight of you."

"You bitch." His anger had congealed, and was a hot weight in him. His feelings were blunted. He threw the handle spinning into the depths of the woodshed, getting a slight satisfaction from the clatter it made. Slowly he turned his back on his wife and walked deliberately away, going into the house.

Inside he breathed more easily. Confused and dully angry, he walked from room to room, a certainty growing within him. Again in the sun parlor, near the littered secretary, he stopped; stood rigid and still. He recognized the thought that was in him and nodded gravely once, gravely agreeing with himself. And then he put the thought aside and returned almost automatically to the papers which lay there.

—ulhu Iä! Iä! Yogg—

. . . the moon draws wrong has the wrong horn draws wrong has the wrong horn draws wrong has the wrong horn draws wrong has the wrong horn this very night this night evermore this very night evermore this night evermore darkness Cthu—

Had feared that the cows, being alarmed by the Occasion and the pasture already sere in this deathly September, wd. go dry, but have so far maintained their milk, giving 3 or 4 quarts per diem. Some will freshen soon. The sky continues very red at eve (tho' sometimes with green or purplish streaks intermixt) so that the dry weather will probably hold. Mister Peter much concerned with his Chemical researches, very abstracted, the indifferent success of his attempts making palpable effect on his disposition. Gloomy at times, oftimes mistrustful. The weather presently having fretful effect on everyone.

And for a number of nights Peter had kept watch alone, sitting at the kitchen table, smoking his wife's cigarettes one after another—not tasting them—and drinking ugly black coffee that he brewed himself until two in the morning. Sheila had gone to bed long before and slept stubbornly. Then he went up and to bed, but did not sleep; lay wide-eyed in the darkness in the bed apart from his wife, careful not to touch her. He was filled with disgust. . . . And now this night he sat alone again, silently smoking and gulping down the acrid coffee until four in the morning. Occasionally he nodded deliberately, still assenting to himself. Finally he rose and turned off the bare overhead light—there was already a dim light outside—and left the kitchen. He was going to murder her. As he went through the smaller downstairs sitting room, he took the long poker that leaned by the blackened empty fireplace. It was cool and weighty; he was vaguely gratified by the heft of it. He held it forward away from his body, as if he were guiding his way with it like a flashlight. Then through the sitting room and through the long dark hall and, one by one, silently up the stairs.

He paused a moment before the bedroom door, then eased the latch over and let himself in. The air was cool but smelled warm. He found the fuzzy outlines of the furniture, instantly aware of Sheila's muffled form in the bed. She was breathing deeply, sighed now and again in her sleep. He drew near the bed. She was on the other side, scrupulously away from his place, her back turned toward him. She slept, but her body was tense. Her hair gleamed and he stared at it, trying to find the base of her skull. He would like to snap the nape-nerve, to be finished at once.

He struck. She rose from the waist instantly, her eyes wide and unseeing, staring, silent, terrible. She flopped back, roiling, still silent. He struck, he struck.

He had murdered her. The poker dropped. He stood by the bed, regarding it uncomprehendingly, the confused pool, sheet and cold thigh and litter of stain. It had got colder; he clasped his arms round his chest, trying to restrain the trembling of his body. He could not see what lay in the bed, the arc of shoulder and the hair not bright now and the huddle of fouled sheet, but he could not stop staring. He turned, stumbled, going to find his clothes in the dark, and he got them on somehow. He would not turn on the lamp. In the mirrors, even with the light behind him, he seemed hardly there, his body as gauzy as the light, something made to poke holes through. There was a bad smell, rich and chalky. He kept swallowing, but a rancid film stayed in his mouth and throat. He was very cold; now his body seemed capable of feeling only terrifying extremes.

He went out, down the hall, down the stairs, through all the house without feeling his way, his footsteps numb and certain, now his own. The clotted dingy light was everywhere, a grimy dawn was yawning up. He coughed, and spat on one of the curd-colored walls, but his mouth was still adhesive with a clumsy film. He reached the side door and even put his hand on the cold knob, but did not turn it; turned himself instead and went marching back through the downstairs rooms, through room after room, avoiding only the narrow darkened hallway which led to the stairs. In mirrors, glassed doors, cabinet windows his figure appeared, disappeared; and he kept rubbing himself with his palms, as if his body was all a various itch. He did not observe but perceived all the furniture, which perceived him silently, knowing, darkly wise. In the sun parlor he found that he had halted, had turned round and round, stood facing the two whited oblong sister pillows. I SLEPT AND DREAMED THAT LIFE . . . He uttered unresonant laughter, the sound coming flat out of his mouth, inexpressive, hard. Through the glassed door to his left he could make out the heavy squat form of the diseased piano. Again he turned round and round. Then he went through the house once more to the side door and entered to the outside.

Nothing lifted, there was no sense of release, relief. The light seemed no brighter out here, and still hung to him like dank cloth. The sun was not yet up; over the eastern hills was only a lighter grayish smear. The two vertical walnut trees in the lower side yard looked massive and glassy, and the full branches let fall on the lower trunks a dimness—not a real shadow—vaguely shaped like an automobile. He averted his gaze. He went under the dark side of the house out to the dirt road and walked along it for about twenty yards. The prospect was larger, the mountains colorless on the north sky, the nation-shaped fields below him cut through with the smoke-shaped stream, but it seemed no less narrow; it seemed all miniature, enclosing, funneled. In the gray light perched a single gleam of orange-yellow light, steady; it seemed round, but it streaked from the kitchen window of the tenant house. Without hesitation he began to walk the winding descending road, drawn to the single patch of flame on the landscape. He had not thought Morgan would be awake.

He didn't know the time. The hour whitened slowly, but the landscape remained iron-colored, the bad light pervading the dew. Twice he had to stop; he struggled in the wet weeds at the roadside and leaned forward against the bank of the road, clenching the orange clay tightly. He fought to keep the support of his legs. Then he pushed himself into the road again and went along, one numb foot before the other. He got there, paused on the edge of the road above, then let himself down into the yard with a loose ugly shamble. The house looked small now, heavy, squat, diseased. On the tin roof the dew had begun to coagulate, to run off in thin streams. As he went into the shaky eaveless little porch a splash of dew fell on the back of his neck, ran icy under his shirt.

He opened the door, didn't knock, and stood limned there. Morgan was absent. The air was still almost unbreathable, the rancid wood range already cooking, and the flies already industrious, swarming on him immediately. The shaky kitchen table covered by the rubbed dull oilcloth, and on the table the kerosene lamp shedding a glow so yellow and small that it seemed unlikely now he had seen it from the road. Even as he wondered about it, Mina leaned to the screw and turned the wick down, out of sight. The glow was gone. A thread of black smoke rose heavily out of the lamp chimney. They were alone in the gritty sullen dawn light.

Gray in the gray light, her face seemed as impenetrable, as noseless, as he had again and again remembered. Now it was luminous almost, and looked somehow as if it were floating forward. And again her figure, flat and square, without dimension, was all filled with calm waiting, complacent as stone. And again her eyes rested on him, simply remaining still, and he felt enveloped in the gaze; those eyes seemed large as eggs. Her raddled hair hung loose, black as onyx, aggravated the luminescence of the smooth face.—Now in the steaming kitchen he felt hot.

Her voice was soft and thick as cotton. "You're about the worst-looking mess I ever saw," she said. "I never seen such a mess as you are."

He didn't answer, had begun to shudder again. The oily fishy odor stuffed his head.

"You better come here and set down," she said. "You've got a bad case of something, I guess. You sure do look like a mess."

He sat across from her in a creaky little chair, the cane bottom drooping. He slid his hands aimlessly about on the oilcloth.

"You just set there and I'll get you some coffee. It looks to me like you sure could use it. I don't reckon I ever seen anybody in worse shape."

Involuntarily he cowered away. He was sitting by the range. She would have to cross by him to get the coffee. He didn't want her to come near him.

She rose and started toward the stove, but stopped. A slow smile seeped into her inexpressive face. "But it looks like to me you could use something that'd do you more good than coffee. They's a jug back here I'll get. That's what'd do you more good, I bet anything." She turned and went through the door behind her. He heard her displacing a box, rummaging among things which must have been cloth. She returned, holding a gallon jug by its stubby neck, swinging it easily by her side, brushing the black cotton skirt. Her calves were full and muscular, olive-colored. She set the jug on the table, not letting it thump, and went by him to the stove. He twisted away from her, his buttocks clenched tight in the sagging chair. She brought a thick chipped coffee mug back to the table and poured it about half full from the jug. She laughed humorlessly. "I don't reckon a Leland would want to be drinking out of a jug," she said. She put the cup gently before him and turned the handle round toward him. "There you go."

It smelled and tasted oily, of rotting corn. He swallowed it eagerly; and immediately droplets of sweat were on his forehead. He knew absolutely that he was going to be ill, sick to death. He drank again. He had never been more grateful for something to drink.

It was going to be a hot day. Now it was full dawn, and the kitchen was filled with the warm dank religious light, yellow. She stood across the room by the open bedroom door. He felt he saw her with fine clarity, totally, every inch. He wiped his forehead with his blood-smeared wrist. He felt sticky.

Part II

ONE

The little house, so humid and rickety—everywhere you stepped the floor gave a little and creaked—was always full of movement. The old man came and went incessantly, God only knew what his errands were. The mother was almost motionless, she moved her great bulk but seldom, and even standing still she occupied much space; sometimes it seemed to Peter that the air of the house and the movements of body and mind of all the others were loaded by her presence, that somehow she affected even his blood. Mina was always coming and going too, she came to Peter and went away. "I got to look after you," she said. "Somebody's got to take care of you."

He lay in the shabby shaggy bed in the little room that seemed mostly a storeroom. Or he would wander from room to room, keeping away from the windows and open doors; and then he would return to Mina's bed and sit straight, holding his knees with his hands, watching with fixed gaze the unchanging splotched opposite wall. He kept drinking; he had not halted in the three weeks—was it three weeks now?—he had been here. Mina kept bringing moonshine to him, wearing on her face an impassive but still wearily sardonic expression. He loathed the oily raw taste of the stuff; he gulped it quickly and breathed with his mouth open. At night she bore him down in the torn greasy quilts and made love: silent as standing water. It was he who might cry out, her fingernails in him and her cold cold teeth on his shoulder and neck and face. He struggled desperately not to make a sound; when he did

100

groan, his throat hoarse and tight, he was able later to persuade himself that he had made no sound. Mina was relentless as cold wind, she had no feelings, no passion; she seemed to perform with a detached curiosity.

He was continually in a clear acid delirium. Things leaped forward and would get brighter, so clearly he saw them. The unsteady table, the chipped dull blue porcelain coffee pot, the barred iron bedhead, all had outlines strong and burning. Now he lay in the wadded quilts and thought of her father, his face round and red. If you suddenly jabbed him with a pin behind his ear, wouldn't his face pop and go to shreds like a balloon? He drank, and speculated that if you grasped a man's mouth by its corner, you could rip away his meaningless little grin and expose to daylight the real expression on his face. And what would it be? Disgust? A terrible pitiless joy? Anything at all? But it couldn't be done, the grin was too greasy to get a grip on. He drank quickly and regretfully. Or at times he would suddenly find himself on his knees, holding the bars of the bed's footboard as tightly as he could. "Our Father who art," he would say. "Our Father, Our Father, Our Father, Our Father." He could get no further. He would bang his head against the bars until broad red welts appeared on his forehead. And then he would sweat and roll like a pig on the floor. Now tenderly he felt his cheeks; his face must be all ravaged with his own beatings and with Mina's cold teeth. He didn't need a shave. He couldn't remember shaving. Had Mina shaved him? Nausea rose in him to think of her standing with a razor at his face.

Or he would talk, feverishly but clearly; he would actually hold forth with true brilliance, he thought. He spoke about the tragic inevitable division between the cultural aims of a civilization, any society whatever, and the aims of the religion which that culture included. He told how he had at last come to recognize the necessity for a diseased temperament in the understanding of any religious code. He slapped the table softly with open palm. "It's only through suffering that one comes to realize this," he said. "Only through the purest, most intense sort of suffering." He wagged his head gravely. "That's how I have come to know the things I know." At these times he felt he was sixty-five or seventy years old, and a benevolent paternal feeling washed through him; he felt oddly protective of people. They would watch him with

slow eyes and stolid expressions. He would expound elaborate theological justifications for suicide, for extreme poverty, for every emotional
and physical excess. Sometimes he merely sat in the broken stained
stuffed chair in the living room and stared into the tiny fireplace, where
lay yet the powdery ashes of the last fire of the winter. He would mutter
continuously to himself then, but he wasn't certain what he was saying.
It seemed to be a long disquisition on the nature of fault, whether it
was ever entirely personal. But he would suddenly break off and shout
for help, for it seemed to him that he had become very small and that
he lay smothering in the pinkish-gray ash. Mina would come in and
press his shoulders into the chair with her cold dark hands. "Hold on
there," she said. "You're all right. You just hold on there." She kept
her face steady above his so long that he couldn't avoid looking up into
it. And then he couldn't look away, and he was awed into silence. Into
this unending monologue would creep nonsensical words, words he did
not know, an unknown language of despair. "Yogg Sothoth . . . Cthulhu
. . . Nephreu . . ." Then his mouth tasted bad, and he would drink
again.

It was early July; it was scorching. In the fields the weeds—there
didn't seem to be any crops growing—drooped lank and fat in the sun,
and there was the continual sawing of insects. Sunlight was hot and
heavy in the air, and the tin roof banged like firecrackers sometimes,
expanding in the heat. For a while there was no rain and the road was
muffled with pinkish-yellow dust, which would rise in long tall plumes
as cars passed and then settle, coating the leaves of the weeds and bushes.
At night it was cooler and quieter; the crickets sang, but the darkness
made the sound seem distant. Then he heard the stream running below
and the infrequent splash of something small and dark entering the
stream. He hoped it was one of Morgan's muskrats.

Visitors were incessant, and Peter kept out of their sight as much
as possible, where he could collect himself. They were mostly farmers,
large taciturn men with large weathered rancid faces. He was startled
to think how long it had taken him to realize how Morgan made his
real living: he was a bootlegger. Somewhere on the farm his still was
smoking away, digesting and distilling corn. He was even rather amused
to think that Morgan must have to buy the grain from some of his

customers; he certainly didn't grow the stuff himself. Was it a profitable business, was Morgan—for all his outward poverty—actually a wealthy man? This thought too was amusing. And now he could account for the endless supply of the alcohol that Mina was fetching him.

But he didn't like it when on some evenings there would be six or seven of Morgan's customers gathered in the hot kitchen. Then he didn't move, but lay stockstill in the raddled quilts, frozen like an animal trying to camouflage itself. He had to guess the number of them from the guttural muttering he heard and the occasional solemn clomp of a heavy shoe. Often enough there were furtive wheezy giggles uttered, and sometimes there was a single voice shouting, not words, but merely a sound of . . . of . . . of fearful surprise, of quick pain, of pained delight. None of these kinds of sounds, and maybe all of them together. What? He struggled to imagine what Mina was doing in there among them. It would be Morgan's idea, that Mina would encourage the men to drink. But he would not find out, he would not move to look. She would come in now and then to check on him, to bring him liquor if he needed it. She would toss a quilt over him and tuck it tightly and contemptuously under his chin. Her blouse would be unbuttoned at the top and when she bent over the bed he observed her small thick inexpressive breasts. Her skin would be warmer than usual from the heat of the kitchen, but it was still cool.

The next day there was a long massive July storm. It was the first time the light hadn't seemed unbearable to him and he had gone out onto the narrow back porch which ran the length of the house. A cool wind, and the yearning stirring of the wild cherry tree below the house, the limbs asway; flies swarmed out of the wide air and gathered on his face and arms, and he didn't brush them away. He sat in a slouched slat-bottomed rocking chair and moved nothing but the forefinger of his right hand, with which he tapped his knee slowly and steadily, in time to a rhythm by which he felt the storm was gathering. Very gradually he accelerated his tapping. Dark gray on gray: the sky was bunching its muscle; it was slow and broad as dreamless sleep. There seemed miles of air between the big first drops of rain. Then it was all loosed at once, noisily drenching the tin roof. The first stroke of lightning was blinding; it seemed that the nearest western hill cleft open, the lightning ascended the skies like something scurrying up a crooked ladder. There was no warning rumble, the thunder issued immediately all in a bang. He dropped to the worn boards of the porch on his hands and knees, heaving and shuddering like a shot dog. Momentarily he imagined the air full of electric particles; if he breathed, his lungs would be electrocuted. Then he was up and ran stumbling into the darkened living room and stood by the fireplace, clutching the daubed stream rock with both hands. He turned round and round. Then he put his hands in his pockets and walked quite casually to the corner of the room and pressed his shoulders against the walls, pressed his face hard into the corner. He kept quivering, but he felt that now it was all right to breathe. When Mina passed her damp fingers along the back of his neck he didn't move at first, but then turned around suddenly, his eyes unseeing and his face blanched. She grasped his shoulders and steered him into the stuffed chair before the fireplace, and he sat there watching it, turned away from the murderous storm. An inky ooze spread on the walls of the fireplace, the rain running down the chimney sides, and an occasional drop fell straight down the chimney, fell into the powdery ashes with a sound like someone letting out his breath suddenly. He gave no sign that he observed anything.

Later he had calmed a great deal, but was very voluble and seemed joyfully excited. The storm had gone away, but trees and the roof were letting down the final drops. The landscape burned with the reflected sunlight. "Look," he said, "look, it's true what they said, that God does speak to you out of the storm cloud. I was sitting there, and my ears had never been more closed. It came to me when I was sitting there that I was dead, as dead as anyone buried in the ground. It seemed to me that I would like to struggle to come alive again, to make myself alive somehow, but I didn't know how. Even if I knew how I wouldn't have dared, I didn't have courage, I didn't have the strength to find courage. God spoke through the sky to me, and then I was dead, but I came back to life. I had to be killed first, you see, truly killed. The trouble was, you know, not that I didn't have courage to come to life, but that I didn't have courage to be truly dead. I had to accept that I was dead before anything good could happen like that for me. And then when it thundered I knew I *was* dead, and I remained dead for a long time. Whole ages passed while I was dead—I just vaguely knew they were passing. I was in a void, you know, I was where it was all darkness and empty space. Then at last I felt the breath of God, I actually felt it." He ran his fingertips gently, reverently, across the back of his neck. "Here, right here. I literally felt the breath of God pass over my neck."

Mina held him folded in her slow gaze. "That was just me," she said. "I was just trying to get you to pay some mind."

He appeared not to have heard her. He smiled in painful bewilderment. "But I can't remember the words," he said. "Not exactly, anyway. Not the exact words . . . Isn't it strange that I should forget the words? I can remember all sorts of other things, and none of that is important now. It's very strange, don't you think?"

"Anyhow, you're okay now," she said. "I guess I better get you something to drink."

He shook his head, absently impatient. "I want to think," he said. He felt he was on the verge of remembering, if not the words he so badly needed, then something equally important, a revelation.

Mina went off; she smiled carelessly. He sat where he was and slowly, helplessly, watched the bright event flicker in his mind and go out. For a panic moment he couldn't remember even the flavor of what had happened to him; but something at least seemed to come back, and he felt happy again. Now he was sure that an important event had occurred, something happy and eminent. That was enough. You had to be happy with what you got, he thought. No use expecting too much, it wouldn't be handed to you on a platter.

He rose and went to find Mina in the kitchen. "I think that was a good idea you had about having a drink."

She stood with her legs apart, her hands on her hips. "You reckon?"

"Yes." He chewed his upper lip.

"I don't know about that," she said. "I don't see why I always got to be hauling liquor to you, just whenever you want. I don't hardly see no good I get out of it."

He looked at her uncertainly. "Well . . ."

"If I was to expect you to look after me hand and foot, you wouldn't be doing it, I don't reckon. I don't see the good I get out of it at all." She gazed steadily on his face.

"Well . . ." A slight perspiration came on his forehead.

She put her fingertips against his chest and shoved him backward lightly. "You better go and sit down," she said. "I'll bring it to you, I guess, when I get a chance."

He went back and sat waiting, sadly puzzled. What made her act like that, anyway? What had he done? He rubbed his left side slowly and thoughtfully with a vague circular movement. Lately he had a recurrent pain, sharp at times but mostly a blunt heavy ache, and now it seemed to have settled there. The room was much too bright; there was too much light outside, as there always is after a storm has cleared.

In a while she came, bearing a quart Mason jar of the slightly yellow alcohol. No glass or cup this time, he would have to drink it from the jar. "There you are then," she said. "Is there anything else I got to do to keep you satisfied?" When he looked up at her his face was unknowingly appealing. But she had no mercy.

He wiped his mouth and drank. It was too warm, almost hot, and his stomach surged in an effort to reject the stuff, but he made it stay down. He clenched the jar tightly with both hands and a few drops sloshed on his soiled shirt, a shirt stiff and filthy. The ridges of the edge of the jar rattled against his teeth. He felt better now, but had cleanly forgot the whole day, everything that had happened. It was gone from him immediately and silently, so that he sat drinking blankly for a time with no sense of loss. He was very tired. And then the feeling of having forgot something important began to gnaw in his mind and he became uneasy. He set the jar on the floor and began to rub his face with his hot palms. His chest and legs began to itch too and he scratched energetically. He shifted his feet about and tipped over the jar. He looked at it stupidly for a moment and then jerked down to set it upright. The oily liquid oozed slowly over the worn floor, and the odor of it rose all about the chair, surrounding him entirely, a heavy invisible curtain. There was only about an inch of it left in the jar and he swallowed it down quickly, as if it too might be lost to him. Then he held the jar languidly, and empty tears came into his eyes and rolled down his face. He was motionless, not sobbing, but hopelessly weeping and weeping, without sign of surcease. He was so stupid, so stupid. She wouldn't bring him more after he had wasted it; she was implacable. Maybe he could keep her from knowing about it. And as soon as he thought, he was getting his shirt off. He was on his knees, trying to soak up the liquor with his shirt, which became black and smelly instantly. He turned to wring it out in the fireplace.

"Now what is it? What do you think you're doing now?"

He jumped to his feet, dropped the wet shirt on the chair. He shook his head mutely.

"Get that goddamn thing off the chair," she said. "What kind of a mess have you made now?" She was calm as ice, her voice expressionless.

"Nothing," he said.

"You ain't been getting sick, have you? Is that the kind of a mess you're trying to clean up?"

"No," he said. "It's nothing."

She came closer. "Oh. You've went and spilled that shine I brought you. What did you want to do that for? You was the one wanted it yourself. I got no call to go hauling liquor around for you."

"It was an accident."

"You don't make no sense to me, did you know it? I can't hardly get no sense out of you at all."

"I'm sorry about it. I didn't mean to spill it."

"It ain't hardly the craziest thing you ever done, now is it? You ain't been doing nothing but crazy things around here. It's enough to drive ever' one of us crazy. And look how you was mopping it up. What are you going to wear for a shirt now? Or didn't you think about that?"

He was still holding the soaked smelly shirt. He looked at it mournfully. "I don't know."

"I don't think you got anything to know *with*," she said. "You ain't got no brains, that's all."

He grew sadder; it was clear she wouldn't let him have any more to drink.

"Let me tell you what I want you to do with that shirt. You take it in there in the kitchen and put it in the stove. I don't want to see no such of a mess as that around here. You go on and do it." When he got to the kitchen door she said, "I guess we'll just have to put you on a water ration."

He went on in. He couldn't find the handle to insert into the stove eye to lift it. He opened the high shelf on the range and took out a table fork; reversed it so he could lift with it.

"Now what do you think you're doing?" She had come to the doorway.

"I couldn't find the handle for it."

"What? I can't hear for you mumbling like that."

"I couldn't find the handle," he said.

"It's right there on top," she said.

"Oh." He put the table fork back and got down the handle and lifted off the eye. A few coals were live in the bottom of the firebox. He stuffed the shirt in—it didn't seem likely that it would burn—and set the eye back. He got the handle out and held it, a curious warm cast-iron thing, the tip of it shaped like a square-toed shoe. He imagined hitting Mina with it; he would put blue and red streaks on her face, he would make blood come.

"You just better not, buddy boy," she said. "You better not even think about it. You just put that goddamn thing down and come on back here. I sure would like to know what's got into you. You're the craziest damn thing I ever seen. Go on, I said, and put it down."

He hesitated no longer, put the handle on top of the shelf and came to the door.

She was back in the living room, regarded him with cold amusement. "There ain't nobody in the world would be afraid of you no more. You couldn't hurt a cat, and you can just go on pretending all you want but all you can do is just make trouble, make a little mess here and there. That's all. Nobody is going to take you serious." Again she came to him and put her fingertips on his bare thin chest and pushed him lightly backward. "I guess the best way I can think of to keep you from making trouble is just to put you in bed and let you drink. I don't guess you can bother anything there but yourself." She pushed him again. "You go on and get in the bed. I'll be there in a minute and baby you."

He went. He sat on the bed and stripped off his shoes and socks and pants, and then lay back wearily, wearing only his soiled underpants. He lay on his side and tried to go to sleep, but his nerves were acrawl with tiredness and unreleased anger, and he didn't want to close his eyes. He breathed hoarsely. Then she came in, carrying another of the endless jars of corn whiskey. "Here," she said, "and if you spill this or make a mess it's the last of it you'll get to drink in this house, I can tell you. I got more things to do than keep putting up with you." She set the jar on the floor by the side of the bed, and as she straightened she looked flat into his eyes. "I mean it," she said. Then she left, closing the door firmly behind her.

He waited a few moments, until his breathing had slowed. He tried not to think how much Mina had begun to frighten him. Why was she like that? He had done nothing to her, not really. He leaned and took up the fruit jar. Gray and white, but slightly tinged with yellow, Sheila's pert face looked at him through the whiskey. She was smiling: a fixed stiff smile. His hand shook; her face wavered. He was doing well, only a few large drops splashed on his belly. She was smiling. He turned the jar around and peeled the wet photograph off the side, where Mina had stuck it. She had taken it from his wallet. Now he wished he had hit her, that he had made the blood come. Sheila's face was draped between his fingers, the paper all limp, wet. He felt that no one had ever been so abjectly miserable as he; and he let his head roll on his chest from side to side. The photograph wouldn't come loose from his fingers; he shook his hand hard again and again. But he was still extremely careful. He didn't spill any more of the liquor, he had to preserve himself somehow. Finally he wiped the photograph off on the quilts, as if it were a sort of filth which soiled his fingers. Then he leaned and set the jar down carefully, and then lay back, still, his arms along his sides. He began to moan, and it got louder and louder. It got louder, and it didn't sound like a moan any more. He was moaning like a cow gone dry; moo upon moo, and he couldn't stop it. He might have gone on for hours.

But Mina came back in, came straight to him. "Hush up," she said. "Hush up that goddamn noise." She slapped his face hard. "Just hush up now." She slapped him again, harder this time, and he heard mixed with his own hollow fear a tinny ringing sound. He began to breathe more steadily, and the noise subsided to a moan. She slapped him once more, not so hard now, and turned away. "I'm goddamn if

you just wouldn't drive anybody plumb wild with all of your craziness."
She went out.

He lay moaning for a while, and then managed to collect himself.
The photograph was in wet bits, tangled in the quilt. He began to
console himself with the jar.

Or there were times he would be gently melancholy, even rather
humorous; would smile sadly but not bitterly and speak in a calm even
voice. "The *lachrimae rerum*," he would say. "There's something in
the part of a landscape you can see from a window that gives you the
clearest idea of what Virgil's phrase really means. The way the window
limits the landscape, you know; it intensifies the feeling of being able
to see the universe in miniature. Which is what you do when you think
of those two words, though I don't think you do it consciously at all.
But in the back of your mind somewhere there's a real picture of the
smallness of physical existence, of its real boundaries; and there's a
corresponding sense of the immensities of the void, of nothingness,
which encloses physical existence and to which it really belongs. And
then to include the human personality, oneself, in this small universe
is to see oneself really minuscule." He chuckled softly. "It's all a question
of proportion, you know."

"You're as full of shit as a Christmas turkey," Mina said.

He nodded and smiled gently. He felt very old. "I don't mean to
bore you," he said, "but I know I am. But you can see—can't you?—
how hard it is for me to keep my mind alive, to keep it going. With
the weight of the circumstances, well, with the way I am now, I feel
I've got to keep my wits about me somehow. I know these are nothing
but foolish empty speculations, but it begins to seem more and more
that my mind won't operate on the material that's given it. The things
that happen more and more don't mean anything, and I can't make
them mean anything. And as limited as my life has been—and it's
always been severely limited—I was always able to make something
useful out of a few events. By 'useful' I guess I mean intellectually
edifying or . . . or morally instructive. That's what I mean, in fact:
every event that happened to me was a moral event. I could interpret
it. And now I can't. It seems to me that a morality just won't attach
anymore; events won't even attach to each other, no one thing seems

to produce another. Things are what they are themselves, and that's all they are. Or maybe I'm just troubling myself to no end. One of my troubles always, too many useless scruples."

"Scrooples," she said.

She had got his checkbook from somewhere, and she got him to sign all the checks, blank. He didn't hesitate; it couldn't have mattered less. He felt a detached mild curiosity about the purposes to which she would put the money, but he didn't question her. He knew she wouldn't have told him, and anyway he had no use for it. What could he buy? He himself had been sold, sold out.

The days got hotter. The weedy field below was noisy with grasshoppers. The sun was white as sugar and looked large in the sky.

Sometimes he was very depressed, kept a strict silence. He thought of suicide, thought of slashing his wrists. He pictured his long body lying all white and drained. Perhaps there would be a funeral for him in the brick house, in the dark disused sun parlor there, his body lying in a soft casket beside the disordered piano. But he knew that that was all wrong. There was no doubt he would be cast just as he lay into an open field and left to ferment in the sun. Muskrat food. Yet this seemed appropriate; it was, after all, a proper burial, wasn't it? He wouldn't expect any more than this for himself. In fact, he would stop expecting.—It would take him entire hours to think through a daydream like this, and then he would be mollified but sullen. His body would feel too heavy.

And in the bed too she was relentless. He came away nerveless and exhausted, his face and neck and shoulders aching with the cold bitter hurt. Why, why? Whatever she wanted there finally, it was nothing his body could give, poor dispirited body. She was not satisfied; even blood, he discovered, would not satisfy her. What was it she wanted? How could such stolidness be so demanding? He burrowed against her, spent his last, came fighting for breath. His heart would feel ready to burst; convulsed, convulsed. And it was unhealthy, the whole business.—Or afterward he would fall into a deep sleep and dream bad dreams which once again he could not remember; but felt in his sleep still the fishy breath of her and the oily taste of her skin. —Or he would have one of the blinding headaches, his mind riven like a stone with the pain. What was it she wanted? There was nothing left.—He would not admit that he cried out in her grip.

After dark the visitors would come again, every night of the week. This time he was drinking in the living room, and Mina let him stay there, didn't lead him through to the bedroom. She closed the kitchen door. He sat in a stupor in the soiled chair and heard without listening the shuffle and thump of the big shoes, the muttering. Finally he rose and went out on the back porch. It was cooler than he'd thought and stars of the deep summer were spread all over the sky; no moon. The night smelled good, snug odor of weeds and flowers and field earth and the cool smell of the running stream. It was the first night he had been outside, and going down the bowed wooden steps he felt slightly elated. He stretched out his arms; he felt he had forgotten until now the feeling of bodily freedom; it was as if a woolen musty coat had been snatched from him. He wandered about in the sparse lower yard, swinging his arms, and looked up at the stars, held still as if tangled in a net, among the small leaves of the wild cherry tree. A faint breeze moved the branches and the stars moved too, seemed to jiggle quietly.

He went round the right corner of the house, going up toward the roadbed. The light from the single small lamp in the living room—it sat on a small table next to the stuffed chair—fell on him as he passed the living room window and caused him to appear pink and insubstantial. It was a queer sensation to stand here outside and look into the room he had just come out of. He could almost see himself sitting there in the chair, drawn and sullenly silent. Such a pitiable figure he made, or so contemptible a figure. The quart jar sat by the lamp; he had drunk half of it. He went up into the road, not walking steadily, but sliding his feet before him as if he moved on snowshoes. In the gravel of the road he found two small rounded stones and he held one in each hand, squeezing them slightly, reassuring himself of their solidity, their reality. Then he threw them high away into the field below. The kitchen window framed an irregular rectangle of orange light on the sloping ground, and once more he heard that unfathomable intense cry and was attracted by it to the bare kitchen window.

He stood angled away from view. The room was choked with large forms of men. Along the edge of the table next to the window a hand lay asplay in the lamplight. It looked huge. The freckles on the hand seemed large as dimes, the distent veins thick as cord. It didn't look like a hand, but, oversized, like a parody of a hand, an incomprehensible hoax. Against the far wall, by the door to the bedroom where Peter slept, a tall farmer leaned. He was dressed in blue jeans and wore a cotton plaid shirt, the sleeves rolled to his biceps, exposing long bony forearms and sharp elbows. His face was narrow and small for his body, seemed as disproportionately small as the near hand seemed large. His nose was prominent and sharp, but his eyes under the shaggy eyebrows looked shrunken, aglitter with concentration. He gazed fascinated at something out of Peter's view, and he licked his thin mouth with a sudden flicker of his tongue. He rubbed his chin with the back of his wrist. Then he moved forward to the table and took up a jelly glass half filled with corn whiskey and drank it suddenly. It spilled a little from the side of his mouth and darkened his shirt, and as he stood by the table close to the lamp his shadow loomed big and fell dark on the bedroom door. Then he stepped back and leaned against the wall once more; and he had not once moved his fierce gaze from what he stared upon.

Peter wanted to see, but he was afraid Mina would see him. Then what? It would be bad. He had to go all the way back up to the road and skirt round the patch of light. Again he picked up a stone and kept rolling it in his hands. His hands were damp with mounting excitement. What was it that everyone in the world knew but he? There was something grave and black being kept from him, and he could feel how important it was, how imminent, and he was desperate to know. There were two other men aligned against the west wall, by the door to the living room. Both wore bibbed overalls. One, a blondish thickset man, wore a faded red sweatshirt, looked yellow in the yellow light. He too stared—as did his companion. His face twitched and he was almost smiling, but not happily; in anticipation, perhaps, as one smiles involuntarily the moment before a vaccination. The other wore a rough blue workshirt, the collar open below the high bib of the overalls. He was taller and looked older than the other man. Spriggy gray hair lay on his chest. He wore an expression almost as unmoving as Mina's, but his stare was as intensely fixed as the others'. Morgan himself stood by the outside door, his hands in his pockets. His face was red as always, his eyes filled with lazy mischief.

Mina had her back toward him. At first he could not make it out: her dark tangled hair on her shoulders; the blouse loose, obviously open all down the front; her thigh olive and bare beneath the edge of the table. He could not see her waist. She was reversed, sitting backward in the chair, straddled on the short fat man who sat round the other way. Her bare leg swung rhythmically and not idly, and it seemed to Peter that she was singing, singing softly music he could not hear. Astraddle, her leg moving to and fro. She gripped the farmer's shoulders and stared intently into his face; it was the way she treated Peter when she was calming him from one of his bad hours. The red fat face was thrown against the chairback, the mouth was open, and the lips tightened and relaxed like a pulse around the dark cavity; lips were frothy and saliva trickled gleaming from one side of the mouth. And now the mouth began to open wider and then almost to close: a fish drowning in air. Mina's naked leg swung easily but more quickly now. And now the muscles under his eyes twitched, this tic rhythmic also, and the man's breath was a hoarse clatter in his throat. Still gripping his shoulder with her right hand, Mina reached behind to the table without looking. She drew forth a snake which was limp at first and then grew taut. She held it just below its head and it wrapped about her forearm. It was brown and splotched with a darker brown; he didn't know what kind it was. She held it apart from her for a moment and then began slowly to bring it toward the man's face. Below the edge of the table her leg swung ever more quickly. The farmer breathed a big bubble of spit; his breathing was louder now. Mina knew when. In time she brought the snake to his face, rubbed it slowly on his cheek. The mottled body writhed carefully, a slow cold movement of the skin without a catch. The man cried out, but the sound seemed not to come from him, but to fall from everywhere out of the hollow air of the kitchen; the sound totally itself, pure unintelligible feeling. "Iä! Iä!" he cried.

Mina spoke gravely and quietly. "Iä!" She spoke in affirmation.

It was over. Again she held the snake apart from them, and then leaned her head forward and put her mouth to the man's neck. When she straightened, the white oval impress of her teeth was plain to Peter.

Her leg had stopped swinging. She unbound the snake from her forearm, just as she might take off a spiral bracelet, and dropped the thing carelessly on the table. There it crawled a moment and then lay still; Peter thought that it might be dead now. She got off the lap of her victim easily—it was like crossing a low stone wall—and stood on the other side of the table straightening her black skirt. She brushed her thighs slowly with her fingers. The drab blouse still hung open all down the front and one small solemn breast peered blindly through the window at Peter.

He stepped back quickly out of the light. He turned his back to the window. They had begun talking again. He went again, avoiding the oblong of yellow light, to the road and came back down into the yard. It felt much cooler now than when he had first come outside. Passing the dimly lit living room window he glanced inside and then stopped. At first he couldn't understand, but looking more carefully, he saw that it was he himself who sat in the ugly stuffed chair. His gangly body was all angles and still. There he sat, uncomfortably asleep, the quart jar still half filled beside him. He stood looking for a few minutes until it all came clear; then he went on, round the house and up the steps; entered the living room and went to sit in the chair. He arranged his body carefully in an angular repose. It was all going to be a bad dream, one of the terrible dreams which caused the sweat to stand on him unmoving and cold. He arranged himself carefully, according to plan, and almost immediately he fell asleep, breathing easily and regularly, not stirring. He stirred once, only slightly, when that hard inexpressive cry sounded again; a different voice, and this time followed by an outbreak of hoarse laughter.

TWO

*I*n early August Mina found what she wanted. Now the heat was tortuous. The sky pressed more closely than before, the landscape seemed flatter, rolled out before the eye, baked, seamless; in the metal heat the different kinds of plants were not to be distinguished. The great white sun was cluttered with yellow and black specks.

"I got somebody who can drive us," Mina said. "I'm sick of this place. I don't want to hang around here forever."

The short blond boy leaned against the doorframe, relaxed and indifferent. He always had about him a liquid uncaring gracefulness. His arms hung at his sides and smoke rose along his body from the cigarette he held in his fingers with a cool exquisite droop. His name was Coke Rymer. Peter, sitting in the stuffed chair, looked at him. He detested Coke Rymer thoroughly; he hated him. He couldn't remember when the fellow had shown up, yawning, glancing about with watery blue eyes which seemed to take in nothing and yet seemed always observing, observing without curiosity. The dark-streaked blond hair was gathered upward in a stiff greased pompadour and was bunched behind in a shabby d.a.

"Coke here can drive," Mina said. "He can take us anywhere we want to go."

Peter nodded. Why was she telling him? She didn't care what he thought about it; she had given him up, for a while at least. He sat in

116

his chair all day, slept in it at night; had denied himself Mina's bed, or had been denied it. "What good are you if you can't fuck?" she had asked, and the question had no answer, of course. He couldn't care, either; for the moment at least that was one ordeal he was spared. Many things in him were damaged; one thing in him was broken, but he didn't know what exactly, was hardly interested. He had gone stale in the ability to suffer, but was certain that Mina knew it; she would find some way to rouse him again. He could contemplate without rancor long intense days of pain, thought of it dispassionately, as if it were a solid library of books that he had to read through.

"I can drive anything with wheels on it," Coke Rymer said. "Take you anywhere you want to go, honey." He had a thin watery tenor voice which wavered on the verge of a grating falsetto. "Just point me on the road and we're gone."

Peter nodded again. What difference did it make?

"They's some things I got to look after first," she said. "But it won't be long now." She sidled through the door by Coke and went through the kitchen into the back bedroom. She'd grazed him with her thigh.

The blond boy stood where he was, watching Peter with nonchalant eyes, not moving except to puff slowly at his cigarette, which was burned almost down now. Peter was thirsty again; these last few days that he hadn't been drinking the corn whiskey he couldn't seem to get enough water, made innumerable trips to the bucketed dipper in the kitchen. He rose and went toward the door, and Coke Rymer shifted his stance slightly, setting his right foot in the opposite corner of the doorsill. Peter stopped immediately before him, looking carelessly into the pasty blond face with its fixed smile, a meanly dissembling expression. He was indifferent; it wasn't worth it. He turned about and went out the other door onto the porch, down the steps into the yard.

The heat was impossible; stuffed the air like metal wool, would abrade the skin. The copper clangor of the sun filled his ears. There was no breeze, not a hint of it, not even a current in the air. It was so still and hot he felt a match flame would be invisible here in the open. The roaring heat quite overpowered the sound of insects. Under the rough cotton shirt—it was one of Morgan's which Mina had brought him—his ribs trickled with sweat. He walked into the unmoving shade of the wild cherry and stood looking across the glaring fields to the tall glaring hill beyond.

He heard footsteps on the sagging porch steps and turned. Coke Rymer came toward him through the brassy light. In the heat the blond body seemed to waver like steam, to have less weight than a normal human body. He stopped before Peter once again, still wearing the creepy unmeaning smile. "Was there something you was looking for out here, baby?" He inclined his head gently to one side.

He shrugged heavily. The only thing he noticed was how silly this boy was. How old was he, anyway? He couldn't be over nineteen or twenty, was probably seventeen or eighteen. Merely a beer joint hood, cheap as a plastic toy; something you could wind up and let scoot across the floor, its movements predictable and dull: before long the stretched rubber that made it go would snap and you'd throw it out. What use was he to Mina? He couldn't see what she saw in him. He began to turn away to go back into the house.

Coke Rymer put a wet hand on his shoulder. "Wait a minute, feller. It ain't polite to go walking off while somebody's talking to you. I don't much like it when people don't treat me polite."

He turned again. "Get your hand off," he said. His voice was drowsy.

"I don't much like people giving me orders, neither. Especially when it's some chicken bastard like you. I don't know what you're doing, hanging around here anyhow. Why don't you just cut out while you got the chance? There ain't nothing to hold you here. If I was you I'd just point myself on the road and get gone."

Without hesitating, almost without thinking, he aimed a kick at the blond boy's knee; missed. His foot caught him on the lower thigh.

Coke Rymer blundered backward a couple of steps. "You're right mean, ain't you? By God, we'll see about that." But in the middle of his speech his voice cracked into a hoarse falsetto, and this as much as the kick seemed to anger him finally. He clenched his fists and held them apart close to his body and lowered his head and charged at Peter like a clumsy yearling.

He was calm as wood, unthinking. Again he didn't hesitate, but stepped forward and brought his elbow up fair into Coke Rymer's face. It jolted through his arm like an electric shock, but he disregarded it. This sort of pain was meaningless; the whole struggle was meaningless. It was simply one more task he hadn't asked for but which he had to get through.

Again Coke Rymer staggered back. Peter had clubbed him on the forehead. The yellowish skin reddened, but Peter guessed that it wouldn't bruise or cut easily. "You . . . son of a bitch." He was gasping. Peter could almost feel in his own lungs the weight of the heat the boy sucked in. He came at Peter again in exactly the same way, but then stopped short and threw an awkward punch with his left hand, catching him on the biceps.

He was surprised at the lack of force in the punch and, without bothering to guard himself, stepped backward. Coke Rymer came on unsteadily, and they began circling. In the intense heat it was like fighting under water. Coke made innumerable foolish feints with his fist and kept gulping the hot air. Peter backed slowly, keeping his eyes dreamily over the boy's left shoulder. Somehow that seemed a very clever strategy. He could draw the kid off guard and step in when he pleased. He was momentarily delighted. The mechanics of this struggle, inept and silly as it was, had begun to interest him. He felt a paternal pity for the boy, for his stupidity and awkwardness; it was too bad how he was floundering himself to fatigue out here in the heat. Surely this boy ought to be smarter about fighting than he was. He was still backing, and now he made a feint himself; stepped forward and flicked a short left jab.

He had surprised him. Coke Rymer hadn't been touched, but stumbled over his own feet and fell backward, rolling in the dust. He came up breathing hard, his T-shirt caked with the reddish grit. Lips apart, he breathed through dark crooked teeth. He looked warily about him and again assumed his ludicrous boxing pose.

It was too much. Peter giggled, then laughed hard. He smiled at the boy, fondly amused for the moment. He turned abruptly and walked toward the porch steps, and would have gone back into the house if he hadn't heard Coke Rymer come stamping after him. He looked and ducked; began backing again slowly and carefully. The knife was shining in Coke's hand; the boy held it loosely but confidently. This was different, he could kill him with that knife, he was that silly. Peter felt completely at a loss, kept his balance gingerly and made himself stop looking at the weapon. Where had he read that you mustn't look at the knife but at the man's eyes instead? Some stupid crime novel probably. He wasn't at all certain that it was a wise policy. Out here, even in the broad light, Coke Rymer's eyes were all iris; the pupils had diminished to mere dots. Now he was frightened. He remembered the boy's queer clumsiness and thought of it as his only advantage; he was backing slowly and weaving, careful to keep his balance. He tried his former tactic, stepping forward suddenly and feinting a jab, but it was a mistake. Coke Rymer leaned out casually and pinked him in the left shoulder. He jumped away and began circling again. The cut itself hadn't hurt much, but in a few moments it began to sting; he hadn't realized he'd been sweating so hard. He took a quick peep over his shoulder and then broke and ran, ducking under the floor beams of the porch.

The space under the house was wedge-shaped, the building resting almost on the ground in the ascent of the hill, stilted up on crooked log lengths down toward the west. It was dim and silent under here but not cool. The air was no easier to breathe, stuffed with dust, stagnant. His body remembered it as the air that had stuffed the black attic room before. He ran up a little way under the house and stopped and turned. He couldn't see about him yet; he watched the open space beneath the porch where Coke Rymer would come through. Casual appearance of legs in the blue jeans with the broad glass-studded leather belt, the soiled T-shirt. He heard the boy giggling furiously.

"Why don't you run one time, you bastard?" Coke Rymer said. "I'd just like to see how good you can run." He broke down into giggles. He held the knife at his side, then began carelessly whittling at one of the porch steps. "If you think I'm going to go crawling around in there after you, you're crazy as hell," he said. "That ain't my way, to go crawling around under a house for some chicken bastard. No sir, baby, I just don't cotton to it. Me, I'm just going to wait right here till you come out." He jabbed the knife into one of the log supports and let it remain, near at hand. The sound of his high voice under the house was hollow, had an unearthly whistle in it. "I'll wait right here, me, if I have to for five years. And when you take a notion to come out I'll cut your ass good." More giggling. Slowly the boy took a pack of cigarettes from the pocket of his jeans and lit one.

Except for the open end of the porch the space beneath the house was sided with raw boards which let streaks of light between them. His eyes were becoming accustomed to the dimness. He was half bent now and to get comfortable he would have to squat; he didn't want to do that, he didn't want to see that yellow fixed face. The dust was thick, came almost to his shoe tops. He maneuvered about a bit, trying to find a measure of comfort, and glass snapped under his foot. Looking, he saw bits of a broken Mason jar.

"I'd sure like to know what the hell you think you're doing under there," Coke Rymer said. "There ain't no way out for you, sweetheart, except by me. Why don't you just face it?"

He moved to his left and squatted. Now the boy's face was hidden by the porch steps; visible were a blue knee, a hand laxly holding a burning cigarette, the knife protruding from the log support. He waited to grow calm again, to steady his breathing. He thought of trying to get out, going quietly and keeping the steps between them, but he knew it was no good. The boy, standing, would see him; he wouldn't get halfway down into the yard. But if he waited here long enough Mina would stop them. Surely she wouldn't let the blond boy kill him. . . . But why not? What did he know about her, anyway? She was unfathomable. The simple fact that she countenanced Coke Rymer at all was unfathomable. All her motives were buried under the ocean. He sighed.

Moving to the left still, still trying to get out of his sight every part of Coke Rymer and the knife, he struck with his foot something solid and metal. At first he couldn't find it, buried in the deep dust. He dug in and dredged it out: a handle for a water pump. It was lovely, it was about two and a half feet long, dull iron. It had a very slight S curve and the end of the handle was smooth, his hand fitted it perfectly. The opposite end of the handle tapered to a flat iron plate which contained three quarter-inch holes evenly spaced. He imagined how the holes would whisper when he swung the weapon. It fitted his hand perfectly, it was proper. He held it before him, admiring the heft and the subtle curve of it. Suddenly in love, he wagged it before him.

Now he could go out. He could keep the steps between him and Coke Rymer—if he could just move silently under the house (the dust would muffle the noise)—and he could come out standing and ready to fight. He went forward on his knees and crawled toward the light. He pushed the pump handle gently along before him, breathed shallowly and quickly, not wanting to sneeze with the dust. When he reached the edge of the house, he took a ready grip on the handle, then rose slowly to a crouch.

The boy was talking again; he talked a great deal, Coke Rymer. "I'm telling you, sweetheart, I don't mind waiting five years for you to come out if I have to. I got all the time in the world." He stooped and flicked the live cigarette butt under the house, into the dust.

Peter came out immediately; his eyes had got used to the light. The boy heard and turned, plucking the knife from the log with the quick careless movement one would use in striking a match. They stared at each other over the descent of the sagging steps; it was a moment or two before Coke Rymer glimpsed the pump handle. "What's that thing you've got?" he said.

He began to edge round the steps.

"That won't do you no good, just a ole pump handle. I got something here can cut your ass good."

But he didn't come forward; kept still, watching the swing of the handle. Was *he* going to duck under the house now? That would be too much; Peter thought he would laugh himself sick if he drove the boy to ground like a rat, as he had been driven. No, now Coke began to sidle away from the porch, going back down into the yard.

"It won't do you no good. I can throw this here knife." Almost without looking, and with the one hand, he reversed the knife, holding it lax between thumb and forefinger about halfway down the blade. But there was no conviction in his eyes, and his voice was again teetering on the edge of a falsetto. Peter jumped forward and poked him in the stomach with the handle, holding it like a broadsword. Not a hard blow, but telling, assertive of his advantage. The watery blue eyes bulged; the yellow face splotched with red.

"Throw down the knife," Peter said. He was surprised; his own voice was whispering and rough. "If you throw the knife down I won't have to knock your brains out."

"Hell you say. I ain't putting this knife down for no son of a bitch. I throw it anywhere, it'll be in your belly."

But surely it was obvious, even to the boy, the superiority . . .

"Go on, go at it. I want to see you kill each other off." Mina, of course. She stood on the porch watching and now began to let herself gently down into the broken rocking chair. She rocked complacently, enfolding the whole scene with her still gaze. "Go on," she said. "Kill each other off, why don't you? Ain't neither one of you worth what it takes to keep you alive. It's been a long time since I seen a good fight. Let's see you do it."

They looked at one another helplessly. Their animosity was smothered completely.

She saw it too and laughed, a hard flat faceless laugh. "And I guess it'll be a good long time before I ever see another good fight, if it's up to you two. You ain't hardly got no fight in you, have you?" Again, the flat hard laugh.

"Aw shit," Coke Rymer said. He stuck the knife listlessly into the porch steps. "I can take care of honeybunch here any time I want to. He don't bother me none, him and his goddamn pump handle. I can take care of him without batting a eye."

Peter knew better; he was silent, vowing not to let the handle out of his sight. His life was bound to it now; he could see the connection as simply as if it were a glittering chain, a handcuff which held him to the junked iron. For a while now his life had been bound to iron, and the necessity of the handle didn't surprise him; it was inevitable.

"I don't know whether you can or not," Mina said. "Mr. Leland might be some tougher than you think. What I do know is, you ain't going to try it no time soon. It ain't something I'd just let go on and on. Work to get done around here. We got to get packed up to leave and you got to help get it done."

"That's all right with me," Coke Rymer said. "I'm ready to go anytime, anywhere you want to."

Peter was ascending the steps, clutching the iron tight. It was the only thing solid in him now. His legs trembled, and his empty right hand. The delayed fear in the struggle with the blond boy had settled on him now and his heart staggered in him. His seeing was blurred with fear. He stopped at the porch edge, Mina watching him, amused.

"And what do you think you're up to?" she said.

He licked his caked lips. He was careful to look away from her face, over her head into the shadowed sullen air. "I'd like to have a drink," he said.

"I guess you don't mean water then," she said. "I guess you mean you want liquor."

"Yes." He was still not looking at her.

"What makes you think you'd get any? What have you done to get any? Have you done anything for me lately?"

"No." He spoke slowly. "No, but . . ."

"But what?"

His mind was empty. He let his shoulders rise and drop. Helpless.

Coke Rymer spoke, his voice at once belligerent and whining. "I don't see why you want to put up with him. What do you want with some crazy old drunk anyhow?"

"Hush," she said. "Me and Mr. Leland's still got lots of things to do together. Don't we, Mr. Leland?"

He nodded numbly.

"Even if you can't fuck no more."

He nodded again.

She rose easily and came toward him and he sank back in himself, though his body didn't move. Her silvery eyes held the whole range of his knowledge; she placed her hand casually on his penis, withdrew it without haste. "No. Not anymore. But there's always something else, ain't there? Why don't you just go and set down in the rocking chair and I'll see if I can't find what you're looking for. Something'll put hair on your chest." She grinned. "Make a man out of you." She stepped lightly away and went to the door and turned. She spoke to Coke Rymer; her voice was sharp and peremptory. "Quit that fiddling around and come on in here. They's work got to be done if we're ever going to get going."

"All right," he said. "I done told you I'm ready to go." He stopped his scraping of the notched edge of the porch step and folded the knife and put it into his pocket. He came up the steps with his buoyant grace and followed Mina into the house, pausing only to give Peter a single swift foul-natured glance.

Peter giggled. That one last glance had so much about it of the impulse of the hindered child who sticks out his tongue. That was Coke Rymer, all right: a spoiled child. Spoiled, soiled; but also despoiling, assoiling. He darkened the heavy brightness of the air, and even in his total blind paleness there was a dimness, as of a furry rot-inducing mold. He tipped the rocking chair forward and back, but the motion augmented the queasiness that his belated fear had brought on and he stopped quickly, sat in the shadowed porch gazing out. The settled heat had not moved. The limbs of the wild cherry tree dropped, the sharp leaves looked buttery in the sunlight. He was simply waiting, and in a while Mina did appear, holding one of the too-familiar jars loosely at the ridged top.

"Here now," she said. "Here it is, you can drink it. But I don't want to see that you've poured none of it out or spilled it or wasted it, or you'll never see another drop from me as long as you live."

She went back into the house. He looked through it at the landscape, which was streaked and crazed and looked even hotter through the yellowish liquid. He began to drink, drank steadily, and within the hour he was delirious and lying on the porch in fetal position, his hands clasped tightly between his knees. He was prophesying in a loud voice, heedless. And then he began to whisper. "Mina's right," he said, and the sibilance of his whisper was echoed in the sibilance of his clothing as it rasped on the boards of the porch. He squirmed on the floor but made no progress. "Mina's right about the snake. We live as serpents, sucking in the dust, sucking it up. The stuff we were formed of, and we ought to inhabit it. We ought to struggle to make ourselves secret and detestable, we should cultivate our sicknesses and bruise our own heads with our own heels. Where's the profit in claiming to walk upright? There's no poisonous animal that walks upright, a desecration.

It's better to show your true shape, always. It's better to s— . . ." But now he had squirmed forward, to the edge of the porch, and his forehead knocked against a supporting post. He raised his head and began to gnaw feverishly at the base of the post. The wood tasted of bitter salty dust. He closed his eyes and kept gnawing until the fit had passed off him and then he lay weak throughout his whole body. He was sweating, the bitterness of the post streamed out his pores; and a fine-edged clarity possessed him. He felt unutterably ashamed, and he turned his eyes toward the door, knowing already what he would see, his face and mouth and ears burning with fearful shame.

"Ain't you something?" Mina said. "Ain't you a sight?" She didn't laugh, but turned away and disappeared again.

Grasping the post, he pulled himself shakily upright and shook his head hard, trying to clear it. He staggered to the rocking chair and folded into it and began to drink again. That was Mina's way, that was always her way: she simply appeared and disappeared when she liked, everything was always under her control. He remembered that only a few weeks ago he had daydreamed that when she had finished the life of his body she would have it discarded—dumped—in the fields under the brutal sun. Naked to the corrupting heat . . . Now he realized that he wouldn't be so lucky. That fate had been reserved for his wife's white body; Sheila, whom he had murdered, lay out there somewhere, going to pulp in the southern weather. Trying to turn the thought away, he turned his head, shook it hard again. He didn't have to guess about Sheila; Mina had told him what she had had done, repeated it again and again. Of course. . . . Mina would always do exactly as she pleased. Coming and going, her movements admitted of no prediction, except that she would continually find him in the moments of his worst shame. Now he had guessed that this was her motive in keeping him, to observe how far downward he had gone. He had become a queer experimental animal; Mina used him purposely to try to gauge through him the fiber of the whole species. And he too felt a chilly detached curiosity. How far into this rushing darkness could a man go? When he had devoured his heart, what was there to push the machine along? At what point was this machine no longer recognizable as himself? He glimpsed a blurred moment of illumination: at that bodiless point—whenever, wherever it was—that the humanity in him melted, disappeared, the universe rested. At least one universe, the humane one. In this momentary half-vision (which he could hardly believe he had been granted) he felt obscurely the presence of other systems, other universes, to which humanity—his humanity—was irrelevant. Mocking crowded points of corruscation. Infinite coldness. He shook his head for the third time and drank again, feeling gratefully the flush of the liquor leap upward in his body from his belly.

THREE

*T*hey were traveling. They had loaded Peter into the back seat with the same uncaring gesture they had loaded whatever it was Mina was carrying into the trunk of the car. He sat numb while they made the final preparations, overwhelmed by the all-too-familiar look and odor of the machine. It was his car, of course; Mina had taken possession of everything that had once belonged to him and Sheila. No question about her purposes with his possessions; she would waste them totally and carefully. He observed the scratchy ribbed felt overhead, the frayed latticework of the seat covers. Wouldn't it be funny if the dome light worked, now that Mina had the car? It had never once worked when the car was his. He wondered if the little leather-bound copy of the Gospel of St. John was still in the glove compartment; surely Mina would have no use for that. He was still slightly drunk; he sat carefully steady and kept his hands clasped between his knees.

They were simply leaving, no good-byes. Neither Morgan nor his wife—who was almost never seen in the house—came out to speak or to wave. She and Coke Rymer finished what business they had inside the house (without doubt she bore Coke Rymer, too, desperate down into the rancid quilts) and got into the car. He drove and she sat listlessly, her bare arm stretched along the top of the front seat. She glanced about with a placid curiosity. Peter had none; sat stolid, feeling the pour of warm air on him, heaviness of the moving landscape. Behind the car the reddish-yellow dust rose solid as wood and then dispersed to separate particles. Peter looked behind once to see the tenant cabin tossing, as if swimming away in the yellow haze.

They passed the big brick house, the house of the murder, and Peter turned his head. There, it had loomed before him suddenly round a sharp curve of the road and stood shocking in the glacis of the hill. He turned his head. Even the single glimpse of it disturbed, served to force into his gullet the sour taste of the guilt he had been so long now trying to swallow and to keep down. No specific memory—nothing so acutely defined—but a shapeless huge nausea overwhelmed his nerves, and he kept his head turned. He simply would not remember, he denied it all.

On this road it was farmland all the way. On a board fence bordering the roadway, a large gaudy metallic-looking rooster flapped wings and crowed, too late in the day. The racking crow sounded mechanical. Through the bottom fields the creek wandered, not appearing very different from where it ran by Morgan's cabin. Sunlight burning in ovules on the glassy leaves of poison oak. Two white butterflies involved in hectic acrobatics. The passing in and out of the shadows dropped by massy oaks. Splotched cattle on the splotched hills. Barbed-wire fences, the weathered posts leaning awry, sagging rusty wire. Hot gray roofs of squat chicken houses. Barns red and gray, looking fat and hollow at the same time. The neat white houses and the battered tenant cabins, each garnished on one side with lines of hung washing, spectacular in the breeze. Noise of flung gravel, of wind.

And then they hit pavement and Coke Rymer drove faster. The wind that poured in on Peter cooled and increased in volume. Coke was intent on his driving; he drove savagely but with a flashy accuracy, carefully watching the road before him, though he never seemed to look into his rearview mirror. Nor did Mina glance into the back seat at Peter. Now and again she would draw her fingers slowly along the top of the front seat; she was caught up in her own listless thoughts, and even the slight curiosity she had at first shown in the passing scenery had vanished. Peter let himself relax; the first motion of the car had made him feel faintly ill, but now he let himself drift with it, tried to enclose the oblique movements of the machine in his body and, lax now, felt that he had partially succeeded. It was not a good car, an old

one—it was what he had been able to afford—and it quivered mercilessly and, after a full stop, shuddered alarmingly climbing into the
gears. He ought to have got a new car long ago, but there hadn't seemed
a real need and, of course, there was the question of money. Even
now, he didn't know what the need for the car was. He had no notion
where they were headed, except that the direction was easterly, out of
the mountains. He didn't even know whether Mina had planned a
definite destination. She was perfectly capable of truly aimless movement, he thought, but then he knew the thought was false. Even if
there was no destination, her moving would never be purposeless; all
her energies were bent to a single purpose, she never swerved. This he
had observed again and again—and a lot of good his observation was.
What this purpose was he had never fathomed, so that all her actions
were mysterious and sometimes seemed almost crazy; but he didn't
doubt that there was a single principle which would bring it all to him
clear if he once could grasp it. These thoughts made him restless and
he shifted his feet on the floorboard, feeling for the solid presence of
the pump handle. He touched it with his toe and was grateful and
comforted. He glanced down at it, permitted himself a faint smile in
the roaring windstream. He planned to take care of the weapon, to
polish it till it gleamed, and then—and then a light oil bath to prevent
its rusting again. He pondered. And perhaps too, a rubber grip for it;
he would need only a few inches from a rubber garden hose. . . .

He felt that he really ought to know Mina's purpose: it seemed so
closely dependent on Peter himself. There was a reason, yes, why he
had been subjected to what he had. The idea of punishment formed
in his mind, but the idea of the crime for which he was being punished
would not come. It was not murder—ah, that was a mere word to him
now; the memory of Sheila herself had disappeared, to leave only an
impression of bright sheeny light, no person at all—no, not murder,
but something more terrifying, something previous to anything he could
ever remember, previous, he sometimes thought, maybe to his whole
life, previous to his birth.

Regular monotony of the passing telephone poles, dark, spearlike.
The shadows slipped through the interior of the car like spears. Now
racing the candescent threads of railway track which lay along the road.

He could follow the progress of the stretched shape of the sun as it zipped on the iron. Impression of heatless light. And then they caught up with the train, passed the red caboose, went exhilaratingly by the rollicking freight cars. He heard them bounding along the track. *Rocker unrocker rocker unrocker.* Passed the diesel engine which let go with its ugly sour horn. Shot through narrow concrete bridges. Up and breathtakingly down dark wooded hills. Coke Rymer was taking the secondary highways; Mina must have asked him to keep off the broad fast interstate system. Again Peter couldn't guess her reasoning; it was no less public the way they were going. Cars came toward them and slipped by, momentary as a wink. Trucks loaded with heavy paper bags of fertilizer lumbered along before them, and Coke Rymer cursed, slowing suddenly; Peter was always certain they would bang into the trucks. He cowered inside himself; imagined smothering under a flood of smelly fertilizer.

They rode on and on. Occasionally they would pull into a nondescript service station for gas, or Coke Rymer would say, "I got to go to the little boy's room," or "I got to powder my nose." His coy silliness, something always grim about it. Mina would go into the station and return, bringing Peter a soft drink and cheese crackers with peanut butter. The cellophane packages were always dusty, he wiped his fingers on his trousers. But he ate and drank dutifully. Four empty soft drink bottles rolled clinking together on the floor. In one station Peter went to the restroom, and there, in the acrid odor of the disinfectant, looked out the window before him, a narrow slot in the white concrete block wall, and thought absurdly of escape. But there was nothing to escape from. He was not a prisoner, not held by force. He was simply bound to Mina wholly; he was his own prisoner, he could escape by dying, by no other way. He uttered an involuntary sob, zipped his fly, lurched out. The sunlight struck his eyes like a slap.

It got later, the sun was behind them. The eastern sky was orange, wild with queer cloud shapes. Still they went on. The land got flatter, and towns were glimpsed before they were arrived at, the lights making ghostly white aureoles on the horizon. The young men were out, dolled up, restlessly courting the girls. Gay convertibles; shaggy fox tails pendent from radio aerials. One little town like the others, all flat on the landscape like stamps pasted in an album. Sharp brick buildings in the evening light; they looked like biscuits set out of the oven to cool. And yet it all fitted. The landscape was perfectly integral. Across the slim horizontal rows of cotton or cane, the weathered vertical form of the farmhouse seemed truly correct: its gabled porches, its uprightness, its bony angularity. On the whole land a somnolent watchfulness, a waiting for the night, for coolness, for the justice of stars. They passed drive-in movies, and the great flat faces of strangers fluttered away in the darkness; they were quickly oppressive, these visions of bright love and violence, a tipsy staggered glimpse of the secret heart of the land. Peter felt conspicuous and embarrassed at seeing the great screens; it was like peeking into bathroom windows.

It had begun to cool, but he still felt hot. His body was gritty with dust, filmed over with evaporated sweat. The oncoming headlights burned his eyes, scraped on his exacerbated nerves. They kept driving on and on, and he wanted to cry out for them to stop it, to stop it: they were going nowhere, there was nowhere to go. Why couldn't they let up? Why was it so necessary to squash oneself to a handy ball and keep torturing it along over the flimsy landscape? He leaned and picked up the comforting pump handle and held it tightly across his lap. He gripped it hard, not to let go, and the tightness began to seep out of his chest. He ran his finger along the clear curve of the metal; it was he, this weapon; he could punch holes in the world, he possessed heroism kept carefully in check. He settled his head back against the seat. His eyelids flickered. He dozed resistlessly, still gently fingering the pump handle.

In the sharp restive dream he was a spider; no, a daddy longlegs. He scoured in jagged lines over the fields, searching out water with an unerring hunger. His size was protean; grew monstrously; diminished. On the skin of the great water, when he found it, he would drift in coolness, the big overhanging leaves of the weeping willow would keep away the sunlight. The soft fields were singing softly. In the harsh embittering dream was a peaceful dream, of waters shot with healthy shadows, of the rounded spaces under trees enclosing as with cool arms. But in the heated fields his six-legged unstable body was painful, crazy. All his eyes had nowhere to look; a glazed glare held his vision with unbreakable force. He moved crookedly; he did not want to move. There was no reason for it, there was no purpose in it. The six-legged machine was its own volition, and he a prisoner trapped. It came to him that this at last was the true image of his sickness, and in his sleep he was somewhat mollified. The sweat ceased to trickle down his sides from his armpits and his grip on the pump handle gentled.

"All right, honey, you can climb out of there. You've got the place we're looking for."

He was awake immediately. They had stopped. Coke Rymer tugged at his shoulder through the open window. He didn't know where they were. It was full dark and cool. All round the car were trees, sibilant in the night breeze. He clambered out, stiff and dizzy, and raised his head to look at the sky. Random stars pierced the foliage, and the tree limbs moved now to sweep them from sight. He flexed his arms, held them out straight, rotated his neck on his shoulders. He breathed deep, grateful, but when he walked forward he staggered, the stiffness still in his legs.

Mina was leaning against the front fender, resting easily. Nothing bothered her; she knew where they were, why they were here. "I hope you had a good nap," she said. "That might be what you're good for, you know it? Just to sleep. You might could get to be a real expert."

He turned away from her, scratched the small of his back with both hands.

"Or you could drink liquor," she said. "I forgot about that. There's two things you can do, right there."

He wandered away from the car, heading ignorantly into the darkness.

"Where do you think you're going?" Mina said.

"I'll be back in just a few seconds," he said.

"He's going off to take a leak," Coke Rymer said. "Do you want me to go with you, honey? To hold your hand?"

It was dark and cool, and he began to feel better, not so heavy. His body was still sticky with travel, and as he stood to urinate he listened hopefully for the sound of a stream nearby, water to slice away some of the road dust. No sound of water, but a sound, the night breeze hazing the foliage, like water; and even this seemed to help, to refresh.

There . . . Now he did feel refreshed, and as he walked back toward the car he permitted himself a vague half-smile, thinking, *I woke and found that life was duty.*

They were waiting, still standing by the car. "We're going to sleep in the back. You can sleep in the front, if you want to," Coke Rymer said. "The steering wheel gets in the way, that's why."

"All right."

"Or if you want to, you can sleep out here on the cold ground. I don't give a damn what you do."

"All right," he said.

His acquiescence robbed Coke Rymer of anything to say. He stood uncertainly. "Well . . ."

"Oh goddamnit, come on," Mina said. She caught the blank boy by the arm and opened the car door and propelled him into the back. "If it was up to you-all, I guess you'd just stand around talking all night. There's better things to do than that." She turned. "Why don't you just take another nice little walk? I don't reckon they's anything around here to eat you up. So all you have to do is just not to get lost. You can take a little walk and watch out where you're going." She got in and closed the door.

He didn't feel that a nice little walk was what he needed, he was tired. But he'd better go. He put his hands in his pockets and started away, heavily desiring alcohol. How much easier the trip would be if there were something to drink. Mina would know that, and yet she had allowed him nothing. . . . He tried to put it out of his mind, but this resolve simply made it all the worse; his very neurons seemed to cry out for the stuff. The breeze had not abated and now it was cooler than he wanted. He hunched his shoulders forward. He walked aimlessly, noticing nothing about him. Now and again he looked up, walking on, and the stars seemed to float backward over the various shapes of the trees. He kept wondering if he had come far enough, if he had been gone from the car long enough to satisfy Mina. Finally he turned back and began to retrace his path. It wasn't difficult here; the undergrowth was sparse, the trees were mostly large and well spaced. Two or three times he wandered off the track and had to extricate himself from patches of bush and briar.

But there was no real trouble, and he got back too soon. He came to the edge of the little clearing where the car sat and there he stopped, hearing Coke Rymer's choked muttering from the back seat. He let himself clumsily to the ground and sat with his legs crossed, listening. Again he let himself smile, irony without joy; and he waited. The low whistling intake of breath he heard, the unnerving muttering: all the cruel mechanics of the lovelessness of the deed. He waited knowingly, certain of what would come. And he heard it: Coke Rymer's anguished last outcry, uttered twice and enveloped in the breezy darkness. Coke too was under the pain of it. Snap. O, her cold cold teeth, the fishy breath of her. It was unremitting and continual; she was relentless. He smiled with solid satisfaction for the first time in a long while. She had no mercy, none. Now it wouldn't be very long before Coke Rymer was like Peter, not male; he wouldn't be able to fuck anymore. He would be broken, a figure paper thin. . . . Abruptly he hankered after his pump handle. He should have brought it with him, he felt frightened without it. It was his weapon, and if anyone ever needed a weapon, it was he, for surely there had never been anyone so utterly defenseless, so helpless and so caught in incomprehensible dangerous toils. The land and sky looked upon his helplessness.

What was ever going to satisfy her?

He lingered; waited until what he hoped was a decent time had elapsed—smiled, a third time, because the word "decent" had come into his mind—and then rose, brushed absently at the moist earth that clung to his trousers. He went to the car, walked round the front and opened the door at the driver's seat as quietly as he could. It remained dark in the car, the dome light didn't work, not even for Mina. He looked into the back. Coke Rymer lay squashed against the seat, already asleep and breathing heavily, wearily, through his gaped mouth. Mina lay on the outside, propped on her elbow, taking up most of the room. She wasn't even disheveled. She regarded Peter with her pale, almost luminous eyes; spoke in a level, quiet—but not hushed—voice. "Well, did you have a nice walk?"

"It was all right," he said. There was a glitter of petty triumph in his voice that he couldn't keep out, and he hoped she wouldn't notice it.

"Good for you," she said. "Get some exercise, that's the best way to get your strength back."

He leaned in and began to crawl across the seat on his hands and knees. He wanted to have the steering wheel at his feet.

"You know," she said, "it wouldn't bother me none to turn old Coke out of the back seat here. He's just going to sleep like a dead man. If you was to want to come back here and try your luck for a while, I'd roust him out." Her voice was lazy and impassive, her eyes two gray patches. "You reckon you feel up to a little more exercise?"

All his little happiness melted away. "I'm afraid not," he said.

She sniffed; sheer disdain. "I didn't reckon you would."

He lay down, then squirmed around to close the door; got his position back and lay there, sour and painful. He needed fiercely the pump handle, but he was determined he would not ask her for it. He lay awake, holding his genitals in his left hand. But sleep at last caught him, held him silent and dreamless and he woke into the daylight without rancor, feeling rested. But he thirsted harshly for Mina's dispensed alcohol.

In the early afternoon they came to Gordon, a town not different, so far as Peter could tell, from the scores of towns they had passed through. The surrounding countryside was flat, and on the easterly breeze was a whiff of brackishness; it couldn't be many miles from the ocean side. Grass struggled to grow here, and the earth was often bare, a pinkish-white dust blanketed over packed burning clay. Here clay land was changing over into sandy land; the two soils melted together. The sunlight too seemed powdery, thick on the leaves of magnolia trees, collected in drifts like burning snow in the upper crevices of boxwood shrubs.

"Well, this here's the town you wanted to get to," Coke Rymer said. "Where do you want me to go from here?"

"Just drive us around a little and let me look," Mina said. "I'll let you know where I want you to stop."

"Well, you're the doctor."

"That's right," she said.

The streets of Gordon were quiet. Cars were parked along each side of the main street, pocketed when it was possible in the shade of tall oak or magnolia trees. Grave-eyed Negro children passed on the sidewalks, swinging wet bathing suits by their sides. The houses here were mostly white wooden houses of two storeys, but here and there were small brick duplexes with the silvered boxed air conditioners protruding from the less sunny windows. Through the main square of the town ran two railroad tracks, side by side, and the town was truly divided by them. On the east side of the tracks the moneyed houses began to grade finely down into grudging respectability and then at last into frank poverty. The asphalt pavement narrowed and was broken along the edges. Here were the one-storey white frame houses, held off the naked dusty yards by unpainted concrete blocks.

"You can turn here," Mina said, and Coke Rymer obediently turned left into a red jolting dirt road. The sloping ditches were filled with black cinders, and the houses were no longer white, but stained brown or weathered gray. They were in a Negro section, and there were no longer signs at the corners telling the names of the streets. Here the streets were nameless. There was an occasional shabby grocery store, its false brick siding plastered over with advertisements for soft drinks and headache powders.

"Right here, now," she said, and he braked the car, let the motor idle. They had come out of the Negro section into a beaten-down poor-white area. On the right was a squat white house, but Mina was observing the house on the left. It was small, looked as if it would contain four rooms or so; the rough oak siding was stained a dark brown, as dark almost as creosote, and the white trim was mostly battered away. The unfenced front yard was as bare and dusty as the others. The roof was gray galvanized tin, no different from the roof of Morgan's house back in the mountains. Peter saw nothing interesting about the place. There were a hundred, a million others which would mirror it without a scrap of difference. . . . But it was what Mina wanted, what she must have been looking for.

"You can turn off the car," she said. "This here's the place we been looking for."

He turned off the motor and they climbed out, leaned resting against the heated metal of the car.

"I don't see what's so wonderful about this place," Coke Rymer said. "Who is it lives here, anyhow?"

"They don't nobody live here," she said. "This is where we're going to live."

The blond boy shrugged, sucked his front teeth. Peter was at first bewildered—it made no sense, none—but then he was grateful. They could move the stuff in the trunk of the car into the house, he would help move it, and then Mina would give him something to drink.

FOUR

When Peter woke, his gangly frame was shuddering all over, not just from the morning cool, but because this was the condition of his awaking body. He struggled with his limbs. The chains clashed and thumped on the splintery kitchen floor. He didn't want to open his eyes. The early sunlight would strike like a bullet into his brain. The smell of slopped liquor, of chewed rancid scraps of food, hung in the room, only slightly freshened by the raw air that poured in. A window was broken or maybe somebody had left the door open. The light was on his eyelids, forming behind them a coarse abrasive red curtain which made his temples ache. An uncontrollable belch brought up the whole fetor of his gut and while he struggled to breathe, keeping his mouth open to dissipate the deathly taste, droplets of sweat popped out over his whole length, dampening his shirt and pants which were already salty and sour from the weeks before. He gasped.

Then he lay still, trying to listen, but all he could hear was his own thick choked breathing. When he held his breath he could hear only the blood swarming in his ears. But no one seemed to be awake but himself; he had to lie still. If he woke them, moving his chains loud enough to wake them, they would kick him to bits. He tried to place his head, without moving his arms and legs, so that the sun couldn't get at his eyes. It was no good. The day had already begun its dreadful course, the sun was poisoning the sky. He felt the baleful rays sink into his pores. His spine felt as if metallic cold hands squeezed it intermittently. He couldn't get his face out of the sunlight.

He lapsed into a fitful red doze, but was jarred awake by the fear of rattling the chains in his sleep. With her big mouth Mina would tear his Adam's apple out of his throat. She would spit it on the floor and crush it with her big mean heel, like killing a cockroach. He could almost see her unmoving face hovering over his, feel the cold fishy breath of her; her teeth would be like hundreds of relentless needles. He whimpered helplessly, but stopped it off, constricting his throat like a ball of iron inside. If he began whimpering hard he couldn't stop and it would get louder and louder until the moos came on him, and then they would beat him until he stopped. He stopped the whimper. His chest already felt jagged inside where they had kicked him. He fought to make all his muscles relax from the quivering, and stream on stream of tears rolled down his face. If he opened his eyes the tears would shoot sharp spears through them.

But he was so tired he was almost inanimate. He fell into a yellow sleep, bitter with a drilling electric sound and the smell of black mud and fish. He dreamed that he had no face at all and that his eyes were unseeing dark splotches on his gray stony back and that he swam forever through this world of solid objects which were to his body liquid. In the dream there was nothing he could touch, his body was mere extension without knowable presence.

Again he came awake, now with the black thirst upon him. The sunlight no longer filled his face, and yet he did not think that he had slept long. He felt a warm presence. At first his eyes wouldn't open, and he thought that they had clicked them shut forever with locks and he thrashed around, beginning to whimper again, not caring about the chains now. He got his eyes open, though they were still unseeing, but it was hard to breathe. He blew his breath out hard and an inexplicable chicken feather blew up and stuck on his cheek. He gagged. Then when he could look it was all dim, but behind the dimness was a bright white ball with the hurt strained out of it.

He could not think anymore. Everything in his head was gone. At last he realized he was looking at the sun. It shone through the dark gray cloth, reddening faintly the stretched muscles of the legs which arched over his face. He knew them already, Mina's plump steady legs, taut curve at calf and thigh, arrogant, careless. He looked up the pink-tinged insides of her legs. He knew he had always been right. There at the X of her where her woman-thing ought to be was a spider as big as a hand, furred over with stiff belligerent hairs straight as spikes. He couldn't stop looking. His gullet closed and his chest began to strain for air; he could hear it begin to crackle. His throat opened again, but it was hard to breathe because the whimpering had started. It started loud and he knew there was no hope stopping. The moos had got to come now; and then they would kick him to bits.

"Hush up, just hush up," she said. "Can't you never take a joke?" With the hand which wasn't holding up the front of her skirt she reached down there and plucked the spider away. She held it free above him and though he could see it was only a toy, only wire and fuzz and springy legs, he couldn't keep the whimpering back. It got louder; the moos had got to come.

She dropped her skirt and leaned her face over him, rolling it a little so that he could see she was disgusted. "Well, there then," she said. She shook the toy spider in her hand and then dropped it on his face.

He tried not to, he clenched his teeth and tried to keep it back, but the noiseless loud fear poured out of his mouth, moo after moo of it, pure craziness. He was so frightened he couldn't hear himself, and he heard Mina calling:

"Coke! Coke! Come in here right now. Come in here."

Before she had stopped shouting the watery blond boy came in. He didn't even look at Mina but simply put the heel of his boot on Peter's chest and ground his foot round and round, pushing down hard. The blond boy pushed harder until Peter couldn't breathe any more, and he had to stop mooing. Then the boy squatted and sat on his chest, bouncing his weight up and down so that he couldn't get out his fear. He drummed his arms and legs, banging the chain links, rubbing them across the floor.

The blond boy began to slap his face first with one hand and then with the other. "What's my name?" he said.

"Coke."

He slapped him again and again. "What's the rest of it? What's my full name?"

Peter was cold with unknowing. He formed sounds but no name emerged from them.

"Come on, baby. Stick with it. What's my full name, now?" The slapping had got progressively harder.

"Coke Rymer," he said.

"*That's* my baby," the blond boy said in a soothing tone of voice. "That's a way to go." He stood up with the meaningless nonchalance he always had about him. "We'll get you a drink now, okay?" Without pausing for an answer he kicked Peter hard on the side of his neck. "That's a baby," he said.

He groaned at the kick, but after the first uttering of pain was out he subsided into the whimpering which finally became only a strained silent heaving of his chest. He kept looking up at Coke's liquescent blue gaze; his own eyes were charged with pain and fear but not with hate. He would never have any more hate.

Apparently satisfied, Coke Rymer knelt and began to unlock the chained cuffs at his wrists and ankles. He was still murmuring soothingly. "All right now, you're coming right along. You're going to do all right, honey, you're going to do all *right*." When he finished with the locks he handed the bunch of keys on the long chain to Mina. She dropped the chain loop over her head, tucked the keys into her cotton blouse and buttoned it up. She stood away from the two of them, her arms folded. Coke Rymer hoisted him to his feet and held him up until he seemed steady enough to stand by himself. He stood wavering, his head dropped almost to his chest and lolling back and forth; floundered across the room and leaned backward against the flimsy dinette table. He stroked carefully at his wrists; there were scarlet ichorous bands on them where the broad iron cuffs had rubbed the skin away. It made him feel very pitying to see his poor wrists like this.

"Huh," Mina said. "You ain't hurt. That's nothing."

"We'll get him a drink of liquor," Coke Rymer said. "That'll fix our little honeybunch up before you know it. Make a new man out of him." He swung open one of the rickety wall cupboard doors. Inside, it was full of empty bottles and broken glass. He brought down a pint bottle of murky stuff and shook it, looked at it against the broad light that streamed through the open door. "What'll you give me for this?" he said. He showed his dim little teeth in a stretched smile.

He could barely grunt. It sounded like gravel rattling in a box.

"Oh, go on and give it to him," Mina said. She watched him patiently, as if she was curious. Of course curiosity would never show in that locked face.

The boy held it out to him and he waited a wary moment to see if it would be jerked away. He got hold of it in both hands and then momentarily just stood clutching it out of fear of dropping or spilling it. He drank in short convulsive swallows. It tasted thick and mushy and warm, but it had a burning around the edges. As he lowered the bottle he lowered his head too and then again he stood clenching the bottle and, with the muscles of his chest, clenching his insides too. He had to keep it down, couldn't let it get away from him; he stood taut from his heels to his chin. After a long time the writhing spasms stopped. Again sweat came out on him all over.

Mina was still watching him. She spoke in an observing even tone: "They's chicken blood in that liquor."

He was still stuporous; her face was as blank to him as paper.

"You was the one done it yourself," she said. "You was the one pulled that chicken's head off and crammed that neck down in the bottle. I guess you didn't know it, but that's what you done. It was just last night." In the morning sunlight her eyes seemed paler than ever.

Coke Rymer sniggered.

He looked clumsily at the bottle in his hands, then put it carefully on the table. He was a long way past caring now. He stood still, waiting and dazed.

She stirred her feet and began talking to the blond boy. She had the full relaxed air of someone who has just seen a difficult juggling trick performed successfully. "Me and the girls has got to go off," she said. "I got to get me something to wear for tonight. You better keep your eye on him good while we're gone and see he gets this place cleaned up some. Don't let him drink too much of that liquor so he can't do nothing. You better get him something to eat at dinnertime too. We got to make him eat something."

His mind was clearing some. The narrow avenues of what he knew of his labors and his fear had emerged a little from the wet smoke. He understood that she was talking about him but that he didn't have to listen. And then he had to. She was telling him something. "Go on in there and wake them girls up," she said. "We got to get going."

"Wait a minute," Coke Rymer said. He turned to her. "I want to show him something." He came across to where Peter stood and spread his hand flat on the table, his fingers wide apart. "Look here," he said, "I want to show you something." He fetched a big folded knife from his pocket and let it roll in his hand. When he moved his thumb a sharp crying blade jumped from his fist, circled in the air. Peter moved back a little, trembling. The knife was Coke Rymer's man-thing, he didn't want it to hurt him; he didn't want to see it. Coke Rymer laid it on the table and twirled it around with his index finger. He was giggling. He picked the knife up at the end of the blade, pinching it with his thumb and forefinger. "Look at this," he said. He hesitated and then flipped the knife quickly upward. It spun round and round, a flashing pinwheel. When it came down the blade chucked into the tabletop in the space between the third and fourth fingers of Coke Rymer's left hand. He giggled. The knife quivered to stillness.

"That's enough of that stuff now," Mina said. "I want him to get some things done today. I don't want you messing around and playing with him all the time. He's got to get some things done."

Coke Rymer folded the knife and put it away. He turned toward her. "You want me to take away that ole pump handle?"

"I reckon not. You just quit deviling him and leave him alone. He's enough trouble the way he is already, without you picking at him."

"I wasn't hurting him none."

"Just leave him alone, I said." She spoke to Peter. "I thought I told you already to get them girls out of bed. I ain't got all day to fool around with you."

He slouched forward, going reluctantly toward the bedroom. He wanted her to make sure the yellow-haired boy wouldn't disturb the pump handle. She ought to stop him. The pump handle solaced him with its length and its fine heaviness in his hand; he loved to stroke along the long subtle curve of it; he liked just to have it near him, to hold it out before himself, admiring its blazing shininess and its heft. Hours and hours he had spent scrubbing and shining and oiling it. He knew that Mina derived a clear satisfaction from knowing that it was his man-thing, and he thought she ought not let Coke Rymer dally with it.—He couldn't understand the blond boy. There was nothing in him, nothing at all; he didn't understand why Mina tolerated him.

He lumbered through the narrow doorway into the living room. In here the light was dimmer and didn't bulge in his head so much. The torn shade was pulled almost down in the north window; little chinks and blocks of light shone in the holes. Through the west window he could see the squat cheap white frame house across the street, all yellow in the sunlight. One pillow lay staggered on the floor, dropped from the springs of the stained greasy wine-colored sofa across the room; along the top of the sofa back all the prickly nap had worn away. On the black little end table was the radio, which was on—the radio was always on—but now nobody had bothered to tune it to a station and it uttered only staccato driblets of static. There were a couple of broken cardboard boxes in one corner of the room, and a few sheets of newspaper were scattered on the floor. On the east wall beside the door were dime-store photographs of Marilyn Monroe, Jayne Mansfield, and Elvis Presley, all dotted with flyshit. At the edge of the sofa and in two corners of the room were blurred remnants of the pattern which had once covered the dull rubbed linoleum.

The bedroom was to the south of the living room and he entered without knocking. A dark green shade covered the single bedroom window and in here it was much dimmer than in the living room. He had to wait until his eyes adjusted to the darkness. Heaped together in the small bed in the corner—the big double bed on the left was Mina's—the girls stirred restlessly, sensing in their sleep Peter's presence in the room. He went to the bed, grasped a protruding pale shoulder and shook it as gently as he could. The startled flesh moved under his nerveless hand. "Whah." He shook her again and she mumbled some more and sat up. Because of the bad light her sharp face looked detached, a soft lantern. It was Bella. Her black hair came forward, hiding her face; she shook her head, raised her arms and stroked her hair back over her shoulders. Only her face and her breasts stood visible. Her breasts were like featureless faces; they bobbed softly as she fixed her hair. Enid shifted in her sleep, turning toward them, and flung her thin arm over Bella's gentle belly. She stopped manipulating her hair and for a moment stroked carefully the arm which lay on her.—He knew that this too was one of Mina's satisfactions, that Bella and Enid were after the woman in each other.—Then she tapped Enid's arm. "Sweetheart," she said, her voice thick and throaty from sleep, "wake up. Mina must want us to get up. Come on." Enid dug deeper into the bed.

Bella looked up at him, her gaze abstracted, visionless. Momentarily it seemed to him that there was something she wanted from him, and the thought frightened him. He stumbled back from the bedside.

"What do you think you're doing?" she said. Her voice was regaining its natural sharpness. "Go on away. Go get where you belong."

As he went out the door he saw Bella resume her loving ministering to Enid.

Mina was talking to Coke Rymer in the living room, and Peter went straight through and on through the kitchen out to the back porch. He wanted to check his pump handle, to see if it was still where he had hidden it—that was the one thing he could remember from the day before. The porch cracked and swayed under his footsteps, the boards weakening with rot or termites. A double handful of big blue-and-green flies was flocked on the carcass of the headless chicken that lay there. They skipped about on the queasy body, making a noise like muttered swearing. Already the air was hot, viscid, and the singing of the flies seemed to increase the oppressiveness of the heat. He nudged the chicken with his bare toe and the flies swirled up in a funnel-shaped pattern and then settled again immediately. With his forearm he wiped his mouth; he couldn't understand how he could do something like that. All the glare of the sun seemed focused on the murdered bird.

He stepped down into the fluffy dust of the back yard. The yard was small, and underneath the dust was burning packed clay. A ruptured hog-wire fence unevenly straggled the rectangular borders, and here and there long shoots of blackberry vine poked through. In the north corner of the yard was the little low weather-stained shed from which he averted his eyes without even thinking about it, with the strength of a habit enforced by sheer instinct. He went around the edge of the little porch, which was laid out at the back of the house like a perfunctory throw rug, and peeked underneath, where the pile of daubed stones supported it. There, crosswise in a space between two joists, lay the pump handle. He hadn't realized until he found the handle that he'd been holding his breath and it came in a swoop out his mouth and nose, all too heavily redolent of what had happened to his insides. He wiped his mouth. He got the pump handle and stood and held it before him, hefting it warm and solid in his hand, beholding it in the sunlight. He examined it all over for a speck of rust or dirt, but it was clean and shiny as quicksilver.

"Well, so that's where you keep it then? Well, that's all I wanted to know."

He looked up. Coke Rymer was standing at the edge of the porch, leaning against the post support and whittling slowly at the edge of it. Dismayed, Peter stepped back.

Coke Rymer showed his meaningless grin; his teeth were little and yellow. "That's all in the world I needed to know, where you keep hiding that ole pump handle."

He stepped farther back, gingerly swinging the bright handle like a pendulum in front of his legs. He decided that if the watery blond boy got down into the yard after him he would hit him, he would make blood come. Already now he was whimpering.

The other folded his knife and returned it to his pocket. "Aw, hush up. I ain't going to hurt you." He grinned again. "You better come on in here now and get started on this stuff Mina wants you to get done. She's liable to get mad if you don't, and I guess you don't want her to get mad at you. You'd be a even more pitiful sight than you are if she was to get mad and get ahold of you."

Still he hung back, but he had stopped swinging the pump handle. He clasped it fondly across his belly.

Coke Rymer looked at him. "Aw, you can bring that old thing with you. What's it matter to me?" He turned and briskly went inside.

He shuffled unsteadily up the two creaky steps onto the porch. He didn't mind the work so much. He was just hoping they wouldn't make him eat the gooey soft-fried eggs and toast for lunch.

FIVE

*I*t wasn't long until September. In another one of his moments of clarity he sat inspecting his body. A good view of it; they dressed him now in only these tattered blue swimming trunks, no matter the weather. The boards of the hated floor were sharp with cold in the mornings, and sweated dirt streaked his body like paint. On his lower shoulder were still pieces of the silvery quarter-moon scars that Mina's teeth had left on him, but now these were beginning to be lapped over by the tattooing. Where he wasn't filthy dirty he was gaudy as a comic book. They had begun at the base of his spine. He had lain stretched on Mina's bed, grasping the iron bars hard and weeping without control, while Coke Rymer, nervous and sweating and cursing him, held the nervous hot electric needle and Mina stood calmly watching. "No, not there, you're not doing it right," she had said. "No, you're not doing it right." And then she would lean over and touch softly the spot she wanted decorated and Peter's body would jerk, as shocked as if her cold finger were the burning needle again. "Yeah, yeah, I see," Coke Rymer would say, his voice querulous, whining asperity. "If I could just get this son of a bitch to hold still." The sweat dripped oily from his face onto Peter's back and then ran itching down his side. It was maddening. At the end of the first session they had got a couple of mirrors so that he could see the handiwork. He rose weakly from the bed, where the imprint of his body was wet and vehement. He looked where they

148

directed and he couldn't help crying out, "Is that all? Is that all?" in anguish and impotent rage. In the mirrored mirror was his skin and on it only a small misshapen yellow circle, about the size of a quarter, with an indistinguishable dark head in it and letters—he supposed these marks were letters—in a tongue he had never seen. It was a coin on his spine, or the sun, sardonically injured. Was that all? The intolerable waiting and the nervous pain, just for that?—But now he had got used to it, it was no more than being swarmed over by a troop of red ants. They all took turns, Coke and Bella and Enid, but he wept no more under the needle, the artwork had come to seem necessary to him, and he was coolly curious as to how it would turn out. The little gold coin—or maybe it was a sun—had been obscured almost; in his mirrored skin he had to search hard to find this starting point in the crawly fantastic turf his back had become. On his back nothing was what it was, there were no demarcations, no outlines; nothing was formed, it was all in the process of becoming. Except here a large eye, marbled and fluid; there a crippled hand, the fingers webbed together with sperm. Scattered purple lumps which might be grapes, but pendent from nothing, not attached; knives which looked melting but still cruel; blue fernlike hair; smeared yellowish-white spots, which might be stars dripping down the soundless void, spots of startling silence on this raucous grating jungle, the polychrome verdure suggesting an impossible pointless fecundity and even the odor of this, but the whole impression transitory as dew. Here, was this an inky bird struggling into shape? Really, were these great fish? Or bared unjoined tendons? Was this a clot of spiny seaweed? . . . A worm? . . . And now lapping over his shoulder onto his chest, covering over the scars of Mina's bites, these looked like green licks of flame, upside down.

In a muffled flimsy way Peter could share their clear pleasure in the work. It was Bella's turn now, and now that they laid him on his back to perform he observed the intense concentration in her bladelike face. She used the needle as carefully as if she were making a painful embroidery, and he felt obscurely flattered. When she worked on him she had about her none of the contemptuous stupor she used with the men that she and Enid brought to the house. But of course she had no interest in the men except for their money: a dark manner she had, and her body smelled always of earth, of the sandy dirt outside, beaten clangorous by the sun. Mina too was intent on the tattooing, though her face, forever closed, wouldn't show her interest. But Peter knew it was there, and felt a crazy gladness. Clearly he was being prepared, clearly he was being readied, although he didn't know for what. But that finally was unimportant to him. He guessed that his evening performances, which he could not remember, were growing in intensity and in absurdity, and that he was gradually fixing for some simple horrifying climax to it all; but he didn't care. The careful progress of the tattooing gave him the feeling of being new-made; his old self—perhaps his only self (that was all right too)—was being obliterated; it was almost as if he were being reborn, inch by inch, and this feeling was effervescent in him, sometimes buoyed him over his hard depressions and the moments when he let go and felt himself falling, falling, falling through the void shaft between all the atoms.

He was sitting on the tiny back porch, the pump handle near, and the early afternoon sunlight was on his chest like thick cotton. The air seemed sugary and the scores of heavy flies fumbled about in it. Enid came out of the house to sit beside him; hitched her skirt over her white thighs and let her legs dangle in the sunlight. He didn't squirm away. He wasn't afraid of Enid, felt even a sort of melting pity for her: she was nothing, she was airy, empty as air, and herself fearful. She was blond very much as Coke Rymer was blond, but she was thin and graceless, had no cruelty in her. But still, he had furtively to move his hand and touch the pump handle. There; he felt better.

Her voice was a singsong whisper. "I always have to do like you do," she said. "I have to do whatever Bella tells me to, just like you have to do whatever Coke tells you to do. It's funny, the way it is."

Peter didn't answer. It hurt to talk; his throat had been stripped raw by the drinking.

Her legs flashed when she moved them in the light. "And Bella and Coke have to do what Mina wants them to. It's funny." She shrugged; her shoulders were thin as dry leaves. "But I don't care what they do, they can't do anything that would really bother me."

He almost spoke. He wanted to tell her that she just didn't know, that they could do things to her she couldn't imagine, she would have pain and humiliation she could never understand. And worse, she would be deprived the solace of her outrage, she would have none.

"I guess I'm next too," she said, "I know it. When you're all gone, I mean, when they're finished with you, they'll start on me. But I really don't care, because I've put up with just about everything already."

He dropped his head sadly. It was all too clear that she referred to his death. He wondered for an instant why she had been told, and why they had kept it from him, for surely his foreknowledge would be the most closely observed part of their treatment of him. But he discarded the thought: she had not been told, no; she knew about his death in the same way that he did, for he had known long ago, even before the death of Sheila. He corrected himself. Before he had murdered her . . . But Enid was still mistaken; there were things in store which would pain her impossibly. She was made for a victim too: empty and pliant as air, she had neither will nor way to strike back. Even so, he must admire her courage. She could guess something of what was coming, at least, and still she kept a resigned composure. Of course, any kind of courage was of no use without some allegiance to, some tenacity for, one's life, and Enid was void of these. To the end she would simply be what she was already, a ready-made victim. And perhaps it would be easier for her. He had sometimes thought that it would be much less painful for him if he could just resign himself, could just accept without struggle whatever black looming entry they'd shove him through next. . . . And a darker thought rose to the surface: he wondered if Enid was being set as an example to him by Mina. Was her acquiescence, for all its show of courage, one of the final temptations for him? Were they trying finally to rupture in him a last thin shard of integrity, an integrity which must disturb Mina but which he could not himself discover? Or was this thought a single piece of self-flattery? The doubt in his mind was like a hard iron ring and, as ever, he hefted up his shiny pump handle for some kind of affirmation. And now it was not enough. Self-pity welled in his heart like empty tears to the eye. The pump handle too, like every other object, like everything but his tough chains and the boards of the floor and the quivery tattooing needle, was losing its presence. It lacked its former heft, its authority. It was going away from him; now he was going to be entirely alone.

Enid pushed lightly off the edge of the porch and went round in front of him up the steps into the house. He listened to the whisper of her bare feet on the wood, over the linoleum. And he heard Bella's sharp voice accost the blond girl as she entered the living room. "Here's Enid now, and she's a pretty thing, isn't she?" A piercing voice, a throaty male tenor, Bella's. "You ought to put some meat on your bones, honey," she said. "You're just a bag of bones. I still love you, though, because you're so blond. I always was crazy about blondes. You'd be just about perfect, I think, if you'd just put some meat on those bones." She was silent for a moment, and Peter could picture the scene: Bella was sitting in the balding sofa in her long brown dress, her legs crossed like a man's, ankle laid across knee, exposing her long stale dusty thighs; and now she stubbed out her cigarette with a single jab of her wrist, sharp. "Come here," he heard her say. "Come here to Mama."

He sighed. The afternoon was blazing away; the sun had dipped lower, but the light was still white, still hot. It didn't seem the sun had moved, but that the landscape had ached upward after it, as if the heat that had soaked through the dust into the pressed earth was not enough, would never be enough. In the center of the world was a fast deep iciness, pure recalcitrant cold, which could absorb the whole heat of the sun and every point of light; yearned after it. This coldness impinged upon him; he had felt its approach and now he felt it so imposing that his body shivered, anticipated.—The hand of every natural thing was turned against him, he knew it. The pump handle felt light as balsa wood, bodiless. There was no point at which his body was in contact with the world; his body garish, he floated a garish emptiness.

But something with a weight was dipping into his shoulder. He looked. Coke Rymer's hand upon him, and he rose as steadily as he could, not wanting the boy cruelly to help him to his feet. But he lurched into him—it was almost impossible for him to keep his feet anymore—and Coke Rymer shoved him sharply backward and smacked his left jaw with a sharp elbow. "Goddamn you," the boy said. "By god, I'll learn you." He slapped him across the eyes and then took his hand and led him inside.

His vision was dazed with tears. Something in his head bored like a big auger.

Coke Rymer leaned him against the spotted kitchen wall, the way one might prop a board up while he turned to something else. The blond boy stepped back to look at him, but even in his mean eyes most of the cruel interest was gone. This handling of him was routine, and the performance was much too far along for the routine to carry interest. Now all was bent toward acceleration, toward the meaty ending.

"Well, honeybunch, can I give you a drink?"

Coke Rymer's figure swam blurry before him; he tried to fix it tight, but couldn't. He shook his head. He couldn't drink anymore. His body would no longer accept the stuff; he couldn't keep it down and there was no comfort in it.

"You sure now, sweetheart? Used to be, you'd hanker after a drink some."

He kept mute and still.

"Well, okay then, whatever you say. Come on in here."

He led—half carried—Peter into the darkened bedroom, and Peter fell almost gratefully into Mina's wide bed. Voluntarily he grasped the bars of the bedhead, readying himself for the tattooing session. It was Coke's turn once more; Mina stood away, slightly behind him, ready to supervise. Bella turned on the naked overhead bulb, and the room went stark and shadowless. Peter gazed down at his long body with clinical interest. He hadn't imagined that his thin being could grow so much thinner; he was all angles and knobs. His ribs were distressingly evident, stiff, stiff as fingers of the dead. When he breathed his skin seemed to move reluctantly over his ribs, he could almost hear a susurration. Ah, poor body, with its single destination, powerless and expectant. Coke Rymer reached to a cord at Peter's navel, snapped it loose, began to maneuver the tattered bathing trunks from his waist.

He squirmed and croaked.

"Now don't start that goddam meowling," Mina said. "You just hush up. Because they ain't nothing you can do about it anyhow."

Only disjointed croaks he could muster from his throat.

"Hush. They ain't nothing there that could hardly get hurt, is there? You ain't got nothing down there to be touchous about. Just you keep quiet."

The bare bedroom was filling with men. They jostled together, unreal, tough-looking; they wore sport shirts or white shirts open at the collar. He couldn't count them, the light from the big bulb jabbed his eyes. He thought that he recognized some of them; they were customers, the men the whores brought in. They had red faces, baked, hoodlums from the town of Gordon, scoured, God knew how, out of the beer joints and hamburger joints, and brought here for the spectacle. They didn't speak; they were silent except for an occasional single whisper and an accompanying titter.

Coke Rymer gave a final tug and the swim trunks came off his feet. "There, by God," the blond boy said. Peter watched him; he was trembling and sweating. He was more fearful than Peter, and somehow it made sense. Coke still had to fear Mina, but Peter didn't any longer. No matter what happened to him, he was well out of that. It was a strange funny thought, but when he laughed he uttered only a scraping gurgling sound.

"Hush up," Mina said. "I ain't going to tell you no more."

He clenched his teeth, he could hear the unnerving rub of them together; he was going to keep silent, not from fear of Mina but in the hope of frustrating Coke Rymer. He knew that Coke hoped for his pained reactions, that they were a great part of what he had now to subsist upon. He too was losing grip. After she was finished with Peter and with Enid, it would be Coke's turn. Peter began to wish that he could see it, he would like to know how Coke would bear up under what Mina had planned for him. Whatever it was, it would be different from Peter's treatment; and he guessed that it would be worse. Abruptly he felt a queer sympathy for the boy, who was pushing forward now through the ring of strangers, bearing the black-handled needle with its black cord dangling; abruptly he was glad that he wouldn't have to watch the spectacle of Coke Rymer's going. As the blond boy squatted by the bedhead, grunting, to plug in the electric needle Peter glanced at the top of his sticky hair. He felt that he almost smelled the bad nerves in him. It was a performance for Coke as well as for Peter.

He held the bars of the bedhead as tightly as he could, as Coke Rymer stood above him, leaning forward in a sort of triumphant uncertainty. But those bars seemed to go away from his grip; like the pump handle they had lost substance. In all the world there was nothing in which he could touch, find his maleness; all drifted.

Mina came closer. She was ready to begin. She put the tip of her index finger on her cold tongue and leaned and touched Peter's chest just below the right nipple. "There," she said. "You can start right there."

Coke turned about and sat on the edge of the bed, pressing it so that Peter slid slightly against him. "Scoot your ass over," Coke said. His voice had become the uncertain liquid falsetto once more. Peter shifted. Coke leaned sidewise over him; he was already sweating heavily and the oily drops fell from his forehead onto Peter's belly, trickled into his navel.

He held on as tight as he could and kept silent as long as he could. From the circle of the strangers came an occasional restless unsurprised mutter. . . . Perhaps they had expected more from him; he was being too quiet to please them, and he didn't want to please them. But in a while he was muttering hoarsely; they all peered at him more closely. He couldn't see very well what Coke was up to with the needle; it hurt his neck to look because of the way he had to crane. There was a murky green-and-purple band filling in from right to left across his chest, joining the place where the tattooing had already lapped over his shoulder. Around the tattooing the bare skin was flushed, heated, swollen; the design, if it could be called a design, appeared on him like a great lurid continent thrusting itself out of the sea. The upper part of his chest was numb, but it afforded him no real relief. He had ceased muttering, though. The only sounds now were the intense breathing of the five or six men gathered about and the warm steady hum of the electric needle, like the flight of a hornet near away in summer air. Not enough was happening; he felt Mina's boredom, and he wasn't surprised when she wet her finger and placed it high on his left cheek, not far below his eye.

"There," she said. "Start there again."

Coke Rymer held the needle above Peter's neck and turned to look at her. "How come you want me to start up there now?" he said. "Ain't I done enough work for one day?" His voice, the watery feminine whine.

"Work; you don't know what it means, work. You don't know what the word is. You go ahead now, like I showed you."

He turned back to Peter. His hand was shaking savagely. For the first time Peter felt that he saw in those wet blue eyes an attitude toward himself that was not indifferent, nor fearful, nor contemptuous, but almost fellowly, almost sympathetic. And this discovery was more frightening than any other. If this sort of feeling could be roused in Coke Rymer, it meant that the edge really was close, was nearing steadily.

"Here we go then, sweetheart," Coke said. "Hold on to your hat."

At the first prick of the needle he jerked his head aside, sputtered with stifling pain. Enid was standing at the foot of the bed, and through his pinched eyes he saw that her mouth was working, rounding and widening on breaths of air, though she made no sound. She had in her eyes a full wasted pity. He thought that she had better keep it for herself; Mina was killing two birds with one stone.

Coke grasped him harshly with his left hand under his chin; his fingers were tight on the spit glands under his ears. "Goddamn your eyes," he said. "Hold your head still."

He acquiesced in his mind; he wanted as little trouble as possible, he wanted it to be over soon.

But when the needle was at his cheek again, his head recoiled. He couldn't help it. Now his body was taut with apprehension, and warm liquid streamed down his face, across his mouth. Taste of salt. When his head moved, the needle must have ripped his cheek. He looked at Coke in despair. He had made him angry, he hadn't wanted to. It would be easy for the boy enraged to plunge the vibrant needle into his eye.

But Coke turned away, turned toward Mina. "I ain't going to do it no more," he said. "I'm tired of it. You can do it your goddamn self."

She didn't smile, but her voice was levelly humorous. "All right. That's fine. I guess you've had a hard day and I feel real sorry for you. You give Bella that needle and then you can go and lie down and take a little rest." In the blazing room she was the only cool thing. "I'll be around and tend to you in just a little while."

Bella poked her way through the waiting unreal circle of men. "Give me the needle," she said. "I never have believed that you had the guts of a weasel. . . . Isn't it true that he shamed him in a fight once?" She asked the question of Mina. "Isn't that true? That Coke was afraid of something like *him?*" She gestured toward Peter with the needle she had taken from the blond boy. It was still running, humming.

Coke rose from the bed and pushed his way clumsily through the group. He rubbed his streaming face. Mina took his place on the edge of the bed, a neat aggressive motion.

"I won't be able to do it, I can't hold it still," Peter said. But the words became mere grating gasps, formed from pain and fear.

Mina surveyed him from the foot of the bed. There seemed clear in her steady eyes the knowledge of what he was saying. "That's all right, honey," she said to Peter. "Don't you worry about a thing. We'll take care of you fine." She touched two of the near men in the circle and they looked at her, waiting, shamefully scared. "Take hold of his feet," she said. "Hold him down good and tight."

They grasped Peter's ankles, unhesitating; pressed them so hard into the lumpy mattress that he had to let go the bars of the bedhead. His forearms were prickly with exhaustion, his wrists felt all injured tendon, his palms were bruised scarlet.

"You-all grab his hands too. We got to stop him from jumping all over the place."

One of the men, fantastic and red-faced as the others, took Peter's right hand, bent his elbow hard, bringing his forearm under his neck, and then took both wrists together, one atop the other; held them crossed hard with his knee. His face was unreadable. He steadied his stance by holding to the bedhead.

Bella took Coke's place at the bed edge. She took Peter's chin with thumb and finger and turned the torn cheek toward her. "Look at that," she said. "Coke's made a mess of this, it's just a mess."

"You can let that part go then," Mina said. "You'll have to start lower down." She wet her finger, leaned over the foot of the bed, touched him where it would be most sexually excruciating; but there was no longer sexuality in him. She straightened, her eyes still plainly bored; and from the strangers a murmur of . . . Was it satisfaction? They were expectant.

He nodded. It was as he had thought; there was no way out of Mina's thinking. He came at last to anticipate her every maneuver, horrified because she had so usurped his mind. It was his own head that labored so to produce his own humiliation.

Bella rose and moved lower on the bed.

The moos were on him, implacable, but now they didn't care; they let him sound away, absorbed in their work. He kept passing out and rousing again to consciousness. The world was flaring brightly before him; gasping and flickering down again. It was the most fragile tendril that held him tied to it all.

At last they brought him back again for the final time. Coke Rymer had returned, and he helped one of the strangers hoist Peter to his feet. They almost dropped him; he had no control.

"That's all, sweetie," Coke said. "That's all there is."

Mina came forward and looked him over. They held him pinioned by arms and shoulders. He couldn't see her well, he didn't look at her face, but felt the cold wash of her gaze on all his body. "Wouldn't you like to see how it turned out?" she said. "I believe you've improved a whole lot." She spoke to Coke and the other. "Bring him over here in front of the mirror."

They dragged him standing before the wardrobe. He saw the image; nodded wisely. His legs were still naked, untouched by the needle, but they were no longer his, no longer even supported his body. They looked irrelevant and alien, detachable. The remainder of his body was obliterated; it had been absorbed entirely into another manner of existence, a lurid placeless universe where all order was enlarged bitter parody. Even his bare skin where the needle had not tracked was a part of it all, and the bloodstain over his face was integral, was assuredly important. His body now was a river, was flowing away. He nodded again.

"Well, now," Mina said, "I'm glad to see that you like it. I think it does you a lot of good myself." She spoke to Coke Rymer and the other man. "Well, take him out there where I told you to."

Immediately they began dragging him toward the door. The line of strangers fell away and they went through into the living room, turned, went through the kitchen. It was dark and no cooler. The stars looked close and hot, and in the darkness were clumps of darker shadow. He breathed deep, convulsively; he felt almost as if he had been holding his breath for hours. No, but in the air he had been breathing had been no sustenance for his lungs. The porch floor creaked as they shuffled across it; the board steps cried out. He was not resisting, but he couldn't aid them, either. There was nothing left in his body. He had no body.

Shuffling in the thick dust they took him across the barren ground. He gazed upward and the sky looked narrow and vile, hurrying against him. They were taking him, he knew it, to the low weather-stained shed. There the god permitted his being at times to obtrude into perception. He had feared the obscure shed and the altar with all his deep and fearful hate, but now he was hopeful for it. He wished that he could move toward it under his own volition. Coke Rymer unlatched the shabby raspy door and they flung him in. He fell on his back, and for a few minutes lay still. He knew that they wouldn't come in to help him sit up; they wouldn't enter at all. Coke Rymer gazed at him through the door only for a moment; threw him—it was like throwing a foul scrap of meat to a dog—a limp mock salute. "Well, bye-bye sweetheart," he said. "I guess I won't be seeing you for a while. Might be a good long time." He turned and followed the other man, both forms dissolving into shadowed night. They left the door open, dark gray rectangle scratched with the wiry lines of blackberry vines. He heard Mina coming; and he pushed himself backward through the dirt floor littered with wads of paper and corncobs.

She leaned forward in the low door, putting her hands at the top to hold herself. "Well, there you are now," she said. "You look like you're comfortable. You look like you're going to be all right. You're all right, ain't you?"

He couldn't answer.

"Well, you look all right to me. I'll just leave you here and I'll be back in a little while."

All he could make out of her was her luminous gray eyes, spots in the darkness. He nodded, he was sure she could see him.

"Yeah, I knew you knew I'd be back." She laughed, a slight dry sound, humorless. She stepped back; shut the door lightly; shot the solid latch forward.

He waited. He heard her going away, and then he heard nothing for a long while. Then, a faint rustling in a far corner: a rat, perhaps. And then again silence, disturbed by his own unsteady breathing. Inside his chest it was as painful as outside. In here it was inky dark and his eyes did not grow accustomed to it. He could barely make out the shape of the silly altar, loose boards of uneven lengths laid over two rickety sawhorses. Very gradually his breathing grew in volume, stertorous, bladed in the throat. It grew and grew; he could feel the passage of it on his skin. It was not his breathing. He understood. He opened his mouth to breathe. The galaxies poured down his throat, thick tasteless dust he could not spit out, could not vomit. The breathing was icy on his skin; impression of swift wind continually on him, but the dust of the floor not stirring. Slowly he raised his hands to rub his face. It was cold and dry and felt not like flesh, but like wood or leather. It was himself no longer. . . . Point of vague light somewhere in the air, but then not light: a circle of blackness, a funnel that sucked all the light away, even the light of his body which was glowing with a faint phosphorescent pulse. He looked into his body, looked through it: wide clots of dust, a thin winking membrane where the nebulae were being born. . . . Something solid out there. An angleless wall without protuberance; no, not solid; a bending wall, breathing upon him.

Eye.

Tooth.

Glimpsed and then erased, wiped coolly from vision.

The god Dagon assumed the altar.

Reptilian. Legless. Truncated scaly wings, flightless, useless. The god Dagon was less than three feet long. Fat and rounded, like the belly of a crocodile. He couldn't see the mouth hidden away under the body, but he knew it: a wirelike grin like a rattlesnake's; double rows of venomous needles in the maw. On this side a nictitating eye, but he thought that on the other side there would be no eye, but merely a filmy blind spot, an instrument to peer into the marrow of things. The visible eye gray, almost white. A body grayish-pink like powdery ashes. Chipped and broken scales covered it, tightly overlapped. It breathed and this took a long time. The froglike belly distended, contracted.— The reptilian shape was immobile; there was no way for it to move upon the earth.

He recognized the god Dagon.

An idiot. The god was omnipotent but did not possess intelligence. Dagon embodied a naked will uncontrollable. The omnipotent god was merely stupid.

Peter laughed, his teeth shone in the dark.

He confronted the god. The presence of Dagon displaced time, as a stone displaces water in a dish. Surely hours elapsed in the stare that was between them.

Merely a ruptured idiot stubby reptile.

The god Dagon went away. Suddenly winked out; whisked.

At last Peter relaxed. He smiled in the dark. He had faced the incomprehensible manifestation and he still maintained himself; he was still Peter Leland. He blinked his eyes gratefully, casually turned his head from the altar. He heard Mina coming and turned to face the door, still smiling in the dark, uncaring and relaxed. She opened the flimsy door and entered without hesitation. In her right hand she bore Coke Rymer's man-thing, faintly gleaming. She took a handful of his hair in her left hand and Peter knelt forward on his knees and raised his head. Happily he bared his throat for the knife.

SIX

*P*eter Leland died and came through death to a new mode of existence. He did not forget his former life, and now he understood it. The new vantage point of his psyche was an undefined bright space from which he could look back upon this little spot of earth and there see the shape of his life in terms not bitterly limited by misery and fear. At his death he did not relinquish the triumphant grasp of his identity he had acquired in encountering Dagon face to face. He had come through. In this surrounding brightness there was no time, and he watched his career unfold itself again and again beneath him and he laughed, without rancor and without regret. Now his whole personality was a benevolent clinical detachment.

He understood suffering now and the purpose of suffering. In an almost totally insentient cosmos only human feeling is interesting or relevant to what the soul searches for. There is nothing else salient in the whole tract of limitless time, and suffering is simply one means of carving a design upon an area of time, of charging with human meaning each separate moment of time. Suffering is the most expensive of human feelings, but it is the most intense and most precious of them, because suffering most efficiently humanizes the unfeeling universe. Not merely the shape of his own life taught him this, but the history of all lives, for from here he perceived with a dispassionate humor the whole of human destiny.

Metaphor amused him—and this was necessary, for in this place

162

metaphor was a part of substance. Here he had no properly physical form apart from metaphor. And now it seemed his task to find and take his likeness in every possible form in the universe; he was to become a kind of catalogue of physical existence and of the gods. There were metaphors for everything: sometimes all his past life appeared to him in the image of a gleaming snail track over a damp garden walk; or a black iron cube, two inches square; or a shred of discolored cuticle; or a frayed shoelace.

No regret and no anger in him, no nostalgia for the painful limits he had metamorphosed out of. He was filled with an unrepressed motiveless benevolence. He contemplated with joy the unity of himself and what surrounded him. He deliberated what form his self should take now, thinking in a tuneless dreaming fashion of every possible guise. Galactic ages must have passed before he finally gave over and took the form of Leviathan. Peter took the form of the great fish, a glowing shape some scores of light-years in length. He was filled with calm; and joyfully bellowing, he wallowed and sported upon the rich darkness that flows between the stars.

The Gaudy Place

Arkie

C onsider Arkie.

    (But it breaks your heart.)

Teacher used to tell him he didn't exist.

Arkie shook his head angrily. "Yes I do. I do that." Immediately belligerent. He wasn't sure what it meant, *to exist*, but he knew that whatever it was it was no good for Arkie. Some sort of con, he bet. Arkie would bet you.

"You got a driver's license?"

"No."

"You got a social security number?"

"No."

"Birth certificate?"

"I don't know. Maybe I got that."

Teacher grinned. "And no school records and no vaccination scars and no doctor's records and no dentist's records. I guess you don't even have a mailing address."

"I got places I can get letters."

"How do you know? You never got any letters. You can't be sure, can't be sure of anything." He still grinned that skinny grin. He got a Herbert Tareyton between thin trembling fingers and took a long time getting it lit. "Don't you see?" He coughed: sound like metal scraping metal. "Officially you don't even exist. Nothing proves it."

In a desultory voice: "I do though." Arkie was bored now.

"Have you got a real name?"

164

"James Parker McClellan."

"Not that anybody ever uses it. And how old are you?"

"Sixteen."

"*Horse*shit. You can tell the cops that when they come around checking. You're fourteen years old. Fifteen, maybe. You wouldn't know which yourself."

"Gimme a stab."

"Maybe in a minute I will." He propped his chin on a shaky hand. "What's your mother and father's name?"

Arkie shrugged and went away, leaving Teach sitting at the bar. Teacher was a fat waste of time always. This was in the Ace and ten-thirty in the morning and there was nothing moving, nothing, or Arkie wouldn't have spent this long with him. All the time he'd known Teacher he'd never got a thing out of him, not a penny. Teacher was 0, absolute. Not a teacher anyhow. Everybody called him that because he always wore this grimy corduroy jacket, color of dago red, with cigarette burns in unlikely spots. The jacket had wide side pockets, and always in one of the pockets was a paperback book, a gangster or a fuck or a cowboy. Teach sat in the bars and read the books until he got too blind drunk to see the pages. But talk. He'd talk. Jesus God, he'd cave your ears in.

He looked into the other room, the bigger room with the dance floor, but nothing was happening. A tall guy with an open white shirt and a dirty apron was bending over a mop bucket. Arkie could smell the bitter disinfectant even from where he stood.

"Hey, John, you seen Clemmie?"

The big fellow looked up without straightening his body. He had a wide face, white as sugar. "Not since last night I ain't. She ain't been in this morning yet."

When he went back through the other room Teacher had already planked open a book and was staring at it, leaning his head on his left hand. Arkie made out not to look at him, silly bastard. He went out the door into the cool sunlight of early May. He had to shield his eyes, glancing across the street a few doors up and down. Juanita's Place didn't look any more lively than the Ace, the whole scene was a cold deck. This was the very worst time of day, with the hardasses at their nine-to-fives and the pigs still laying up. Most Arkie could hope for was to run into some hungover gungho who still had a few bucks and maybe juice him for a couple of quarters. If he was woozy enough. More likely all he could get was a cold drink here and there off the bread men or beer men or meat men on their daily rounds. He hated these hours, nothing moving, and the joints not really wanting anything to move yet, trying to get last night's crud off the floors. Arkie never felt right until about two o'clock in the afternoon, when the bars closed their solid front doors and the air-conditioning went on and the soft lights came up, the game machine lights and the juke lights. Just wait till he'd found his con and got a little dump laid by: you wouldn't see Arkie all day till the moon came out. . . . It was awful what a headache he got from sunlight.

He jingled the coins in his pocket, turned right abruptly and down Gimlet Street he went, listlessly jingling. Today he'd staked himself to seven bucks, feeling when he'd got up this morning that he was going to be lucky or unlucky, pretty big one way or the other. (He hoped to hell.) Seven, man, was a heavy one-third of what he had in the world. But with an hour's maneuvering he'd upped it by only fifteen cents, piling trash bottles out on the curb down at the Rebel Cafe. Gimlet Street ran up a steep slouched hill, and Arkie was going down, past remnant goods stores, secondhand furniture stores, past dingy newsstands, upholstery shops, sandwich factories. Three blocks down he turned right on Flint Street, starting uphill again. It was a hilly goddamn town, Braceboro. Bunker County was a hilly goddamn county. The whole western slab of North Carolina was nothing but rocks, briars, and goddamn hills.—But suppose he'd turned left coming out of the Ace. Four short blocks and he would have been standing in the Braceboro town square where he could have inspected a big green metal statue of a guy on a horse. Zebulon Johns, it said on the marble base of the statue. Patriot and Philanthropist. 1834–1906. Green Zeb, Arkie knew, was some kind of old-time gungho (holding a sword) and politician. Pieraker. All statues were of pierakers. . . . That's the kind of crazy apple this town was, rotten at the heart, but bright and shiny on the outside, jacketed with golf links and shopping centers.

He went into the Big Bunny. Squelch was behind the counter, a short red-haired bulgy man. His arms were folded, his big steel-rimmed shoe was propped up on the drink cooler.

"Squelch. Like you for a quarter."

No, he wouldn't move. Not a flicker.

"Come on."

You might as well talk to the fireplug.

"Come on, Squelch. A little action. Make it a dime, make it a dollar, If I ain't like you I rare up and holler."

Heavily he unfolded his arms and refolded them. Gave Arkie a clear bottle-green eye. "See you for five." Squelch had a soft voice, low, and it always sounded ominous.

"Christamighty."

He could almost take it. He could use the cash and he could ride the stolid barkeep for a month about losing it. If he won. But five bucks, no, man. Today was Friday and come Monday night old man Johnson was going to stomp up the stairs and gouge him seven bucks for that farthole he called a room. And if Arkie didn't have it he could just punch the t.s. card and head for citizensville. Sleep on the sidewalk with Dick Tracy and Orphan Annie tucked under his chin. . . . Well, no, it really wasn't all that bad. If it gave plumb out, he could pile in with Clemmie or one of the other pigs, as long as they weren't jockeying a john. But what kind of life was that for a man?

"You know I can't go no five bucks. Bring it down to man-size." Arkie did his little dance. "If you fly too high, Then you sure gonna die."

Squelch spent a long time getting ready to talk. "Been a slow week, Arkie. Here it's Friday already. I ain't got time for no chickenshit bets with ever gutterpickins that comes dragging in."

"Ah hell." Dispirited, he straddled one of the short bar stools and twirled twice around. "Gimme a stab."

He took the Camel from Squelch and got it safely lit before he let the mild careful whine seep into his voice. "You got no call to cuss me like that, you know it? Gutterbaby or whatever you said."

Squelch shrugged.

"Hey." Now his voice was lively again, enthusiastic. "Did you get the line yet?"

"Not yet."

"What'll you give me to go and get it for you?"

"It ain't in yet."

"It'll come in in about an hour. I'll run and get it for a quarter."

"What for? You know Walker's just going to call it in here. The fuzz ain't hooked into his phone no more."

"What's the good of taking a chance like that? A quarter's the cheapest bail money you ever went."

"Let's just wait and see if he calls." He leaned slightly forward and began to sound confidential. "He'll know whether it's safe or not. He always knows how it stands. See? He's got to know. That's how he got where he is."

"Ah hell."

Day to day, minute to minute, vain hopes were what Arkie fed upon. Two months ago, Danny Walker, who received the out-of-state gambling odds on all the sports for the Braceboro bookmakers, had found out that his telephone was going to be tapped. Every day for two weeks Arkie had earned fifty cents a stop for bringing the line to Walker's customers. Harder work than you'd think, because Walker was jittery and wouldn't allow Arkie to write anything down. But he never forgot: "State and four; Villanova and eight; Florida State and two . . ." He could jabber it off like a radio announcer, faster than they could take it down, and never a mistake. He could carry policy numbers too, all in his head like that. Those had been rich days for Arkie; that was something else he hadn't forgot. And every now and then Walker would have another case of nerves and Arkie picked it up, but it was nothing solid, nothing regular.

"Ah hell." These were sour sad hours.

Squelch started picking his teeth.

"I'm on the move," Arkie said. "I'll see you later."

"Yeah," Squelch said. "I'm damn sure of that."

Big Bunny my ass. Big wad of nothing . . . And the harrying painful sunlight . . . Back on Gimlet he turned right again, still going downhill, edging into mule territory now. Here it looked more interesting, the traffic noisier, people talking, even a juke blaring away in one of the joints. But Arkie had the educated eye, knew it all already. There was nothing here but mules, standing around with their hands in the pockets of their bib overalls and mouthing at each other and spitting big resounding gobs of tobacco juice. They would squeeze a quarter or a dime till you could slide it under the nail of your pinkie. Mules were what Arkie called truck farmers. They parked their dented pickup trucks at the bottom of the hill, where Gimlet joined Rance Avenue, and sold their produce off the truck beds. Open-air market. They were all dumb bastards. Arkie wished that he was getting just a little piece of what they all had to pay in to Burn Ryan so they wouldn't get their produce slopped and trampled, not get their tires slashed. He shrugged tiredly. That wasn't for Arkie, that heavy stuff. He had just turned fourteen (according to his own cloudy reckoning) and he was little for his age.

(Not that you could tell from his face. He looked whatever age you thought he did.)

He wandered into the Lucky Star and spoke to the first guy he saw, a mule sitting at the bar with a cup of mud. He was the mule type perfect and complete. Dumb from hairline to clodmashers. Lean, freckled, sandy-haired; the faded bib overalls and a red sweatshirt gone gray under the armpits.

"Hey. Match you for the piccolo," Arkie said. Piccolo, that was mule talk for the juke.

The guy looked him over, up and down, and Arkie stood easy, carelessly smiling. This was where you had to move very slowly; nothing scared away quicker than a mule.

"What are you going to play, then?" The farmer had to consider this a canny question. You wouldn't catch him putting up a good hard-earned ten-cent piece for some kind of city trash music he couldn't stand to listen to.

"Ever what you like," Arkie said. "Bill Monroe. Mac Wiseman. Lester and Earl."

"Just for a dime?"

"For one thin dime."

Look at him. Tight bastard had already sold his rutabagas and his pockets were probably running over with dump. But spend more than a dime? Not till it snows green money out of the sky.

The guy fished a quarter out of his bib pocket. Arkie listened to the change rattle, a good double handful. Arkie made sure the mule saw him staring at the ceiling while he was shaking the coin in his loose fist; but he saw too that it was going to come heads. Arkie, man, he's got those sharp eyes. He pulled a dime from his pocket, turned it once and laid it on the counter.

The guy wouldn't uncover yet. Grinned at Arkie like he'd just sold him a bushel of rotten turnips at an outrageous price. "You're like me, that right?"

"You got it right," Arkie said. "I'm matching you." Patience, Lord, give us patience.

"Play that there piccolo, boy."

Arkie had put down tails.

"Well," he said, "I'm damn. You sure can't win em all." He picked up his dime and went back toward the juke. "What would you be wanting to hear?"

"They got 'Foggy Mountain Breakdown' on that music box?"

"They got it."

They had it always, they're going to have it on forever.

He punched the buttons and came back and sat on the stool next to the farmer and ordered a Pepsi in a glass. "And could you give me cube ice in that, Bill?" He turned to the farmer. "Can't stand this mush ice in my cold drink," he said.

The mule was still pleased with himself; he hardly heard the fiddle and the banjo. "You can't win em all," he told Arkie. Still grinning like a jack-o'-lantern.

"That's the dying truth," agreed Arkie. He shook his head ruefully and got out one of his own loose cigarettes and lit it. He let the index finger of his right hand curl over the edge of the glass and rest gently on the ice cube floating in the soft drink. "You bring some truck into market this morning?"

"Yep."

"How's the market going?"

"Pretty good. Ought to get better."

"Who's watching your stuff for you now?"

"I reckon my brother is. Leastways, that's what I left him doing."

By now his finger felt cold enough to turn the trick and Arkie casually wiped the wetness from the finger on his pants leg. He really didn't care about the other chance; God knows, he didn't have the stomach to sit out in that sunlight this morning, nursing some dumb mule's rutabagas. Suddenly: "Hey. I bet you I can hold this cigarette longer than you can. Hold it like this, I mean." He held it lengthwise, the burning end pressed against his index finger. He made a horrible painful face and dropped the cigarette almost immediately.

When the guy started grinning again Arkie knew he had him. If there was one thing mules had confidence in it was their goddam calluses. "All right," he said. "How much you want to bet?"

"Dollar."

"Well, all right," he said. "You sure are one betting man."

"Can't help it," Arkie said. "I got it in my blood." He picked up the cigarette from where he had dropped it on the bar. "I'll go first." He held it between thumb and forefinger for thirty seconds. The mule watched him intently, but he didn't quiver a muscle, nothing showed in his face. Finally the live coal began to tingle through the coldness, and Arkie handed over the cigarette. "There you go," he said. "Thirty seconds by the wall clock."

The mule wasn't so dumb he thought he could do it, but he had to give it a try. He got seven seconds before he flung it down. "They's some kind of trick to that," he said resentfully.

"Ain't no trick. Just takes willpower."

"Yeah? Let's see your hand."

Arkie showed him. Nothing to see.

"It's some kind of trick or other."

"No it ain't, I'm telling you. The secret is, you got to think about something else while you keep hold of it. The secret is, not to think about it." He drank down his Pepsi in two heavy swallows and rose. "Well, I be seeing you, old-timer. You take it easy now."

"Wait a minute." The farmer was pondering; he wanted at least a piece of his dollar back. "What say we match one more time for the piccolo?"

"I can't stay to listen," Arkie said. "I got to go and see a feller. But I'll match you for the dime."

"No; match for the piccolo. We'll go for a quarter this time."

"Well," Arkie said, "if you think it'll make you happy."

They matched.

"Well, hell," the mule said. "This ain't my day. This ain't my day and that's the living truth."

"You can't win em all."

Arkie departed.

Stupid, Christamighty stooopid.

And with mules it took practically forever. Look how much time and money he'd spent just to juice one slow farmer. Half an hour it took to make the dollar, just jollying the guy along. And then you had to count out a dime for the bait, that first bet on the juke, and then another eleven cents for the cold drink. In half a day's hard scrabbling he'd come up with ninety-four cents, and that was including the work he'd done with the trash bottles. A man could starve; buddy, you know it for true. Somewhere, Arkie was certain of it, somewhere there was a real fine con, not a big one, but a good solid one that it didn't take a lot of capital to get off the ground with. A good solid con he could work by himself. It had to be by himself; anybody you went in with was older and a lot bigger than you. So they paid you off in bottle caps and if you tried to mention anything they stomped your ass around the block. He was going to ask Clemmie to ask Oxie for him. That Oxie, everybody knew about him, and a lot of people said they knew him, but hardly anybody really did. Clemmie knew him: she was one of Oxie's whores. And Arkie knew Clemmie. That would be his in. And if anybody had a con up his sleeve it was Oxie. Smart. Hadn't he come off Gimlet Street and got away clean? He wished he already knew Oxie; he wished they were a.h. buddies; wished he could call him on the phone right now this minute.

Where now?

He was beginning to feel a little hungry but it was close on to the lunch hour already. The hour that was either too early or too late for Arkie. When people were eating Arkie wasn't welcome in the cafes or joints. Everybody was too busy, running around taking orders and frying and wiping the tables and counting up the dump. They didn't want Arkie around trying to juice the eaters, getting underfoot and balling up the timetable. And they didn't want to take the time out to get him his cheeseburger. (Well done, with mustard and lettuce and tomato. No onions: Arkie was continually meeting the public.) But after lunch it was time to start drinking again and then they didn't care what he did. Actually they rather liked having him about. Good for business, if you looked at it right. He upped the take on the pinball machines and the bowling machines, the jukes and the pool tables. He was always matching for drinks. He kept people joking and hollering and talking and drinking, with his poems and that little dance of his, and that was maybe the best thing he did. Because when the johns were talking and laughing they weren't fighting, busting up the windows and bar mirrors and furniture. All that was fine. But not at mealtimes.

(Arkie: he could be an annoying little prick too.)

It was getting along in the day and he still hadn't run into Clemmie. No telling what that meant, he just never knew. She might simply be laying up—she was lazy enough for two mauds her size—or she might be in the hospital with a busted jaw or lying in a muddy ditch somewhere with her throat ripped open. He shuddered. The mauds had it tough. He didn't like to think about it. Let's see: last night before she went off she had gouged him for a dollar. (So. He was more or less used to that from Clemmie.) He hadn't been able to place the john she had picked up; a stranger to Gimlet. He had looked all right, short, blue-eyed guy, pretty well dressed. But what did that mean? Not a goddamn thing. By the time a maud found out that the john was crackers, had some weird hang-up and was going to slice her, it was far too late. He didn't like to think about it. Not that it was any skin off Arkie's ass, not really; but he kept thinking about Clemmie in lots of different ways. He felt that something might be going to pan out there.

He wandered through the truck market. The crowd was thinning out now, though the housewives kept driving up in their shiny cars, still for Godsake dressed in pajamas and housecoats. Hair in funny-

looking curlers. What made them get out of the sack? If he had that
kind of money . . . Parked at the curb was a brand-new dark green
Buick with the windows down. The dame that owned it was across the
street, probably stridently trying to screw a mule down on his rutabagas.
Arkie could just picture her. The windows were down, but there were
no keys in the ignition. Arkie wasn't thinking about stealing the car,
just because he didn't know how to drive. (How could he have learned
that?) But he knew where he could have peddled the keys for a couple
of bucks. *Hyook.* He hawked up and spat on the back seat, on the dark
gray new-smelling felt. They hadn't got the plastic on the upholstery
yet.

Here among the mules the number of flies had increased. Arkie
rubbed his nose with his wrist, not caring for the smells of vegetables
and jonquils and fresh earth. The sunlight seemed worse. When he
cut the corner of Rance Avenue he was in the shadow of the buildings
and he felt a lot better.

Up this hill and down, up this hill again.

If you went down Gimlet, then you had to climb Rance. . . .
Arkie's universe was minuscule, actually comprising an area of about
fourteen blocks, although he knew of course that there were other places
he could go when he wasn't trying to gouge the dime, the quarter, the
dollar. (When would that be?) But, you know, fourteen blocks is a pretty
big territory, and this was the place where you could go not only round
and round, you could also go up and down. On Gimlet Street you
could go so far down you would never see daylight again. . . .

Now he had reached his goal, the Teeny Tavern. Every now and
then he would hole up in here over the lunch hours. It was a little
bitsy place, about twelve feet wide and twenty feet long, stuck between
a rundown tailor's shop and the warehouse for a roofing firm; Arkie
could use it because it was too small to serve meals. Nothing to eat in
here but stale potato chips and pretzels and peanut butter crackers in
the dusty jar. Drink your beer and get out. When Arkie entered the
little white-haired man behind the counter didn't come to see what he
was up to. He was deaf and nearsighted and mostly oblivious to what
went on; he seemed to be going over again and again in his mind
something that had happened to him a long time ago. A nervous tic

kept jerking below his right eye and now and then his lips flinched, trembled, as if the little old man were trying to form a word that had never been spoken on this human earth, a single word that would cleanse, heal, and transform. . . . Arkie had a notion about him: once upon a time, years and years ago, some maud had given him the screw and this old guy was still trying to figure out what had happened. This was the kind of con Arkie longed for: one that warped the mind, so that twenty years later you were still blinking your eyelids and wondering where it had gone wrong.

No machines in here, except for an old beat-up Silvertone radio that Arkie had never heard turned on. No action of any kind in here. Guzzle your suds and get your ass out. Arkie dragged a slat-bottomed chair away from a table and sat, tipping the chair back against the wall. He shifted and reshifted; folded his arms; crossed his legs. And then he dozed off, dreaming.

—What does Arkie dream about?
—O Lord, please, let's don't talk about it. It's too garish and disconnected and bewildering. The kind of fantastic jungle no sound man will ever set foot in.
—But when he dreams of Arkie, how does he see himself?
—Just the way you and I do. As taller and stronger and wiser and tougher than he is on Gimlet Street.
—Is that all?
—That's enough. It's more than enough.

In an hour or so he was awakened by voices, but he didn't open his eyes immediately. Arkie had learned after various unpleasantnesses that it was best to play possum after napping until he'd remembered exactly where he was. Oh yeah . . . The Teeny . . . Nothing was going to bother him in here. A couple of drivers for the roofing company were taking a break, came in to snatch a beer before going back on the job. He rose gingerly and stretched, replaced his chair and went out. What time was it? And where, goddamnit, was Clemmie? He slouched into Diamond Billiards and got a cold Pepsi from the machine. Wanted to wash the sleep-film out of his mouth; it made him feel greasy all

over. Wandered to the back table to look at Johnny Wyzscysky practicing.

The skinny paste-faced young man glanced at him. "Here you go,
Arkie. Bet you a quarter I can lay the four in the left side."

The purple ball was resting on the lip of the left corner pocket.
The cue ball was against the rail slightly below the left side pocket.

"Come on," said Arkie. "Who you think you're trying to hustle?
Me, I seen you do it a hundred times."

Click.

What about hustling pool? No, man; not Arkie's style, he wasn't
built for it. Patience, that's what he lacked. His nerves wouldn't take
it. . . . As he stepped out the door he almost bumped smack into
Clemmie. When she saw him she pranced away and made as if to
hurry on.

"Hey, kid, there you are," Arkie said. Made it sound jaunty. He
always had to jolly her because she was five years older than he and it
gave her a lot of edge. She continually put him off his stride, so that
he felt like a little kid around her sometimes. "I been wondering where
you at."

"Well, if you don't know where to find me by now you got to be
pretty dumb." She had a pleasant throaty voice; it sounded like rich
cloth tearing.

He hesitated. "Well, you know. I wouldn't want to come right
busting in on you in your pad and screw things up."

She shrugged.

Oh goddamn.

"That's all. I just don't want to ball things up."

Now at last he'd found Clemmie and he felt acutely miserable.
Despite the cool early season she wore only a black skirt and a transparent
nylon blouse. Through the filmy cloth he saw goose bumps on her
upper arm. A breeze with a chill in it moved her odd-looking hair.
"Come on," he said. "I'll buy you a cup of coffee."

She shrugged again, but came along anyway. Slowly though, so
that Arkie felt he was just dragging along. She was a good four inches
taller than he (that was, he thought, a lot of the problem right there)

and she was wearing rickety spike heels. Each time she took a step her right ankle quivered; Arkie saw this but didn't know whether she noticed it.

They went into Dillard's Place and he ordered one black and sweet for himself and one light without for Clemmie. They sat in a slick plastic-seated booth. Dirty cotton batting bulged out of the tears.

"If you're wanting that single from last night I ain't got it with me." O Lord, if that was how she was going to begin . . .

"How? Didn't the john pay up?"

He knew immediately he'd said the wrong thing. Because of his helpless anger.

She stared at him disdainfully; sniffed. "Jimmy, you mean? My boyfriend Jimmy from last night? He's a *real* fine feller and yes he did let me have a little money for right now. But then I had to go and loan it all to Agnes. Agnes said she was having a hard time trying to make ends meet. Of course she's always talking like that but I thought I ought to help her out." She lifted her chin an inch or so but kept those green eyes on Arkie's eyes. "I don't know of nobody else that's going to."

"Yeh yeh. Don't worry about that." Arkie hadn't even been thinking about his dollar. She'd already gouged him for—what? At least ten or so. He knew he was never going to see it again. "I was just wondering how you was getting along, if you was all right."

"Just fine, thank you. Why wouldn't I be all right?"

"Nothing, no reason. I just got to wondering." This was the day he couldn't say one correct word. He looked at her, the tall thin girl with the bladelike face. Her features were as definite as if they had been chopped from a block of wood and her fine dry electric hair was unmanageable, fell about her shoulders like a handful of oat straw. She had bound a soiled green ribbon around underneath and tied it at the crown of her head in a coy bow. But it looked odd, off center. Arkie decided to make his move. It wasn't the best time, but now it didn't look to get any better. He leaned suddenly toward her, sliding his elbows across the table. He jarred his coffee cup and it slopped over, darkening his jacket sleeve. "Oh goddamn." He snatched a paper napkin and dabbed disgustedly at the bright blue rayon. "Goddamnit."

She giggled.

"What's so fuckin funny?" He got another napkin and began mopping at the table.

"You. You're pretty funny. Looks like you've sort of got the jitters."

He dropped the soggy napkin into the ashtray. "Gimme a stab."

Because she was still laughing at him she could obey without loss of face. She took a package of Chesterfields out of her worn red clutch bag.

He lit one and took a couple of deliberate puffs. He wasn't going to speak until he'd regained his composure.

She tried to get him going. "Now as you was saying—" But she began giggling again.

Why was it she every time had him by the short hairs? "Well . . ." He pulled his ear lobe. Tried a tactical change. "Look. You're a good friend of Oxie's, right? I mean, you really got some stretch with that guy, ain't you?"

"I guess I know him about as good as I need to."

"Well look. I don't see Oxie so much here of late. You know? He don't come down on Gimlet the way he used to and I was just wondering if you might ast him something for me." He caught her frown and rushed on nervously. "Of course I could ast him myself if I seen him. Me and Oxie are just like that." He crossed his fingers and held them before her face until she looked at them. "Asshole buddies. But I don't get up his way so much; little off my ground up where he is. I was thinking maybe if you was to see him before I did maybe you could ast him. It wouldn't be nothing."

"I don't know as how Oxie would want to be bothered a whole lot. He's awful busy these days, down at the courthouse and one thing and another."

"Yeah, I know Oxie's a mover, all right. You don't have to tell me about that guy. But this wouldn't take no time and it wouldn't cost him a penny, not a red cent. All I want is, if you could just ast him to let me know a little good action. I want to find me a little action that don't cost too much to set up. I don't mean just cheap, though. I can get up about a hundred without no sweat." He rode over this stark lie easily and gracefully because he didn't expect her to believe it. Not that he was trying to jive her. But this kind of lie was acceptable currency. They both knew what he meant by it. "Now that wouldn't be nothing to him. You know as good as I do how smart Oxie is. Got a hundred pieces of action buzzing around in his mind that he ain't even interested in. Just going to waste. All I need is something to give me a little start."

She kept shaking her head. "I don't think I better. I don't reckon I ought to bother Oxie with something like that. He's awful touchous these days, you don't never know. It don't take hardly nothing to set him off. . . ."

But Arkie had stopped listening; he was merely watching her mouth wiggle. He'd already known how she would answer.

". . . I declare that man is jumpy as a sack of snakes, you can't tell from one minute to the next. . . ."

Now, without preamble, Arkie made his move.

"Listen, Clemmie, if something was to happen between you and Oxie, how about letting me be your stringer?"

She was staggered, seemed tipsy for a moment. Her fierce green eyes looked slightly glassy. "What? What was that you said?"

He took a quick deep breath. "I said, if something was to happen, if something was to go wrong between you and Oxie, how about me coming on as your stringer." Arkie didn't know that he was speaking very loudly.

"What are you talking about? What in the goddamn hell? You don't know what you're talking."

"I guess I do."

"I guess I don't. I know I don't. You." Was she spitting? No. But that was Arkie's impression. "You're just a silly little runt, that's all you are. You wouldn't be good for nobody for nothing."

"Why don't you think about it?" He was beginning to whine. "That's all I'm astin, you just to think—"

"Shut your mouth."

She was leaving. She rose jerkily, pale with anger, and the two stainless steel spoons rattled on the bare table. She towered over him and her mouth was thin and twisted when she talked. "And you needn't to think you can talk to me like that. Like I was one of these damn Gimlet Street whores. You. That's just how fucking stupid you are."

She stalked away. Her figure looked set, harder and sharper than ever.

Arkie sat shaking. He was impotent with icy rage. He took out one of his loose cigarettes, but then stuffed it back into his pocket, crumpling it. Now he felt upon him the amused glance of the counterman and he turned about, staring at him savagely.

"What the hell *you* looking at?"

His amusement became heavier. "I'm looking at exactly nothing," he said.

Arkie got up; lurched. Clemmie not a whore; not one of your Gimlet whores, she said. Man, that had to be the wildest pipe he'd ever heard. She was the crawliest goddamn maud on the turf. If a john had any sense he wouldn't touch her with a ten-foot cornstalk.

—What now, Arkie. What you up to now?
—Shut up, he says. Blow it out your ass, why don't you.

But as he ducked once more into the raucous sunlight he was wearing a cold secretive smile. He was still ahead of it, after all. He knew things she didn't know. Arkie had hard scrabbling, he had to keep his ear close to the ground, he had to know where it was at and he had to look ahead. Clemmie didn't look ahead, she thought she had it laid in the shade. And why? Because she was counting on old hotstuff Oxie to take care of her. But Arkie could see it coming, clear as a neon sign. Oxie was going to cut her loose and it wouldn't be long from now. That guy was leaving this part of the world, going up. He was going to cut loose from both Clemmie and Agnes. Agnes: she was nothing anyhow but a goddamn mooch. Arkie would bet you she didn't turn up a clean fifty bucks a week. And look at Clemmie's drawbacks. All poison; tough and mean. Had a temper like a buzz saw. And how she got her kicks was stirring up and circulating little jealous intrigues among the pigs. She could start a fight standing alone in a ten-acre field. Trouble on wheels with rhinestone spokes. Arkie could see where things were going and how it was going to happen and he had to get dibs. Once the word was out that Clemmie was loose there would be gougers aplenty after her, and after Agnes too; heavies, the kind of guys Arkie couldn't go up against. Couldn't hold his own in that kind of rub; he had to get in first, that much was clear. . . . Goddamnit, why couldn't she see that this was her best move? He was doing her one fat favor if she only knew it. Look. He wasn't going to smack her around or stomp her ass to get his rocks off. Arkie wasn't that kind of guy. And look. He was close in to things, knew where to find the best setups. Oxie was a million miles away. When she ran out and hit those days on the thin crust, who was going to stake her? How about for that matter the ten bucks he'd already staked her to? . . . Well, he'd made up his mind: he'd put it to her again. Soon. He tried to think how much time he had left, and it didn't seem much. . . . He felt a bit feverish. The sunlight was a precarious weight on his head, oppressive as thirst.

In Maxie's he ate a cheeseburger and drank a cold drink and then decided to get another sandwich. Uusually one satisfied him, but he'd had a rough morning. And so his meal used up almost all the money he'd made today. There was a game of liar's poker in progress in one of the booths and he joined it gratefully: not only a chance to pick up some dump; he could get his mind off Clemmie for a while. There were six guys at the table but Arkie had seen only one of them before. Didn't know his name or have any kind of book on him; just knew him as a hefty lug always nervously snickering. So Arkie went gingerly for a time, cagey among strangers. After having made certain early on that he was a buck to the good, he idled, picking up a couple and dropping them as the mood struck him. In a while everyone had become familiar with the serial numbers of the bills they'd been playing with and they traded with Donald at the bar for a new batch. When Arkie was dealt his new bill he palmed it and substituted his lucky dollar. This bill he always carried with him and wouldn't think of spending; he didn't even count it in as part of his stake. The bids went round a couple of times with Arkie innocuously silent, and then the big giggly guy bid three sixes.

"I got to raise that. Six sixes."

"Who many?"

"Uh. Six."

"Get serious."

"Mess with a wife, You get trouble and strife," Arkie said.

They had to wonder what the hell that meant.

"Well, I'll challenge six any day of the week."

"Fair enough," said Arkie. "You want to raise it? Challenge for five dollars this here one time?"

The hefty fellow shied off for a moment. It was possible to have six identical digits in the serial number of a dollar bill, but who'd ever seen them? He considered the possibility of a ringer, but how? The barkeep had brought the bills to them.

"Five dollars, hell. What do you think I am?"

"I don't have no idea," Arkie said. "I been kind of wondering."

The big guy giggled; reddened; gave him a bad look. "Buddy, you finding out. I'll go you for five. You remember it was *six* sixes you said."

Archly: "Was it six? Um. Any you other gentlemens feel like putting up for five?"

No no. But they would challenge for the regular single. . . . Okay. . . . Everybody in?

He tossed the bill on the table. "Read em and weep."

The man across from him picked it up. "They're all there," he said, "every last one of them." He passed the bill to the hefty guy. "I be goddamn," he said. He flung it down. "That cleans me." Gave Arkie another bad look. "It's a good thing I get paid tonight."

Arkie seemed to pay no attention when his winnings were passed to him. He picked up his talisman dollar and gazed at it as if actually seeing it for the first time. "Six damn sixes," he said. "I wouldn't never of believed it." He wagged his head. "It's for goddamn sure this one's got to go out of the game." He reached into his pocket and pulled out the dollar the bartender had brought. "Here," he said, "let's trade it with a new one." And he put his lucky bill back into his pocket.

They played another half hour before breaking up. Arkie kept it exactly even, not winning and not losing. When the fellow sitting next to him rose to go he offered to buy him a final beer.

"No thank you. I got to be getting along. Later than I thought."

"Well, maybe next time," Arkie said. Feeling expansive. The guy seemed like, you know, like a pretty good john and you could never tell when you might be running into him again. A little Mazola made it that much easier.

He was feeling much happier now. His early impulse to stake himself to seven dollars had proved right; this was his lucky Friday. Even the hassle with Clemmie hadn't wrecked it completely.

But as he was going out he was stopped by Donald the barkeep.

"Okay, Arkie, I got to have me a piece of that."

"Piece of what?"

"Piece of the change you picked up. I've seen you pull that lucky six dodge in here before."

"What's it to you?"

"It's goddamn enough to me. You sit in here every day taking up ass-room and conning my customers and slopping up the tables. It's worth a piece of change to you just so as I don't blow the whistle on you ever time you come through the door."

The careful whine. "Aw come on, man. It ain't no harm to you."

Donald leaned toward him. "How'd you like to be kicked out of here for good and all?"

"I'll give you a single," Arkie said. "Honest to God, I didn't pull down all that much."

"Lay it right here in my hand."

Arkie forked it over, muttering savagely, but it really hadn't much daunted his spirits. You had to expect it now and then; the kickback was a routine part of the action.

Still traveling Rance Avenue. Making the rounds, making the rounds. A huge fat woman with a mottled face was standing on the sidewalk, just beneath the edge of the awning of a used-furniture store. She blocked his path. Looking up into her eyes, he felt a momentary bewilderment.

"Hello, Arkie," she said. "How about splitting a pipe with me? You want to split a pipe?"

"Not today, I gotta make hay."

He sidled around her and went on, but she'd clawed at his nerves.

. . . Goddamn hophead. Ooh, think of them eyes. Everything about her looked wrong. . . . Who was she anyhow? That was the worst of it; he couldn't put a name to her. Seemed like he'd seen her around the street but he couldn't place her. She knew him all right, though; stepped right up and called him by name. He felt a quick glow of pride. Damn right she knew him: everybody knows Arkie. He's a mover, people could tell he was going places, they kept their eyes on him. . . . Uhhh. Maybe that wasn't so awful good, to have everybody know your name. It meant the fuzz would know you too. They would come around balling things up simply because they could finger you.

Good news, bad news. Came down on you like rain.

He visited the Okay and the Blue Star, the Champagne Club, Tommy's Joint, Ed's the Happy Time, Dr. Feelgood, and the Neptune Room. Making the rounds. He began to feel better as the sun got lower. The neon went on and the soft lights and weariness settled like veils of cobweb over the faces of the bartenders. The pigs came out in droves, batting their mascaraed eyes at any ambulatory entity not wearing a brassiere. He juiced a couple of gunghoes for three quarters, picked up a dime matching and another quarter at nineball, dropped a dime on the traveling Coke bottle. (You'd think for Godsake St. Louis would have taken it, but the john had a Tallahassee. He should have seen that.) He got a guy on the doorknob trick for half a rock. Just making the rounds. Arkie did his little dance.

He wandered back into the Ace, making the first full circle of the day. Clemmie and Teacher were sitting at a table. She was talking earnestly to him in that low rich voice and he seemed to be paying earnest attention but he was dog drunk. Arkie knew it. Why for Godsake did she want to talk to that silly bastard? Fat waste of time . . . He felt a twinge of fear. What if she told Teacher what Arkie had said? The dumb son of a bitch would mouth it all up and down the street. That would be pretty funny, oh yes it would: that Arkie himself had given out the word that Clemmie was unattached, that Oxie was going to cut her loose. Arkie would hang himself. Don't trust nobody, especially the mauds: how many times did a man have to be reminded?

"Greetings and hallucinations, brother," Teach said to Arkie.

"Howdy, gang," Arkie said.

"I ain't talking to you," Clemmie said.

"That just busts my heart," Arkie said. "I can't tell you how bad."

They resumed their jabbering. Clemmie lowered her voice so that Arkie couldn't hear.

He shrugged.

A couple of drunk johns were standing at the bowling machine. Arkie eyed them for a while, patiently gauging how far gone they were, and then he picked them up and juiced them for an easy buck and a half before they quit on him. But then he couldn't help rubbing it in. He stood with his back to the machine and jauntily tossed the plastic ball over his shoulder. The machine registered a strike. When he looked at their faces, he regretted immediately what he had done. They weren't so drunk they wouldn't remember that. He'd just had his last slice of action with those two. (It was that goddamn Clemmie; she was eating his nerves up.) Trying to take the edge off the johns' resentment, he did his little dance; his loafers scraped and crackled on the gritty linoleum tile.

He sang, "Fried cornbread and cold coleslaw, I'm traveling down to Arkansas."

Arkansas: that was how Arkie got his nickname.

Arkansas . . .

Man, was there really such a place as that?

Ough.

Clemmie had found herself another fight. Some tough-looking maud in a blue dress had come over to the table and the two of them were shrieking at each other. Fur was going to fly, clawful after clawful. Teacher, the chicken bastard, wanted of course no part of it and he was trying to get away. Arkie laughed. It was worth money, watching him trying to sneak around the girls.

Suddenly the maud in the blue dress reached out and snatched at Clemmie's blouse. A button popped loose. Trying to scratch her tits off.

Not much there to scratch, Arkie reflected.

Clemmie stood up, totally enraged and searching blindly on the table for a beer bottle. But Arkie got there and lifted it out of reach.

"Wait a minute, womens," he said. "Throw some water on this here brush fire."

"Get out of my goddam way," Clemmie said.

"Simmer down. Because if you don't the cops'll come in and simmer you down. That what you want? You want the fuzz in here?"

"I'm going to bust her head in, that's all."

"Now you hush, just simmer down one damn minute. . . . What's it all about anyhow? There ain't nothing worth fighting about." He turned to the other maud. "How did this ruckus get started?"

"I'm just letting this here fleabit whore know she's going to keep away from Jimmy. He's way too good for something like her. Jimmy's my steady. We been steady a long time before he ever laid eyes on her."

"I don't take that off of nobody," Clemmie said. "I'll bust her fucking head in."

"Come on," Arkie said. "You don't want to do that. You'd just feel bad about it later on."

He turned to the other. "Clemmie didn't know nothing about all that. How was she going to know that? Anyhow, it don't do no good to fight about it. Be better off if you just let it ride."

To Clemmie: "Come on. Let's go get us a cup of coffee down at the Bluebird."

"I ain't backing down from this bitch." She flailed at the girl halfheartedly, but the table was between them.

"Quit that," he said. "You ain't backing down, you just showing some sense for a change. Come on now." He tugged at her arm and reluctantly she came with him. He was surprised.

At the cash register she turned. "You needn't to think you're getting away with anything. You can make by God sure that you're going to get yours."

"All right," said the other coolly. "I'll let you know where you can find me." Color of victory in her voice.

Arkie led her out. At last the sun had set and the stars had arrived. A mild breeze stirred about them as they stood uncertainly on the pavement.

"I'm going back in there," Clemmie said. "I ain't letting her get away with that."

"Calm down. She ain't worth wasting your time on. Get your hands dirty."

They walked for a while, breathing heavily.

"Don't you worry none, buddy," Clemmie said. "I'm going to settle with her and no two ways."

"Damn right."

"Look here. One of my buttons is off. I don't know where I can find one to match. . . . I'll settle with her. She'll wish she never heard of that Jimmy's name."

"Damn right. Later on, though. Make her worry about it a while first."

They sat hunched over coffee cups. The monotone glare of fluorescent lights enlarged their features. Man and woman; not many times Arkie had it like that. The Bluebird was drab and quiet and Greek, mostly an all-night coffee stop for cab drivers. You wouldn't come here for a good time: too much light and a dull juke.

He kept talking, soft and low. His mind raced. "And see, that's exactly why you need somebody like me for your steady stringer. Oxie now: he's getting too busy with other stuff to look after you right. He don't know what's going on down this way anymore. Truth of it is, he's plumb got away from Gimlet. Take tonight now: if I hadn't been there to tell that bitch off, you'd of wound up in a fight." He was proud of himself, putting it like that. Once he got started he could speak as elegantly as any mayor. "You'd be up to your ass in trouble, and over something it wasn't worth dirtying your hands. A pig like that . . . Just one more good reason you need somebody like me around, somebody I mean that'll stick close. You see what I'm getting at."

She gazed into his eyes and smiled sweetly. "What if I was to tell Oxie what you said, how you were talking to me?"

He leaned away from her, contorting his body angrily against the back of the booth.

"Goddamnit, Clemmie . . ."

Sometimes it seemed that all she was good for was to ball up the pitch. She had that grainy streak in her. . . . His mind ran furiously. Suppose she did tell, what then? It would mean one of two things: either Oxie would send some big goddamn razor around to stomp Arkie, or he would simply hurry things along, seeing that the news was already out, and cut Clemmie loose that much sooner. Actually, either way was all right. If someone was coming to get him Arkie would find out long before it happened (because you can't send muscle without making noise); he would quietly duck the scene, hole up somewhere. Or if he decided to get rid of Clemmie sooner, then it would be that much sooner she'd see how Arkie was smart, really on top of things. Okay, then.

He made himself relax; yawned ostentatiously. "Go ahead and tell him. It don't make no never-mind to me."

"Ain't you afraid what he might do?" She looked at him with a newly serious curiosity.

"Oxie don't scare me none. What I been trying to tell you, he don't know this territory near as good as I do. Got too many other things on his mind. He don't scare me even a little bit."

She kept watching him. Maybe after all she was beginning to get the message. "Anyway," she said, "sooner or later you'd have to settle up with him. There wouldn't be no way out of that."

Sometimes it occurred to Arkie that maybe Clemmie wasn't hampered by a lot of brain power.

"No, now damnit, don't get it all fouled up. I ain't trying to ball up any arrangements you-all might have. All I'm saying is, if it does happen, you know who you can come to. It ain't no more than just a friendly offer."

She seemed mollified. "Well. I'll remember what you said."

"Good. Fine and dandy. That's all in the world I want you to do, keep it in mind."

"Let's get out of here." She looked about distastefully. "This place is so dead it's spooky."

"All right," he said. "But let's don't go back to the Ace. I'm getting good and sick of that joint." Always the diplomat; he knew if she spotted the pig in the blue dress she'd start the fight where it left off.

"Let's go down to the Bunny. Maybe Agnes might be there. I need to see Agnes about something."

"Let's go."

The Big Bunny had come alive, crowded and noisy and wet. When they entered they were greeted loudly, beerily welcome. The regular crowd had gathered and they saluted all familiar faces more or less in the same fashion.

Clemmie went immediately to sit on someone's lap.

Someone yelled at him, "Hey, Arkie, tell us a lie."

"Wash your mouth out," he yelled back. "I never told a lie in my life."

"Arkie. Match you for the juke."

"Match you for the quarter," he countered.

He ran up a score of 5837 on the Space Patrol pinball machine and put seventy-five cents into his pocket.

You couldn't keep him down now; he couldn't remember when he'd been so happy. He felt confident about his whole life and he offered to match Squelch for that five spot, but now the stolid barkeep chickened out of the bet and Arkie ribbed him unmercifully. "And I thought you was a sporting man," he said. Even when Clemmie gouged him for another single and left with a drunk john he didn't much mind.

"Screw the women, screw the law, I'm traveling down to Arkansas." He did his little dance.

In a while he felt hot and too keyed up and he stepped out on the sidewalk to settle his nerves before taking another round at the pinball machine. He saw that the sky was filled with cool stars. Suddenly it occurred to him that this street, Gimlet Street, could take you anywhere in the world, it was joined to all the other streets there were. He shook his head, grinning. Arkie couldn't go. This was his territory. He was chained to Gimlet and he was chained to Clemmie, that green-eyed girl he was so helplessly in love with.

"River gonna rise, creek gonna thaw, I'm traveling down to Arkansas."

I Am One of You Forever

The Overspill

*T*hen there was one brief time when we didn't live in the big brick house with my grandmother but in a neat two-storey green-shingled white house in the holler below. It was two storeys if you stood at the front door; on the other side it was three storeys, the ground floor a tall basement garage.

The house was surrounded by hills to the north and east and south. Directly above us lay the family farm and my grandmother's house. Two miles behind the south hill was the town of Tipton, where the Challenger Paper and Fiber Corporation smoked eternally, smudging the Carolina mountain landscape for miles. A small creek ran through our side yard, out of the eastern hills. The volume of the creek flow was controlled by Challenger; they had placed a reservoir up there, and the creek water was regulated by means of the spillway.

At this time my mother was visiting her brother in California. Uncle Luden was in trouble again, with a whole different woman this time. Maybe my mother could help; it was only five thousand miles round-trip by train.

So my father and I had to fumble along as best we could.

Despite the extra chores, I found it exciting. Our friendship took a new and stronger turn, became something of a mild conspiracy. New sets of signals evolved between us. We met now on freshly neutral ground somewhere between my boyhood and his boyishness, and for me it was a heady rise in status. We were clumsy housekeepers, there were lots of minor mishaps, and the tagline we formulated soonest was: "Let's just not tell Mama about this one." I adored that thought.

He was always dreaming up new projects to please her and during her absence came up with one of masterful ambition.

Across the little creek, with its rows of tall willows, was a half-acre of fallow ground considered unusable because of marshiness and the impenetrable clot of blackberry vines in the south corner. My father now planned it as a garden, already planted before she returned.

We struggled heroically. I remember pleasantly the destruction of the vines and the cutting of the drainage ditch neat and straight into the field. The ground was so soft that we could slice down with our spades and bring up squares of dark blue mud and lay them along side by side. They gleamed like tile. Three long afternoons completed the ditch, and then my father brought out the big awkward shoulder scythe and whetted the blade until I could hear it sing on his thumb-ball when he tested it. And then he waded into the thicket of thorny vine and began slashing. For a long time nothing happened, but finally the vines began to fall back, rolling up in tangles like barbarous handwriting. With a pitchfork I worried these tangles into a heap. Best of all was the firing, the clear yellow flame and the sizzle and snap of the vine-ribs and thorns, and the thin black smoke rising above the new-green willows. The delicious smell of it.

After this we prepared the ground in the usual way and planted. Then we stood at the edge of our garden, admiring with a full tired pride the clean furrows and mounded rows of earth.

But this was only a part of the project. It was merely a vegetable garden, however arduously achieved, and we planted a garden every year. My father wanted something else, decorative, elegant in design, something guaranteed to please a lady.

The weather held good and we started next day, hauling two loads of scrap lumber from one of the barns. He measured and we sawed and planed. He hummed and whistled as he worked and I mostly stared at him when not scurrying to and fro, fetching and carrying. He wouldn't, of course, tell me what we were building.

On the second day it became clear. We were constructing a bridge. We were building a small but elaborate bridge across the little creek that divided the yard and the garden, a stream that even I could step over without lengthening my stride. It was ambitious: an arched bridge with handrails and a latticework arch on the garden side enclosing a little picket gate.

He must have been a handy carpenter. To me the completed bridge appeared marvelous. We had dug deep on both sides to sink the locust piers, and the arch above the stream, though not high, was unmistakably a rainbow. When I walked back and forth across the bridge I heard and felt a satisfactory drumming. The gate latch made a solid cluck and the gate arch, pinned together of old plaster lathe, made me feel that in crossing the bridge I was entering a different world, not simply going into the garden.

He had further plans for the latticework. "Right here," he said, "and over here, I'll plant tea roses to climb up the lattice. Then you'll see."

We whitewashed it three times. The raw lumber sparkled. We walked upstream to the road above the yard and looked at it, then walked downstream to the edge of the garden and looked at it. We saw nothing we weren't prideful about.

He went off in our old Pontiac and returned in a half-hour. He parked in the driveway and got out. "Come here," he said. We sat in the grass on the shoulder of the culvert at the edge of the road. "I've been to the store," he said. He pulled a brown paper sack from his pocket. Inside I found ten thimble-shaped chocolate mints, my favorite. From another pocket he produced a rolled band of bright red silk.

"Thank you," I said. "What's that?"

"We want her to know it's a present, don't we? So we've got to tie a ribbon on it. We'll put it right there in the middle of the handrail." He spooled off two yards of ribbon and cut it with his pocket knife. "Have to make a big one so she can see it from up here in the road."

I chewed a mint and observed his thick horny fingers with the red silk.

It was not to be. Though I was convinced that my father could design and build whatever he wished—the Brooklyn Bridge, the Taj Mahal—he could not tie a bow in this broad ribbon. The silk crinkled and knotted and slipped loose; it simply would not behave. He growled in low tones like a bear trying to dislodge a groundhog from its hole. "I don't know what's the matter with this stuff," he said.

Over the low mumble of his words I heard a different rumble, a gurgle as of pebbles pouring into a broad still pool. "What's that?" I asked.

"What's what?"

"What's that noise?"

He stopped ruining the ribbon and sat still as the sound grew louder. Then his face darkened and veins stood out in his neck and forehead. His voice was quiet and level now. "Those bastards."

"Who?"

"Those Challenger Paper guys. They've opened the floodgates."

We scrambled up the shoulder into the road.

As the sound got louder it discomposed into many sounds: lappings, bubblings, rippings, undersucks, and splashovers. Almost as soon as we saw the gray-brown thrust of water emerge from beneath the overhanging plum tree, we felt the tremor as it slammed against the culvert, leaping up the shoulder and rolling back. On the yard side it shot out of the culvert as out of a hose. In a few seconds it had overflowed the low creek banks and streamed gray-green along the edge of the yard, furling white around the willow trunks. Debris—black sticks and leaves and grasses —spun on top of the water, and the gullet of the culvert rattled with rolling pebbles.

Our sparkling white bridge was soiled with mud and slimy grasses. The water driving into it reached a gray arm high into the air and slapped down. My father and I watched the hateful battering of our work, our hands in our pockets. He still held the red ribbon and it trickled out of his pocket down his trouser leg. The little bridge trembled and began to shake. There was one moment when it sat quite still, as if it had gathered resolve and was fighting back.

And then on the yard side it wrenched away from the log piers, and when that side headed downstream the other side tore away too, and we had a brief glimpse of the bridge parallel in the stream like a strange boat and saw the farthest advance of the flood framed in the quaint lattice arch. The bridge twirled about and the corners caught against both banks and it went over on its side, throwing up the naked underside *of the planks like a barn door blown shut. Water piled up behind this damming and finally poured over and around it, eating at the borders of the garden and lawn.*

My father kept saying over and over, "Bastards bastards bastards. It's against the law for them to do that."

Then he fell silent.

I don't know how long we stared downstream before we were aware that my mother had arrived. When we first saw her she had already got out of the taxi, which sat idling in the road. She looked odd to me, wearing a dress I had never seen, and a strange expression—half amused, half vexed—crossed her face. She looked at us as if she'd caught us doing something naughty.

My father turned to her and tried to speak. "Bastards" was the only word he got out. He choked and his face and neck went dark again. He gestured toward the swamped bridge and the red ribbon fluttered in his fingers.

She looked where he pointed and, as I watched, understanding came into her face, little by little. When she turned again to face us she looked as if she were in pain. A single tear glistened on her cheek, silver in the cheerful light of midafternoon.

My father dropped his hand and the ribbon fluttered and trailed in the mud.

The tear on my mother's cheek got larger and larger. It detached from her face and became a shiny globe, widening outward like an inflating balloon. At first the tear floated in air between them, but as it expanded it took my mother and father into itself. I saw them suspended, separate but beginning to drift slowly toward one another. Then my mother looked past my father's shoulder, looked through the bright skin of the tear, at me. The tear enlarged until at last it took me in too. It was warm and salt. As soon as I got used to the strange light inside the tear, I began to swim clumsily toward my parents.

Three

The Beard

*U*ncle Gurton's beard had a long and complex history, but I will try not to bore us with much of that. Enough to say that it was a fabled beard and that when my father and I heard that Uncle Gurton was coming to visit we were thrilled at the prospect of viewing the legendary fleece.

"How long is that beard of his now?" my father asked my grandmother.

She smiled a secret smile. "Oh, I wouldn't have no idea," she said. "But he's been growing it for forty years or more and ain't once yet trimmed it. That's what I hear tell."

"And he's coming here to our house to visit?" I asked.

"That's what Aunt Sary says in her letter." She held up the scrawled bit of paper, but not close enough for us to read the writing.

"And when is he going to get here?"

"She wouldn't know about that. You'll just have to wait."

"Hot damn," my father said. "If this ain't the biggest thing since Christmas. We're going to make that old man plenty welcome."

"Now, Joe Robert, don't you be deviling Uncle Gurton," she said. "Leave him in peace."

"Oh, I wouldn't harm a hair of his face," he said. "When you say he's coming?"

She smiled again. "You'll just have to wait till he shows up."

*   *   *

Show up is exactly what Uncle Gurton did. We heard no car or truck arrive, and he didn't walk into the house or knock at the door. One Tuesday noon he was just there, standing under the walnut tree in the side yard and staring at our chopblock and pile of kindling as if he'd never seen such objects upon the face of the earth. An apparition, he simply became present.

The three of us raised our heads from our dinner plates at the same time and saw him, and a spooky feeling came over us.

"What in the world is *that?*" my father asked.

"Uncle Gurton," said my grandmother in her serenest voice.

His back was toward us, so that all we could tell was that he was a very tall man, his white head bare, and dressed in faded overalls and a green plaid shirt, as lean and narrow as a fence rail, and warped with age and weather. Then, as if presenting himself formally to our gaze, he turned around.

I was profoundly disappointed. The famous beard that he had been working on for forty years and more, the beard that was the pivot of so many stories, was tucked down inside his overalls bib.

My father and I had made bets whether it would hang down to his belly button or all the way down to his knees, and now we couldn't say.

But even apart from his beard he was an extraordinary-appearing person. His arms were too long for his shirt sleeves and his hands dangled out like big price tags. His overalls legs were too short and his skinny legs went naked into his high-topped brogans. His long hair was white and hung down both sides of his ruddy sharp-featured face. The beard, as purely white as a morning cloud, went down behind his overalls bib, and what happened to it after that, what it truly looked like, only Uncle Gurton and the almighty and omniscient God could say.

"Jess," my grandmother said, "go out and welcome Uncle Gurton to the house."

"Please, ma'am, no," I said. Uncle Gurton was too famous in my mind. It would have been easier to shake hands with Lou Gehrig.

"He does look kind of fearsome," my father said. "I'll go gather him in."

He went out and talked and Uncle Gurton gave him one short

nod and then they came into the house. When the old man entered our small alcove dining space he looked even taller and odder than he had outdoors. His head nearly scraped the low ceiling.

My grandmother told him how glad we were to see him and how we hoped he would stay a long time, and asked him to sit and eat with us. Which he did with right goodwill. She brought flatware and a glass of buttermilk and a plate piled full of green beans, cornbread, and fried rabbit. Then she sat down at the end of the table and began to question him.

"How is Aunt Jewel getting along?" she asked.

Uncle Gurton smiled and was silent.

She waited a space of time and asked, "How is Cousin Harold doing?"

He gave her a smile as warm and friendly as the first, and as informative as a spoon.

In a while she lit on the correct form. "Has Hiram Williams got him a good tobacco crop set out?" He smiled and gave a vigorous affirmative shake of his head. After this, she asked questions that could be answered yes or no, and Uncle Gurton would nod a cheerful Yes or wag a downcast No.

And all during this exchange he was feeding voraciously. Great heaping forkfuls went into his hirsute mouth with mechanical accuracy and rapidity. A sight awesome to behold. My father kept filling his plate and Uncle Gurton kept emptying it. My father described it later: "The way he was forking at it, and with all that hair around his mouth, I kept thinking it was a man throwing a wagonload of alfalfa into a hayloft."

He finished by downing a whole glass of buttermilk. We came to find out that buttermilk was his sole beverage, breakfast, dinner, supper. He never touched anything else, not even water.

He edged his chair back from the table.

"Uncle Gurton, won't you have a little something else?" my grandmother asked.

"No thank you," he said. "I've had an elegant sufficiency; any more would be a superfluity."

That was his one saying, the only one we ever heard him utter, and he was as proud of it as another man might be of a prize beagle.

He said this sentence at the end of every meal, and we came to realize that he got mighty upset, his whole day was lusterless, if you didn't ask him to have a little more something, and give him occasion to say his sentence.

My father's mouth flew open like a phoebe's after a fly. His eyes lit up with surprise. "Would you mind saying that again, Uncle Gurton?" he asked. "What you just said?"

Uncle Gurton gave him a sweet warm smile and disappeared.

I don't mean that he dissolved into nothingness before our watching eyes like a trick ghost in a horror movie. But he evaded my father's request with one of those silent smiles, and when we had got up and scraped our dishes into the slop bucket and stacked them on the drainboard of the sink and turned around, Uncle Gurton was gone. His chair was angled back from the table, his red and white checked napkin folded neatly and laid in the seat, and he was nowhere to be seen. If it weren't for the soiled plate with the knife and fork primly crossed and the empty streaked glass, we might not have believed that he had been there. No footsteps of departure, no sound of the side door, nothing.

"Our Uncle Gurton has got some interesting ways about him," my father said.

"Poor old soul," my grandmother murmured.

This habit of absenting and distancing himself we learned to know as an integral part of Uncle Gurton's character, as one with the man as his silence. You would sight him on the ridge of the pasture above the farther barn, his stark figure scarecrowlike against the sky and leaning into the wind, and then if you glanced off into the pear tree to see a bluejay, he was no longer on the ridge when you looked again. Snuffed out of the present world like a match flame. Translated into another and inevitable dimension of space. What? Where? When was he? He was an enigma of many variations, and his one answer, silence, satisfied them all as far as he was concerned.

"There's one thing, though, you can be certain of," my father said. "He won't miss a mealtime."

And this was true. As soon as the first steaming dish of corn or squash or squirrel burgoo was set out, Uncle Gurton *arrived* from whatever mystery world otherwise absorbed him.

My father kept testing him. "Uncle Gurton," he said, "this afternoon Jess and me have got a little fence mending to do along the back side of the far oatfield. Restring some barbwire, reset a few posts. How'd you like to go along and keep us company?"

There was the smile, sweet and friendly and utterly inscrutable.

My father rephrased the question. "I mean," he said, "would you be willing to go along with us, maybe lend a hand?"

Uncle Gurton nodded.

My father leaned back in his chair. "That's fine," he said. "We'll go catch us a smoke out on the porch here after lunch and then we'll go on over to the oatfield."

What distracted us? When we finished eating and tidied up a bit, Uncle Gurton was gone again. The folded napkin, the crossed knife and fork; and no Uncle Gurton.

"I'm going to get me a moving picture camera," my father said. "Because I want to find out how he does that. I believe that it's a truly rare gift that he has."

He pondered the matter all the way out to the fence line, the roll of barbwire hoisted on his shoulder and bouncing on the burlap-sack pad with every stride. I walked at his side, toting the awkward posthole diggers and the wire stretcher. "I put the question to him wrong," he said at last. "I didn't ask him was he actually going to go with us, but was he *willing* to go."

"What's the difference?" I said.

"He was willing to go, all right, but he was even more willing not to."

At the top of the high second hill of the pasture we turned to look back. There in the dusty road between the house and the first barn, as steady as a mailbox post, stood Uncle Gurton.

I dropped the posthole diggers with a loud clatter. When we looked again, the road was empty.

"No, a movie camera wouldn't capture it," my father said. "It would take some kind of invention that is beyond the capacity of present-day science."

*   *   *

We were resting from the fence work. We sat in the shade of a big red oak and watched the wind write long cursive sentences in the field of whitening oats.

"One question we don't need to ask," my father said. "Whether he sleeps with his beard inside or outside the covers. Stands to reason that a man who would tuck his beard down in his overalls will sleep with it under the covers."

"How long do you reckon it is?" It was the thousandth time I had asked that question.

"Before he got here, I would've guessed it was a foot and a half," he said. "And then when I saw him first, I'd've said two feet. But now the more I don't see it the longer it gets. I've been imagining it four or five feet easy."

"You really think it's all that long?"

"I've got to where I'll think anything when it comes to that beard."

"If it's that long he has to let it run down his britches leg," I said. "Which one you think, left or right?"

"Kind of a ticklish decision," he said. "Maybe he divides it up, half down one leg, half down the other."

"You reckon it's the same color all over?"

He gave me a level look. "Jess, for anything I know, it's green and purple polka-dotted under them overalls and he's got it braided into hangnooses. But I'll tell you what. I'm bound and determined to see that beard, every inch of it. I'll never sleep easy again till I do."

"How are you going to do that?"

"I'll let you know."

It was three days later, the hour before suppertime, when he revealed his grand and cunning design. He took a thumb-sized blue bottle out of his pocket. "You see this? This is our beard-catcher; this is going to turn the trick."

"What is it?"

"It's a sleeping draught I got from Doc McGreavy."

Doc McGreavy was our veterinarian, an old man who lived with his wife in a dark little house three miles from us, at the very end of the road where the mountainside pines took possession and human habitation left off.

"What are you going to do?"

"Slip it in his buttermilk. When he goes to bed he'll sleep as sound as a bear wintering in. Then we'll have us a look at that beard."

"You think it'll work?"

"Doc says it'll lay a horse down, he's put many a horse to sleep with it. I'll give Uncle Gurton just a little bit. We won't be hurting him any."

"You sure?"

He was impatient. "Sure I'm sure."

And so at supper my father kept close watch on Uncle Gurton's buttermilk. When he had drunk off the first glass, my father picked it up. "Here," he said, "let me get you some more, Uncle Gurton." He tipped me an evil wink and I knew he was going to drop the powders.

Uncle Gurton nodded and flashed the friendliest smile in his smile box, and when the buttermilk came he drained it in two swallows. My father looked so gleeful I was afraid he'd bust out laughing and spoil it all.

Then I was afraid he'd got hold of the wrong powders because nothing seemed to be happening. Uncle Gurton was as bright-eyed silent as ever and was forking into the stewed tomatoes with devastating effect. But in a few minutes I saw that his eyes were growing faraway cloudy and the lids were drooping.

"Have another piece of cornbread," my father suggested.

"No thank you," he said. "I've had an elegant sufficiency—"

But he didn't say on to *the superfluity* and we knew we had him. He rose from the table and stumbled through the kitchen and out the door, headed down the hall for the stairway. He didn't cross his knife and fork on the plate, and the checked napkin lay on the floor where he'd dropped it. My father retrieved it and laid it by his plate.

My grandmother followed his progress with curious eyes. "Uncle Gurton is right strange-acting. I wonder is he feeling poorly."

"Aw, he's okay," my father said. "He's just plumb tuckered from appearing and disappearing out of thin air all day."

We cleaned and stacked our dishes and then retired to the side porch where my father smoked his cigarette after meals.

"We going to see the beard now?" I asked.

"Better give him a little while, make sure he's sound asleep. Let's go out to the shed a minute."

In the woodshed he took a dusty kerosene lantern off a hook and shook it to hear if there was oil in the reservoir. He reached an old motheaten blue sweater off a nail and wiped the cobweb off the lamp. "We'll need this if we're going to be good and sneaky," he said. He brought the lamp and the sweater and we returned to the porch and he smoked two slow cigarettes and we watched the first stars pierce the western sky. The far hills went hazy blue and then purple-black.

"Let's go," he said, and we opened the forbidden door and tiptoed through the dark sun parlor. The souvenir teacups rattled on the glassed-in shelves. It was stale in here and dusty. I was afraid I'd sneeze and trumpet our crime to the world at large.

We entered into the dark stairway hall and stood for a moment to listen. My father struck a kitchen match with his thumbnail and lit the wick and let the shell down. The pale orange light made our shadows giant on the walls, and everything was strange in here in the hallway, all silent, and in the stairwell above in the hovering darkness. I felt a way I'd never felt before, like a thief or a detective. My breath was quick, the pulse tight in my temples.

We climbed the stairs one careful step at a time. Our shadows fell behind us and washed up on the far wall and the shadows of the banister posts spun like ghostly wheel spokes. My father held the lantern by his side in his left hand and I hid in his right-hand shadow, moving when he did.

We paused at the top of the stairs and he raised the lantern. The door to Uncle Gurton's room was at the end of the hall and we edged toward it. Every snap and squeak of the floor made me fearful; I was certain we'd be discovered. What could we say to Uncle Gurton or my grandmother when they found us? I realized, maybe for the first time, that my father wasn't always the safest protection in the world.

At that fateful door we stopped and held our breaths to listen. My father began to ease the door open, turning the knob slowly, slowly, until it ceased and the door swung open upon blackness. We heard the sound of heavy breathing and I felt relieved to know we hadn't poisoned the old man to death. My father had wrapped the wool sweater around the lantern and now he rolled it up from the bottom, showing a little light at a time.

We needn't have been so precisely stealthy. Uncle Gurton's mouth was open and, lying flat on his back, he uttered a gurgling half-snore. We could have dropped a wagonload of tin kettles on the floor and he wouldn't have stirred an ounce.

I was impressed by how Uncle Gurton lived. There were a few shirts on hangers in the open closets and one shirt hung on the back of a chair by the foot of the bed. In front of this chair his battered brogans sat, a sock dangling out of the top of each. And that was all I saw there. He led a simple existence.

My father handed me the lantern and we advanced to the edge of the bed. After giving me one significant and thrilling glance, he began to turn the sheet down from under the old man's chin. We were dismayed to discover that Uncle Gurton slept in his overalls. He wore no shirt; his naked freckled arms lay flat beside him, but the blue denim bib still hid what we had schemed so anxiously to disclose. My father rolled the sheet down to Uncle Gurton's waist, then leaned back from the bedside.

He gave me another look, this one of bewilderment and frustration. Little beads of sweat stood on his forehead. I shrugged. I was ready to leave, figuring Uncle Gurton was just one too many for us. He was a coon we couldn't tree.

But we'd come too far for my father to let it go. He reached and unhooked the gallus on the far side; then loosed the one nearer. Then he inched the bib down.

We were not disappointed; it was everything we had come to see. A creeklet of shining white lay over Uncle Gurton's skinny chest and gleamed in the lantern light like a drawer of silver spoons. It was light and dry and immaculately clean—a wonder because we'd never known Uncle Gurton to bathe. We'd never seen him do much but eat.

I thought the beard was marvelous, and I couldn't regret all our trouble and terror. It was like visiting a famous monument—Natural Bridge, Virginia, say; and I felt a different person now I'd seen it.

But the great question went begging. How long was it? We couldn't tell, and there didn't seem to be any way to find out unless we stripped him naked or tugged the beard to light by handfuls.

We stood gazing dejected until the beard began to move. It was a movement hard to distinguish. At first I thought it was flowing away to the foot of the bed like a brook, and then I thought it was rising like early mist over a pond. My father clutched my shoulder and I knew he saw this motion too.

Then suddenly it was out upon us, billow on billow of gleaming dry wavy silver beard, spilling out over the sheet and spreading over the bed like an overturned bucket of milk. It flowed over the foot of the bed and then down the sides, noiseless, hypnotic. There was no end to it.

I felt it stream over my shoe tops and round my ankles and it was all I could do to stifle a shriek. I dropped the lantern and my father bent and picked it up before it could set fire to the beard, to the house. We retreated, stepping backward quickly, but always facing the bed. We were afraid to turn our backs on that freed beard.

Now over Uncle Gurton's torso it began to rise into the air, mounding up dry and white and airy. It was like seeing a frosty stack of hay rising of its own volition out of the ground. Little streamers of beard detached from the mass and began to wave in the air like the antennae of butterflies. They searched around the tall flat headboard of the bed and went corkscrewing up the curtain drawstrings. In just a moment the beard had curled in and out, around and over, the chair in the middle of the floor like wisteria overtaking a trellis.

At last my father said something, speaking out loud. *My God*, was what he said.

"Let's please leave," I said. The flow of beard was up to my calves now and I was afraid it would start wrapping around my legs the way it had gone over the chair. Then what would happen?

"Go on," my father said. "I'm right behind you." Then he pointed and said *My God* again.

Over the bed the beard had climbed until it was like a fogbank, only more solid, and threatened to topple forward. But it was still sliding underneath in sheets off the bed like a small waterfall, and now out of that misty mass and down over the edge of the bed came a birchbark canoe with two painted Cherokee Indians paddling with smooth alacrity. Above them, out of the mist-bank of beard, flew a hawk pursued by a scattering of blackbirds. We heard a silvery distant singing and saw a provocative flashing and then a mermaid climbed out of the beard and positioned herself in the streaming-over straight chair. She did not seem to see my father and me, but gazed into some private distance and sang her bell-like song; the hair that fell over her shoulders, hiding her breasts, was the same color as Uncle Gurton's beard.

Behind the mermaid's singing all sorts of other sounds emerged, squeaks and squawks, chatterings, chitterings, muffled roars, howls, and thunderings: the background noises in a Tarzan movie. In the corner of the room was a sudden and terrific upheaval and a great mass of beard lifted to the height of the ceiling, then subsided to ominous silence. We glimpsed the movement of a huge indistinct bulk beneath the surface, moving stately-swift toward the far wall.

"What's that?" I whispered.

My father said *My God* once more and then murmured, "I believe to my soul it's a damn big white whale."

"I really think it's time to get out of here."

"I do believe you're absolutely right, Jess," he said. He pointed at three dark sharp triangles cutting through the surface. "Sharks in here too. Well, that settles that. We'd better go, I reckon."

He slipped the lantern bail up over his shoulder and dropped the old wool sweater. It floated for a moment on the surface of the silver hair and suddenly submerged. Something had snatched it under, I didn't want to know what.

We made our way to the door, lifting our feet high, and after a minute of straining together, managed to push the slowly closing door against the wall. The river of beard was already out into the upper hall, spreading both ways along the corridor. We stopped at the top of the stairs and my father unslung the lantern from his shoulder and held it up. The beard was flowing steadily down the steps, and the footing on the stairway looked plenty treacherous.

"What do you think?" I asked.

"I don't know. I don't trust it."

"I know what," I said. "Let's slide down the banister."

"Yeah, that's the ticket," he said. "I'll go first and hold the lantern for you. You can see your way down better."

"I'll go first."

"Stay right here and watch if I get down okay." He clenched the tin wire bail in his teeth. Then he straddled and lifted his feet and slid to the bottom pretty nifty. But he hit the newel post there hard and I knew if he hadn't had a mouthful of lantern bail I'd have heard some hair-singeing curses. He got off and stepped back, holding the lantern with one hand and rubbing his ass with the other. "Come on," he said, "you can make it just fine."

But as I was getting set to mount the banister, my left foot tangled in a wavelet of beard and I pitched forward. I was sure I was drowned or strangled, but my right hand on the banister held me up and I twisted over and got hold with my left hand and pulled myself up. Then I got on and slid down.

"I was worried about you for a second there," he said. "Come on, let's go."

"I was a little worried myself."

The beard was only shoe top deep down here and we went padding through it into the little sitting room, then through the kitchen hallway and out the back door.

In the yard stood a startling black apparition, but when my father held the lantern toward it, it was only my grandmother standing straight and narrow and angry in a wine-colored bathrobe. "What have you boys been doing?" she asked.

We said nothing and turned to look at the house. The upstairs windows were packed solid white with beard, and there were trailers coming out of the downstairs kitchen windows, and from the chimney a long flamelike banner of it reached toward the stars and swayed in the cold breeze.

"We just wanted to see Uncle Gurton's beard," I told her.

She clucked her tongue. "Well, do you think you've seen enough of it?"

My father looked at her and gave a deep and mournful sigh. "Yes ma'am," he said. "I've seen an elegant sufficiency. Any more—" He choked on a giggle like a bone in his throat. "Any more would be a superfluity."

Six

The Storytellers

*U*ncle Zeno came to visit us. Or did he?
Not even the bare fact of his visit is incontestable. He was a presence, all right; he told stories, endless stories, and these stories worked upon the fabric of our daily lives in such manner that we began to doubt our own outlines. Sometimes, walking in the country, one comes upon an abandoned flower garden overtaken by wild flowers. Is it still a garden? The natural and the artificial orders intermingle, and ready definition is lost.

But the man who effected such transformation seemed hardly to be among us. He was a slight, entirely unremarkable man given to wearing white shirts with frayed cuffs and collars. That is, in fact, how my memory characterizes him: a frayed cuff, a shred, a nibbled husk. If he had not spoken we might have taken no more notice of him than of one of the stray cats which made our barn a sojourn between wilderness and wilderness. His hair, his face and hands, I cannot recollect. He was a voice.

The voice too was unremarkable, except that it was inexhaustible. Dry, flat, almost without inflection, it delivered those stories with the mechanical precision of an ant toting a bit of leaf mold to its burrow. Yet Uncle Zeno had no discernible purpose in telling his stories, and there was little arrangement in the telling. He would begin a story at the beginning, in the middle, or at the end; or he would seize upon an odd detail and stretch into his stories in two or three directions at once. He rarely finished a story at one go; he would leave it suspended in midair like a gibbeted thief or let it falter to a halt like a stalled car blocking the road. And he took no interest in our reactions. If the story was funny our laughter made no more impression upon him than a distant butterfly; when we were downcast at a sad story, he did not seem to realize it. His attention was fixed elsewhere. My father and I got the impression that he was not remembering or inventing his stories, but repeating words whispered to him by another voice issuing from somewhere behind the high, fleecy clouds he loved to stare at.

That puts me in mind of . . .

These six flat monosyllables will be spoken at break of Judgment Day; they are the leisurely herald notes which signal that time has stopped, that human activity must suspend and every attention be bent toward discovering the other leisurely country words which follow. This is the power that beginnings have over us; we must find out what comes next and cannot pursue even the most urgent of our personal interests with any feeling of satisfaction until we do find out. The speaker of these words holds easy dominion.

That puts me in mind of—Uncle Zeno said—Lacey Joe Blackman. You know how proud some folks are of what they've got—he said— cars and fine houses and such. Some folks are proud of their wonderful hunting dogs, like Buford Rhodes was, but I ain't talking about him but about Lacey Joe Blackman. Lacey Joe was proud of a watch which come down to him from his daddy and Lacey Joe kept it on him for fifty years or better, and he couldn't say how long it had been in the family before his daddy. It was real old-fashioned, a big fat bib watch in a silver casing and been around so long the silver had wore thin on it like a dime. Even when he got to be seventy-five years old Lacey Joe was liable to tug his watch out and flip up the lid and give you the time of day, you didn't need to ask.

Lacey Joe had a well-known name as a hunter, maybe only Turkey George Palmer had killed more brutes, and Lacey Joe would go on a hunt anytime night or day—deer, bear, groundhog, you name it. Go a-hunting pissants I reckon if they was in season. They ain't much bear hunting in these parts anymore, I remember the last time Lacey Joe went.

Setback Williams had sold his big farm down on Beaverdam, as he was getting on in years, and him and Mary Sue had bought a little homestead that butted up against the Smoky National Park. No farming on it, Setback was past doing any heavy labor, but there was a little apple orchard in the back, maybe two dozen trees, and old Setback liked his apples and his apple trees.

But there was a troublesome bear ranging in those acres and he liked the apples and the apple trees powerful well too. You know how it is with a bear and the apple trees, gets all excited and he'll go to sharpening his claws like a cat with a settee. Go around and around a tree ripping at the bark and pretty soon he's girdled it and that tree is doomed to die.

Setback had done already lost two trees to this bear and he didn't know what to do. Can't shoot a bear anymore even if he's on your property unless you get permission from the Park Service and they won't hardly never give permission no matter what cussedness a bear has been up to. But Setback called anyhow over there to the Ranger Station I don't know how many times and kept deviling them and finally they were out to his place and allowed as how maybe he had a problem.

What they done was put up a fence, but the Park Service won't put you up no barbwire fence because it ain't what they call rusticlike, they don't want no tourist looking at a barbwire fence. They put up a heavy peel-log fence around the orchard about six foot high, ten times as much work as a good barbwire fence, and Setback took one look at it and declared, Boys, that ain't going to keep no bear off of my apple trees. And it wasn't two days later he went out and there was a bear setting in a tree, looking down like he owned that tree and the U.S. Park Service too. Setback raised a holler and the bear scuttled down and lickety-split into the forest right over the fence. Didn't make no more of that fence than you would a plate of peach cobbler.

So he called the Rangers again and they dawdled and cussed awhile and finally come over and built another peel-log fence, never seen anything like it. This one was fourteen foot high if it was an inch and strong as a fort. Kind of awesome to look at, think about the work them fellers had put into it. But Setback wasn't nothing only suspicious, and a week later he looks out and there was that same bear up in that same tree. Like the King of England on his throne all of gold. Setback ran out and hollered and the bear jumped down and run to the fence. When he got there he stretched up like a man reaching down a jug off a tall shelf and took hold of the middle log about seven foot high and leapt up and then he was over. It was plumb pretty to look at, Setback said, except he was so mad.

He was on the telephone in a jiffy and told them he was going to shoot that bear, National Park or no National Park, and they said No he wasn't. He told them a man has a right to protect his property, especially the apple trees, and also besides his wife was getting scared, that bear coming in on them all the time. That was where he was stretching it because Mary Sue never took fright of nothing, stouthearted she was. Finally they said they'd let him trap the bear as long as he used the trap they'd bring him, and he could hold it and they'd come and pick up the bear and carry it to the farthest-back part of the forest and it wouldn't wander out as far as his apple trees again. He suspicioned that wouldn't work neither, but he was willing to try anything.

The trap they brought him didn't have no teeth, smoothed off so it wouldn't hurt a bear's leg much, but it was awful big and heavy, Setback said he never seen one that big.

He pegged it in the ground out there amongst the trees. Used a locust stake must have been five foot long and a big old drag chain. Covered it over with leaves all proper.

Might be another week passed before Setback and Mary Sue heard the awfulest row and tearing around and uproar. It was the early hour of the morning, not what you call sunlight yet. Bothersome to be woke up like that, but when it come to Setback they must have caught the bear he hustled into his clothes and went out to have a look.

But there was nothing to see but some tore-up leaves and rassled-around dirt. Not one other blessed thing. That bear had pulled that five-foot stake plumb out of the ground. Hadn't left nothing, toted off the trap, the drag chain, and the locust stake, and gone over that fourteen-foot log fence. Hard to believe his eyes, Setback said.

He was back on the phone to the Rangers again, telling them what he was going to do and them saying Yessir right along. Because you couldn't leave the animal with the trap on his leg, him in pain like that. Then he called up me and five others and Lacey Joe Blackman who still kept his bear dogs and always had such a name for bear hunting. And we met over at his place it must have been about eight o'clock in the morning.

The dogs got the scent right in a hurry, all barking to beat Joshua, and we set off in a trot. We kept an eye on Lacey Joe, him going on eighty years of age, but he was hale and spry and after a little bit we figured he would wear us down and the dogs too. Didn't have far to go, though, maybe two miles and the bear was already treed.

An awful big tree too, sixty foot tall anyhow, and spindly at the top where he was at. He was right in the very tip-top, and the tree was bowed way over with him. If it wasn't a pine tree you'd think it might bust. And just enough wind to sway it, and the bear in it, that was some sight. We stood just a-looking for a long time.

Till Setback says, Well, Lacey Joe Blackman, I believe it's up to you to take the first shot. Him being the oldest, and us all thinking he was about half sand-blind and one of us would get the kill. I'll do her if that's what you want, he says, and steps out and raises up his rifle. Which we seen was an old thirty-aught-six must've belonged to Nimrod and didn't even have a front sight. We was all thinking, that bear ain't got no worries just yet, and he steps out and raised up his rifle and didn't take no aim and killed that bear stone dead. Bullet we found out later went right between the eyes.

The bear dropped plummet. Down about thirty foot and then jerked up again. That locust stake he'd been dragging got caught crossways in the fork of a big old limb and held him up there. The tree was bending way over. And the bear hung up like that went back and forth like a pend'lum on a grandfather clock. Back and forth, and back and forth. It was a sight made us all stand there quiet as pallbearers.

And so Lacey Joe Blackman, he pulls that silver-case watch of his out and opens it up. He squints at that bear swinging back and forth and he looks down at his watch, up at the bear, down at his watch. And he says, Boys, if this-here old watch of mine is still keeping right, that bear is swinging just . . . a mite . . . slow. . . .

"Just a mite slow?" My father frowned. "I don't get it. A bear is not hanging in a tree to be keeping time. What does he mean, a mite slow?"

But that was the end of the story, and the end too of Uncle Zeno's talk. He only told stories, he didn't answer questions. The voice he listened to, the voice beyond the world, gave him only stories to report; any other matter was irrelevant. Uncle Zeno turned to my father but his gaze was so abstracted that the chair my father sat in at the supper table might as well have been empty.

That was part of the trouble. Uncle Zeno lived in a different but contiguous sphere that touched our world only by means of a sort of metaphysical courtesy. So how was he able to tell stories? He seemed to absorb reality, events that took place among people, without having to be involved.

"Was Homer blind because he was a poet?" my father asked me next day. "Or was he a poet because he was blind?"

"I don't know what you mean."

"I'm thinking about Uncle Zeno," he said.

"Oh," I said.

"You remember I told you the story of the *Iliad?* Well, Homer couldn't have been a soldier, of course, because he was blind. That's how he came to know so much. If he'd been a soldier, he couldn't have told the story. If Uncle Zeno ever struck a lick of work, if he ever had any dealings with people at all, maybe he couldn't tell his stories."

I could recall vividly my father's retelling of the *Iliad*. He found a magazine photograph of Betty Grable and propped it on the mantelpiece by the gilt pendulum clock and said that Miss Grable was Helen of Troy and had been stolen away by a slick-hair drugstore cowboy named Paris. Were we going to stand for that? Hell no. We were going to round up a posse and sail the wine-dark seas and rescue her. He flung himself down on the sagging sofa to represent Achilles loafing in his tent, all in a sulk over the beautiful captive maiden Briseis. He winked at me. "These women can sure cause a lot of trouble." The account ended ten minutes later with my father dragging around the room a dusty sofa cushion which was the vanquished corpse of Hector.

His excitement enticed me to read the poem in a Victorian prose translation, and I found it less confusing than his redaction, its thrills ordered.

That was the trouble with my father's storytelling. He was unable to keep his hands off things. Stories passed through Uncle Zeno like the orange glow through an oil-lamp chimney, but my father must always be seizing objects and making them into swords, elephants, and magic millstones, and he loved to end his stories with quick, violent gestures intended to startle his audience. He startled us, all right, but never by the power of his stories, always by the sharpness of his violence.

He had grown jealous of Uncle Zeno's storytelling and decided he would tell a suppertime story involving a mysterious house and a haunted shotgun. But his brief tale was so perplexed that we couldn't follow it at all. We were, however, disagreeably shocked when the haunted shotgun fired, because he illustrated this detonation with a swift blow of his fist on the edge of the table which caused the insert prongs of the inner leaf to break off, catapulting a bowl of butter beans onto my father's shirtfront.

My mother and grandmother and I stared at him in consternation as he mumbled and began plucking beans from his lap, but Uncle Zeno, sitting directly across the table, took no notice, gazing past my father's downcast confusion into his portable Outer Space. "That puts me in mind of . . ." he began, and proceeded to tell of a haunted house of his knowledge, atop which the weather vane pointed crosswise to the wind, in which fires flamed up without human agency in the fireplaces, and the cellar resounded with a singing chorus of lost children. We turned with grateful relief from my father's predicament and were soon enrapt by Uncle Zeno's monotone narrative, which now began to include sealed doors that sweated blood, a bathtub that filled up with copperhead snakes from the faucet, a vanity mirror that gave back the images of the dead, a piano whose keys turned to fangs whenever "Roses of Picardy" was attempted. My father too became enthralled and sat motionless among his butter beans until Uncle Zeno concluded. His ending, if that is the correct term, was, "Anyhow—"

That jerked my father awake. "Anyhow?" he cried. "What kind

of climax is that? Did this Willie Hammer ever find the forbidden treasure or didn't he?"

But Uncle Zeno was not to speak again until possessed by another story, and he merely looked at my father with an expression of vacant serenity. My father gave up in disgust and began again to drop his lapful of beans into the bowl one at a time, plunk plunk plunk.

His jealousy grew. He was going to learn to tell stories that would shade Uncle Zeno's the way a mountain overtowers a hill of potatoes. He ransacked his memory, and he begged stories from the loafers down at Virgil Campbell's grocery store, and he began to delve into the volumes of fairy tales and folklore scattered about the house. He borrowed my book of Norse mythology and committed a good half of it to memory. All to no avail. My father was simply too entranced with mischief and effect, and the stories he managed to begin in leisurely fashion soon careered into wild gesticulation and ended with an unpleasant loud noise. "Wham!" he would shout. "I've gotcha!"

But he didn't have us, not in the way he wanted to, and he looked into our startled faces with an expression of expectancy quickly sagging to disappointment. "Well, maybe I left out some stuff," he would say, "but it's still a damn good story. Better than some I've heard lately."

Uncle Zeno said: That puts me in mind of Buford Rhodes and his coonhounds. Buford was a good old boy anyway you want and kind of crazy about raising coonhounds and was an awful smart hand at it. Lived out there in Sudie's Cove in a tin-roof shack with his wife and six younguns and must have been a good dozen dogs. All kinds of dogs, Walkers and Blue Ticks and Redbones and lots of old hounds with the breeding mixed in like juices in soup. One of them named Raymond you couldn't never figure out, must have been a cross between a bloodhound and a Shetland pony. Kids rode that dog all day like a pony, he was that good-natured.

But it was the dog called Elmer that Buford was most proudest of, though Elmer wasn't much bred either, just an old sooner dog. Still he was the brightest dog anybody ever heard tell of. Buford was selling his hides to Sears and Roebuck for a dollar apiece. He'd catch them coons by the score and skin them and tack their hides up to cure. Got

THE FRED CHAPPELL READER

so after a while there wasn't a inch of wall on Buford's house or milkshed not covered with coon hides. So Buford always kept an eye out for old scrap lumber and kept piling it underneath his house to cure them hides on.

That was where Elmer's smartness come in. That dog Elmer was so smart that if Buford showed him a piece of oak board or a joint of pine siding, he'd take off and tree a coon which when the hide was skinned off and stretched would exactly fill out that length of wood. That was what made him so smart and valuable and caused Buford to think the world of him, rather have Elmer than the jewels of Sheba and the wisdom of Solomon.

But then they got into trouble one Tuesday about the middle of September. Elmer happened to wander inside the house while Buford was off somewhere and his wife had left the door open by mistake. Buford wouldn't never of let him in, ruins a good dog to lay around in a dwelling house. But Elmer wandered in this time and seen Buford's wife there ironing the laundry. He took one look at that ironing board and just lit out down the road as fast as he could go and heading west as far as you could point. Buford said later on he didn't know whether Elmer already had a coon that big somewhere he knew about or it just sparked his ambitions.

Whatever, Elmer had set hisself a journey and when Buford got home and heard what happened he took off after him. Dog like Elmer, that smart, can't afford to lose a dog like that. So Buford was traveling west now, trying to track him down, asking questions of anybody he came to, and for a long time he could tell where he'd been. Folks will remember a dog that's got something on its mind. But then the houses got scarcer and not many people to ask, and Buford was getting worried—

My father nodded sagely. "And I'll bet you're not going to tell us anymore. You're just going to leave it hanging there, aren't you, Uncle Zeno?"

Uncle Zeno gazed into his placid abyss.

My father leaned over the table toward him. "Well, I've got your number now. I don't know any Willie Hammer or Lacey Joe Blackman or Setback Williams or those other people you've been telling us about.

But it happens that I do know Buford Rhodes. Hired him one time to do some house painting. I know right where he lives, down there on Iron Duff, and I can drive right to his house. That's what I'm going to do, Uncle Zeno, and check your story out."

This possibility made no impression upon the old man. Why should it? We didn't care whether the story was true and Uncle Zeno didn't care about anything. But the idea that he could actually track down Buford Rhodes and talk to him seemed to give my father gleeful satisfaction.

It occurred to me that my father was preoccupied with the problem of Homer's blindness. Homer had lived in history and told his stories about real soldiers and described in grisly detail battles he could not have seen. But, like Uncle Zeno, Homer had left no trace in the world. Patient scholars were forced to debate whether the poet had actually ever lived. My father was not much interested in getting the details straight about coonhounds; he wanted to see if Buford Rhodes had ever met and talked to Uncle Zeno. The old man was living with us, eating our food and sleeping in the upstairs bedroom, but he was hardly present except as a voice. Like Homer, he was leaving no trace.

And so my father, in the disinterested pursuit of knowledge, was going to interview Buford Rhodes, the actual subject of one of Uncle Zeno's stories. Schliemann, unearthing the first traces of a Trojan site, must have felt something of the excitement my father felt.

My grandmother muttered that it seemed pure foolishness to her, traipsing down to Iron Duff for no good reason, but my father, leaning back in his chair and blowing a happy smoke ring, said, "That's just exactly where I'm headed first thing tomorrow morning."

Actually, he didn't get underway until midmorning, some five hours after rosy-fingered Dawn had streaked the sky with orient pearl and gold. I realize now that he had other necessary errands to perform, but of course he wouldn't give my grandmother the satisfaction of knowing he was doing something useful. He preferred for her to think he was off lollygagging after Uncle Zeno's story.

His absence left me with idle time and, since it was a lovely August morning and not yet sweltering, I decided to forgo reading and wander the hills of the farm until lunchtime. A favorite place for lonesome cowboy games was in a glade behind one of the farther hills of the pasture. An awesome storm had blown over a great oak tree there and I loved to clamber among the fallen branches and look at the jagged tears wrought in the trunk and see what new animal life had come to inhabit.

But when I arrived I found the tree already occupied. Uncle Zeno was sitting perched in an easy place on a big limb. His back was toward me and over his left shoulder protruded the end of the gnarly staff he sometimes used for walking. Never had his figure seemed so insignificant, his shoulders slumped and his head craned forward away from me so that I knew he was once again looking deep into his private void.

He was talking too, out here in the grassy knolls under the soft blue sky where there was not a living soul he could have been aware of to listen to him. I crept up as noiselessly as I could. I wanted to hear what he told himself in private, thinking that maybe the old man was revealing secrets of the earth he alone was privy to.

Here is what Uncle Zeno was saying:—but finally he was lost and he had to admit it. Hated it like poison, he'd never been lost in the woods before and he was hoping none of his buddies would ever hear about it, Buford Rhodes lost in the woods. He had give up on his good dog Elmer and he thought he'd be lucky if he could get back alive hisself. But right then he heard a baying he knew was Elmer and he begun to take heart. Happened though that he was down in a box cove with steep flanks on both sides and an anxious-looking rock-face cliff at the upper end. The sun was a-going down and the moon not coming up yet. And it echoed in there till he couldn't say where the baying was coming from. He started climbing, but by the time he was halfway up the mountainside Elmer lost the scent and hushed. Or maybe Elmer wasn't following no scent, just lost and worrying about it like Buford, but anyhow he shut up and not another sound out of him.

So now Buford was loster than before. He was going to swaller his pride and call for help, but he seen they wasn't no use, he wasn't close to nothing but mossy rocks and sawbriars. He set down there on a rotten pine log and he was feeling about as bad as a man can feel.

Didn't know how long he set there. It got cooler and the moon come up, turning the green leaves as white as snow, and it was as quiet as the bottom of a well. And then he seen somebody, or he thought he seen somebody, the moonlight deceiving. It was a Indian woman. She come at him smiling with her arms down at her sides, and he was awful happy to see her except when he tried to talk he found out she didn't speak nothing but Cherokee, which he didn't speak none of, not a speck. They tried to talk together but soon had to give it up as a bad job. She finally just reached out and took his hand and led him off with her, deeper and deeper into the woods, Buford feeling worse and worse. He was content he'd go with her wherever she wanted, he couldn't do no better.

It was a cave she lived in that she took him to and wasn't a bad cave, nice and dry, with some crevices for smoke to get out, and there was stuff to eat, berries and roots and herbs and squirrel meat. Wasn't the most comfortable place in the world but must have suited old Buford all right because he lived there in that cave with that Indian woman two year or more. Turned out not such a bad life after all, because Cherokee women don't like for their menfolks to do no work, and Buford just laid around and let her wait on him hand and foot. Ever once in a while at night he'd hear that fine hound dog Elmer start up baying somewhere off in the dark and Buford would get up and go scouring around the ridges, thrashing through blackberry briars and laurel hells. But then after a few months he didn't even bother to get up and look, didn't see much point in it anymore.

Went along like that two whole years, till one morning in spring he happened to wake up just when the woman was stepping over him to poke up the fire for breakfast and he took notice of a part of her he hadn't looked at close before and he wasn't what you call pleasured. Looked like a big ole crow had swallered a redbird there. He shut his eyes, and laying there with his eyes shut it come to him how awful ugly this woman was. He never thought about that before and now it started to bother him right much. After breakfast he sneaked away to a clearing where he had a favorite sandstone rock that he liked to sit on and think.

He set there and thought till he was pure gloomy. Here he was, lost in the woods and living with the ugliest woman creation ever made and he couldn't even talk to her. Well, he had plumb sunk into being a forsaken savage, all there was to it. Seemed to him there wasn't no hope for Buford Rhodes in this world anymore, he was lost to the sight of God and mankind. It was a black study he was in, but just right then when he was thinking his darkest thoughts, he heard a rustling over in the bushes—

At this point Uncle Zeno ceased. The story impulse had died in him, or maybe this story flew from this roosting-place across the world to another storyteller, Chinese or Tibetan, who sat waiting for inspiration. Uncle Zeno's audience—the white clouds and fallen tree, the blue daylight and sweet green grass—listened patiently, but the story was over for now. Yet here in the glade was the best setting for his stories, and I felt that I understood him in a way I hadn't before. He was some necessary part of nature we hadn't recognized, seeing him only as a windy old man. But he was more than that, and different. What was he doing now that the story had ended in him? Why, he was sitting on the tree, giving audience to the history of its regal life and calamitous downfall, a story I couldn't hear. I would have to wait until Uncle Zeno was possessed by the impulse to repeat it to us.

I hoped he would never find out I'd been there to overhear him. I turned away quietly and went back to the house and made a lunch of bread and cheese and buttermilk from the icebox. I ate alone. My mother and grandmother had walked over to pay their respects to a shut-in friend, my father was down in Iron Duff playing archeologist-detective, and Uncle Zeno was in the pasture telling stories to the mica rocks and horse nettles.

After lunch I took a book of science out to the porch to read, learning that Sirius was the most luminous star in our heavens and was thought in old times to bring on madness in people and fits of poetic frenzy. I didn't care to read fiction; I'd had enough stories for a while.

My father returned about four o'clock and came to the porch to sit and chat with me. He looked haggard.

"What did you find out?" I asked him.

He rubbed the back of his neck and looked at the pine ceiling. His tone was mournful, puzzling. "Nothing," he said.

"Couldn't you find Buford Rhodes?"

"Couldn't find him, couldn't find anyone who knew him, couldn't find the least trace of him."

"Maybe you went to the wrong house. You might have forgot where he lived."

"Drove right to his front door, where he used to live. House was empty and run-down. Windows broken, doors off the hinges. Holes in the roof. Looked like nobody had lived in it for twenty years."

"Did you ask the neighbors?"

"They never heard of him. Walked down to Hipps' grocery, and nobody there ever heard of him either."

"You must have got the wrong place. Somebody would know him."

"I drove down to ask Virgil Campbell. He knows everybody that was ever in the country. At first he thought he sort of did remember a Buford Rhodes, but the more he thought about it the less he could remember."

"Maybe you got the name mixed up," I said. "Maybe the man you hired to paint had a name like that but different."

"I know Buford Rhodes," he said. "Know him anywhere. Uncle Zeno described him to a T." He snapped his fingers. "I'm glad you mentioned that. I recall I paid Buford with a check. I'll have a record in my check stubs. Paid him seventy-seven dollars exactly. Wasn't but three years ago, I'll go look that up." He rose and walked to the door.

"Where did you eat dinner?" I asked.

He gave me another harried look. "I haven't been hungry lately, Jess," he said and went in to pore through his records.

But this research, too, proved disappointing. He found a check stub for the amount of seventy-seven dollars, and its date would fit into the period of the house painting, but he had failed to list whom he'd written the check to.

When the women returned from their errand of charity he asked my mother about it. "See, here's the check stub," he said, waving it under her chin. "You remember Buford Rhodes, don't you?"

She backed away from the flapping paper. "We had three or four painters working about that time. I don't remember any of them."

"You'd remember Buford, though. Had the kind of beard that gives you a blue face. Always cracking jokes and talking about his hound dogs. Always had a drink or two under his belt no matter what time of day it was."

"That describes every house painter I ever met," she said.

"You ought to remember him, though. Uncle Zeno has got him down exactly. He was some kind of character."

"All I ever meet are characters," she said. "I don't believe that normal human beings show up in this part of the country."

Exasperated, he flung down the booklet of stubs and stamped on it. "How could anybody not remember Buford Rhodes?" he shouted.

"Calm down," she said. "It's not important."

But it was important to my father, and his shouting indicated the intensity of his feelings. I almost spoke up then. I almost told him that the last I'd heard Buford Rhodes was lost in the forest and living in a cave with an ugly Indian woman. I realized, however, that I had better not speak; this information would only cause more confusion.

I was assailed by a wild thought and a goosy sensation. What if Buford Rhodes had ceased to exist upon the earth *because* Uncle Zeno told stories about him? I had entertained odd fancies since overhearing the old man this morning. What if Uncle Zeno's stories so thoroughly absorbed the characters he spoke of that they took leave of the everyday world and just went off to inhabit his narratives? Everything connected with them would disappear, they would leave no more sign among us than a hawk's shadow leaves in the snow he flies above. The only place you could find Achilles these days was in the *Iliad*. Had he ever existed otherwise? Had any of those heroes left evidence behind?

I cried out, "What about Agamemnon?"

My father gave me a peculiar look. "What about him?"

"Didn't you tell me they found his death mask? Didn't you say it was a mask made out of gold and they put it in a museum?"

He answered in a vexed tone. "That's the name they give it, but they can't really prove it belonged to Agamemnon."

"Well, it ain't his," I said. "They've got the wrong man." Because now I was convinced of my notion. Homer and Uncle Zeno did not merely describe the world, they used it up. My father said that one reason Homer was reckoned such a top-notch poet was that you couldn't tell where the world left off and the *Iliad* began. . . . No wonder you couldn't tell.

My theory was wild enough to amuse my father; it was just the sort of mental play-pretty he liked to entertain himself with. But I decided not to tell him about it. He was earnestly troubled by the problem of Buford Rhodes and obviously in no mood for metaphysical speculations in the philosophy of narrative. I could read that much on his face. Then he said, "Come on, Jess. We'd better get the milking chores done."

I rose and followed him willingly. I looked forward to getting the evening chores out of the way and sitting down to supper. I was hungry, with nothing but bread and cheese for lunch, and I was eager to hear Uncle Zeno tell another story. I felt like a scientist now that I'd hit upon my brilliant idea, and I wanted to watch the process at work.

Sure enough, as soon as my grandmother had got through one of her painfully detailed supper prayers, Uncle Zeno began talking, without excuse or preamble, as always.

—and out of the bushes there, Uncle Zeno said, come a gang of six kids, looked to be eight, ten years old, and dressed in washed overalls and pinafores. They kept staring at Buford and he begun to think for the first time how he might look awful strange, dirty and bearded from living in the woods so long. But he kept hisself soft-talking and gentled them kids along until they agreed to lead him back to civilization. These here kids belonged to the Sunday school class of a hard-shell Baptist church back up that way and they'd run into Buford while they was hunting Easter eggs. Turned out he hadn't been as lost as he thought he was, no more than two miles from a little old settlement there, and the congregation had come up here for an Easter picnic. It was just that Buford's mind had been occupied, thinking about that Indian woman and worrying about his good dog Elmer that he hadn't heard bay in more than a year now. Buford just hadn't been taking no proper interest, that was all.

So the kids led him out of the woods down to the settlement and he got started on the right road a-going home. He was dreading to arrive, figured his place must have gone to rack and ruin while he was gone and his wife and children probably in the poorhouse a long time ago. He didn't know what he was going to tell folks and whether anybody would believe him or not.

But when he came in sight of his house, well, he was mighty surprised. The place was all fixed up and just a-shining, better than he ever done for it. There was a spanking new tin roof, and them old coon hides had been tore down from everywhere and the house was painted up nice and white and there was a new Ford car setting by the edge of the yard.

So he reckoned his wife had took up with another man while he was gone and they wouldn't have no use for him around there no more. But he went on up anyhow and rapped at the door. It took his wife a minute or two to recognize him but when she did she was happy fit to bust and hugged him tight and his kids run out in fine new clothes and jumped around, it was the best welcome-home you'd ever want to see.

After they settled down a little bit he got to questioning her. How come you're doing so good, with the house all fixed up and a Ford car in the front yard? And she said it was Elmer. Elmer had found his way finally back home a year ago and seen how the family was doing poorly, so he went out and got hisself a job. Buford said that was awful good news, he was proud of that dog, and what kind of job did he have. She said Elmer got him a job teaching over at the high school, arithmetic and natural science, and drawed a pretty good salary considering he didn't have no experience to speak of. And Buford said a dog that smart didn't need no experience, what he was going to do was get Elmer to show him how to smell the ground and track coon and they'd switch off, Buford would be the dog and Elmer could be the man because maybe that's the way it ought to have been in the first place—

"All right," my father said. "I'm glad to hear some more of that story." He kept rubbing the back of his neck. "But what I want to know is, Where does Buford live now? I've been looking for him all day and can't turn up hide nor hair. Speak, Uncle Zeno. Tell us where Buford Rhodes has got to."

But of course there was no answer. Uncle Zeno looked calmly into his vast inane, contemplating the nothingness that hung between stories. He probably wasn't aware that my father spoke to him. He lifted a slow spoonful of creamed corn to his mouth.

My father leaned back, his sensibilities sorely bruised. "No, you're not going to tell us. I know that. I wish I hadn't asked." He heaved a sorrowful sigh and looked down at his lap. "Well, now I'll tell a story," he said. "It's my turn." He leaned forward again, placing the palms of both hands flat on the table, and stared intently into Uncle Zeno's face. He looked like a bobcat ready to spring. "Once upon a time there was a pretty good old boy who never did anybody any harm. I won't say his name, but he was a pretty good old boy. It happened that he fell in love with a fine mountain girl and married into her family and they lived there in the hills and he worked the farm for them. That was all right, everything was just fine. Except that in his family there was an army of strange uncles who were always dropping by, and they were an interesting bunch, most of them. This good old boy—let's just call him Joe—got along okay with these strange visitors. He liked to talk to them and find out about them. He was interested, you know, in what makes people tick. . . . But there was this one weird uncle—we'll call him Uncle Z.—he couldn't figure out to save his life. Truly he couldn't. And it began to prey on his mind until he couldn't make himself think about anything but this Uncle Z. and how queer he was. . . . I'm sorry to tell you, Uncle Zeno, that I don't know the end of this story. But I think that this good old boy started worrying so much that he finally just went crazy and they carried him off to the funny farm in a strait-jacket." He gazed morosely into the plate of food he had hardly touched. "But like I say, I don't really know the end of the story."

My grandmother reprimanded him, in a tone gentler than usual. "Now, Joe Robert, you don't want to be unmannerly."

He stood up. "No, of course I don't," he said. "If you-all will excuse me, I think I'll go out on the porch and have a cigarette. Maybe clear my head. I don't know what's the matter with me." He fumbled a moment with the knob, then stepped through the door and closed it.

My mother and grandmother looked at each other, and my grandmother said, "Joe Robert's acting kind of peculiar, seems to me. He ain't ailing, is he?"

"He doesn't seem to be ill," my mother said.

"It's Uncle Zeno's stories," I told them. "They get him all worked up. He wants to do something, but he don't know what to do."

"They're only stories," my mother said. "No one is supposed to do anything *about* them."

I wanted to reply, but I couldn't very well tell my mother that she didn't understand my father, that he always had to be doing things, changing the order of the world in some way, causing anarchy when he could or simple disorder if he couldn't do any better.

"Just seems peculiar to me," my grandmother said, "somebody getting all worked up about a few harmless windies." She looked at our visitor with a fond expression. "Why, Uncle Zeno wouldn't harm a fly."

The three of us gazed at him, an inoffensive old man who hardly seemed to occupy the chair he sat in. He seemed ignorant of our regard, and it was clear that what she said was true. He wouldn't harm a fly.

Then his drifting abstraction formed into a voice and he began to speak again. "That puts me in mind of," Uncle Zeno said, "Cousin Annie Barbara Sorrells that lived down toward the mouth of Ember Cove. Had a right nice farm there, about a hundred acres or so, but didn't have nobody to work it, her oldest son dying when he was eight and her other boy, Luden, gone off to California on a motorcycle. But she had her a son-in-law, Joe Robert his name was, and he was a pretty fair hand at farming, she didn't have no complaints to speak of, except that Joe Robert was ever the sort to dream up mischief. . . . Well, it happened one time that her boy Luden had sent Annie Barbara a present, which was a box of fancy candies he'd bought in St. Louis—"

This was too much.

Uncle Zeno was telling a story about us. I knew what he was going to say; I'd lived through those events, after all. His story focused on my father, and that fact disturbed me. My father didn't seem to get along too well with Uncle Zeno as it was, and perhaps he wouldn't be happy to hear that he was now a character in the old man's stories.

I jumped up without even saying Excuse me and went out to the porch. It was as dark as the dreams of a sleeping bear; rain clouds blocked off the starlight and there was only a dim light coming through the dining room drapes. My father was not smoking, but just sitting in a chair shoved flat against the wall of the house.

"Are you here?" I asked.

He paused a long time before answering. "Yeah, I'm right here, Jess."

"Are you feeling okay?"

Another pause, and I could hear Uncle Zeno's mumble drone through the door.

"I'm all right, I guess. Maybe I'm catching a cold. I've been feeling kind of lightheaded. Feel a little weak all over, like I'd lost a lot of weight in a hurry."

"Come on back in and have a piece of apple pie. Maybe it'll make you feel better."

He sat motionless. There was no wind sound, no sound at all except for the low, indistinct mutter of Uncle Zeno's story.

"Apple pie," he said softly. "Well, that's not bad medicine." He didn't move for a while yet. Finally he rose slowly from the chair. But when he took a step he walked directly into darkest shadow and I couldn't see him at all and at that moment Uncle Zeno's story concluded and all the night went silent.

Seven

The Maker of One Coffin

When Uncle Runkin came to visit he brought his coffin and slept in it, laying it across a couple of sawhorses we carried into the upstairs bedroom. But I could never imagine him sleeping. If I crept in at midnight, wouldn't I find him with his bony hands crossed on his chest and his weird eyes staring, staring into the dark? I didn't care to find out; I was frightened of him, and maybe my father was too at first, though he'd never let on. He treated Uncle Runkin lightly, loosely, banteringly, but surely he was bemused by our odd visitor who must have spent the majority of his years preparing to lie forever in his cold grave.

We often hosted wandering aunts and uncles, all on my mother's side, and they intrigued my father endlessly and he was always glad when one of them showed up to break the monotony of a mountain farm life. Especially glad for Uncle Runkin; he had a reputation which preceded him as twilight precedes darkness, and we were not to be disappointed.

He was slight, about five foot eight, and frail looking because he carried no fat and not much muscle. "All skin and bones"; Uncle Runkin was the only person I ever met who fit the description. The bones in his hands and head were starkly prominent beneath parchment-colored skin as tight on him as a surgeon's glove. His head was entirely hairless, and not pink but yellowish. His beaky nose drooped sharply. His eyes were black as coffee grounds and large and sunken in his skull and surrounded by large circles as dark as the great pupils. These eyes looked quite past you, and Uncle Runkin made you feel he saw you without looking; and that was another unsettling sensation.

His motions were grave and deliberate and I never saw him smile. His skin was dry as wood shavings and when he touched any surface there was a slight raspy whisper, like a rat stirring in a leaf pile. Or like a copperhead snake skinning over the edge of a table. Or like a black silk pall sliding off a coffin. I never got used to it; each time I heard it was like looking down into a bottomless well.

I never got used to anything about Uncle Runkin. It wasn't that he tried to discomfit us; I think indeed that he tried not to. But whenever I was in his presence I felt like I was standing with my back to a cliff and couldn't remember where the edge was.

The same uneasiness affected my father, but he hid it pretty well. He teased Uncle Runkin and joked, but it was easier to be sociable with the midnight wind. His jollity went out into the void and no laughter returned. And we were not certain we wanted to hear the kind of laughter that might return; it wouldn't be what you call comradely.

Still my father kept on, gibing and bantering ever more recklessly, his gestures growing ever more strained and awkward. Waving his hands about at the supper table, he tipped over the salt shaker.

Uncle Runkin gave the spilled salt a solemn glance and uttered his most characteristic sentence. "That means that somebody is going to die."

"What? Spilling the salt?" my father said. His desperation was obvious now; he snatched up the shaker and began sprinkling salt all over the green tablecloth. "Fine and dandy," he said. "We'll do away with the whole German army."

"It never is somebody you'd want to die," Uncle Runkin said.

My father gave him a wild look. "Well then, who? Who's going to kick the bucket?"

But he didn't answer; his voice box had silted up again with crematory ashes.

Uncle Runkin found lots of signs for coming death. A black cat crossing in front of you, the new moon seen over your left shoulder, a flock of crows taking flight on your left-hand side, one crow flying against the full moon, sunset reflected in a window of a deserted house, an owl hooting just at dark, a ladder leaning oddly in a corner, the timbers of our old house creaking at night: he knew all these as indications that somebody was going to die, and the way he said *somebody* made you want to reconsider your plans for airplane trips and bear hunts.

My father scoffed. "It would take Noah's flood and the Black Plague to carry off as many victims as he's seen signs for." But I could hear in his voice a shaky bravado.

Uncle Runkin's silly prognostications affected us all, but me— eleven years old—most. I found myself calculating where the new moon was in relation to my left shoulder, and I wouldn't look at the full moon because who knows when the crows might fly? And I began to operate mighty gingerly with the salt shaker. . . . He affected us in other ways as well. I'd never remembered my dreams before, but after Uncle Runkin arrived I couldn't forget them, much as I wanted to.

I thought he would say No, but when I asked to look at his coffin he seemed pleased I was interested. Coffin or no, it was an impressive piece of handiwork, though a monstrous huge thing, as we'd discovered in wrestling it up the stairs. Eight feet long and four feet wide, it was much too large for Uncle Runkin, and he must have lain lonesome in it like a single pearl in a jewel case. The corners were so tightly mitered and joined that I could hardly find the seams with my fingertip. The wood, he told me proudly, came from an enormous black walnut, and the bottom and sides of the coffin were cut from whole slabs. There was a triple molding as elegant as ever you could see at the base of the coffin, and an elaborate cornice at the top with a crisp dentate design. The lid was to be attached with no fewer than eight brass butterfly hinges, and he looked forward to its completion.

It wasn't complete because the lid wasn't finished. Handsome as the box was, it wasn't a patch on what the lid was going to be. The unfinished lid sat on the long worktable out in our woodshed, covered with two blankets of heavy green felt and the weathered old tarpaulin he secured the coffin in when he hauled it in his open pickup truck.

He peeled the wrappings back so I could have a look at his hand carving. Along the edges ran a garland of grapes and apples, roses and lilies, intricately intertwined and delicately incised, down to the leaf veins. In the center was a largish death's-head, and it was interesting how much this skull resembled a self-portrait, only having an ominous hole where he had a beaky nose. Otherwise it was Uncle Runkin to the life. Or death. There was a blank entablature below on which he was going to engrave a motto, as soon as he could decide whether it was to be *Come lovely Angel* or *Sweet Death comes to Soothe* or *How glorious our Final Rest.* Or a phrase that destiny hadn't yet thrown in his way. He was still searching out mottoes. Beneath the blank he'd carved what he called a sleeping lamb, which looked to me like it would dream no more forever. Not quite completed, though the great work had taken him twenty-five years so far. The lid alone cost him seven years, but easy to see it was going to be worth it, rubbed and oiled and varnished and polished until it was as smooth as the inside of an eggshell and dark and satiny.

My father suggested that the motto ought to be *Death, where you been all my life?* But he too admired the coffin and complimented Uncle Runkin. Later he changed his motto suggestion to *Opus 1* because, he said, making that coffin was the sole lick of work the old man had ever struck.

We talked about Uncle Runkin sleeping in his coffin, and we tried to imagine what that would be like. I thought it would be scary but exciting, and I didn't think it would be stuffy in there, but as cool and dark as eternity. I imagined that after you got accustomed to it, you would have peaceful winter dreams and hear voices from beyond the grave.

"What do you think the dead folks are saying?" my father asked.

"I don't know," I said. "I can't imagine that part. What do you think they're saying?"

"I don't know," he said. "But every time I imagine lying in the grave my ass starts to itch."

I wanted to try it. I wanted to sneak into Uncle Runkin's room some hour when he was away and lie down in the coffin and see what I thought about it.

"I wouldn't do it," my father said. "I'm no great believer in signs, but there can't be much good luck in lying around in coffins all the time. I don't much look forward to death myself; it's like knowing you have to go to the dentist."

"I don't think it's like that. I think it would be real quiet." (I made noise in the company of dentists.)

"Well, if quiet is what you desire, you're going to have a riproaring time after you're gone. The graveyard eats up noise like Uncle Runkin eats his supper."

I knew what he meant. Uncle Runkin cleaned his plate so thoroughly that it was surprising to see the design still on it, the little blue Chinese bridge with the lumpy tree and long necked bird. Everything was gone, including the chicken bones, and not even a smear of grease remained. But I never saw him eat, never use a knife or fork or spoon. The plate would be steaming full before him and then the first time I noticed, it would be spotless, and Uncle Runkin wouldn't be chewing but looking at me, or rather beyond me, with unearthly speculation.

"I know what we can do," my father said. "We can steal that coffin."

"What in the world for?"

"Don't you have any curiosity? I'd just like to see what the old man would do when he couldn't find it."

I had mixed feelings about the idea. It was all right to look at the coffin and even to touch it, but when I thought about stealing it, it took a different shape in my mind. Became bigger and blacker and heavier and deeper. I felt we would be tampering with dark forces we knew nothing about, distressing some of the bones of the universe. "I'm not so sure," I said.

"Why not?"

"Too heavy," I said. "The three of us like to never wallered it up the stairs. Two of us wouldn't get it to budge an inch."

"I guess you're right," he said. "I'll think of something, though."

"Maybe you oughtn't to. Maybe Uncle Runkin is one uncle we ought to leave plumb alone."

"Yeah?" He gave me an amused look. "That old man hasn't got you buffaloed, has he, Jess?"

"He's a different kind of uncle from what we're used to."

"Don't worry," he said. "I just now figured out what we'll do."
But when he chuckled softly, I had to feel uneasy.

I don't know what supernatural spell my father was able to exercise
over my mother. It had to be one of nearly unthinkable power for her
to aid him. Probably there was nothing more sinister about it than the
fact that she too had a sense of mischief, usually dormant, which he
was able to arouse on urgent and suitable occasions.

And this occasion was, for my father, an urgent one. The family
had undergone gradual but significant changes since Uncle Runkin
came. There was less casual talk, less casual touching, and less laughter.
We were not absorbed in gloom, all day thinking morose thoughts, but
we had surely darkened and a quiet seriousness began to prevail over us.

It was just the sort of atmosphere my father couldn't abide, and
he may well have felt that he was struggling for psychic survival.

Whatever means he used, they were successful. My mother brought
home one Friday afternoon the skeleton from the health classroom at
her high school. I know she didn't steal it; she wouldn't stray so far
from the straight and narrow. Probably she just asked to borrow it for
the weekend. "I don't know why," she would say. "My husband imagines he's got some use for it."

So we had a skeleton, and a lovely object it was too, properly wired
together, all white and smooth, and its teeth intact. I was curious about
where the high school had got hold of it, and my father said it was a
former fullback on the Black Bears who had run the wrong way in a
game and scored a safety for the Hiawassee Catamounts. "Huh," I said.
He then told me it was a woman's skeleton, an axe murderess who had
chopped up her mother-in-law, her husband, her eleven children, and
the family poodle and then, realizing what she'd done, turned the axe
on herself and committed suicide.

"I don't believe that one, either," I said.

"That's the difference between us and Uncle Runkin," my father
said. "He would believe that story in a jiffy. And you know what he'd
say?"

"He'd say, *In the midst of life we are in death.*"

"That's it exactly," my father said.

He had no very elaborate plans for the skeleton. He was merely going to lay it out in the coffin where Uncle Runkin slept. "That ought to give him something to think about." Then, as an afterthought, he decided to remove from the fuse box the fuse which controlled the upstairs bedroom lights so that Uncle Runkin would have to clump up in the dark to meet his unannounced bedfellow. "I'll tell him something's wrong with the wiring on that side, but that I'm working to fix it. Meanwhile, take every candle in the house and hide them."

This was one of my father's less complicated ruses, and the details were easily arranged. We ate our Saturday night supper in what had become our habitual bemused silence, and Uncle Runkin practiced his usual legerdemain, disappearing every scrap and nitlet of food from his plate. He took his whispery-silent leave of us to go up to his room. My father had already lied about the wiring, and we made an ostentatious search for the candles that I'd stuck away in a feed bin in the barn.

We couldn't hear our uncle, but we sat at the table without talking and felt his progress through the house on our skins. We knew when he opened the hallway door upon darkness and went touching his way down the hall. We knew when he mounted the first step of the stairs and grasped the banister in his dry hand. We could feel every step upward he took and the pause he made at the top in order to get his bearings in pitch darkness. We felt how he inched down the upstairs hall and opened the door to his room and slid in the dark over to the edge of the coffin and began to disrobe.

But after that we knew nothing. Our heightened senses and imaginations failed us at this critical point, and we couldn't say what would happen, but sat hushed, waiting.

We sat a long time in silence. We looked at one another. I don't know what we expected from Uncle Runkin, a bloodcurdling scream, or a crash and shouted curses, or maybe the sight of the old man fleeing naked and bony-shanked out into the October night. Now it seems unlikely that we would have been treated to any of these edifying spectacles; the old man's attachment to the Black Deliverer was more profound than we could fathom, and there was nothing about death that was going to surprise him.

We sat a long time.

Finally my mother said, "Well, Joe Robert, this is one of your little pranks that didn't work out."

He sighed. "I didn't care what. As long as *something* happened, I would have felt better."

"And after all the trouble I went to to get that pile of bones," she said. "You boys go right up to his room in the morning and get that skeleton. I'll be in hot water if I don't get it back to school first thing Monday."

"Yes ma'am," my father said. His voice rang hollow with defeat.

Next morning Uncle Runkin came down to breakfast, all polished and ready for church. He'd tracked down some minor sect of strange Baptists yon side of Turkey Knob, with a preacher who gave sermons on the utter and awful and final power of death over life, and this little cinder block church drew Uncle Runkin the way a rosebush draws Japanese beetles.

During breakfast my father made a couple of feeble attempts. "Did you sleep sound last night, Uncle Runkin?"

He answered Yes in that voice that was like a breath of dying desert wind.

"No trouble with bedbugs—or anything like that?"

He told us No in that same sepulchral voice and my father bent to his plate and took a mouthful of gloomy eggs.

After Uncle Runkin departed for church, my father pushed his chair back from the table and said, "Well, Jess, let's go up and rescue our skeleton." He looked as cheerless as a bloodhound.

Then it got worse because the skeleton was not there in the coffin. Nor anywhere else in the room. Nor in any other upstairs room, not in the bedroom, nor in the storage room. And in no downstairs room. We searched and searched again every nook and corner of every room of the house, and there was no trace of it, not the least little finger bone.

"What in the world could he have done with it?" my father asked.

"I don't know," I said.

He looked at me with a glazed expression. "Look here, Jess, you don't think he ate it, do you?"

"I don't think so," I said, but I had to remember all the squirrel and rabbit and chicken and pork chop bones that were never left on Uncle Runkin's plate.

"I believe he did. I believe the old man ate that skeleton."

"Is that what you're going to tell Mama? So she can tell them at the high school that our uncle ate the skeleton from the health class?"

"I purely don't know," he said.

That was what she asked when she heard. "What am I going to tell them at the high school?"

"I think you'd better lie to them," my father said.

"Lie?" she wailed. "I can't lie to them. I don't know how."

"Nothing to it," he said. "We'll stay up late tonight and I'll teach you."

That afternoon Uncle Runkin made me go with him to look at a graveyard he had discovered. It was an old one, disused and grown up in weeds and sawbriars. Thick mosses and peeling lichen flooded the stones and some of the markers were just thin slabs of shale with the names and rude designs etched in with farm tools, cold chisels and axe bits and the like.

"What did we come here to see?" I asked.

He looked at me in surprise. "Why—everything," he said, and he swept the air to indicate the universe that interested him, the graves and weeds and briars and, I suppose, the grubs and worms munching away underground. "Don't you feel at peace here? Ain't it a shame people have let this beautiful spot go to ruin? Wouldn't this be an awful nice place if you wanted to build a house close by?"

Maybe it was beautiful, but for me it was a graveyard, and I wasn't ready to invest in that brand of real estate. Chill bumps rose on my forearms. "I don't know," I said.

"Let's go around and look at some of the stones," he said, and his voice was dreamy and intimate.

So that's what we did, with Uncle Runkin pausing before each hacked stone in rapt contemplation. He would stare at the stone, read off the inscription silently, stare at it some more, and then wag his head solemnly and pace up the hill to the next. He clasped his hands behind his back like a philosopher.

I wandered with him, feeling bored and dreary.

"Keep an eye out for any good motto I might could put on my coffin lid," he said.

"Well, how about this one here? *Gone but not forgotten.*"

"Look at the name on it," he said. "*Rodney Walsh.* You ever hear of Rodney Walsh?"

"No," I said, "but they buried him in 1910."

"You know any Walshes in this county?"

"No."

"Well, see, he's gone all right, but he's plumb forgotten too. You see that motto a lot, but it just ain't going to do. People don't remember you after you're dead. That's why you have to do it all yourself beforehand."

"How about this one?" I asked. "*She done what she could.*"

"Well, but don't that make it clear she done a right piddling job?"

"Here's one. A *brighter day awaits.*"

He snorted. "What they mean by that? Next Thursday?"

We meandered on among the markers, and each time I would read off the writing he would be right there with a telling critique. I finally had to admire his expertise; he'd pondered on it until he was a connoisseur. And I admired the way he never got depressed by it; in fact, the more gravestones we looked at, the mournfuller the inscriptions became, the better he liked it; and if it was anybody but Uncle Runkin I would have said he was bright and cheerful.

"*Gone to a better place,*" I read.

"How do they know that?" he said. "I bet this William Jennings done a whole lot of meanousness they just never heard about."

"*Grave, where is thy victory?*"

"Suppose this here where we're standing is the battlefield where death and the living had a fight. Who would you say won?"

"*Gone to lighten the dark.*"

"Now that one might have possibilities," he said. "I'll be thinking about that one." He took a little notebook and carpenter's pencil out of his overalls bib and wrote it down. I thought he must have a hefty backlog of that kind of writing by now, and I was pretty sure it was his favorite reading matter, along with Job and the obituary page and the Lamentations of Jeremiah.

The motto he took the brightest shine to was, *In Life's full Prime Is Death's own Time*; he was positively gleeful when we struck on it and wrote it down and underscored it twice. "There's a lot of wisdom on these stones, if people would just take the opportunity," he said, and he was happy enough to be willing to leave for home, which didn't exactly break my heart.

At home he headed directly into the small room off the kitchen hallway where the coal stove and radio were. There was a radio program on Sunday afternoons called "Meditations" that he never missed. It was all slow organ music playing behind a fellow who read passages out of a book of dejected thoughts and it was just the thing to brace Uncle Runkin up.

I went upstairs, hoping against hope that I might locate the lost skeleton, though I knew my father had searched the place over again while Uncle Runkin and I were out. I went into his room and poked about quietly, but found no trace of Mr. Bones. I was attracted at this moment by his imposing coffin there on the sawhorses and went over to it and laid my cheek against its smooth side to enjoy the cool and polish of the wood. I pulled up a chair and looked over into it, and now it seemed inviting, sweet, and peaceful. I'd never been much interested in coffins before, but prolonged exposure to Uncle Runkin had begun to change my outlook, and I thought it might not be such a bad thing to be dead, not having to get up on frosty mornings to milk crazy old cows, not having to learn multiplication or the capital of North Dakota, not having to eat cold fried grits when my grandmother felt trifling.

I tugged off my high-topped shoes and stepped over into the coffin and lay down. It was marvelous at first. The black satin plush was not cool, as I'd thought, but warm and soft; he'd cushioned it with cotton batting. The black plush sides rose up steep in my vision, giving me a view of the ceiling in a box, and the perspective caused me to feel I was sinking down and down, that the world outside was receding. I waited for the sensation to pass but it never did; the ceiling, the room, the house, the farm, the sky kept pulling back from my sight, floating away to some unreachable forever. And I began to think of the coffin as being like the bathysphere of William Beebe, except that the coffin sank not through water but through solid substance, would drop through the floor of the room, down through the foundations of the house, and dive into the earth; and I would be able to look upon creatures never seen or imagined before, animals made of glowing mineral that swam the veins of the world and traced their mysterious lives to mysterious destinies.

Then I fell asleep.

As soon as my eyes closed I was assaulted by a barrage of fleeting dream images. A sky full of stars arranged itself in an unreadable tomb-stone motto. A great silent galleon with black silk sails lifted off an ebony ocean and floated into the sky, straight into the full moon. A flock of crows flew through a snowstorm, then changed into a rain of blood and fell, staining the snowy ground scarlet. A sinister monk opened the orange-lit door in a mountain and stepped out; he was dressed in a loose black robe and made arcane gestures with his bony hands, causing a spiky crop of skeletons to rise out of the ground and giggle.

But none of these visions was frightening; they were comforting, and I began to know that death was the Meadow of Vision, where dream was wrested from the marrow of stars.

One vision, though, was not comforting but disturbing. That was the sight of Death himself. In my dream I was standing in a narrow doorway, which had no building to belong to, in the middle of a barren plain. Nothing was before or behind me but blank wind. His pinched, intense face appeared suddenly out of the air, his sunken eyes burning dementedly, and he recognized me there in my constricting doorway and reached out his paw of lightning and caressed my cheek. I jerked and quivered from the shock of his touch, and yelled an awful yell, a soul-shaking screech.

Death yelled too and leapt back away from me, and it was obvious that he also had been frightened. Death and I had met face to face and scared the pee out of each other. And then it was obvious that I wasn't asleep and dreaming of Death and a doorway; instead, I was awake in Uncle Runkin's coffin and the old man, not expecting to find me there, had cried out in surprise. What he cried was *Yipes!*, just like Dagwood in the funny paper.

Yipes! That's the only time in my life I heard anyone say that word.

Then I heard Uncle Runkin rush out of the room and fly down the stairs. I sat up slowly, groggy from sleep and my harsh awakening, and took my time clambering out of the coffin and finding my shoes and putting them on in the dusk-dim room. From downstairs in the kitchen came the ruckus sound of heated conversation, and it was a sure thing that Uncle Runkin had not enjoyed finding me asleep in his coffin and was down there stirring up the family against me.

I sat in the straight chair and stared at the floor. I knew I was in for some kind of punishment, but I didn't care. I was dazed. After all, I had been out to visit the afterlife and had found it an entrancing place, and so a few licks with a hickory switch held no terror for me, and a month of Saturdays without cowboy movies not much disappointment. If death was as entertaining as it had been there in the promise of the coffin, I could always hang myself and have forever a free show that was better than any cowboy movie.

The noise downstairs went on and on, and I sat there and looked at my shoes until the noise stopped and I heard my father and Uncle Runkin coming up the stairs. When they entered the room my father switched on the light and all the strange thoughts that had been bemusing my mind flew away like a flock of birds at a gunshot.

"Jess," my father said, "Uncle Runkin has decided he can't stay with us any longer. He's got some pressing business in hand and needs to move on."

"That so?" I said, and I looked at Uncle Runkin but he wouldn't look back. He went over to his coffin and smoothed out the plush where I had been lying and inspected all over the wood for damage.

"Yes, he says he's afraid he'll have to be leaving," my father said. "So if you wouldn't mind giving us a hand with the coffin."

"Not at all," I said. "Be glad to."

It was much less a chore to get the coffin down the stairs and out of the house than it had been to get it upstairs. We slid it onto the truckbed and Uncle Runkin went to the shed and got the lid and placed it carefully over the box. We left him there, blanketing his treasure and roping it down tight. We went in and sat at the kitchen table, and my father poured coffee for himself and my mother.

In a few minutes the old man came in. My father stood up and they shook hands. Then he turned to my mother and offered her a slow, dry half-bow. He gave me one soulful burning glance and then stepped out and closed the door and was gone. Didn't utter a syllable. We heard the truck start up.

My father sat down and sipped the coffee. He blinked his eyes. "Whew," he said. "A *load off my mind.* I never knew what that sentence meant till right this minute."

My mother and I nodded. The old brick house felt lighter around our shoulders now that coffin was out of it.

"I have to admit I feel better too," she said.

My father yawned and stretched. "I don't know about you-all," he said, "but Uncle Runkin kind of took it out of me. I think I'll mosey on to bed, no matter how early it is."

That sounded good to me too, even though I'd already had a nice nap not so long ago. I went into my room and read a Hardy Boys for a while, then turned out the light. I was hoping that I would have more of those interesting dreams I'd had in the coffin. But I didn't. I slept lightly, peacefully, dreamlessly.

Until about six o'clock in the morning.

Then I was awakened abruptly again by the sound of someone yelling. This time it was a piercing shriek, a real true bloodcurdler, and it took a moment for me to realize that it was my mother who had screamed, out in the kitchen. I slipped into my pants and ran shoeless, shirtless, to the noise.

My father had just got there before me, rumpled and unbuttoned. "What in the world?" he asked.

She couldn't speak. She leaned white-faced against the doorway of the alcove and pointed a trembling finger.

There, sitting in the open icebox on a plate garnished with lettuce, was a skull. Two chrysanthemums glowed red in its eye sockets. A dead corn snake dangled out of its pearly teeth.

My mother cowered in my father's embrace. "I was just getting milk for our *oatmeal*," she said.

"I can see how it would give you a turn," he said. "I wonder what he did with the rest of it?"

We came to find out that Uncle Runkin had dismantled the skeleton and hid the pieces everywhere around the house. When you went looking for a Mason jar rubber or a length of string you would turn up a toe bone or a metacarpal. There are 206 bones in the adult human body and Uncle Runkin found 3,034 hiding places for them. Just the other day—twenty years afterward—I found in an old tackle box a kneecap. It brought back tender memories.

Ten

Bright Star of a Summer Evening

To the best of my knowledge, my grandmother made but one mild joke in her life and it went out over the radio.

It was broadcast on radio because she had accompanied Aunt Samantha Barefoot to the station for an interview. Aunt Sam was quite a famous person in our mountains, a prize fiddler and banjo player. She and my grandmother were cousins and had been close friends since they were children; so they must have been about the same age. Aunt Sam, though, looked much younger. Her terracotta hair was wild and frazzly, and two blue silk bows perched in it like butterflies on a tile roof. Her freckled face was scarcely wrinkled; her lively blue eyes shone with bright feeling and easy mischief. I got the impression that she was as full of mischief as my father, but that it was more acceptable in her because . . . Well, because whatever she did was acceptable.

Yet for all her mischief and adventurous talk and strange show business clothing, she was demure and straightforward. All the things that had happened to her in the many years of traveling her music had never touched her central innocence. Whatever she did and said was as natural to her as dignity to a cat, and beneath her noisy ways lay a deep reserve of dignity not a bit catlike.

When she came to stay with us for a while, she got out of her long sky-blue Cadillac wearing a calf-length denim cowgirl skirt and a red bandanna blouse and cowgirl boots, elaborately tooled. I made up my mind to take a slow tour of those boots when I got a chance. She tripped up the porch steps like a courting-age girl and wrapped my grandmother in a bosomy embrace. "Oh, look at you, Annie Barbara," she cried. "You haven't aged a minute in seven years. It makes me feel like something a possum has pissed on and buried."

My grandmother returned her hug and murmured endearments, her eyes closed.

Then she went round to each of us. My mother, she declared, looked like a movie star and had a fine reputation as a schoolteacher. She told my father that he would be mighty handsome if he wasn't so mean and trifling. She said it was grand that I read so many books; someday I would be a scholar of high renown. "Oh, it makes me so proud to see all of you that I'm just weeping," she said.

It was true. Tears welled from her blue eyes and streaked her freckled mannish face.

"Just let me get my Kleenex out of the car," she said, and tripped down the steps.

"For God's sake, don't let her get in the car," my father said. "She might drive off and leave us."

But she didn't. She searched in a huge leather bag and took out a handful of tissue and wiped her eyes and loudly, frankly, blew her nose. She came back to the porch, carrying the bag by its shoulder strap like a man fetching a bucket of water. "I'm going to sit down right here in a rocking chair," she said. "Seeing you-all look so fine has made me too excited."

We pulled the rocker up and she sat. Then we made a scurrying effort to find out if there was anything in the world she wanted: coffee, lemonade, tea, breakfast, dinner, or supper. If we had possessed a casket of jewels we would have poured them at her feet. I listened in amazement as my father offered to get a cushion.

"Joe Robert," she said, "my old ass is so tough I can't feel the good of a cushion."

Oh, I liked her immensely. She had already said out loud in front of everybody two words my mother didn't want me to think to myself in a closet. No one paid the slightest mind. I ran through the list of words I was forbidden to say—there must have been a dozen—and hoped she'd light on every one of them before she left. At the rate she was going, it wouldn't take ten minutes.

"Now tell us what-all you've been doing, Sam," my grandmother said.

"I came to find out about you," she said. "You don't want to hear about me."

"We don't?" my father said. "Well, why do you think we paid you to come?"

She giggled, and winked at my mother. "Didn't I say, *mean and trifling?* I bet he keeps you on your toes."

"I'm more interested in keeping her on her back," my father said.

That was a misplayed note and drew brief scalding glances from my mother and grandmother. But the remark delighted Aunt Sam and she laughed deeply and slapped her knees. Then she burst into tears again. "That would be just like what my Dundy might say," she said. "Lord, how I miss him." She dredged up another clutch of Kleenex and scoured her broad face.

I found out later from my father that Dundy had been her husband. He was a comic for the country music shows, prancing on stage in baggy plaid trousers and a famous beat-up hat. His opening line was, *The news is dismal in Limber Junction,* and his best routine was where he confused a veterinary who had delivered a foal with a doctor who was delivering his wife's first baby. He had begun in show business as an old-fashioned claw hammer banjo player and, when that style went out of fashion, had started telling the ancient cornball jokes country music fans liked to hear. ("Why didn't he tell new jokes?" I asked.— "If it's new, how would you know it was funny?" my father said. "Nobody's laughed at it yet.") It is the ordinary fate of comics to make everyone merry but themselves, and "Neighbor Dundy," as he was called, was a deeply sad man whose melancholy resulted in suicide.

This was but one of the misfortunes that darkened Aunt Sam's life. When she was seventeen years old and in the middle of her first road tour her father and mother and younger sister had perished in the fire that razed the old homestead in Cherokee County. Her youngest brother had lived on two years in agony before the mercy of his death.

The older brother, formerly a brakeman, was paralyzed from a railroad accident. Her grandmother had died when Aunt Sam was a little girl, but her grandfather, at age seventy, had been shot in a boundary line dispute.

"And look how strong she's stood up under all that," my father said. "She knows how to live with her feelings. When she wants to cry, she just cries right in front of everybody and goes on with her business. When she wants to laugh, she doesn't hold back an inch."

Mostly she wanted to laugh and I noticed that after a day or so she began to hang close to my father, waiting for him to drop an observation or pull a rusty that would send her into purest gales. This was something of a strain on him because my father didn't think of himself as a funny man but rather as the earnest purveyor of unwelcome home truths. When his humor lost its sardonic edge, it was likely to become weakly silly. He was willing, however, to try to entertain Aunt Sam, and mostly failed. Then she realized what was happening and withdrew a little and was rewarded with the uncommon spectacle of my father's ordinary behavior.

Which now consisted in great part of trying to tease Aunt Sam into playing music for us on her fiddle or guitar or banjo. "I don't believe you've got it anymore," he said. "You've lost the touch. You've been deceiving those dumb hicks at the fairgrounds and the square dances."

She was adamant. "I made a solemn vow to myself," she said, "that I wouldn't play the first chord while I was here unless Cousin Annie Barbara joined in with me."

So then it was up to my grandmother and this was a startling revelation to me. "I didn't know she could play any music," I said.

"Oh but she can," Aunt Sam said. "When we were girls she could play circles around me."

"I didn't know that. I never heard her play nothing."

"She made a solemn vow too," Aunt Sam said. "A long time ago. But I wish you could have been there, Jess, a long time ago. She was so bright and handsome and talented in the music. I used to simply worship her. . . . But of course you weren't thought of yet."

"He never was thought of," my father said. "He's just a by-product of the automotive age."

"Well, let's get her to play some, then," I said. "I want to hear it."

"You'll have a hard row uphill to persuade her," she said. "I've been trying for forty years and more."

"Why won't she play?"

"I'd better let her tell you. I'm not sure I understand it."

But she wouldn't tell me. My grandmother pursed her lips and shook her head. "It was a promise I made and I ain't to go back on it," she said.

"What kind of promise?"

"It was a personal promise," she said, and that's all she would say.

I had to go to my mother for enlightenment and she told me it was an old grudge my grandmother had always kept against her father. This was another hard revelation, that my grandmother had had a father. How was it possible for anyone ever to be older than she was? I had a sudden vision of my family lined up in a single file that stretched backward in time to Noah, each of them with an older and more Sorrells-like face. It was an image not inspiring in the least.

"Why was she mad at her daddy?" I asked.

"He stopped her from meeting the Queen of England," she said.

"How was she going to do that?"

"When she was fourteen she was already playing in the band for the best square dance troupe in the mountains. The dancers were invited to a festival in Scotland and they were to dance before the queen and then be presented to her. It meant a lot to Mama. It meant a lot to everybody, taking our music and dance across the ocean for the queen to enjoy. Her heart was just set on it. I've heard Aunt Minnie Lou tell about your grandmother practicing her curtsy in front of a mirror. For hours and hours."

"And her daddy wouldn't let her go?"

"Your great-grandfather Purgason was a stern old man with strict ideas," she said. "He was afraid that she'd spend the rest of her life in music and dancing."

"What's wrong with that?" I asked. I tried to picture my grandmother singing in front of audiences, dressed up like Aunt Sam and peppering her pious sentences with some nifty cuss words, but I soon gave up on that job, light-years beyond the limits of my faculties.

"I don't know that there's anything wrong with it," my mother said. "But people had different notions in those days. My grandfather was old-timey religious. He thought the music and celebrity would be bad for your grandmother's character, that she would turn out to be a shallow and thoughtless person." She made a little squirrel-like noise of exasperation. "Can you imagine anybody thinking that about your grandmother?"

"No ma'am," I said, and I couldn't. In the recent hours my imagination had blown all its fuses. "Couldn't she go without his permission?"

"Oh, she'd never do that. She'd never do anything without her father's blessing. Aunt Samantha took her place in the band."

"Aunt Sam has met the Queen of England?"

"The way I heard it was that Mama swallowed her disappointment and took pains to coach Aunt Sam in the music, showed her how to play some of the difficult passages and so forth. You'd think there would have been bad feelings between the girls about it, but there never was." She paused to look out the kitchen window where a robin scavenged the circle of bare ground around the chopblock. "Don't you think your grandmother must have been a brave young girl?"

"What was she like, the Queen of England? What did she say?"

"You'll have to ask Aunt Samantha about that," my mother said.

"I'm going to," I said.

"Be sure and ask her when your grandmother is someplace else," she said.

But there was no need for that, as I learned from Aunt Sam. When she had returned from the festival in Scotland, she told my grandmother all about it many times in microscopic detail.

"What was she like, the Queen of England?"

"She was nice," she said, "an awful nice lady."

"How big was her crown?"

"She wasn't wearing a crown. She had on a white garden party hat with silk flowers and white gloves on her hands."

"How did people know she was the queen, if she wasn't wearing a crown?"

"Oh, it was easy to tell she was the queen," she said. "Nobody ever made a mistake about that."

"What did she say to you?"

"She said, *Thank you for coming.*"

"What else?"

"That was all she said."

"What did you say?"

"I didn't say anything. I just curtsied. Your grandmother showed me how to do that. We practiced it till my knees buckled."

"Didn't she invite you to come over to the palace for supper?"

Aunt Sam smiled. "No. I think maybe she wanted to and then it slipped her mind. There was a big crowd of us, it would have been a hard lot to feed."

"I'd like to meet her," I said. "I'd give anything to meet the Queen of England."

"Maybe you will someday," she said. "I hear she takes a keen interest in scholars of high renown. You keep on reading your books."

It seemed a plausible idea. The Queen of England had to be a busy person without much time to read. My plan would be to read the longest and most difficult book in the world, the book that nobody else ever read, and then go and tell her what was in it. She'd be glad to have that information.

"I guess you'll never forget about meeting the queen," I said.

"There's a lot of reasons I never will," she said.

These interrogations of the grown-ups had to take place over a period of four or five days because the house had become a restless and confusing place. Word had got abroad that Aunt Sam was visiting us and her local fame brought in a steady stream of visitors, more people than I'd seen in one place since my grandfather's funeral. And the telephone jingled incessantly, as if the tribe of Uncle Luden's girlfriends had rediscovered our number. No one seemed upset by all this confusion, not even my father. In fact, we took a fine pride because Aunt Sam had come to stay with us, as it was well known that she had many important friends in fancy places and could drop in for a visit on anyone she'd mind to.

She showed a nice patience with all these people who were mostly strangers. Some of them she had known from years gone by and she greeted them with effusive warmth. Others laid claim to some tenuous obscure connection and she never denied them, though she didn't pretend to remember. "Law, honey," she would say, "I hope you'll forgive me, but I just can't recall. My old memory has got as weak as butterfly farts."

Of course, everyone asked her to play a good old tune or two, but she turned them down without hurting their feelings. If they persisted, she explained that she had made a personal promise having to do with her cousin Annie Barbara, and they had to be satisfied with that. It was obvious to anyone that Aunt Sam wasn't a deceiving person, she didn't waste her time trashing folks.

A lot of people came because they had heard her on the Grand Old Opry radio show which came out of Nashville, Tennessee. That was a show I'd never heard, the one radio program my grandmother forbade us to tune in. I'd never thought before why she wouldn't allow it, but now it was plain that the music stirred memories in her and fancies about what might have been and perhaps the old resentment toward her father. She wanted to keep her mind concentrated on running the farm and on Jesus, and, until Aunt Sam had showed up, she had quietly succeeded. Now, though, you might see her hanging back from the circle of admirers around her cousin, gazing with a mild but wistful speculation.

Who can fathom the motives of others? People in this world will do anything, for reasons you couldn't trace in an eternity of trying. But young as I was, it seemed to me that I did understand a little of what Aunt Sam was up to. Her friendship with my grandmother was close and warm, but she felt there was a flaw in it, a hairline fracture no one else would notice but which remained a tender spot between the two of them. Aunt Sam had determined to mend that fracture, to seal the friendship whole again, and she had decided that the act which signified completion would be for my grandmother to play music once more. It was a symbolic gesture, no more than that but no less too, and important to Aunt Sam.

I imagined that I began to understand a little. She was wealthy and famous, but Aunt Sam was lonesome too. She missed having a family. This realization made me think of my family and though it didn't entirely reconcile me to the irksome fact, I began to feel somewhat mollified. And I thought that if it was in the cards that I had to have a family, I wanted Aunt Samantha Barefoot included.

One of the telephone calls had been from a radio station in Asheville. They wanted Aunt Sam to come to the studio for an interview, and she agreed to do it if she could bring a few friends. "Would you like to see a radio broadcast?" she asked.

"Yes," I said.

So then we were all in her big Cadillac, dressed in our Sunday best, riding to station WWNC. "Wonderful Western North Carolina," the announcers added, after giving the call letters, and of course my father always transformed the letters to different phrases: *Wildest Werewolves in North Carolina*, *Woolly Worm Night Crawlers*, and so forth.

At the station they gave us a short tour, showing us banks of exotic knobs and dials and switches, and a wall of photographs of famous people who had visited: Uncle Dave Macon, Little Jimmy Dickens, A.P. Carter, Woody Guthrie, and platoon of others I'd never heard of. The proud young man showed us a blank space in the wall and said, "Here's where we'll put Miz Barefoot's picture." She was to be inserted between the Blue Sky Boys and Henry Wallace.

Then he led us into a room with two rows of folding chairs. We were to sit here and watch through the big soundproof window. Aunt Sam said that my grandmother was to be interviewed also and asked if they would need a voice check. My grandmother said that they wouldn't need a voice check, whatever in creation that was, because she didn't intend to talk on the radio.

There followed a long and predictable argument which Aunt Sam finally won. She told my grandmother that she was about to go on tour with a new group, the Briar Rose Ramblers, and they desired all the

publicity they could get. She wanted her cousin to say a few words for
the sake of local appeal; she didn't want people thinking she was some
Brooklyn musician who had learned everything she knew from records.
It was a matter of good business, she said, and that sentence was the
clincher. My grandmother was proud of her business acumen. Didn't
she always get the best prices going every Saturday for her ten pounds
of butter and three dozen eggs?

It was quite exciting and I suffered only one punishing disappointment. The interviewer was an announcer named Reed Bascom, a short
bald pudgy man with mushy hands. From his radio voice I'd pictured
him as looking something like Johnny Weismuller, only more sophisticated. Worse than that, he patted me on the head.

We sat in the chairs and watched the interview through the window
and heard it from a small loudspeaker overhead. It mostly went off very
well. My grandmother marched to the microphone with the same tight-
lipped grittiness she might evince for a leg amputation and when she
was introduced to the radio audience, said, *Hello, folks* distinctly.

Almost all the questions were asked of Aunt Sam, and my grandmother's main task was to stand by the microphone without passing
out. When Aunt Sam explained that she was in these parts to visit her
kinfolks, especially to visit her cousin Annie Barbara Sorrells, Mr.
Bascom turned to her and asked a bland question or two. She answered
succinctly and firmly.

Then he asked what sort of musical instrument she performed on
and she replied, "Oh, I just play second fiddle to Cousin Sam."

That was her joke, the only one I ever heard her make. No one
laughed or so much as chuckled, not even my father. We were stunned.
I have an image of the three of us sitting in the little room with our
mouths gaped open like coal scuttles, but surely this picture is a later
emendation. We were actually too shocked to open our mouths.

"Now that's a promise, Annie B.," Aunt Sam crowed. "I'm going
to hold you to that!"

Mr. Bascom appeared confused by this exchange and turned again
to Aunt Sam to conclude the interview. It finished up pretty smooth
except for one awkward moment when he said that some people claimed
country music was getting too commercial, too far away from its old-

time folk roots, and Aunt Sam replied that some people didn't know cow shit from cake batter.

The remaining remarks were hastily spoken and Mr. Bascom gave a signal to the engineer and the ON THE AIR sign went dark and they came into our little room. There was some busy leave-taking, Aunt Sam signed a publicity photo she had brought, and we went away.

Driving slowly home, Aunt Sam hummed a song. Her happiness shone in her like candlelight and she said once more, "I take your words as a promise, Annie Barbara, and I'm holding you to it."

My grandmother looked out at the green and yellow fields sliding beside us like a cool river and said nothing. We knew, three of us knew, that her first joke had been her last.

But if Aunt Sam considered it a promise, then so it was, and my grandmother would gnaw live rattlesnakes sooner than break a promise. The evening before she was to leave we all gathered in that sacrosanct corner of the house, the musty sun parlor. My grandmother hadn't touched a string instrument in nearly fifty years, but she agreed to accompany Aunt Sam on the piano. The piano was in disastrous condition since no one in our house played anymore. The keys were chipped and broken, the strings green and rusty, and the notes that were not out of tune were mostly ciphers.

Nevertheless the bargain had been sealed, and my grandmother sat on the wobbly stool while Aunt Sam stood beside her with her fiddle and struck up "Come All You Fair and Tender Ladies." It sounded very strange, and not entirely beautiful. They played two choruses and then Aunt Sam sang.

> *"Come all you fair and tender ladies,*
> *Take warning how you court young men,*
> *For they are like a bright star of a summer evening,*
> *They first appear and then they're gone."*

Her singing transfigured the music entirely. She had a dark contralto that sounded like it had mellowed in an oak barrel for slow decades, a voice as rich as damask soaked in burgundy wine. The song began to take on strength and shape. In the middle of a chorus Aunt Sam stopped singing and fiddling and all the music was my grandmother's harmony chords with so many notes missing. She played on, hesitant but unfaltering, and those wistful broken chords sounded like the harmony that must lie beneath all the music ever heard or thought of— tremulous, melancholy, constant. It was a music you might hear down in the autumn grass on a cold hillside. Then Aunt Sam joined in again and the song finished out with a lingering sweetness.

We were silent for a long space.

Then came the rottenest moment. My father said, "Well then, if that's the song you choose, I'm going to get Jess to sing. I want to hear 'The Green Laurel.' That's got a verse in it I'm partial to."

I fought against the suggestion like a wild dog, but it was no use. Nothing would do but for me to stand there in the middle of the floor and sing. I did it. Staring down at the scraped and battered toes of my shoes didn't help much, but it was less embarrassing than to look up and see Aunt Sam and my grandmother holding hands like schoolgirls and listening to me in seraphic rapture.

I made sure to include the verse my father wanted to hear:

> "I have often wondered why women love men,
> But more times I've wondered how men can love them;
> They're men's ruination and sudden downfall,
> And they cause men to labor behind the stone wall."

My face burned like a comet; I mumbled and choked. I couldn't sing then and I can't sing now. If I could sing—sing, I mean, so that another human being could bear to hear me—I wouldn't sit scribbling this story of long-ago time.

Helen

*I*t seemed that there were four of us in a hunting cabin high on a mountain near the Tennessee border, Uncle Luden, Johnson Gibbs, my father, and me. And it seemed that it began to snow the second day we were there; in the late afternoon little bitter papery flakes came down in nervous spirals. It wasn't supposed to amount to much, but when we woke early the third morning there was well over a foot of the fluffy stuff, driven in scallops by a bluff wind. We decided to wait our deer hunting until the weather improved.

But it kept on snowing.

We amused ourselves with poker and setback and eating. The others drank a little whiskey, but I was too young. We didn't worry, but by that evening had started to feel a little cabin-bound. Our manners grew gentler; four of us in close quarters might prove a tedious business.

That night we stayed awake late, swapping lies and jokes about hunting, cars, sports. The others pulled a little more steadily at the whiskey, and a cozy lassitude suffused their talk and there were long passages of silence.

I began to feel a little as a stranger among them. They knew different things than I did. It seemed that they were willing to tell me, but I didn't know what to ask. If they had talked about women I would have had some questions, but they never entered upon the subject. I thought it curious that they hadn't; maybe they were regarding my youth. No, that wouldn't be the reason.

After midnight the pauses lengthened and the comfy drowsiness deepened, the fire sinking to orange-and-red embers. They decided it was time for bed. I was still wide awake, but did not demur. I kicked off my unlaced boots and stripped off my shirt and heavy pants and climbed into a top bunk. There I lay on my back with my hands beneath my head, staring at the ceiling in which I could barely make out the board edges and pine knots. I heard the wind sifting the papery snow in the oak trees and laurels.

They fell asleep one by one, their breathing steadied and slowed and purred. Now and then one of them would shift in his bunk like a log shifting in a campfire. I lay thinking of many things, but nothing of winter. In my mind was the light of summer and its grass smells and sweat and dusty roads. I thought a little why we had come here, what it would be like to kill a deer.

My thoughts were interrupted when Johnson Gibbs in the lower bunk spoke in his sleep. I couldn't make out the word the first time. He spoke again, thickly but comprehensibly in the reddened dark: "Helen." Then he said nothing more, but now there was true silence in the cabin, no one turning or half-snoring, and I realized I was holding my breath. I let it out carefully. And then Uncle Luden asleep in the top bunk on my right spoke the word: "Helen."

I could tell from his voice that he was asleep, and at first I thought he was only repeating in dream the name Johnson had uttered. But wouldn't it have changed in his mind, undergone the usual alchemy? Maybe it was someone they both knew, someone they happened to be dreaming about at the same time. It was a farfetched notion, but it amused me and I elaborated upon the fancy for a while.

Then I heard my father in the other lower bunk roll over and mutter a word. I couldn't hear it distinctly, only a liquid nasal murmur: ". . . llnn . . ." But now I took it for granted that it was a transfiguration of the familiar name Helen.

There was a woman I had never heard of before and she was powerful in their three lives. No, that was not possible. There was no secret like that for them to share. They didn't share secrets anyhow.

The room waited; I couldn't hear them breathe now. The fire had gone all down, only a pinkish gleam furred over with gray ash.

Suddenly—all at the same time—each of the three stirred in his bed. I couldn't see them, but recognized from the sound of the movement that they now sat bolt upright in their bunks, their hands flat on the mattresses. They were still not awake, but each of them stared open-eyed and sightless into the space of the room in front of the fireplace. As one man they gasped, like divers coming out of the ocean. They remained sitting, all three, breathing hoarsely, staring and not seeing.

I couldn't see them. I couldn't see anything, but I knew what they were doing. I too stared forward into the room, straining to see . . . what? I knew I couldn't look into their dreams, I had no desire to. But the tension caught me up, and I tried to sculpt from the darkness a shape I might recognize.

Little by little—yet all in a single instant—I saw something. I thought that I saw. Framed by glossy black hair, a face appeared there, the features blurred by a veil and yet familiar to me, I fancied, if I could remember something long ago and in a distant place. Then there was no face. If something had actually appeared, it lasted no longer than an after-image upon the retina. But if I had seen something, then it was her, Helen, I had glimpsed.

Now the others lay back again. Their breathing slowed and quietened. Now they would dream no more of Helen; each would follow his own strange travels in the forests of dream; their sleepings would no longer touch.

I was disturbed most of all by the unplaceable familiarity of the vision. Who was this woman with thick black hair and those penetrating brown eyes? I thought and thought with no success and grew irritated and tired of myself. The room began to gray with predawn light reflecting from the snow and I fell asleep and dreamed of summer and a bright yellow field of oats.

I woke to the sound of sausage sizzling and water pouring. They were all up and about, and I scrambled down quickly and got dressed. In the kitchen, the only other room here, they went about their tasks, a little dull maybe from the evening whiskey. They gave me good-morning as I sat at the table and began to observe them closely.

No secret seemed to obtain among them. They were as open and *careless as ever before. Even so, I felt myself at a distance from them, left out, and I felt too a small gray sense of shame, as if I'd gone through their pockets while they slept. But nothing passed among them that I could detect.*

During breakfast my father informed me that we were leaving. Though the snow had stopped, they had decided the weather was no good for hunting and that we were returning home. I nodded dumbly.

They packed up and I packed hurriedly and went back to the cast-iron range to wash the tin plates and cups. They stripped the bunks and swept. When I finished washing up and had damped down the cookstove fire, I sat at the table while they loaded the gear. They waited in the car and still I sat there, gazing about the cabin.

In a few minutes I heard the sound of boots on the rough porch planking. The door opened and Johnson Gibbs stood solidly in it. His blue eyes were very bright. There was full sunlight now and it made a burning glare on the snow. Against this harsh light Johnson's figure loomed black, black as velvet, blackly burning, and his voice sounded deep and hollow:

"Well, Jess, are you one of us or not?"

II

Short Stories

Moments of Light

Mrs. Franklin Ascends

Nov. 1. 1762. I arrived home from England. B.F.

*D*eborah Franklin noted this newest entry in the household account book with satisfaction. She leafed through a few back pages, observing her own sparse entries: "pair of purpill shoes for Salley—7 shillings, 6 pence," "my cash did not quite hold out this month," "a Blew necklis for Salley and a Jet Necklace for my Self," "goodeys for my pappy 2 Jars—6 pounds." She was not going to admit to Mr. Franklin—no, now *Dr.* Franklin—that she had deliberately made a mare's nest of the household expenditures in order to see them set straight again. It happened almost exactly as she had imagined. Soon after entering the house he had called for the book, looked through it, and then registered his arrival in the firm delicate script that meant, *No more of this.*

But her husband was a discerning man. He must have seen that the disorder of her accounts was her expression of longing during his five-year absence, for he knew how clever she was with money. After all, she had helped handle the print shop accounts in the old days, when the family labored to make its fortune. This time he hadn't complained, had not even twitted her, but she thought she recognized a familiar light in his eye. She closed the book and laid it on a shelf of the cupboard. They would speak of it later.

No time to talk now. The house was confusion from cellar to attic. Five cabs were lined up before the house, and servants struggled in from the street with boxes, trunks, and packing cases. Already guests had gathered to the house to attend Benjamin's return to America, and

261

the happy Doctor stood in the front hallway, animatedly chatting with Mr. Collinson and Mr. Neave while almost negligently directing the disposition of all those parcels he had brought from abroad.

Deborah gave him a critical attention. His sojourn in England had altered his appearance much less than she had supposed it would. He had gained weight. He was fifty-six years old—she in her mid-fifties had plumpished too—but surely the miseries and terrors of an ocean voyage would diminish any man. Deborah could imagine the sea only as a great watery desert filled up with tempests, monsters, and shipwreck, and nothing would ever dissipate her fear of it. . . . His hair had receded and his features had somewhat sharpened, but his essential kindliness shone through. In fact, he had acquired a more spiritual appearance altogether. He had always tended toward the avuncular and now it seemed more pronounced. It came to her that this was what "Pappy" had always been, everybody's concerned but amusing uncle.

He saw her watching and, excusing himself, led her aside. In his fondly joking manner he said, "Deborah, my dear, I had better tell you that I have begun to make up a dinner party for tonight."

"With this house in such a state? And with the servants taken up carrying all this stuff about? Dr. Franklin, you must know that a dinner party is impossible."

"I had thought it might be impossible, so I have invited only four. With us, six."

"After your long absence am I to see so little of you?"

"My dear, I promise that you shall see all that there is to see." So saying, he clasped her round the waist and hugged her tightly.

"La, Dr. Franklin, you must not excite the feelings of a woman who has been so long widowed by distance." She disengaged herself, but she knew that she was blushing, and was observed blushing by Mr. Collinson and Mr. Neave, who now turned away from this *scene* to engage in private discussion. Taking advantage of their good manners, she kissed her Pappy pertly on the cheek.

He slipped away, crying, "Peter! Take particular care of the small square boxes. They contain those glass bowls, and they are to go directly to the attic. Be very careful."

Deborah turned out of the confusion of the hallway and went

toward the kitchen. A soup of leeks, she was thinking; and she recalled that he was partial to turkey, and there was a smoked turkey on hand; and she could send for oysters. As for wines he would inform her, and it was probable that he had brought some special vintages from abroad.

Then she was momentarily dismayed, remembering the descriptions of dinners in her husband's letters. He had acquired a new cleverness in eating, and how would her severe colonial cooking now please him? She brushed the question aside. Dr. Franklin had come home and so must do with home fare.

In the kitchen she got out pen and paper and made a list and read it aloud—with appropriate glosses—to the kitchen maid and sent the girl off to market and bakery. She put on an apron and busied herself. As she worked, pieces of news began to arrive from other parts of the house.

"Master's compliments, and he desires you to remember his fondness for a turkey."

"Pray tell Dr. Franklin that goose more suits him."

"Master sends this length of silver lace and requests you to observe the workmanship. He says that if it pleases you you are to do with it as you like, but that if it does not you are to cast it into the fire."

She regarded the expensive stuff at arm's length. "You may tell your master that this lace may possibly do to trim small-clothes for a gentleman who rates himself too handsomely."

Of a lace cap with silk ribbons: "Tell Dr. Franklin that us scullery maids are not to be corrupted by such finery."

Of an English silver tea set: "Inquire of your master if these are implements for some new chemical experiment with which he will disfigure my house."

"Master says you are not to tease him anymore, for he is weary with travel and heartsore and his feelings quite tender."

"He will feel better once he has eaten good *American* food."

And so the afternoon passed off, in bustle and badinage.

It was an odd dinner party. Mr. Collinson and Mr. Neave returned, and Mr. Whatley and Mr. Lining arrived, and Deborah was the only woman present. Dr. Franklin insisted that she sit at head of table, and paid her such exaggerated polite attention that she was quite overcome with shyness. However persistently she might return her husband tit for tat in private, in company she had not his ease and facility and she took retreat in the merciful covertness of femininity.

Dr. Franklin had found a white Bordeaux of which he was proud and after the obligatory gesture to the King proposed many pretty toasts to his wife. These she managed to acknowledge in good countenance, though once she could not resist remarking, "Gentlemen, I doubt my husband would be so merry if he had spent these last five years at home, where he had belonged."

Benjamin smiled and bowed and drank.

The soup was brought in and the talk turned away from domestic subjects. The men were anxious to give and receive news, especially political gossip, of which Dr. Franklin had acquired a great store. The guests professed surprise at finding their host so conversant with colonial affairs, some of his news being new even to them. "But all news comes to London," he said. "After all, London is the center of the civilized world." And with that he stole a secret glance at Deborah, but she affected not to notice.

Why should he tantalize himself? His feeling that moving his family to London would be a step of great advantage was already known to her. Mr. William Strahan, her husband's London friend, had already acquainted her by letter of Dr. Franklin's notion, and she was certain that Strahan's letter had been written at Benjamin's suggestion, if not under his personal direction. But if his heart was set upon her moving then his heart must break. She would not lose her life in the ocean, not for any mortal man, not even for Pappy.

After the oysters he seemed to grow weary of political talk and asked for news of the Philosophical Association. At once the talk veered to topics scientific, and Deborah's attention waned. Of all her husband's many interests these investigations in natural philosophy least attracted her. Some of them indeed dismayed her. In the matter of lightning rods, for example, though it was comforting to know that Benjamin had made the house secure from the power of lightning—a thing which no other man had ever conceived of doing—still it was alarming to pass on the stairway his bell-and-chain system during a thunderstorm.

She had seen the passage there so filled with white electricity that a person might well read a letter by it.

Deborah was not so silly as to consider herself an ignorant or a superstitious woman. She had not the advantage of the classical tongues, nor any of the higher mathematics, nor even of accepted English spelling. (This latter lack Dr. Franklin did not conceive to be a failing of hers but one inherent in the language, and he was working to devise a pattern of phonetic spelling in which women and men would be equally at home.) But she well knew that she was more soundly accomplished than almost all the men with whom she dealt daily. She could read and write and cypher, knew something of geography and modern history, and had proven herself successful as a commercial and as a domestic manager. Even so, Benjamin's endeavors in science awed her and with her awe was mingled a shadowy dread. She could well enough understand the excitement which overtook these gentlemen when they began to talk of natural philosophy, for after all they were concerning themselves with the warp and woof threads of creation. But wasn't there some fear in that? Mightn't they some day pull one of the threads awry, or break one, and so disturb the whole fabric?

Her thoughts had wandered far from the converse of the company, but now she took fresh notice. Dr. Franklin had borrowed Mr. Neave's half-filled wineglass and set it next his own empty glass. From his vest pocket he produced a lump of chalk and dusted his fingers with it. Then, rubbing the lips of the two glasses, he sounded a humming chord.

"Dr. Franklin has a new invention!"

"No sir, it is not new," Dr. Franklin said, "nor is it my invention. Yet I believe that I have introduced many improvements upon Mr. Puckeridge's model. Perhaps I do have some reason to claim the invention as my own. The great thing is to increase the stability of the separate bowls so that a constant pitch can be maintained."

Mr. Lining said, "I don't see why it mayn't be regarded as a new invention. There are other cases—I am thinking of the plow and the rifle—in which the basic principles have been long in practice, and yet improvements have so altered them that we may well regard them as new inventions altogether."

What were they speaking about? This rendering of tones by the rubbing of glasses was certainly no new thing in the world. It was an amusement of children, and Deborah remembered that she as a child had one day kept at it so constantly that she had got her ears boxed. It was nothing new at all; the quality of the tone was a bit unsettling, and that was all the peculiarity in it.

She recalled that sometimes before she had thought about the *boyish* character of a great many of these experiments in science. Indeed, the excitement which came to the gentlemen when they began to talk of science reminded her of the exhilaration of boys on holiday. She knew of course that an intellectual amusement could have strong practical applications, but there was something a little callow about this whole subject matter. Something in fact just a little sad.

"Have you decided upon a name for this new instrument?" Mr. Collinson asked.

"That problem caused me some concern," Dr. Franklin said. "For a long time I had in mind to call it a *deboronica*, in tribute to the dulcet timbre of my goodwife's voice."

She looked down at her plate. Dr. Franklin was being ironical. She knew that among some she had reputation as a termagant, but it was unimportant to her as long as Pappy approved her *private* character.

Finding she would not speak, he went on, "But I confess that the ungainliness of my coinage—*deboronica*—would defeat the purpose of making a new name. I therefore settled upon *armonica*, from the Italian *harmonia*, attempting a compliment to the beautiful harmony of the Italian language."

Mr. Neave brought forth an objection. He thought he remembered hearing opinions from medical men to the effect that continued performance upon glass instruments set up such a vibration within the performer's body that it interfered with the vital fluids. He had even heard it declared that long exposure to such performance might eventually lead to madness.

"I have heard this theory," Dr. Franklin said, "and I cannot believe that it is correct. I have myself practiced upon my armonica for longer than four hours by the clock and have never felt the least ill effect."

He paused and gave a soft smile. "Of course, there is always a likelihood that I am quite lunatic."

Deborah spoke up. "If this be so, then I am sure that my husband is the gentlest and most sensible lunatic who has ever managed to escape from the Bedlam of Europe."

"Hear hear!" cried Mr. Neave.

"My dear," said Dr. Franklin, and he drank to her. He then laid before them the proposition that of all sciences the two upon which the salubrity of mankind most depended—medicine and agriculture— were the most laggard in development and the most ill-defined in aim. The assemblage began to pursue this topic, and Deborah's musings fell away once more.

Now she was tired and distracted and she hoped the dinner party would end soon. For dessert she had prepared a trifle, and though she was reluctant to have it brought in before receiving some sign from her husband, she went ahead. It was received with hearty approbation and even, she thought, with genuine pleasure. She watched as the men ate and talked, thinking how these social exchanges were arranged. Although no outward deference was shown to her husband, and certainly, no sign of sycophancy, yet to an onlooker it was obvious that it was Dr. Franklin who initiated each new turn of discourse and who elicited any interesting response from the members of the company. It was also obvious that the other men were mostly unaware of his gentle management.

The party began to break up. The mood had changed from excitement to expansiveness to a slight melancholy. When Dr. Franklin rose the other men rose, but Deborah went with the company only as far as the dining room door, trusting to her husband the duties of shepherding the guests down the stairs and into their greatcoats and out into the raw autumn night. Deborah reseated herself at the table in Mr. Collinson's chair, and stared tiredly at the leavings of the meal, the smeared pewter plates and smudged glasses. She listened to the farewells, and then to her husband reascending the stairs.

He returned and gazed at her and went to the sideboard where he poured two small glasses of blackberry cordial. Handing one to Deborah, he sat in the chair next hers. "I am afraid this day has been very tiring for you," he said.

"It has been a full day," she said.

"Perhaps I was mistaken in arranging a dinner on the evening of my arrival."

She sipped and meditated. "I think that some such affair may have been necessary to you in order to dissipate gradually some of your journey-nerves."

"You are wise."

"I am not. I can only conjecture as to how I might feel, returning after long absence through such danger."

"The danger was little."

Surely he was not going to broach the subject of her removal to England at this moment. . . . "I consider the danger sufficient and the effort exhausting. Dear Pappy, you must be tired out of all capacity."

He laughed softly. "Madam, I doubt not you know me better than that."

She did indeed.

He drained his glass and stood, taking her hand. They went downstairs together, and in the foyer Dr. Franklin instructed Peter that the servants were to retire, that what remained to do could be done on the morrow. They went together to her bedroom and made ready for bed by candlelight. After Deborah climbed in, Dr. Franklin snuffed the tapers.

In the dark they lay, caressing and murmuring endearments. After a while they took pleasure of one another and fell asleep.

The soul of Deborah Franklin was adrift in the waters of sleep. Her tiredness was so thorough that her mind seemed to have departed her body entirely. She slept happy and peaceful, but it was a dark deep sleep, almost as if she had been drugged. In her dreams were pictures which would ordinarily have been frightening, glimpses of amorphous sea monsters and of the grandeur of continental courts, but this time they did not alarm her; these were images of dangers already passed through and conquered. Perhaps at one point her mind did vaguely realize that there was some stirring in the bedchamber, but this sensation was soon lost in the flow of her dreaming. In her deepest sleep she flung her arm out, and it did not touch her husband. He was not with her in the bed.

Just as her sleeping soul was attempting to accommodate this information, she became tranquilly elate. A choir of angels was singing. First one voice, a low soprano of the most beautiful timbre, sounded a single sustained note; and then other voices joined one at a time. There was never any music like this, celestial, supernal. It sounded not only in the mind and the mind's ear, but also in the body's very blood and bone.

She sat bolt upright with open eyes—though she was still not truly awake. She had never expected to be so utterly happy. For now her heart's profoundest wish had been accomplished. She and Benjamin, Deborah and her dear Pappy, had died together. In the long November night they had expired in their sleep, and now they were transported to heaven. Somewhere in the great passage over to death they had got separated for a moment, but she knew that he was nearby; he was just above her and she could climb up to him in a trice.

She rose from bed and drew a robe about her and went out into the hall to the stairs. She was neither truly awake nor truly asleep, but in a vague state between. As she ascended the stairs—treading softly, her heart sweet with fulfillment—the music of heaven grew louder, absorbed her whole being.

She went up and up. A pane of light glowed on the edge of the top step, coming from beneath a door. She never hesitated, but stepped to the top and opened the door inward.

It was no scene she could have expected, this smallest anteroom to the Many Mansions. It looked in fact exactly like the attic of her house, lit softly by a single oil lamp. And here was no chorus of angels, but only a small plump man hunched over what looked like a child's coffin filled with queer glass bowls. She watched as the man pumped a treadle attached to the box, driving the larger and smaller glass bowls round and round. He touched one bowl and then another, unleashing the music of the spheres.

The man's figure was painfully familiar. "Benjamin?" she murmured.

He turned. The light of the oil lamp gave a nimbus glow to the white hair standing out about his head. "Deborah? My dear, I'm sorry if I have disturbed you. It was on my mind to see if my armonica was broken during the voyage, and I knew that I could never rest without finding if it was in working order."

Oh, this was too much! Must Dr. Franklin always be arranging everything? Even the musical entertainment of their afterlife? Deborah bit her lip. *She was exasperated.*

Thatch Retaliates

At last Mr. Tidrow departed the company of Toby Milliver and Hyde Prescott. In Pasquota Province, at a point in the trail marked only by a tall plane tree, he reined his horse—the other two knew everything they could desire to about that horse!—into the bushes at the right of the track and disappeared. The primeval Carolina forest swallowed him in an instant.

If only Mr. Tidrow had once stopped talking, his presence would have gladdened his comrades measurably, for he knew the roads and trails and was a woodsman able to alleviate some of the discomfort of wilderness travel. But ever since they left Williamsburg, he had talked incessantly of his plantation with all its animals, slaves, and crops; and he talked about himself, telling of his past history, his lineage, his bravery, his hunting skill, his amorous adventures. He dinned the other two men and gave no quarter. At one point Mr. Milliver had leaned over his horse and whispered to Mr. Prescott a rhyme he had made:

> "My Friend, thou hast but subjects two:
> The one is Thou, the other You."

Prescott was not partial to rhymes, but this one stayed in his head, repeating itself to the rhythm of his horse's hooves.

Before Mr. Tidrow turned off to become one with the forest, he gave a great many instructions about direction, about how to keep dry, and about whom to ask for in the town of Bath, which was their destination. But they had listened to him for so long that they were less grateful for his information than for his imminent absence.

Now Toby Milliver and Prescott rode along in a silence broken only by the cries of this wilderness. They had reason to talk to each other, as they had only lightly introduced themselves at the outset of the journey, but the attraction of silence had become as a Siren to them and they rode for a long distance without speaking. It was a mild September day of the year 1718 and an agreeable breeze moved the treetops and grasses along their path. The breeze blew in from the seacoast a few miles distant on their left-hand side.

They refreshed themselves with silence like thirsty men watering at a spring. Then when they had had enough, Toby Milliver inquired of Prescott the nature of the business that brought him to Bath. Prescott replied, somewhat guardedly, that his business was of a private nature merely, that a maiden aunt had suddenly died some weeks ago, and that he traveled in order to look after the disposition of some properties. He returned the question to Milliver and was astonished to find that his companion was a bookseller and was journeying to see into the possibility of establishing a printshop and an outlet for printed volumes. He tugged his earlobe, and then: "My dear Milliver, how long have you resided in America?"

"Since March only, sir," Toby said. "I arrived at Jamestown from London. But already I begin to feel comfortably at home here in the colonies."

"And have you visited Bath before this time?"

"Sir, I have not. What can you tell me of it?"

Prescott looked at the round little man who sat a horse so precariously. Toby struck him as an excessively cheerful person, a man who was always smiling. "I hope you will not take it amiss," Prescott said, "if I say that I find your expectations rather sanguine. For while Bath town is well established so far as colonial towns are capable, it is still a raw country settlement, and many of the polite accomplishments of London have still to take root here. Reading may well be counted as lacking."

"I do not expect to obtain success at once," said Toby Milliver.

"I am content to make my way gradually. I see as the important thing to make printed materials available. Then those who are able to take advantage may do so, and others, seeing what pleasures and benefits accrue from reading, will wish to acquire the talent."

"I am doubtful of it."

"And sooner or later the machinery for printing shall become a necessity. When I acquire machinery and can found a press, I shall count that as security against my future."

"I fear, Mr. Milliver, that you much mistake the character of Carolina, at least in its present state."

"As I say, I harbor not much delight in its present state. 'Tis the future state that gives me to hope."

A shadow darkened Prescott's mind. "The future, sir, is not so easy to make out." He forbore to say further and again they rode silently for a space.

Then Toby Milliver began to speak at length, gently chiding Prescott for his lack of faith in the colonial character, and pointing out to him the learned achievements America had already gained. He spoke of the establishment of the colleges of Harvard and William and Mary, of the writings of the brilliant Mather family, of Thomas Hooker's contributions to theology, and of many other matters. He was surprised and amused at the enthusiasm which Toby brought to bear upon this catalogue of names, most of which Prescott found either slightly familiar or totally unknown. At last he said, "You have said enough to convince me that a bookseller might do well in our northern colonies, but here in the Carolinas it is a different country. Much of the venerable learning of America that you speak of would be fresh news to the inhabitants of these parts; nor would it be the sort of news they are most anxious to hear."

"But surely, sir, the character and intellect of our southern gentlemen cannot be so thoroughly rated below those of our northern? Surely a little geography cannot see so much change in men?"

"I cannot account for the great differences between Boston and Bath, but I understand that these differences exist. Of course, this is my first visit to Bath also."

Toby said, "I see the difference as a difference in opportunity. No one has endeavored to introduce here the first necessity for learning. And that is why I see all my opportunity before me."

Prescott said, "Perhaps I am just not very optimistic by nature. Others have told me so."

As daylight declined and shadows deepened, the breeze increased. The tops of the oaks turned silver as the underleaves showed and a soft tumbling resounded through the woods.

"Mr. Tidrow might tell us now if rain portends," Toby said. "Are you a prognosticator of weather, Mr. Prescott?"

"I believe we shall be dry," he said, "but we might begin to look for a place to settle for the night. It is not long till dark."

In a while they came to a stream and watered the horses and then, finding a patch of tolerably dry ground, they made preparations for the night. Prescott managed to get a fire going. They boiled tea and dined on salt pork and ship biscuit. Afterward they lay at their ease, propped against their saddles. The heavy American darkness moved in the trees, and they heard rustlings they could not place and the voices of beasts they could not identify. All round them towered the ancient mysteries of the night, so deep and secret that the two men began to feel like children. They were profoundly moved and wished that Mr. Tidrow were with them again, let him chatter on as he would.

Prescott asked, "Does it really seem to you that this place needs so many books?" The firelight on his face scored the creases, causing him to have an even gloomier expression than before.

Toby paused, then laughed. "At this moment it seems more appropriate to learn how to wrestle bears and crocodiles. But it will appear different in the morning. And Bath town is after all not a part of the forest. In our age, Mr. Prescott, this wilderness is being pushed back. Here round our fireside are materials enough for a score of books of natural history, if you or I could interpret."

"But in the event of bears or crocodiles, I am content to let others stay here to write them. Perhaps we shall find out about any such monsters here during the night. Sleep well, Mr. Milliver."

Milliver knocked out his small clay pipe. "Then, in the face of such impending danger, I do desire you to call me Toby," he said.

*   *   *

The morning rose, cool and half-misty. The sun marked solid columns and delicate filigrees of shadow within the mist, and everything was freshened, the ground, the air, the plants. They declined to take breakfast, anxious to be on their way. The experience of another night in these savage trees they anticipated with no pleasure. They mounted as soon as they were able and rode briskly along the way. The horses' hooves gleamed with dew.

They now resumed some of the topics they had pursued yesterday. His uneasy night in the woods had not dimmed Toby's enthusiasm. His new America was, he maintained, opportunity not only for himself and other enterprising gentlemen like himself, but for everyone in Europe. He saw the colonies as a fresh beginning, a place where the old mistakes did not have to be repeated, where new forms of government might be tried, where institutions could be thought out beforehand, *founded upon reason* rather than upon old superstition and custom. *Reason* was in fact to be the guildmark of America, for every man is first guided by self-interest and can only injure his affairs with unreason. Therefore, injustice and prejudicial opinion and baseless cruelty could never importantly take root here, for each man's personal welfare was posed against them.

As he talked Hyde Prescott began to feel a warm fondness for the little round man. Toby was without doubt one of the greatest fools to be met with in the world, yet his enthusiasm was embracing rather than starkly fanatic, and the future he depicted was a delectable improbability. In Toby's company Prescott found himself thinking again and again, If only what you say could be so. And he found that he suppressed some of the melancholy remarks that rose to his lips in order not to dampen the spark of his companion. Prescott's experience of the world was broader and longer than Toby's, but, he reflected, that did not signify that it was wiser. He had met men who seemed to travel scatheless through the vicissitudes of circumstance, and perhaps Toby would be one of these. Nevertheless, he could not help interjecting demurrals now and then, pointing out that the old Adam was still heartily at work in every man and that a newfound landscape could hardly be a panacea for all the ills of human character.

To this Toby agreed readily enough, but claimed to think that the great flaws of personality both in the state and in the individual were historical products rather than inbred propensities. He put the question: "And don't you think, Mr. Prescott, that if we are to form new schemes of government it is better to establish them upon the parts of men we consider best rather than upon the worst? For if a government establishes itself as mostly to oppose criminals, then that society shall never have lack of them."

"But," said Mr. Prescott, "if a government does not make and enforce laws against the criminal, then it is resistless before him."

Toby referred this objection to his theories of self-interest. The object of every life was contentment, and when opportunity was plentiful, as here about them it was, society could be troubled only by a few aberrant members, a minority so small that it could be handled almost perfunctorily.

The countryside had changed during the course of their discussion. The tall trees, the oaks and beeches, had become smaller and fewer. The slight rolling hills had given way to flatness and the crumbly humus turned into patches of sand and marsh. Along their left-hand side lay a broad tidal marsh, wind dimpling the reeds. Birds were more readily seen, herons and red-winged blackbirds. And the bracing smell of salt was in the air.

Toby ventured that they could not be far from their destination.

"I think not," Prescott said, "but then we do not know how far this marsh extends. Here the ground seems none so suitable for planting a town."

Thus he struck up a new subject, and they talked of the requisite soils and waters for towns, until they came to a little wooden bridge across a murky channel and the town of Bath lay before them on the other side.

It must have been fully eleven o'clock in the morning, but the streets of the town were mostly silent. Even the few children they encountered gazed at them silently, big eyes in dirty faces, and ran to hide when they passed. The early brightness had clouded over and the sandy streets of Bath, which were wide enough, looked dim and constricting. The several houses and establishments on each side seemed almost lifeless. What they had observed of the place so far seemed forbidding to Toby's schemes of enlightenment.

Prescott gibed him: "Before you teach these citizens to read, you must first rouse them from bed."

One lad of about twelve with ragged dirty yellow hair stood in the road, and they asked him the way to the inn. He merely shook his head, staring down at his feet until they rode past him.

"Upon my word, Mr. Prescott," Toby said, "I don't believe he is acquainted with the word *inn*. What manner of place have we come to?"

Six hundred yards before them the street appeared to end at a sandy point of land with a sparse stand of pine trees. Through the trees they could see water, the wide estuary bay shining gray-brown. As they were going toward it, they heard from behind them a strange half-musical sound, as of someone mumbling and singing at once.

But when they twisted round in their saddles to see, the street behind them was empty. Before they could articulate this eerie experience, a man emerged from between two houses on the right, and went up the street the way they had come down. He went quickly, walking with a peculiar half-hobble.

"Sir!" called Mr. Prescott.

But the man did not abate his pace, gave no sign of having heard.

Toby sang out, "Sir, sir! I say there!"

The man slackened momentarily and over his shoulder threw them one brief frenzied glance and a snarl and hurried on his way.

Toby and Mr. Prescott reined their horses round and looked at one another in astonishment. For the appearance of this personage was wild indeed. He was a shortish swarthy man who, when he had glanced at them, had shown a countenance almost obliterated by a long heavy black beard, a beard done up in filthy curls and ringlets which stuck out from his face in every direction, so that he might have sat as a true model for the Medusa or some other fabulous monster of antiquity. His clothes too were filthy and spotted with grease, his gray linen shirt and long maroon doublet. His soiled tricorn hat was twisted awry so that the peak jutted over his left ear. His eyes were small and dark but the two companions observed them well enough. Such strange fierce disordered eyes they had never seen before, and they concluded that the man was either mad or much under the influence of strong drink.

They accosted this apparition no further but merely watched him go along the edge of the street, still murmuring his crazy chant.

And then on the opposite side of the street a door opened and a man stepped out. This was a tall redhaired man in his shirtsleeves who held in his left hand a naked saber. He cried out to the wild man: "You there, Thatch!"

But the other did not return his greeting nor even so much as look at him.

"Thatch!" he cried. "I stand to tell you you are but a cowardly villain and I defy you."

Other than to quicken his pace slightly, the man Thatch gave no indication of having heard.

The redhaired man called his name once again and, still receiving no sign, bent down and picked up a stone and flung it at the uncouth figure. The stone struck him sharply on the shoulder and rebounded into the street. Once again Thatch looked shortly, gave an ugly snarl, and then disappeared between houses suddenly, like a stoat going to earth. "Ah," said the redhaired man. He seemed greatly disappointed and gave the empty air before him two wicked whistling cuts with his saber.

Toby and Mr. Prescott were amazed and not a little frightened by these first signs of social intercourse they had seen in the town of Bath. They looked at each other in wonderment, and then all about them, at the street and the houses and the roofs of the houses. Were those pale shadows in the dark windows peering faces?

Prescott took his courage up and greeted the redhaired man, who answered in surprise, evidently not having noticed the travelers until now. "Sir, could you lend some assistance to two bewildered travelers?"

The man shook his head, as if to clear it of confusion, and advanced toward them.

Toby reined his horse hard back.

"I hope, sir," said Prescott, "that you intend us no harm with your sword."

He stopped and looked at the saber in his hand with an expression of sudden remembrance. Then he examined Toby and Mr. Prescott appraisingly. "I intend no harm to any honest gentlemen," he said, "if any are to be met with."

Prescott considered it prudent not to interpret this remark as an affront. "I believe you shall find us as honest as any," he said.

"As honest as any is scant credentials in these parts. But, seeing that you are strangers, let me be heartily your servant. I am no permanent resident here either."

"Can you tell us of an inn where we may put up? For we are fatigued with travel."

"There is no inn," he said, "but only a pair of taverns. Yet there is an ostler too. If you will await me but a few moments I shall be glad to guide you."

"Sir, we are grateful," said Toby.

The redhaired man returned into the house. He was gone some little while, and Toby and Mr. Prescott began to grow apprehensive. Then he came out again, no longer bearing a weapon, and dressed now in a black waistcoat and sober gray doublet. "Please come this way, gentlemen," he said, walking toward the south, toward the pine trees and the bay.

They dismounted and walked beside him, leading the horses.

He offered his hand. "I am James MacCollum, formerly a lieutenant of the King's Army, and now in America to visit my only relations."

Mr. Prescott introduced himself and Toby and gave a brief account of their circumstances, to which MacCollum listened with attentive respect.

These details being out of the way, Toby at once asked who might be that curious personage MacCollum so disliked.

"Do you not know? Why, gentlemen, that is the infamous Edward Thatch, one of the arrantest villains that God has ever suffered to creep upon the earth. He is called Blackbeard, and is a notorious freebooter of these waters."

Prescott was consternated. "Is that he indeed? The bloody pirate of the street ballads?"

" 'Tis he."

"I have heard much report of him and could not help suspecting that most I heard was exaggerated."

"Mr. Prescott, it will be an ingenious man who can exaggerate the perfidy and atrocity of Thatch."

"You must be very brave, Mr. MacCollum," Toby said.

"I am none so brave. It is the way of the soldier to fall back upon the habit of his training. . . . But here we are at the ostler's. Let us see what can be done."

They had arrived at a low rough stable with a mud and stone foundation. Here MacCollum took charge, relaying instructions to the truculent stableman, and bargaining with him strictly. At last he turned to Prescott, saying, "I think we have got out of him what satisfaction can be had."

"I am content indeed," said Prescott. "I could never have done half so well."

"Nor I, certainly," Toby said. "And now if you will direct us to the tavern we shall enjoy recompensing your kindness in brandy."

"Ah no, gentlemen, no taverns. You are to follow me back the way we came. I have arranged with my cousin that you are to come there directly, where there is meat and drink in plenty."

He would accept no refusal, polite nor vehement, and so back they went.

MacCollum had not deceived them about the plenitude of food. Laid out for them on the dining room table were cold joints of venison and mutton and several sorts of fowl and both salt and fresh fish. There were different vegetables also, including an exotic pottage of turnips and bread. Toby and Mr. Prescott found it difficult to do full justice to the repast while at the same time satisfying the civilities of introduction to MacCollum's family.

This family was comprised of MacCollum's cousin, Mr. William Jameson, and his wife, their two older girls and two younger sons. These were pleasant and amenable people, eager to learn all they could about the two travelers and about the conditions of the road and about Virginia, especially about Williamsburg, where they had a family connection. Prescott found that he often must answer with his mouth full, for Jameson or his wife would ask him a question and then urge him on to his plate.

Finally Toby and Mr. Prescott had eaten all that they could and the assemblage went into the dining room to talk more at leisure. Prescott found that he had to make most of the conversation, for Toby, settling on a footstool in a corner, was immediately taken up by the boys, especially by the younger one who brought Toby his cat Silversides to admire. Which Toby did at length, with a learned gravity. Prescott meanwhile was able to learn something of the conditions and circumstances of his hosts. Jameson was a Royal revenue agent whose duty it was to inventory and collect taxes upon whatever cargoes passed through the port of Bath. His wife Elizabeth, plump and merry-eyed, was the daughter of a local planter and retained a countrywoman's complaisance and unruffled humor. Now, though, the family was less happy than it was wonted, for the two girls were to leave on the morrow for Charles Town in South Carolina. Their departure was in fact one of the reasons for the visit by their Uncle Jemmy, whose duty it was to see them there safely into the hands of their mother's brother. Jameson and his wife were so downcast when they spoke of the girls' leaving that Prescott could not forbear asking if it would not be better for their maternal uncle to come to visit Bath. There was danger in women traveling alone, for all of MacCollum's obvious bravery.

"I am afraid, sir, that will not answer," MacCollum said.

"No, alas," said Elizabeth, and at that moment all the vivacity left her face.

Jameson said, "Mr. Prescott, the gravest danger to my daughters is here. So long as the cutthroat Thatch thrives hereabouts no young women are safe, in their lives or in their honors."

"Is this Blackbeard so terrible as is said of him? For surely no man since the Tartar Khan receives such bad report."

"Sir," said Jameson, "it is hard to say that Thatch is now the evilest man in the world, for his first mate Israel Hands may vie to share that name with him. But it is certain that between them they carry off all title."

And the three, Jameson and Elizabeth and MacCollum, began a recital of the crimes of Blackbeard. It was a long and disconnected

story—for many of the pirate's movements were mysterious and sometimes weeks passed when he was not heard from—of deception, blood-
shed, rape, and pillage. The daughters, sixteen-year-old Elizabeth and
fourteen-year-old Marie, sat on a divan clasping tightly each others'
hands and blushing at some turns of the narrative and trembling in fear
at others. Some of what they told was familiar to Prescott in different
form, but much was new. All of it was a maze of numbing horror and
bloody squalor.

Prescott was dumbfounded. "Great God!" he cried. "Can nothing
be done in remedy against this man? Cannot the Governor of the
province bring the militia and drive him off?"

Jameson said, "Well, sir, we have no standing militia, though one
might be raised. But that is not the heart of the problem."

"What is its heart?"

Jameson attempted to speak, but then only raised and let fall his
hands in resignation.

MacCollum answered. "The heart of it is that Governor Eden is
very probably in league with the madman."

"The Governor of the province is leagued with the pirate? For
what purpose?"

"That is any man's speculation," MacCollum said. "I can think
of no reason but personal gain."

"Is the Governor a poor man?"

"Governors are never poor men. Only he has not enough wealth
to satisfy him."

"Then he is a rascal worse than Thatch. Cannot this news be
known to the King?"

Mr. Jameson interrupted: "Gentlemen, we must not be overhasty.
It is probable that Governor Eden, having no military force at his
command, may have no choice in the matter; or he may have decided
that friendship with Thatch is the safest protection for the province."

"That," said MacCollum fiercely, "is always a foolish mistake."

"You say true, Cousin," Jameson said. "I believe the alliance has
already cost Eden much grief. There is not a wife or daughter among
the gentry with whom Thatch has not taken some detestable license.

It has raised much resentment against the Governor among his powerful friends."

"I don't wonder at it," Prescott said. "This town finds itself in a perilous position. I do wonder, Mr. MacCollum, that you dared put yourself in such danger with your challenge to Thatch. Mayn't he have killed you?"

"I was to take pains he shouldn't," MacCollum said.

"But has he not some of his gang nearby to set upon you?"

"We know that they are aboard ship in an inlet south of the bay. It was an excellent opportunity to deprive them of their leader."

"But now might he not come back to retaliate upon this family?"

Jameson said, "Oh, we shall defend ourselves victoriously in our houses, if it come to that, and my daughters once being gone. But it is not Thatch's way to attack a position defended. Sneakery, sir, that is his way of combat."

"You see, Mr. Prescott," MacCollum said, "we are not dealing with a Sulla or a Hannibal. This man has no conception of the military honor. Because of this fact alone, I should not have fear of calling him out by himself at any time."

The conversation then turned upon other subjects, topics less disturbing than Blackbeard, and length of travel began to tell in Prescott and he felt drowsy. He must have given some sign of his weariness, for Toby then came up and entreated him to take a turn about the town with him.

Jameson instantly put himself at their service. "There is not much in Bath town to look at," he said, "but I shall be glad to guide you."

"Oh no, sir," Toby said, "you have accommodated us too much already. Besides, my friend and I have some matters to discuss before we take leave of one another, which we must do on the morrow. Our talk would prove very tedious to you."

"Yes," said Prescott, "you have much preparation here in getting your daughters outfitted to travel. I think we shall have no trouble in finding our way about."

"Very well," Jameson said.

The subject which Toby wanted to broach was their staying the

night at a tavern, for he feared that their host would try to insist upon
putting them up, and this would be too heavy a burden on a family
already greatly troubled. He had begun to speak in low tones as they
went out the door and, as they walked south, the way they had headed
earlier, he spoke more loudly.

Prescott replied that he wanted no persuasion, that it was evident
that Mr. Jameson was cumbered with concern and should be spared
the duty of entertaining strangers. He suggested that they find a tavern
at this moment, take lodging there, and return after disengaging from
the Jamesons.

They were interrupted.

"MacCollum!" It was a thin tenor voice, almost a screech. They
turned to find the pirate Blackbeard, who was running full tilt upon
them. His appearance had altered for the worse since their earlier encounter. He was sweating freely, and his eyes were more wildly excited
and his face scarlet. And a noisome smoke now wreathed his face and
rose round his head, for the madman had set fire to the pointed ringlets
of his beard. Truly he was a fearsome sight; he looked like a devil
painted on a Chinese screen.

Blackbeard cried out, "MacCollum! You look upon your last sight
this side of Hell." He halted and stood facing them a scant four yards
away, and they had opportunity to observe that a brace of pistols now
hung round his neck.

Prescott, remembering Mr. Jameson's remarks and Lieutenant
MacCollum's composure, decided to put up a show of bravery. "We
are neither of us MacCollum, sir. If you would like satisfaction from
the Lieutenant, I believe that he shall be happy to content you."

He could speak no further, for Thatch, uttering a choked half-
shriek, snatched out a pistol and fired it.

The ball struck Toby Milliver in the chest. He tumbled backward
into the sandy street and lay writhing, convulsed with pain. A great
bloody hole was in his chest and blood began to gush from his mouth.
He sucked desperate breath in whistling gasps. The ground about him
was spotted with blood and dust rose all round where he struggled.

Prescott forgot to defend himself. He knelt in the dirt beside Toby and tried to clasp him steady in his convulsions. His mind was only a red confusion. The hollow report of the pistol still rang in his ears and the mingled smells of gunpowder and frying hair made him quite nauseated. He held Toby by his shoulders. His friend's face was tallow-colored and suffused with sweat, while his neck and chin were smeared red. Toby clutched at his coat.

"Easy, man," said Prescott. "Try not to wrestle about so."

Toby's eyes widened and he seemed to want badly to say something, but could not.

Black boots, the toes scuffed and torn, obtruded upon the edge of Prescott's vision. When he looked up he found himself staring directly into the muzzle of a pistol. Behind it loomed the face of Blackbeard, more demoniacally contorted than ever. Prescott realized that his final moment on earth had come and he regretted bitterly that his last mortal sight should be the face of this cruel lunatic. He closed his eyes. He willed himself to think of the gray patient face of his mother.

Thatch pulled the trigger, but the piece failed to discharge.

Prescott opened his eyes in time to see the pirate, grunting like a pig, draw the pistol back. Then he was whipped with it across the right side of his face. The pain was furious. Prescott barely escaped losing consciousness. He was flung over on his left side, away from Toby, but managed to prop himself up on his hands. He lost all knowledge of the pirate, for he could see nothing. All before his eyes was a haze of patched red darkness. He fumbled about blindly.

It seemed a long time before he was aware of the presence of people about him. Had someone come to aid them at last? It must be so, for he felt himself lifted to his feet and helped along the ground. Still he could see nothing, and was at the mercy of his ministrants. They lifted him along, his feet touching the ground lightly and unsteadily.

There was the sound of a door, and the coolness of an interior.

He felt himself settling onto a bed or divan, and then he lost consciousness at last and knew no more.

He woke to a great tearing pain in his head, but the pain did not obliterate his memory. He remembered everything that had happened until the moment that he was struck. His heart was filled with fear and outrage, so possessed that the pain was not so deeply felt. He started to sit up but was pushed back gently by hands unmistakably feminine.

"Please, Mr. Prescott, the surgeon says that you are to keep very still."

"Mrs. Jameson?"

"Yes sir. I am here to see after you. You are my charge and must do as I say."

Prescott could make out her form but dimly, though she was close enough to him to hold his hands. He disengaged his right hand and felt his head, discovering that a bandage covered his crown and was brought down over his left eye.

"Please, Mr. Prescott, lie quiet. You mustn't do so." Mrs. Jameson took his hand away from his head.

He lay quiet a few moments, trying to recover more of himself. Then he remembered Toby. "Mr. Jameson, how is my friend?"

"The surgeon is with him now. . . . Please, you mustn't excite yourself."

"But does he still live?"

"He still lives, Mr. Prescott, lying yonder on my dining table."

"Then he may recover? I had thought such a wound would be certain death."

"I am afraid Dr. Lee does not allow that your friend shall survive this night."

"Are we then in the drawing room?"

"Yes."

Gently, vaguely, Prescott pushed aside the woman's restraining hands. "If you please, Mrs. Jameson," he said. "You must help me up. I am going to Toby."

"Mr. Prescott, Dr. Lee says you must not indeed."

"Madam, I must go to my friend if he is dying. The surgeon must be gainsaid, and I must go to him." He sat up. Fierce lightning strokes of agony broke in his head. He strove to show no sign of pain, to deceive her. "Toby is my friend," he said. "He is my responsibility in this place. I cannot have it on my conscience that I did not go to him."

He made an unsuccessful attempt to stand, but fell back. On the second try he succeeded, Mrs. Jameson aiding him. She took his left arm across her shoulders and put her right arm about his waist. The floor beneath him felt as unsteady as a ship's deck and queasy curtains of dizziness wafted before his eyes. But they managed to make their uncertain way toward the adjoining room, toward the candlelight and sharp shadow.

They gained the dining table, and MacCollum and Jameson moved aside to allow them to move to it. On the other side stood a man whom he took to be Dr. Lee, the surgeon. The doctor gave him a glance of stern reproof but said nothing.

Prescott looked down at Toby. His friend lay on the dark oaken table, a candelabra at his head and two large single candles at his feet. Even with his injured vision Prescott could tell that Toby's hour was near at hand. All his upper chest was only a ruin of bloody linen and his face was white, silvery with perspiration, and his eyes were sunk back dark in his forehead. His breathing was terrible to hear, weak but jagged; his breathing was like broken stones. He could not turn his head at their approach, but asked, "Are you here now, my friend Prescott?" His words, though clearly formed, were almost inaudible.

"I am here."

"I am dying, Mr. Prescott."

"You cannot know that, Toby."

"I am dying, but still I hold—" He could not finish. Shuddering wrenched his body and did not subside for some little space of time. "I still hold to my notion," he said, and his voice had weakened more. "What has happened to me is an accident of mistaken identity. . . ."

MacCollum spoke harshly. His voice sounded loud as cannon in the obscure dining room. "That was no mistake. That was Thatch's knavery. He knew well enough that you were not I. The man—"

Dr. Lee cut the lieutenant short with a quick wave of his hand.

Toby gathered his strength to speak once more. "It is accidental, it is not of the essence." The sibilant word whistled in his teeth.

No one spoke.

Two or three minutes must have passed. And then Toby indicated by his expression that he wished Prescott to listen more closely. The pain raged like a fire in his head, but he managed to bend his unbandaged ear close to Toby's mouth. The words were long in coming, they were soft as snow falling in the deep wilderness, but still Prescott understood them. Toby said, "I remain a friend to Reason in this place."

Then he died.

The involuntary jerk of his right foot toppled a candle off the table. Its flame streaked the shadow like a falling star. Then it went out, and a little more of the relentless American nighttime entered the room.

Moments of Light

— 1 —

During Haydn's first London sojourn honors fell upon him like snowflakes settling upon a public statue. He was adored, worshiped, idolized. He was invited, or rather importuned, to fêtes, balls, dinners, concerts, tours, to every sort of occasion. But though a naturally sanguine man, Haydn was then fifty-nine years old and long ago had learned to order his life. His pressing concerns were, as he put it, "first my health, and 2nd my work." He tried to take all things in stride, to accept some invitations deliberately and to refuse others delicately.

His first year in London passed and the attention paid him did not abate. It seemed that no amount of information concerning the Maestro could sate the appetite of the newspapers; nor, spreading himself ever so widely, could he satisfy the eager expectations of polite society to see him. He grew tired sometimes, but—keeping close watch upon himself—never so exhausted that he was irritable or unable to compose.

He was long past the time when his head could be turned by flattery and, anyway, it was simply not in his nature to be affected by currents of social fashion. This, after all, was the man who, when asked at the Austrian border his profession, replied: "Tonkunstler." The customs official, having not the faintest idea what a Composer might be, wrote down "Topfer"—Potter. Haydn observing this error was serenely amused, and reflected that if his work could attain the solidity and shape of dishes and pots he should consider himself successful. Franz Joseph

Haydn was the man who exclaimed at the age of eighty-one, "Am I to die so soon? I have just begun to understand the wind instruments!"

It must be a great advantage for an artist to have such a steady disposition, to have the kind of emotional balance that we most often imagine scientists to have. But then in Haydn's time the scientist and the artist were not thought of as antipodal creatures. In the eighteenth century it seemed only inevitable that the advancement of learning and the refinement of the senses should go forward hand in hand. In fact, in England Haydn's music was praised as "pleasing to every scientific ear." And the foremost astronomer of the time, William Herschel, had in his earliest youth been trained as an oboe player, and later had become organist at Bath, composing seven symphonies which he finally consigned to a cheerful oblivion.

That Haydn and Herschel should meet was taken for granted. They were both amiably social creatures, they were Germans residing in England, they were nearly equal in years, and they were the preeminent geniuses of their respective endeavors. Eleven years earlier, in 1781, Herschel had discovered the planet Uranus. He had at first mistaken the new member of the solar family for a comet and only arduous observation and painful computation had shown that it was indeed a planet. This was news of enormous scientific and theologic import, since it completed the mystical number of seven planets, and George III rewarded the wide-browed astronomer with an annual stipend in order that he might pursue his researches without fret. Herschel pursued them assiduously, contributing important papers on the parallax of fixed stars and on the motion of the sun, and beginning the notes for his grand treatise on the construction of the heavens.

It was thought that the two great men would take pleasure in each other's acquaintance; Herschel's musical background must count heavily in favor of a close friendship.

But Haydn procrastinated.

Week after week the composer found excuse to put off the historic encounter. There was first this pressing appointment to be kept and then another; he had promised to hear this violinist and that cellist; he must make an excursion to hear this cathedral organ and the other church choir. And finally and always, there was his work; he had accepted commissions he must deliver; and a lady had brought him some verses he thought promising for a cantata. There was no doubt truth in all that he said, but at last even his less intimate friends perceived that he was reluctant to meet his celebrated compatriot.

Why?

It was always easy for even those who knew him well to overlook a steadfast peasant strain in Haydn's character. He was descended of no very illustrious parentage, and the fame and fortune he enjoyed he had wrested by force of talent from a world sweetly indifferent to the success or failure of one *fiddler* or another. New discoveries in the supralunary heavens seemed to be reported almost daily in these years and they disturbed profoundly the four-square conservative fabric of Haydn's nature. It was a good thing to have moved up in society, but having moved up Haydn observed many things he disapproved of. He had met butchers with more gracious manners than shown by counts; he had known carters who had a broader knowledge of the world than princes. Here at the top of the social order and at the forefront of philosophic investigation Joseph Haydn discovered an inconstancy of direction which quite dismayed him.

Herschel was one of the foremost disturbers. Those big glasses he had made sought out ever newer and farther objects in the sky, stars multiplying in the heavens so rapidly as to make the mind ill. Thinking of these discoveries, Haydn felt as if he were looking dizzily down from a great height, looking down upon a flimsy earth from the top of the Tower of Babel. Simply this: Haydn was a little frightened what such a man as Herschel might say to him.

Dr. Charles Burney brought them together. This officious musicologist wrote to Herschel to expect them, and to distract the composer's fears took him in the early afternoon to a horse race. At Ascot Haydn fell in love with the English horses, with their lightness and grace, and he admired the English easiness with the animals. Smitten with colors, he observed the jockeys, "lean as greyhounds, and clad in silks of pink, green, blue, red." He came away from the horse race flushed with excitement.

They were received by Herschel's sister Caroline, herself a famous discoverer of comets, and taken immediately into the library where

William awaited them. He greeted them smiling and with hearty hand-shakes, not bowing. Seeing him, Haydn was obscurely relieved to find that he was taller than his host and for this reason began to feel quite gracious.

They took port, an English habit Haydn had learned to forbear.

Burney at once struck up a pompous political topic. The other two men appeared to listen attentively to this recital of unfamiliar names, but with sidelong glances they were taking the measure of one another.

What did they see?

Haydn, described in the newspapers as a *fiery angel of harmony* and so forth was one of the most ordinary-appearing men God had ever fashioned. He was neatly dressed in a suit of dark gray velvet and his fastidiously powdered wig had not been in the least discomposed by the excitement of the afternoon. He had a musician's aristocratic long-fingered hands which contrasted violently with the strong plain features of his face, with the heavy blunted nose and the thick weathered lips. But Haydn's eyes were remarkable. They expressed a highly intense life force, but at the same time those dark brown eyes overflowed with calm. A person looking into Haydn's eyes would be overcome with a feeling of deep certitude and serenity. What things are there in this world? What terror and joy, what agony and beauty, what order and disorder? In Haydn's eyes were the knowledge and foreknowledge of all of it; a man felt flooded with the sense of the rightness of things. Not one furtive glimmer in those brown eyes betrayed the apprehension of Haydn's soul as it looked upon the queasy humorless future.

When he looked at Herschel, Haydn saw a man alert, independent, and resolute. At this moment he formed no further opinion.

Dr. Burney leapt like a cricket from politics to letters. He spoke of Fenelon's *Entretiens sur la Pluralité des Mondes*. "Do you recall," he asked Herschel, "the passage in which he imagines the worlds of the Milky Way to be so close together that pigeons might carry lovers' messages from one world to another? Dr. Herschel, you have destroyed many a pretty fancy with your observation of the immeasurable distances between planets."

Herschel smiled. "I should be distressed to learn that I have interrupted any discourse of lovers," he said.

At this his sister Caroline laughed and came to kiss her brother
on the cheek. She then excused herself and took leave of the company. Dr. Herschel explained that Caroline was engaged in a series of
elaborate astronomical calculations and could spare little time during
these weeks.

Haydn was delighted to discover that Herschel still spoke with a
thick accent. He felt more and more at ease.

Burney pursued his notion. "But don't you think it at least possible,
sir, that much of the poetry of our lives will be in retreat under the
advance of science? Why, sir, even the symbol of poetry, the winged
horse, no educated child can now countenance."

"Doctor Burney, surely that particular emblem, and many others
with it, was never intended by the poets to be taken literally. It is merely
a way to paint in one phrase both the power and the graceful lightness
of the poetic art."

"Even so, Doctor Herschel . . ."

"And we must never forget how much our present state of scientific
knowledge is indebted to the writings of the ancient poets." Herschel
now spoke at length of the atomist theory as it was received from
Lucretius, of the botanic wisdom to be found in Homer and in the
Georgics. He began to grow quite impassioned, and Haydn noticed that
a new energy interfused his body and animated his regular placid features. Herschel shifted to the new experiments of Joseph Priestley in
America, experiments which demonstrated that the air contained the
combustible substance *oxygen*, and that air possessed weight and mass
and hence offered resistance to objects in passage through it. "Well
then, Doctor Burney, you will recall that in the fourth book of the
Aenied, at the funeral games dedicated to Anchises, an arrow is shot
from the bow with such force that it bursts into flame. Mr. Priestley
has shown us that if an arrow could be so constructed as not to break,
and that if it could be driven with sufficient force, then it would indeed
catch fire. To me that is a near proof that the ancients possessed a great
body of scientific knowledge that we are now in process merely of
rediscovering. I begin to have grave doubt that anything *very* new is to
be known."

"But perhaps," said Burney, "the genius of the Roman was able to pierce the veil of Nature at this point, just as in the Fourth Eclogue he was able to see past his proper time into the future of our western societies."

To this proposition Herschel assented readily, but maintained that this supposition would more reinforce his point than weaken it.

Haydn discovered that he was taking the liveliest interest in this topic to which he could add nothing, not even an intelligent question. The little astronomer whom he had feared as a bugbear unruly and impatient was in fact charming company whose enthusiasm only served to season his conversation.

Doctor Burney fastened once again upon his original contention. "And yet some ideas of great beauty have to be discarded. Surely according to the laws of your own discipline we must now give over the venerable notion of the Music of the Spheres."

Haydn watched Herschel expectantly.

"Come now, Doctor Burney," Herschel said. "Simply because a young child has learned to fashion a toy cart and to pull it behind him, we do not expect the King to give up his carriages. I consider that astronomy is only in its early infancy and that many many years must pass before we attain to a true appreciation of the Harmony of the Universe, which is surely the conception of greatest grandeur the ancient world could claim." Still speaking to Burney, he turned to face Haydn. "If we discard the Music of the Spheres, then we shall reduce our Maestro's art to a series of pleasing noises. In the deepest part of our beings we reject such a proposition, do we not?"

Burney was complaisant. "Sir, I will hold that I am well bested in the argument if we can vindicate the ways of Haydn to man."

Haydn made a noise of polite demurral, yet still failed to speak.

It had now grown fairly dark and tapers were lit. The three gentlemen sat at their ease, talking of one thing and another until dinner was announced.

They dined without benefit of the fair sex. Herschel gave plausible explanations for the absence of each of his family, but Haydn received the impression that the Herschel clan was simply bored by a long procession of nobles, geniuses, and virtuosi breaking in upon their lives.

He felt sympathy for their predicament, which was very like his own, but did not repent that he had come. . . . They devoured plaice and a chicken and an excellent venison.

Afterward, they returned to the library for port.

Haydn felt at last obliged to say something of Herschel's profession and celebrity. He complimented him effusively, mentioning various circumstances in which he had heard Herschel's name bruited on the continent; and he congratulated him on the profession of stargazing which, he said, he imagined to be one of the pleasantest in the world, thus always to be searching out new moments of light and volumes of new worlds.

Herschel was at immediate pains to disenchant his guest. "I doubt you would find it a happy profession upon close acquaintance," he said. "First, there are the computations which are very fine and tedious, but without which any amount of gazing is fruitless. And then the observation itself must take place out of doors in every sort of weather. I am often wracked with ague and stiffened with cold. Then there are the problems of constructing these big glasses and of working around them in the dark. Many times my brother and I have suffered accidents which might well have proved fatal." And he went on to tell how once, stumbling in the night, he had imbedded a hook deep above his right knee. To free himself he had had to give up a good two ounces of flesh to the iron. He added with some pride that the attending physician told him that a soldier with such a wound would be entitled to six full weeks in hospital.

Haydn was surprised. Nothing about astronomy was as he had pictured. He had imagined that an astronomer sat indoors at his ease, poked his tube out through a window, and there waited like a fisherman for something astounding to take place at the other end of the sky. All these mathematical details and physical hardships he could not have guessed at. Especially he was impressed by Herschel's suffering cold weather, for dearest of all things to the composer were his health and well-being.

Burney was seized by a sudden fancy. "Doctor Herschel," he cried, "if there are other worlds with men on them, may we not think that they too are employing telescopes? Perhaps at this very moment they are searching out our own world with their glasses."

"They must inhabit nearby to see us," Herschel replied, not at all excited by the notion. "They must live in the Moon or in Mars or Venus. Or they must have very powerful glasses indeed. For you must not imagine, Doctor Burney, that it is an easy matter to catch glimpse of a planet within all the shine and empty space of the heavens."

"Let us say that they live in Mars," Burney said. "I can imagine them scanning our own orb anxiously, looking for traces of men like themselves."

Herschel said placidly, "It is easier to imagine that than it is to imagine a race of men who would have no curiosity about the stars. If there are men on the other worlds we may suppose that they are looking somewhere, though perhaps not at us."

Burney was silent for some moments and then said, "See here, if there are such beings as Mars-men, I would give anything to hear their music. Indeed, I would give whatever I have."

The other two men smiled, and Herschel then told of the two twelve-foot telescopes he had made for the King, who had paid one thousand guineas. He spoke of the twenty-two-foot telescope and finally of the new forty-foot telescope which had so broadly opened the skies, showing star upon star without number. Even he, Herschel, could not have guessed at the depth of the local universe nor the extent to which it was populated with bodies.

"Is it so very full then?" Haydn asked.

"No, Maestro, it is in the main empty, the distance between star and star being so incalculably great. But there are so many more stars than anyone had suspected. It is just that it is all so much *larger* than we could have thought. . . ."

"May we not have a look at these wonders?" Burney asked. "For I consider it a gross breach of manners that a Mars-man is looking down upon me and I am not looking back at him."

"By all means, let us go to the telescope," Herschel said.

He led them out into the June night, soft and purple and scented. Burney kept chattering ebulliently, but Haydn was downcast. His fears had returned.

— 2 —

It was the most beautiful of late spring nights, velvety warm. Now that they were crossing the lawn under the shell of stars even Doctor Burney fell silent. They had a wide view of the sky here, for all the bordering trees had been felled to give access of vision. Here and there a last glowworm drifted sparkling.

Against the purple horizon the telescope presented a startling aspect. It was seated within a tall open-work pyramid of joists, cross beams, and ladders, stark against the sky like the skeleton of some monstrous insect. At the huge mouth of the instrument open to the stars were two platforms, a smaller above a larger. The other end rested upon or within a little hut situated within the base of the pyramid. The tube of the glass was thicker in diameter than Haydn had expected. As they mounted the ladder to the first platform Haydn—a little breathlessly—remarked upon this.

Herschel did not reply until they had reached the safety of the platform. Then he said, "The diameter often surprises those who have only heard of its length. Before the optical part was finished and the tube lay yonder on the grass, many visitors had the curiosity to walk through. Two of those so moved were King George and the Archbishop of Canterbury. In their passage the Archbishop happened to stumble slightly on one of the interior supports. The King then reached him his hand, saying, *Come, my Lord Bishop, I will show you the way to heaven.*"

They ascended to the second platform, and here Herschel pointed out to them the complex and ingenious arrangement of pulleys which enabled the telescope to be brought into position by a single man, who need be no Goliath. He showed them the great lens and explained his strategy of polishing it by means of a troop of men wearing numbers. He told of the hardship and frustration that accompanied so many of the smaller details of workmanship. Burney and Haydn expressed proper surprise and commiseration at the intricacies of construction.

They descended and stood on solid ground once more.

"Are we now to see into the skies?" Doctor Burney asked.

"Yes," said Herschel, and he led them into the hut, and up onto the viewing platform.

This was the moment that Haydn had dreaded. He was overtaken by a misery so acute that he neither noticed his surroundings nor heard the dialogue that passed between Burney and Herschel. The depths of his mind cried out to the musician that he must not look into this instrument, that whatever he was to see beyond the pale of the moon would have only a disruptive influence upon his nature, that it was his task to think calmly upon the business of timbre and tempo, of chord progressions and tonal transitions. He could not tell himself what he thought, but he had a vague picture in his head of suns and worlds and comets bulging against the bar lines of a score sheet, of the stave lines broken and lying loose like pieces of string.

Herschel had now finished the operations necessary for viewing, and he stood back from the aperture. "Sir?" he said, inviting Haydn to take his place.

Haydn refused.

The astronomer gave him a look full of astonishment, but his astonishment immediately changed to sympathetic alarm. "My dear sir!" he exclaimed, rushing to Haydn's side. He took the composer's hands. "Why, my dear sir, you are all a-tremble. Here, you must sit down." There was a small straight chair at the edge of the platform and he drew it up.

Haydn sank into it gratefully.

"Maestro, are you ill?" Doctor Burney looked extremely anxious.

Haydn attempted to speak but could not.

Herschel hurried back to the telescope. Into a speaking tube that trailed down from the platform, he said, "Caroline, will you please bring wine and some cakes here? Our guest has taken a bad turn." Then he came back.

Burney was distracted by this machine. He ran to it and cried, "Ho! Miss Herschel, are you there?"

"Please don't shout, Doctor Burney," Herschel said. "You will deafen my poor sister. The tube is designed to carry a normal speaking voice." He turned to Haydn, who was now regaining his color and some of his composure. "Can you tell us what is the matter?"

"It is nothing, it will pass." He lied: "Now and again I am taken with a spell of dizziness."

"Are you certain? Our physician, Doctor Ormond, lives not far."

"No, please. It is nothing serious."

Caroline arrived, bearing a platter with a bottle of claret and some little apple cakes. She appeared sharply concerned about him, and, proffering him a glass of wine, murmured something he could not quite hear.

He drank off the wine greedily; a burning thirst had come upon him. He thanked her. She replenished the glass and offered him one of the little cakes, but he could not take it.

Burney looked upon him curiously and said with an air of bemusement: "You are well, you look entirely recovered now."

"Yes. It is nothing." He *had* recovered and there was nothing to be done, but still they fluttered around him until he began to grow a little irritable. "Please, I am *gesund.* . . . I am sound, I am sound."

"Not mere sound," Burney said. "You are music itself."

This lame joke restored the equanimity of the company, and they began to leave Haydn in peace. Herschel and the eager Burney withdrew to the telescope, and Burney was instructed how to view. As soon as he looked into it he became voluble, exclamations pouring out of him like steam from a tea kettle. He waved one hand freely and Doctor Herschel hovered at his side, evidently a bit worried about danger to his machinery.

Caroline stayed by Haydn; and he was grateful, for he was always soothed by the presence of women. He asked her of her astronomical accomplishments and how she came to be so extraordinarily learned. She mentioned something of her father Isaac's instruction and of her brother's, then passed the subject off and began talking of the domestic arrangements of the household, of the special provisions that had to be taken for a house full of stargazers. Haydn was gratified by this topic and questioned her closely about servants, about the disposition of meals for the odd hours that astronomers must keep, and about the house itself, which he found was rather cramped since the many thousands of pages of observed data had to be stored. He was amazed to know that the Herschels kept their pages of errors as well as the true pages; and she was surprised that when a passage went badly for the composer he simply crumpled the sheet and discarded it.

Burney had at length glutted his eyes, and he now came away, still expostulating and querying.

Haydn heard only Herschel's reply to a final question: "You must believe," said the astronomer, "that in a strip of space fifteen degrees long and two degrees wide I found there were 50,000 fixed stars and 466 nebulae."

These numbers struck a pang in Haydn's breast and his resolution almost failed once again. Yet when Doctor Herschel invited him to try the telescope he marched to it steadily, like a soldier marching in rank. As instructed, he put his eye to the aperture and found the metal still warm from the brow of Doctor Burney.

At first he could see nothing at all, not even darkness. There seemed to be a gauzy gray curtain that withheld his sight completely. Then at last this obstruction disarranged itself, and the stars and immense spaces began to show themselves.

— 3 —

The spirit of Joseph Haydn went from his body through the telescope like liquid sucked up through a glass tube.

He was not where his body was, but his spirit was already in the sphere of the moon. The world beneath him was no longer dark; it shone with various colors, pleasantly, like an artist's watercolor. Presently his spirit was in motion again, faster and faster—or was it that the globe began to revolve faster?—and the colors melted all together and the world diminished in size until it was no larger than a washed jewel, and fell away below him, shrinking to a candescent blue jot and then vanishing entirely. After this it was total darkness and awesome silence for a long while; and then the blackness was punctuated with streaks and points of brilliant white light and there came a rushing sound of swift wind, though nothing touched his body. For he had no physical body.

He no longer felt fear or apprehension, not the slightest tinge. He felt instead expectant, felt that he was about to witness something of great importance. That feeling persisted through the whole adventure, and even later when he recalled, there seemed to be something—an event, an image—of moment just outside his line of sight, just beyond earshot. There was about it forever a feeling of *impendingness*.

Now came a sensation of slowing, though the smears of light, which he took to be star-shapes stretched and tormented by the speed of his flight, began to appear more frequently until the whole firmament was surfeited with blinding light. Here his flight paused and Haydn gazed into that light, the heart of it, which moiled and leapt and reached out arms of lacy fire. If there was heat he was insensible to it and received only the spectacle of the light in its joyful agony, quaking and pulsing as it strove to manifest its being in the same instant that it strove to negate that being. He did not find it mindless. If music and poetry are not mindless, but instead the appreciable workings of personality, then this drama of light was intelligently assertive in the same way.

Franz Joseph Haydn passed through the center of that fire. It felt no more tangible than a cobweb. Beyond it was another absolute darkness, but the speed of his flight was not so terrific as formerly and the space about him no longer seemed boundless but enclosing. He traveled now as if he were struggling against some odd physical property of this space. There was a half-smothering quality in this new area. At last he burst through this odd place. It had seemed a shoddy unfinished plot of creation, and when he returned to pure customary space with the stars ranked before him like pearls in a coronet he felt pleased and refreshed.

A destination became evident. He passed a blue-white sun and three inner planets and his spirit-body began to settle tentatively as a butterfly in a fourth world which rose below him like an immense red, yellow, and black carpet lifting itself. He skimmed along the rim of the sky and came to rest in a city. He thought the city sleeping or dead. He walked, in quite ordinary fashion now, through streets and plazas.

Each object, every building, was cyclopean, and some of the structures he gauged to tower at least a mile above the ground. The geometry was uncanny; angles were acute or obtuse—there were no right angles—and many of the buildings looked to fold back in upon themselves so that their surfaces were both inside and outside at the same time. Every prospect was vertiginous and looked granular to the sight, as if even the minute particles which composed the building materials had been turned askew to one another. The breadth of streets and alleys did not correspond to the immense heights of the city, being narrower than they ought. Yet there was no feeling of constriction.

Most strikingly there was about it an impression of the primeval. The city looked not only the result of sophisticated handiwork, of accumulated architectural technique; it retained evidence of the firstness of things. Truly this city could be read as a kind of history book in which the origins of whatever race that built it were evident, origins to which the city was monument. When he inespected closely the wall of a building he discovered that every inch of it had been chopped out with a rude tool from some mineral he could not recognize.

Haydn walked on.

He was touched by an urgent desire to see one of the inhabitants of this world. Looking about the city he had experienced a feeling of outlandish kinship, and he wanted to meet a member of this ingenious race.

But for a long time there was no indication that the place was inhabited. An easy silence hung over every plane and corner. Then there began what he at first took to be a tremor of the ground, a gentle regular quivering that grew gradually in intensity as he went forward. But it was not a movement of the earth; it was a deep dark music. As soon as he recognized it as music it took his mind as wholly as a gentle spring rain. This was a single slow bass line, sostenuto, of unrepeating tones, resonant and elating. He could not determine its source.

The huge city was widely various in terms of space and structure. He began to think that it was centerless, but as that music continually increased in intensity—though not in volume—it occurred to him that if he came to the source of the music he would find the midpoint of the city.

Under the brilliant blue-white sun colors burned with a hard vividness. Indeed, these colors, primaries with others that Haydn could not name, looked not really to be properties of the surfaces from which they emanated. They seemed to stand slightly away, so that when he touched any wall he pushed his finger through the color, as through a film of oil. Otherwise his body was touchless and reacted with no objects at all. Curious phenomenon, considering that he cast shadow, and not a single shadow, but multiple shadows all tinted with the strong colors that flamed about him.

At last he drew into a large parklike area and saw at once the source of the deep music he had been following. All about, in shapes as irregular as cloud formations, stood huge clumps of spongy fungoid-looking vegetation of different pastel colors. Wide sinuous paths cut through this growth to arrive at a large paved circle of gray stone or metal. In the center of the circle stood a fountain. It rose tier upon tier high into the bright air. It jetted without surcease from the top a shining onyx-black substance, but so steady and continuous was the impulse of the fountain that Haydn could not distinguish whether the substance were water or oil. In fact, it looked like cold black stone as it dropped from tier to tier in strait unwavering streams. It occurred to him then that it was some fantastically complex structure of two materials: the veined leaf-green stone of the fountain, the sheeny black stone in descending arabesque. And from here the music issued; it was still no louder than before, but it was more resonant and permeated darkly his whole figure. When he glanced at his shadows he saw them throbbing and dancing like blown candle flames in helpless obeisance to the music of the fountain.

He was finally able to turn his attention from the fountain and saw beyond the paved area a scarlet ramp, glowing scarlet. It was broad and exhibited the usual irregular angles. The ramp led to another of the irregular structures, this one a double pyramid with the upper section inverted so that it looked like a strange hourglass. The building was dull orange in color, and Haydn thought that if he were going to see one of the constructors of this alien city, it would come forth from here. At this point the wall peeled away upward at the ramp juncture and the creature appeared. It looked like nothing so much as a huge coarse dense tangle of hempen rope. It came down the ramp with a monumental slowness. He could see no means by which it propelled itself, nor could he discover the center of its intelligence nor any organs of perception. But though there were no visible indications the composer was certain that the creature was feminine in gender, and there arose in him a vehement wave of tenderness and awe. His heart went out to it entirely. In his spirit-body Haydn fell on his knees to worship.

But the ground did not receive him.

He did not stop tipping forward, somersaulting, and the landscape surged up before him and washed over his sight in a confused blur. When he regained his equilibrium he found that he was traveling once again; once again he was in the interstellar spaces. The stars and planets and the broad silence welled up about him and quickly disappeared. He was traveling even faster than before, in mere moments traversing vast tracts of the universe. Of a sudden he halted. Floating before him in the void, surrounded by emptiness and a sparse starlight, was a yellowish object not larger than a loaf of bread. He drew closer to inspect it and found that it was a dragonfly, a delicate four-winged dragonfly, made painfully of gold and worked finely to the last impossible detail. There it floated, absolutely apart from everything else that existed, like a tiny planet unto itself. He stretched out his hand to touch it, but before he could do so it fluttered its wings in a deliberate mechanical fashion and, after a soft whir, uttered a series of musical notes, silvery tinkling. Ah, it was a music box traveling along out here in the void. . . . Though he could not place it, the gossamer little tune that the music box played was dearly familiar to him. Dearly familiar and nostalgic, and so rendingly nostalgic, that the simple sound of it returned the spirit of Haydn to his Mother Planet, to the nation of England and the village of Slough, where his three friends awaited him in anxious trepidation.

— 4 —

"So high, so far . . . So high . . . So far . . ." These were the words Haydn heard himself saying as he regained his body and his senses. (He was told later that he had muttered these same words for twenty minutes by the clock.) Once more he was shivering violently, for a heavy chill had come over his body, harsh cold piercing to the marrow.

He had been standing immovable, but now they were able to lead him back to the chair.

"Maestro, Maestro, we must take you in at once. We will send for the physician."

He waved his hand to brush the sentence away.

"Come, you must allow us to—"

"I am perfectly in health," Haydn said. His voice was clear and strong and seemed rather to abash his ministrants. "I feel strong and whole. These seizures of mine have sprung from nothing but force of imagination. They proceed from nothing but a childish fear, and now I find I am indebted to Dr. Herschel for presenting me the means to conquer this fear." He rose and gave Herschel a swift, almost a comic, bow.

Involuntarily they reached out to steady him, but withdrew their hands when the composer made a slight frown.

"You do appear remarkably recovered," said Herschel. "But you will not put my mind at ease until you have at least taken some tea."

Haydn nodded, smiling; he was beginning to be amused by so much solicitude.

They returned to the library and Caroline caused tea to be brought. They kept watching Haydn with kindly calculating eyes, and the composer felt assured he was among fast friends.

As they enjoyed the tea, along with the little cakes Caroline had rescued from the observatory, Haydn told them all. He told them in detail of the spatial journey of his spirit and of the strange prospects he had glimpsed. As he spoke they looked at one another in naked alarm, and then a happy comprehension spread over their faces. The Maestro was simply telling them of a *vision*; it was a *flight of genius*, of the sort that must come not infrequently to an artist of Haydn's magnitude. . . . At several points Doctor Herschel seemed to want to interrupt with questions, but he held himself in check, hearing his guest's narrative to its conclusion.

When he finished talking a sweet lassitude overtook him, and Haydn yawned and stretched his limbs languorously.

Even before he could apologize, Herschel and his daughter had rung for a servant and begun importuning Haydn to stay the night.

He agreed. It would be tedious to try to say them nay, and indeed he was feeling very tired, deliciously so. As he was allowing himself to be led up the stairs, Doctor Burney called to him: "Now I have solved the conundrum. That Mars-man I felt was looking down upon me, that, sir, was you!"

Haydn woke later than usual the next morning. Full sunlight streamed through the little window, shining on the stacked volumes of astronomical figures shoved against the farther wall. When he sat up in bed Haydn noticed a note addressed to him lying folded on the bedside table beside the pitcher and basin. He opened it and read:

> Ur, gleet edd gromious Orban! Lummities org Bok-Fin-lay thum smummute. Morey edd Carti er frankpau losh. Freasly ik frammis tur bergey, edd anoot tur twillig bonest ell.
>
> > Meliesly tarse,
> > Yenrub

—My dear Haydn, during the night I received this communication which I am convinced is writ in the Mars-man dialect. If you will breakfast with me here at the New Genesis Inn, we will attempt to puzzle it out. The Inn is not far. I have arranged with the Herschels.

> > With affectionate esteem,
> > Chas. Burney

Haydn laughed and spoke aloud: "Ah, Doctor Burney, in your company one does not have to seek far for the Mars-man." Then he rose from bed.

Some commentators are not content for the account to end here. Two scholars at least have declared that this acquaintance with the cosmos made Haydn's mind receptive to the music of the young composer Beethoven, who was then twenty-three. Less than a month later, Haydn, on his homeward passage, stopped in Bonn and there heard the *Cantata in Mourning for the Death of Emperor Joseph II.* He immediately accepted Beethoven as a composition pupil.

And Sir Donald Tovey, in his *Essays in Musical Analysis,* asseverates that it was on the platform of Herschel's observatory that *The Creation* was born. Some certain physical symptoms might seem to corroborate this view, for when Haydn came to conduct the premiere performance at the Schwarzenburg Palace on April 29, 1798, he reported his condition in these words: "One moment I was cold as ice, the next I seemed on fire. More than once I was afraid I should have a stroke."—The performance was received with an enthusiasm almost incredible. The audience sat transfixed with fright during the musical description of Chaos. When at last came the line, "Let there be light —and there was light," they rose as one man for a prolonged and deafening ovation. Haydn turned to face his admirers and pointed his baton upward, toward the ceiling. "Not from me," he said. "From thence comes everything."

The Thousand Ways

Love, O love, O careless love,
You broke my heart a thousand ways.

— 1 —

*I*t was about three o'clock in the afternoon of a rainy October day in
the year 1962. In the middle-sized town of D—— in central North
Carolina a young man lay in his bed in a cheap hotel and gnawed at
his pillow and bedclothes in indecision and dismay. He lay on his
stomach and with a feverish indolence tossed his head one way and
then another, his dull blond hair falling in thick spikes on the sheets.
His features, though not delicate, were smooth and a bit indistinct, and
his face—although it needed soap and water and a razor—had an air
of dull expectancy, of frustration. Perhaps his eyes most contributed to
this effect, nervous depthless gray eyes beneath dark heavy lids and long
black lashes which curled upward. His body, however, gave no impression of delicacy; he was five feet ten and well proportioned, had a
fineness of bone at wrist and collar and a skin fairer than the dingy
linen amid which he now lay. He was fully clothed in gray gabardine
slacks and a powder blue V-neck sweater worn over a cotton T-shirt.
He wore black loafers and white athletic socks. His name was Mark
Vance.

No light burned in the small room. From the two gritty windows
a listless whitish light fell upon the stained green wallpaper with its
yolk-colored floral design, upon the dressing table black with dust and
repeated lacquerings, and upon the bed where Mark toiled. Opposite
the foot of the bed against the dim south wall stood a rickety writing
desk. Beside the lamp, whose ivory-colored shade was distantly remi-

308

niscent of hooped crinoline skirts, lay scattered a number of small elegant scientific instruments, their uses as yet unknown to Mark. There were also a few paperbound books of symbolic logic and metaphysics and verse, together with four or five newstand sex novels with titles like *Virgin Madame, Dormitory Love, Sins of Lola*, and so forth. A schoolboy composition book with blue-ruled paper lay there also, and a handful of ballpoint pens. There were the tools of Mark's vocation. In the composition book he was setting down a long eclectic poem about the nature of universal suffering, a list of the names of persons who were harshly injured by love and pity. *Pornography* was the proposed title of this poem. A white earthenware pitcher, mouth chipped in four places, sat in a bowl on the nightstand. In one corner of the room a tiny lavatory announced its presence with the sound of continual dripping.

Outside, the town swam hazily in a fall of fine rain. The tarred roofs of the cigarette factories were shiny black and the streets whispered with the sound of tires rolling through the film of water. Industrial smoke rose slowly, struggling upward. The sidewalks were clotted with slow lurid umbrellas. On the rusty window screen raindrops paused, welled, broke, and ran over, like transparent boils. A red sky began to show in the west under the rim of cloud and long red smears were reflected in the wet streets, which after a while oozed with the various colors of reflected neon as businesses prepared to close shop for the night. It was Friday. It seemed to Mark that the autumnal rains always began on Friday, muffling the anticipated weekend.

The whole afternoon he lay in bed and squirmed, turning on his back at times to stare sightlessly at amorphous rusty splotches on the ceiling, at times lying on his side in a nervous doze, blinded by dry yellow dreams. Sometimes a noise from outside, a sudden squeal of brakes, a siren, an exasperated car horn, touched him like a cold finger and he jerked in his sleep and muttered. Sometimes a sworl in a dream, a black door thrust open, moved his body. And when at last he woke around six-thirty a sticky sweat covered all his face and scalp.

He rolled to the edge of the bed and felt on the floor for cigarettes and matches and began to smoke. With some difficulty he maneuvered the heavy jug from the nightstand to the floor and dropped ash into it. He propped and plumped the pillows; lay back, scratched his sparse blond whiskers and his crotch, searched his ear with his little finger, felt his wrist and carefully, firmly counted his pulse. But then, groggy, he dropped off to sleep again for a minute or so.

He woke when the cigarette burned his fingers and rose, murmuring at the pain, and tossed it uncrushed into the jug. He went to the tall dresser and examined himself in the dark peeling mirror. He lifted back his eyelids and looked at the ball and pupil; bared his teeth with a fierce grimace and looked and opened his mouth entirely and looked there too. At the lavatory he washed his neck and face and hands, then found a coffee mug and brush and rust-spotted safety razor in the dresser drawer. He made up a thin lather and shaved and toweled his face clean. For a shaving lotion, he patted rubbing alcohol on his cheeks and neck. Again he looked himself over in the mirror and tugged at his clothes where sleeping had creased them and pulled spread fingers through his hair, bringing it straight over the left side and patting it down. Counting his money, he found that he had four dollars and seventy cents. He got his room key and went out without a jacket.

In the late dusk the buildings that cast huge gray shadows almost invisible acquired a harder, more solid aspect while the smaller buildings that sat squarely in the dark light rather softened in their outlines. A broad misty rain still fell, stuttering upon hot light bulbs. It pervaded everything, so that it seemed to rain inside those buildings with the darkened windows, as well as outside upon the streets and awnings and signs.

Mark came out of the Malvern Hotel and walked a few blocks and went into the Venus Grill, a long, fairly well-lighted, dirty place just now emptying of the customers who had come in for a meal after their factory shifts. He sat on a stool near the middle of the bar. At the bar end a couple of elderly men sat talking about the new integration troubles over beer long turned warm. He ordered chicken-fried country steak and eggs and cold biscuits and honey from a fat man he didn't know, and while he was waiting George Palinopolous came over from the cash register and talked to him.

"Mark, Mark," he said softly. "Wet enough for you? How are you getting along? You doing okay?"

"Just fine, George," Mark said. "How're you getting along?"

"Tell you the truth, Mark, I'm a little down in my back. This kind of weather don't do my bones a lot of good. My old woman tells me it's a bunch of foolishness, but I know what I feel like. I could have told you on Tuesday this weather was coming." He blinked; it was his habit—a quick flicker of both eyelids, like fingers snapping. "It's kind of a *screwing* pain right at the bottom of my backbone. It don't make much sense to tell somebody, you got to feel it to know what I mean. Of course, I wouldn't want you never to have the trouble, though." He touched Mark on the forearm and blinked again.

"You're getting to be an old man, George. That's your real trouble."

"Huh-uh. No sir. I'm fit as a fiddle, me, except for this being down a little in my back. It was that box of canned tomato juice five years ago, right there in that room." He pointed with his elbow toward an unpainted plywood door at the back. "I saw it come slewing off the top of the stack, and if I'd had the sense God gave a billy goat I'd've let it drop. You know how it is, though: you see something falling, you reach out and catch it. It's kind of mechanical—you can't hardly help yourself. Brother, it sure jerked a knot in me." He winked.

"Mnh."

The fat man brought Mark's food. The steak was submerged in a thin gravy. The pale honey came in a little paper cup. Mark hesitated.

George tapped him on the arm. "Go ahead and eat. I've got to get back to the register in just a minute." He propped a leg up on something beneath the bar and lit a cigarette. "Say, Mark, did I ever show you my girl's picture?"

Mark shook his head. His mouth was filled with egg.

George dug under his spotted apron and brought out a worn billfold. It fell open at his daughter's photograph. A girl in a dark sweater with Greek black oval eyes and a large nose. Mark found her very attractive, especially about the mouth. A full, almost fat, lower lip; clean lines of jaw and chin. Her ears were hidden in the black hair swept back. "Don't that look like a snotty ignorant Greek kid? Don't that look like a brat that will worry her old man to death?" He tapped the plastic protector with a tough thumbnail. "You know this college in town, this Burton's Business College?"

Mark shook his head No.

"Well, it's a nice school, it's a fine business school," George said. "You see it advertised in the papers all the time. And she got in easy, they didn't give her any trouble at all. . . . Say, Mark, this is the only country in the world where something like that could happen. When I came to this town I didn't know ten words of English, me. And now look at that." He flicked the photograph again.

"I'm a great believer in American democracy," Mark said.

"Now you're talking. Say, you know this little girl almost went off to one of the biggest and best colleges in this country? A really big college, I mean to say. If it hadn't've been for my brother-in-law . . ."

"Yeah?"

"Well, Dick got into some of these drugs. . . . He got in pretty deep, to tell the truth." He shook his head. "Well, he's had his troubles. . . . I kind of lay it to those doctors after he had his car accident, but he got to taking some kind of dope or other. . . . Anyway, I almost had the money saved up so she could go to one of the really big colleges, and I bet she would've done all right too. But Dick had some trouble —actually, two-three times he's had a little trouble and it's cost me some money here and there, so when it came down to the wire, time for her to go, I just didn't have it. Irene—say, you ever met my wife, Mark?—Irene said I was crazy to let Dick have the money, she said it wasn't any of my concern." He tapped his forehead with his knuckles. "Can you believe that? Her own brother, her own flesh and blood in trouble like that, and she grudged him the money. We come first: that's what she told me; and I told her, We're not in trouble, but Dick's in *trouble*." He shook his head again, his expression wry. "Tell you the truth, Mark. These women can get you by the short hairs."

Mark finished his meal and looked around for the fat waiter.

"What do you need?" said George. "I'll get it."

"Just a cup of coffee."

While he was drinking the second cup the telephone rang and George beckoned him to it. He blinked the quick blink and handed him the receiver. "Sounds like one of your girlfriends," he said.

"Yes?" said Mark.

"Mark?"

"Yes."

"Mark . . ." Her voice was a deep contralto and in the receiver it sounded more masculine than when he talked to her in person. It was furry at the edges, and she drew vowels out abnormally so that he knew she had been drinking. "You promised you wouldn't forget we were going to have dinner together tonight. Don't you remember? Aren't you coming over? I knew I'd find you in that place on a Friday night."

"I wish you wouldn't drink so much," he said. "You're always drinking."

"Mark, I'm *lonesome*. You catch a taxi now and come on over."

"I'll be there in a while, Norma. I want to walk. And I want another cup of coffee."

"It'll take simply hours to walk. You call a taxi. I'll be waiting out for you. I'll pay for the taxi."

"No," he said evenly. "I want to walk. I'll be there after a while." He hung up quickly and went back to the counter and got a third cup of coffee.

George came over to talk again. George was about five and a half feet tall and was accumulating a queer little paunch of which his belt buckle marked the center exactly. His hair was shiny white on the outside but underneath showed a dark gray. His movements were quick and nervous. Across his face expressions flickered fitfully. He lit a gopher match with a wide sweep of his arm as if he were drawing a sword from its scabbard. "That's fine, a young fellow like you gets out, has a little fun. I wouldn't mind it myself, but you know, after the first four or five years after I was married I didn't care nothing about it anymore. That's what I found out about myself. Of course, I've still got life in me, lots of life." Twice he rapped himself sharply on the chest. "How old would you say I am? Go on, take a guess. How old?"

"I don't know. Forty-one, maybe. Forty-three."

"I'm fifty-four years old. Fifty-four, that's how old I am. I've got three kids in school now, and come next fall my oldest girl goes to a fine business college, right here in this town. How's that for a dumb Greek, huh? Not so bad, maybe."

"That's fine," Mark said. "That's real fine." He stood up and pushed his coffee cup to the middle of the bar. "I've got to be getting along," he said. "How much do I owe you?"

"Mark, Mark . . ." George's voice was full of compassionate re-
proach. "You know better than that. The day you pay for supper in
here is the day I shut the doors. You know better than that."

"Now wait, George."

"Listen, Mark, we've been through it before. I just won't take it.
I know it takes a young fellow a while to get on his feet, to get things
going his way. But where do you think I'd be now if people hadn't
given me a little breathing room back when I was starting out?" He
paused, reflecting. "Of course, they couldn't do it so easy back then.
Money was a lot tighter than it is now."

"I appreciate it," Mark said. "I surely do thank you." With a sort
of dull hurt he wondered for how many meals he actually owed George.

Norma Lang lived in the suburbs of the town of D———, about
two miles from the Venus Grill. Mark walked slowly, stooped forward,
his hands in his pockets. Often he halted to look in shop windows or
to watch a girl boarding a bus or a crowd pouring out of the movie
house, crushed together and murmuring fretfully. The sad drizzle had
stopped and a heavy warm mist stuffed the air, spreading halos about
all naked lights. Traffic gathered in bunches and quickly dispersed. On
his face and hands he could feel the moisture gather and run.

A boy about ten years old stopped him in front of the bus depot.
He was wearing worn corduroy trousers and had huge dark eyes. "Give
me a dime," he said.

"What for?" Mark asked.

"I want to see the picture," he said. "All I need is just one more
dime to get in."

"What picture?"

"I want to see *The Crawling Eye*," he said. "It's about this mad
scientist that kills his . . ."

"I know what it's about. What I ought to give you is a smack on
the butt. It's too late for you to be out. Does your mother know where
you are? You better be getting on home, it's way too late."

"She didn't want me at home, she sent me out. She's who told
me to go to the show."

"She ought to make you stay home this time of night. Didn't she give you some money?"

"I lost it."

"No you didn't. You spent it."

The boy looked down at the pavement and half-turned. He wanted to go now.

"Wait a minute. She ought to keep you home this hour of the night. She shouldn't be sending you out."

"Aw, all she wants to do is get laid. She sent me out of the house."

Mark led the boy by the shoulder to the inside of the sidewalk. He leaned against the depot wall and rubbed one hand in the other over and over.

"What's wrong with you, mister? Are you sick?" The boy was frightened, beginning to gather his body to run away.

"There's nothing wrong with me." He pulled all his money out of his pocket and gave it to the boy. "Here," he said. "That's four dollars and seventy cents. You take it and hide it away. Don't let anybody know that you've got it."

He shook his head gravely. "All I want is a dime. I just want to see the picture."

"No. You keep it. Hide it away."

The boy shrugged and stuffed the money into his pants. He walked past Mark, going west to the movies.

"Wait a minute. What's your name?"

"Joe," he said. He turned and cocked his head to one side. He appeared to feel safer at a distance of ten feet from Mark.

"Joe who?"

"Joe Starret. You sure are a dumb guy. All I wanted was a dime."

"I still ought to smack your butt," Mark said. "What kind of talk is that?"

Joe Starret rolled his eyes upward and shook his head. "It's not but eight o'clock," he said.

"Oh lord," Mark said under his breath. With military precision he turned on his heel and walked away. He said it aloud. "Oh lord." He stopped and produced a filthy handkerchief from his back pocket and wiped his cheeks. When he began walking again he was laughing quite loudly. "You sure are dumb, old Mark," he said.

On Marchand Street it was quiet and shadowy. The light from occasional streetlamps was spattered and absorbed by the piled over-hanging branches of red maples that lined the sidewalk. Red, yellow, and tobacco-colored leaves lay flattened on the watery cement as if collected in a child's book. From the windows of the black houses came the hush-making glow of table lamps or the relentless flutter of television sets. For two blocks he was able to follow most of the dialogue of *Rawhide*, and he turned left on Twane Avenue just as the commercial came on. Over the tops of houses and trees shone the ghostly glow of the town lights, diffused through the mist.

She was sitting within the dark porch. He saw the tip of her cigarette brighten and drop as he came up the front walk. "I thought you'd never get here," she said. "It's been hours."

"I ran into a kid," he said, clambering toward her over the stacks of cardboard boxes and wooden crates and loose junk lying on the porch. Something crunched under his foot, and a length of cloth got wrapped about his ankle and he dragged it slithering along.

"Come on inside." She rose regretfully from a deep wicker chair and opened the screen door behind her. She held a bottle by the neck and lurched against the brick wall as she went in. Mark followed.

Inside it was blind dark. "Turn on some light," he said.

"Let's sit here in the dark," she said. "Think how cozy that is."

"Please turn on a light. I can't even see a chair." He stood still while she floundered through the mess to a floor lamp and switched it on. Shade cocked awry, the lamp shed a dim yellow light; revealed the dirty litter of the room: boxes of clothing, dishes, and newspapers lay scattered on the floor and perched on chairs and coffee tables; book-shelves were heaped with cosmetics, hair curlers, pins, toilet waters; books and newspapers lay closed or spread open on the couch and floor. On the brick mantel a large alarm clock sat, its hands not moving from a quarter past two.

Mark scratched a couple of novels out of a chair and sat. He peered through the open door into the dark dining room beyond. "You didn't fix dinner anyway. You couldn't fix a meal with all this mess."

"I thought we could go out for dinner after you got here. The big problem was to get you to show up. That's always the big problem." She crossed to a bookshelf and picked up an empty glass and peered through it toward the lamp to look at the dirt in it. Then she shrugged and poured red wine into it from the bottle she still held loosely in her left hand. "Do you want some wine?"

"I don't drink," he said stiffly.

Her laugh was guttural, nervewracking. "You look so prim when you say that, the way you tighten your lips: *I don't drink.*" She sat on the couch under the lamp. Beneath her the crumpling newspapers made a sound like a house of cards falling. She sat revealed in the lamplight. Her short hair would have been a bright chestnut color if it had been clean, but now it was filthy, tangled and raddled. At least she had not made up; she always looked so much worse wearing cosmetics. The round face was dark and pitted slightly, the light making small shadows the shape of fingernails upon it. Her eyes were large and set far apart, her nose straight but bulbous at the tip. Her body was short and stubby and too heavy for her height. The wide hand that held the glass at the top between thumb and middle finger had dirty fingernails. She wore a dressing gown of a sulphurous green color. One pocket was torn down the side, the other fat with Kleenex. Beneath the robe a white silk negligee was impressed with all the mounds and creases of her body and was spotted with food, drink, and ash. "Sometimes I think you're the worst kind of prude. A real Plymouth Rock Puritan."

"Why don't you clean this place up? I've never seen a place so filthy. You've been here how long?—Four months? You haven't lifted a finger since you moved in."

"Prude, prude, prude." She closed her eyes and drank. "I'm the only person who ever sees it. Except you, of course." She gave him a coy grimace.

"It's not my delight in life to look at it," he said. "It smells bad in here too." He felt helpless.

"Cigar smoke. Can't get rid of it. I had a bottle of Air Wick somewhere, but . . ."

"I thought I was the only one who ever came here."

"I smoke cigars. I just never smoke them when you're here. I'm afraid I'll shock you, you'll have a stroke or something. You're such an awful prude, you know. The last of the Mrs. Grundys." She giggled. "The last of the big spenders."

"What's so funny?"

"It's a pun on the verb *to spend*."

"What *are* you talking about?"

"Oh forget it." She waggled her hand to indicate the mess. "The expense of spirit in a waste of . . ."

"Shakespeare."

"Right you are."

"You could use a bath too."

"The bathtub is full of blankets and things. I thought you knew that. Remember, I told you once I couldn't lift those things up into the closets."

"I forgot."

"No you didn't. You never forget. You told me yourself that you never forget."

"Well, something like *that* . . ."

"If it's not important enough to remember it's not worth bitching about. Bitch and nag, nag and bitch. Mrs. Grundy."

"You keep bringing her up. Is she kin to you or something?"

"My great-grandmother on my husband's side. Pardon me. I mean, my ex-husband."

"Yeah."

"Don't look so shocked, like you found a snake in the icebox. What do you know about it?"

"Just what you tell me."

"That's enough. If you knew anything besides what I told you, you'd just get mixed up. Good God, Mark honey, the world is full of divorce. You'll just have to bear with it. People aren't going to stay stuck together, that's all. It's just too bad, but that's the way it is."

"I know. You talk to me like I was a child."

She grinned, her wide full mouth pulled white. "You are a child. You're my sweet little honey-baby. This big old world's too mean for you. That's your trouble in a nutshell."

"Come off it."

"You ought to donate yourself to science so they could study you. They'd throw Darwin out tomorrow. Survival of the fittest, my ass. You couldn't survive your way out of a bowl of soup. And here you are alive, without a scratch on you. It's a supernatural gift, that's what. You're a scientific curiosity. Suppose everybody was like you—where would we be then?" She lit a cigarette and frowned. "You know, I never feel at peace except when I'm with you. It's like a vacation."

"Vacation from what? You don't work. You live on alimony in this pig sty."

"I can see that you're not very happy tonight. . . . But you're always charming. I simply can't get over how you're always charming."

"Give me some money," he said. "I gave all mine to some kid on the way over here. I couldn't figure it out. Apparently his mama sent him to the movies so she could shack up with somebody. Eight o'clock at night. Hard to figure. She must be divorced or separated or something."

"Maybe she's not married at all."

"She ought to be kicked. Why does she want to do things like that? That kid's not nine years old. . . . I don't see the sense of doing something like that. You know, he could get run over or something. She wouldn't even know."

"How much money did you give him?" She took a white vase the shape of a conch shell from the coffee table and struggled to get her hand into it.

"Four dollars and seventy cents is all I had."

She stared at the money in her hand. "I have twenty-seven dollars. Will fifteen be enough for you? Howard's late with the check again. I hope I don't have to write and remind him. It's so awkward writing to an ex. I don't know how to sign off. I can't just write *Yours truly* or *Sincerely*. But it's so silly to write *Love*, or *Affectionately*. . . . I'll just write down my naked name. That's what I've been doing."

"It's a tough problem, all right."

She poured more wine. "Oh, what do you know about it?"

A fair question. She had too many fair questions. "Nothing."

"That's right. So why don't you save your moral disapproval? Who handed you the goddamn gavel, anyway? How did you get to be appointed judge and jury?"

"I don't know," he answered earnestly. "But I can't help the way I am. I've thought about it a lot lately, and I still believe that I'm right. I have the right idea about things. Nobody agrees with me. That's all right. They like me. Everybody I know is very nice to me."

"You're not that wonderful. You're no Einstein and no Albert Schweitzer either. You look like a Bohemian prince and you behave like Charlie Brown. That's all it is. That's the whole thing. That doesn't make you any goddamn Socrates."

"I didn't say it did."

"But you act like it did."

"I can't help the way I am. I've thought about it quite a lot, and that's just the way I am."

She dumped the last of the bottle into her glass and came over and sat on the arm of his chair. Turning her heavy body, she stroked his chin gently. "You ought to grow a big soft beard. You'd look just like Jesus, I swear you would." She patted the top of his head. "If I left it up to you, you'd talk all night, wouldn't you? Come on, it's getting late. It's already too late. Let's go to bed." She tugged him by the arm.

He was vexed. "I can't help the way I am," he said.

But he was going with her, not only for the taste of it, the shuddery pleasure. He ached for the momentary necessary illusion of having at least a bit of her fate in his grasp. Of course she would be, as always, perversely resisting. He felt an instant of revulsion; it seemed there was a knot he must untie and could not. His fingertips bled with the effort of untying.

She pulled him to his feet. "Come on." She led him forward, still holding her glass in her left hand. At the door she uttered that shattering giggle. "You're a fucking saint, is what you are," she said, "and I mean fucking."

— 2 —

She woke heavily, as if swimming up out of a pool of warm grease, but at first she wasn't awake at all, merely disturbed in a dream because her outstretched left arm did not find Mark beside her in the bed. When she finally opened her eyes she said, "That son of a bitch," and laughed. Her mouth and throat were dry and crusted with thirst. She felt the ponderous stirring of a terrific headache, which she knew would grow to a tight thunder if she didn't get out of bed immediately to doctor it with aspirin and coffee. She rolled over, clutching backward at the sheet to cover her liquescent nakedness. Over her neck and in a delta on her chest was spread a reddish suntan, but below this, all the way down, her body was white as a boiled egg and felt viscid, hot in the coarse sheets. She closed her eyes, and the sun poured a red haze though the lids. She rolled on her back and began to cough. The coughing fit lasted about five minutes, with tense intervals when she gagged a bit and gasped for breath. No doubt of it, she was sick, not long for this world. Maybe she could change her way of living.

It was probably about eleven o'clock. The Westclox on the night stand read three-thirty, just as it had ever since she moved into this house on Twane Avenue. Three-thirty in the morning, that was; the goddamn dark goddamn night of the goddamn soul. She felt ninety years old instead of forty-five. It didn't feel good, but maybe it was a good idea: the rocking chair, the shawl, the false teeth, lone white hairs sticking out of her chin. It was a good idea but it wasn't *her*; too much like a Jonathan Winters characterization. She groped in the shelf in the headboard of the bed for cigarettes and came up with a handful of balloon hair curlers and a paperback copy of *Pride and Prejudice*. She got the Chesterfields on the fourth try and struggled to get one lit. God, the whole day could go like this. She cursed when she rolled over again and one of the curlers crushed into her hip. She threw it on the floor.

Outside the cool sunlight flashed here and there among the oak leaves like butterflies flitting about, settling one place and then another.

She imagined how it smelled outdoors, but it still didn't make her hungry. She was, however, determined to eat and ran over silly lists of food in her mind until she decided that the only thing she could certainly get down was a pineapple sundae. At first she was angry with herself, but then she began to laugh. Why not? A pineapple sundae was as healthy as . . . as a coed at a football game.

She was so miserable she was almost numb. The headache was motionless at the back of her head, gathering force. The wind stirred the trees outside. She could hear a mouse nibbling at a resonant cardboard box in a near closet and the endless streaming of the broken cistern of the toilet and the creak of the bedspring and the susurration of her breasts against the wilted linen as she breathed. Pondering, she rubbed her hand round and round her wide soft belly. "Mind now," she said absently, "you behave yourself. Be a good little belly."

She fell into a reverie. The tree leaves seemed to chirrup with light under the clear sky. In the upper corner of the window sailed a filmy little cloud. What if all her fantasies came true? What if she were immediately younger and beautiful and worth millions? The thought made her stupid. She got only a fleeting glimpse of a large bright sitting room with all the windows and doors open. Oh yes, and a piano. And flowers on the piano . . . But that was all. It was too great a strain to invent any more details or to concoct a plot for a happy drama to take place in the bright sitting room, a story in which she would be the insouciant heroine. The reverie clouded over and Mark Vance's face began to blossom into it.

The mouse in the closet stopped nibbling and in a moment skittered away into a hole, frightened at something she didn't know about. She heard footsteps, slow and deliberate on the front porch, but they didn't come to the door, and soon she didn't hear them. There were no footsteps. Silence always played tricks with the senses like that. It was a great deep silence. What if the Russian radiation had killed everyone except herself while she slept? Saved by an incomprehensible accident, she was the only person alive on the planet. She would wander city after city looking for company. Some quality of the radiation prevented the corpses from rotting or stinking. Bodies were everywhere: seated at lunch tables, slumped behind steering wheels, reading, propped un-blinking on the johns.

She could no longer put off thinking about how much she loved Mark Vance. It made her sick to think about it. On the bare window the clipped squares of sunlight had got brighter, and a female cardinal, gray but pinkish at the throat, lighted in the firethorn shrub outside the window. She examined her big ugly hands. She was going to hell in a washtub. God, she really had got to take hold of herself or she was going to make a hell of an unpleasant corpse. She imagined herself lying in the purple casket in the funeral home and the living filing by her, taking a quick glance at her laid out there and turning immediately to puke in a big silver bucket the funeral home people had placed nearby. Last of all came Howard. He tried not to, he tried to be nice, but it was impossible and finally he too had to turn to the votive receptacle. He always tried to be nice, he almost always succeeded. It was Norma Lang who was the bitch, but even so she was still dissatisfied with herself. All that bitchiness—where had it got her? Seven Ways to Wreck Two Lives: 1. Be an awful bitch; 2. Get worse if possible; 3. Drink like crazy; 4. Catch something incurable. Four was all she could come up with.

Why couldn't she die in style, triumphantly?

The hangover lolled in her brain like a top-heavy sunflower and she almost gathered enough will to rise, to dress herself. The broken cistern trickled loudly; it sounded worse than usual. She melted back into lethargy. It was sucking the stuff out of her, like someone drinking a soda through a straw. Her stomach felt like a handful of wet cotton stuffing. She lay there like a puddle. What if she had to die with a hangover? She had thought about dying so much she was almost ac-customed to it, but she couldn't stop thinking about it. It was like when she was a child and couldn't stop pulling the scabs off her scratches. Anyway, she wouldn't know when she died. Surely her sickness would snatch away her consciousness first and it would be just quietly going off to sleep. At the end she wouldn't be in her right senses and not really responsible for her lack of dignity. She would be quiet and pitiful, a fat Camille. She didn't weigh so much, but she looked fat. That too was the sickness.

What would Howard say? He would cry, he would bawl like a wet baby. What would Mark do? What would he say? She would never tell him what was going to happen. Let him find out, it was the one thing she was going to reach him with. He seemed to understand her. What put him off? The trees stood still in the full light, the tops piecemeal and polychrome like shredded flags. Now the cistern made a high singing sound. Mark was so sweet, and she always made him feel defensive. He was helpless as a rabbit. No matter what he said, he was always the same, presenting to the world his tender solar plexus, and he never got a punch for it. He could arouse a motherly feeling in the carcass of a dead horse. Partly it was because you knew he was strong —but not tough—underneath; he didn't really need your protection, was merely flattered that you offered it. Partly it was because he was so silly. His main fault was that he didn't spend enough time with her.

She had almost reassembled Howard's face in her memory. It was strange how a person you lived with for a long time—say twenty-two years, to make an even number—left no physical memory. There was a memory, right enough, unforgettable and amorphous as water. His face was a long oval. He had thin lips. Now he had a white bald spot on top which she could not cover with her hand. He wore black-rimmed heavy glasses. He was getting a double chin. He had huge ears with long smooth lobes. Tall, fairly heavy, with large bones and great strength. The only thing soft about him was his feelings. God, she felt awful. She couldn't get the puzzling pieces to fit together to form Howard. She loved him mercilessly. The mouse had come back to chew the box and another one had come to join it. She heard its progress across the closet like something wet dripping across the floor. The running cistern sang like a tea kettle.

It was so godawful filthy, that kitchen, that she knew she couldn't face it. She would starve first. She began to daydream. Two starlings settled in the firethorn and yapped and leapfrogged among the fragile twigs. Along her temples and down the back of her neck the hangover began to glow, like a sheet of tin heated red. Another mouse seemed to have joined the two; the house was riddled with them. Unimaginable, whatever in the closet they were attracted to. She loved him without quarter, he gave up without a fight. It was crazy to hurt him that way, to love him so much without any tenderness. Poor Howard. Poorer, much poorer Norma. "I been sick," she murmured, trying to hypnotize her belly into keeping still.

Maybe the mail had come, maybe his check had come, maybe he had sent a letter with the check. What was he doing at night besides sitting home drinking? Brahms. It came to her. Listening to Brahms, for God's sake.

At last she got out of bed. She could feel the presence of the house about her like a huge fantastic overcoat, presence palpable to the pores of her skin almost, securing her nearly completely from the immense inconsequence of the town, of the world that did not think about her. The house was an arena that was like a lens, allowing her to focus all her faculties upon the condition of being about to die. What beautiful nonsense she was thinking. . . . In her mind it imitated wonderfully the noise of intellectual operation.

She got her arms into the grimy green corduroy dressing gown. One of the pockets of the robe was ripped down one side, the other pocket was stuffed with used tissues. She sat on the edge of the bed. She got another cigarette lit and looked down at her body in the open robe. Running her wide hand over her flesh she felt better without knowing why. The tops of her knees were rough and red; her thighs were too short, but they were not fat—her legs didn't make sense. No, not all her body had failed her; between her legs her body still fought toward life. She patted the crisp triangle of her sex rather in the way she would pet a dog. The good and faithful servant, the bad master . . . Brittle light fell on her naked body in the open robe. Her breasts were large and soft and weighty and were streaked with occasional blue marks as if they had been touched here and there with a ballpoint pen. The light coming through the window looked like big hollow glass bars. Around her belly she put her forearms, as if she were gathering up a bundle of clothes, and it spilled between and over her clasp. Somewhere under the sheets her soiled white negligee lay crushed into a ball.

A little alley road ran under the winking trees behind the house, so she really ought to put up the drapes for the bedroom windows soon. What if someone saw her like this? She smiled. Like a fist slowly opening and closing, her headache seemed to make itself come and go. What if they did, so what? Shouldn't it make a man happy and envious to spy a lady naked in her chamber? She didn't have to be a goddamn Lady Godiva. She fell into a reverie.

Why shouldn't she die calmly and nobly? Who was it who said . . . what was it? Saint Francis, who preached to the birds. She couldn't remember. Well, it was obvious that she wasn't particularly noble. She stood up carefully. She went to the white vanity and stood and watched herself gravely in the mirror. Slipping an arm out of the dressing gown, she let it hang at one shoulder and looked over her shoulder into the mirror, studying the way she was behind. She put her arm back into the sleeve. Unsteadily she made a couple of pirouettes on the balls of her bare feet and dropped a curtsy to the mirror in the approved manner. She crushed out her cigarette in the ashtray on the vanity, and the smoke came out of the ashtray and got tangled in her hair falling forward. She began coughing again.

It was a beautiful day, full of light and mice and birds and silence, and in the house she felt constrained, stifled. It was a beautiful day for, say, a picnic. She began to daydream. What a mess that room was. Clothes and sheets and newspapers were strewn all about the floor; on the vanity a clutter of cosmetics, hairpins, curlers, brushes, cigarettes, all dusted over with spilled face powder. Here and there novels lay open face down. It was too final; she could never bring herself to finish a book. In all those books, what happened after they got married? Or got rich? Or got their just desserts? What happened after they died? "You've got to stop somewhere," she murmured. She giggled. She searched in the drawers for something she could wear without a girdle. She felt too ridiculous squirming into the thing. Ah, the feminine charm. She could get by as Mother Earth, perhaps. If she could dress, she could go somewhere to eat; she wouldn't have to encounter the rancid kitchen. She laid out underthings on the bed and searched in the stuffed closet for a dress. The hangover was horrible. She could stand to lose a little weight; a lot, to be truthful. Skipping a meal now and again wouldn't hurt—she couldn't be any worse anyway. Probably there was something in the refrigerator to drink. She took down a dark blue dress she had once been very fond of.

Her arms felt very heavy and she sat on the edge of the bed. The lengths of sunlight had moved across the room, and the white door stood resplendent, glowing. She hummed a few bars of "These Foolish Things." A bit of brightness was what the room needed, a few pictures; Dufy perhaps. It would be simple enough to slip a slice of cloth around the soiled paper shade of the table lamp. A light candy stripe for the drapery and brass rods with those fancy knobs . . . Jesus God, it was like playing with a doll house.

She couldn't remember the words to the song. "A something something in the next apartment," and the next line was gone entirely. The best thing to do was to take a nap. She could sleep the headache off. When she put her hand on her leg it felt cold. Not today and not tomorrow would be any different. The broken cistern streamed on and on. She pressed her eyes with the backs of her wrists.

— 3 —

At six-thirty in the morning he walked back toward the center of D———. The rain had stopped for good, and now and then drops fell from the leaves and formed in his hair little beads which glittered in the cool light. The sun was reddish-white and not yet up all the way over the edge of the town. It was cool, but there was the promise in the air of a rather comfortable warmth for an October Saturday, a good day for football. He couldn't remember if W——— College played a home game today or not.

He went through the sleepy lobby of the Malvern Hotel, the morning clerk giving him a numb but recognizable nod, and to the stairs at the left of the hall. The elevator had been out of order for the two years he had lived there. At the top of the first flight of steps he found a girl trying to help a man to his feet. The fellow was on his hands and knees, wagging his head back and forth like a sick dog, his red silk necktie tracing a wavy course on the dusty wool stair-runner. He was a huge heavy man with a big tomato-colored face and blondish-gray hair that grew long all around a bald spot the size and shape of the mouth of a coffee mug. He was wearing easily two hundred fifty dollars' worth of clothing, his suit a soft quiet gray.

"What's wrong with him?" Mark asked. "Is he ill? I'll go back to the telephone."

"I've got to get him to bed," the girl said. "He'll be all right if he can get to bed and get some sleep." She pulled at the heavy man, lifting with both hands under one shoulder.

"Up we go," said Mark. He motioned for the girl to move away and got down and got his elbows under the shoulders and brought the man unsteadily to his feet. He had to shift his hold twice because the fellow was so tall; he was at least a hand taller than Mark. He couldn't smell liquor on him. "Take the other side," Mark said.

Somehow they wrestled him to the top of the stairs. "This is the floor," the girl said. They let him stand alone to rest for a moment and then had to grab him hurriedly to prevent his toppling backward down the steps.

"Which room?" he said.

"Two seventeen, I think. The key's in his jacket pocket."

"That ought to be the suite at the end of the hall if this floor's laid out like the one I'm on. Say," he said, "he's not drunk, is he?"

"Oh no, it's just a . . . an indisposition." She was breathing fiercely from exertion. "He'll be all right if he just gets a little sleep. It's happened before two or three times."

Mark held him propped against the door jamb while she took the key from his pocket. Her brass-colored hair fell, hiding her face as she bent to unlock the door. When she straightened she brushed the left side of it back with her right hand, her arm making a lancet arch over her head. A young, pretty gesture. Mark saw that she was only fourteen or fifteen years old.

They got him through the short entryway into the first bedroom and dropped him heavily on his bed, then got his legs up and straightened him out. She took off his shoes and loosened his tie and unbuttoned his collar. The man's shiny blue eyes stared unknowingly at Mark a moment and then closed so quickly as to be almost audible. At first his breathing was ragged, but in a minute or so it became quiet and regular.

She was a pretty girl, perhaps a bit thin, but the bones of her hands and wrists were very small and looked fragile and the light from the south window shone like a candle flame through her brass-colored hair. She wore a dark tweed suit and a white blouse with a small collar that had gray piping along the edge. The suit was rather too old for her but she wore it confidently. The high forehead had wide brightly scrubbed temples. Small and sharpish her chin was, so that her face was less an oval than an inverted triangle. Her ears were translucent as wax. And although she wore nylons on her thin legs, her shoes were smudged black loafers. She wore a silver charm bracelet and an expensive perfume.

"Thank you," she said. "Thank you very much. It was very nice of you to help me." She extended her fine hand.

He held it for a moment. "That's all right. I didn't do anything. Are you sure you don't want me to call a doctor?"

She went to the window and drew the drapes. The room grew dim and marine. "He'll be all right if he can sleep for a while. It's happened a couple of times before that I know of, and probably some times he hasn't told me. He's tired, too. We traveled all night to get here for the football game today."

"Well, he does seem better," Mark said. "He's resting easier. You're tired too."

"Too tired. It's that kind of nervous tired feeling when you can't sleep but just lie in bed with your eyes open, all excited."

"I know what you mean. Come and have breakfast with me. Sometimes you relax if you eat something."

"All right," she said simply. "Only don't let me drink any coffee."

They went down to the hotel dining room. They were the only customers so far, and the dining room was still and dark. They took a corner table by a potted plant with big heart-shaped leaves.

Her father had graduated from W——— College in 1935; this was the first time he had returned. Her name was Edwina Tumperling. No, she hadn't been named after her father; her mother's name was Edwina. She had died six years ago. It had been a terrible hurt for her father— for the both of them; she didn't think he ever *would* get over it. After Edwina his wife had died he began to work twice as hard as formerly, and he spent all his time with his daughter when he wasn't working. He gave her too many presents; for example, he had given her a white sports car, having forgotten that she wasn't old enough to drive and that she didn't know how to anyway. (They were from Texas; he owned automobile dealerships.) "I'm horribly spoiled," she said. "Spoiled rotten."

"You don't seem spoiled," he said. "You must take care of your father pretty well. I can imagine that it's been quite a burden for you."

Well, yes, sometimes it had been difficult, but it was easy to see that he had almost gone to pieces. She was simply happy when she had been there for him. "We've always been awfully close. It's a little frightening sometimes." When she had gone on her tour of Europe and had caught pneumonia in that crummy little place in Provence, her father had telephoned. He had known that something was terribly wrong; he didn't know how he knew. It was really a psychic experience, and it had happened like that other times too. Did he, Mark, believe in psychic phenomena like that?

It was hard to say. There were certainly many things like that which couldn't just be explained away. "I try to keep an open mind about everything. It's hard to find out all your prejudices, though."

She smiled gratefully. "I was afraid you'd think I was being silly."

He protested with some show of sincerity. "Not at all. There have been lots of things like that and lots of them have been investigated."

She smiled. It wasn't just about her psychic experiences; Mark seemed to take her seriously for herself. "Lots of my friends think that I behave too . . . importantly—I guess that's the word—for my age. I believe they think that I put on airs."

"Oh no. That's not very perceptive of them. It's easy to see that the way things are you've had to grow up very quickly. You've had responsibility most of them haven't had."

They ate quickly when they ate, but stopped for long periods to talk in hushed tones and gesture. One rumpled heavy old gentleman had come in to sit across the room from them, but no other breakfasters. The Negro waiter regarded them assiduously from the silver counter but did not come to disturb their talk.

Mark began to understand that despite everything—despite her father's money and the seemingly endless series of friends' names which flashed through her conversation—she was really lonely. There was something genuinely melancholy in the thought of this pretty young girl being lonely, and he was perplexed by the queer jumble of interests she had. First she talked a great deal about "psychic phenomena," then about "astrological phenomena," then she went a long way on "prevision," whatever that was. After a while he began to listen only to the sound of her clear prattling, like the sound of two demitasse spoons struck together. It was a sad noise, really. Where did she come up with all this stuff? What did it mean?

"But then Father never believed in formal school education. He always tutored me himself." She stopped for a moment, and he jarred himself to attention. "You haven't told me a thing about you. You just let me talk on and on about myself."

"I wouldn't know how to tell. I'm a very simple sort of person, but everything's awfully complicated. I don't really think of myself very much, but if I once start I never stop. I don't understand things very easily."

"Oh, I don't believe that."

"I don't really want to talk about myself unless I have time to get my thoughts in good order." He knew it sounded bad, but he didn't know any other way out except the literal truth which always sounded so damaging. "You seem awfully interested in these strange mental powers," he said.

"I've always been interested in psychic and astral phenomena," she said, "but I guess it shows how terribly unbalanced my education has been. He didn't believe in public schools, of course, so there I was around the house all day with nothing to do but read. Except when I was traveling; I've traveled a lot. And there were all those books in the house. My mother was interested in it and she got my father interested. I've had experiences like that too. Some things have happened to me I'm not sure I'd ever tell anybody." She glanced at him quickly from beneath lowered lashes.

He was moved by the gesture; all her overtures were so obvious, she was trying so hard to betray herself. He already felt himself placed in the disadvantage of knowing things about her he thought he shouldn't know. But it was for him a familiar feeling, after all: he seemed to attract unwanted confidences, everyone always told him too much. But then of course that really wasn't true. . . . He simply attached too much importance to hints that were inevitably dropped when strangers were first brought together. Trying too quickly to form an idea of her life, his thought had overshot itself, had gone immediately from extrapolation to blind guess. He was missing what she was saying now.

". . . Queen of Neria." She smiled ironically and shook her head. "That's the bad part of being the queen of a kingdom that's on another plane of astral vibration. You can't tell people you're the Queen of Neria just because they can't see it. They'd just say, Well, if you're a queen, where is your palace? Oh, it's invisible, is it? Oh, I *see*." She nodded her head with parodic graveness.

"Yes." He smiled. He didn't understand it at all.

"And they would think you're trying to make yourself important by claiming to be a queen, when the important thing about an astral kingdom is that it isn't important at all to be a queen. Sooner or later everyone in an astral kingdom becomes monarch. Right now I am Queen of Neria, but as soon as something on this plane of vibration we live in happens to damage my astral projection, I'll be deposed. But there are very few people in the world who would understand. I hope you're not laughing at me on the inside and just not letting it show."

"No, no," he said. "Of course not."

"I didn't think you would. It's easy to tell you're a very kind person in every way."

"Not really."

"Oh, I'm sure. And you want to be sure you never lose that quality, it's such a wonderful quality." She leaned forward over her plate and gave him a long searching gaze. He wished she wouldn't try so hard. "There's a sympathetic quality you have that is given to very few. A person knows right away that she can trust you and put all her confidence in you and you won't laugh at her or hurt her feelings. It's a wonderful gift and it's a wonderful feeling to have with any person. Most people go all their lives without meeting someone like you, someone with this inspiring quality. But you want to make certain that you never lose it. You could lose this quality you have and never know it yourself and you wouldn't know why your life had changed so much. Your life would change completely. But you could lose this quality, or, or it could be taken from you." She settled back in her chair and struck the heels of her palms together once silently. "Oh, you've just got to come by and meet my father when he wakes up. He'll be so happy to meet someone like you. He once told me that I would and that I'd be very glad. . . . And you'd like him, I know you would."

"Well," he said. "That sounds fine. What time should I come by?"

"Oh, say about one-thirty, before the ball game. I'm sure he'll be awake by then. It's going to be simply a beautiful day."

"You must be tired, though."

"I'll have a nice nap, simply a delicious nap." She extended her arms in a languorous stretch and arched her neck forward like a chicken.

They rose. He left a generous tip. They walked back to her room, she humming some tune he didn't know, taking much longer steps than her slight body and long skirt might seem to permit. Before the door to her room he took the key from her and inserted it into the lock. They talked softly.

"I'll see you after a while," he said.

"Oh yes."

"Well . . ." Awkwardly he extended his hand, not wanting to turn on his heel and walk away.

She came to him on tiptoe and put her arms about his neck and kissed him. She searched beneath his tongue with her tongue, which was small and cool. Then she slipped inside quickly, and he stood for a long time looking at the closed door. 217. He shook his head as if to clear it of confusion like a wet dog shaking itself.

He went up into his room, which was in better order now, a maid obviously having attended to it. The bed was made, the cracked pitcher was back in the wide bowl upon the table, clean bath and face towels hung at the tiny lavatory. His sweater he draped inside-out over a chair and kicked his loafers off and threw himself face down on the bed. He lay still for a long time before he squirmed over on his back and placed the pitcher on the floor and began to smoke. After a while he got up and went to the desk and took a notebook from a drawer. With a ballpoint pen he entered a new line of verse in his long philosophical poem. He wrote down the words: *Joe Starret, Edwina Tumperling*. Then he went back to bed and lay tossing, a true picture of despair. Outside the window sparrows argued and squittered in the glassy sunlight. He almost prayed for sleep he wanted it so much.

"Help," he whispered. "Help, help."

Children of Strikers

They were walking, the twelve-year-old girl and the younger bleached-looking boy, by the edge of the black chemical river. A dreadful stink rose off the waters but they scarcely noticed it, scuffling along in the hard sawgrass among the stones. It was a dim day, rain-threatening, and the girl's dun face and dark eyes looked even darker than usual. The boy trailed some little distance behind her and would stop now and again and shade his eyes and look upstream and down. But there was no more reason for him to look about than there was for him to shade his eyes.

Occasionally the girl would bend down and look at something which caught her eye. A scrap of tin, a bit of drowned dirty cloth, jetsam thrown up from the river that poured through the paper factory above and then by the mill settlement behind them. This, "Fiberville," was a quadruple row of dingy little bungalows, and it was where the two of them lived. In the girl's dark face was something harsh and tired, as if she had foretold all her life and found it joyless.

Now she reached down and plucked something off a blackened wale of sand. She glanced at it briefly and thrust it into the pocket of her thin green sweater.

The boy had seen. He caught up with her and demanded to have a look.

"Look at what?" she asked.

"What you found, let me see it."

335

"It ain't nothing you'd care about."

"How do you know what I care? Let me have a look."

She turned to face him, gazed directly into his sallow annoying face, those milky blue eyes. "I ain't going to let you," she said.

He gave her a stare, then turned aside and spat. "Well, hell then, it ain't nothing."

"That's right." She walked on and he kept behind. But she knew he was gauging his chances, considering when to run and snatch it out of her pocket. When she heard his footsteps coming sneaky-fast, she wheeled and, without taking aim, delivered him such a ringing slap that his eyes watered and his face flushed.

"Goddamn you," he said, but he didn't cry.

"I've told you to keep your hands away from me. I told you I wouldn't say it again."

"You ain't so much," he said. "I seen better." But his voice, though resentful, was not bitter.

They walked on a space and she began to relent. "It's a foot," she said.

"What you mean? What kind of foot?"

"It's a baby's foot."

"No!" He glared at her. "I ain't believing that."

"You can believe just whatever little thing you want to."

"I ain't believing you found no baby's foot. Let me see it."

"No."

"Well then, you ain't got nothing. . . . How big is it?"

"It's real tiny."

"Gaw," he said. It had seized his imagination. "Somebody probably kilt it."

"Might be."

"They must of kilt it and cut it up in little bits and throwed it in the river." He was wild with the thought of it. "It was some girl got knocked up and her boyfriend made her do it."

She shrugged.

"Ain't that awful to think about? A poor little baby . . . Come on and show it to me. I got to see that baby foot."

"What'll you give me?"

They marched along, and he struck a mournful air. "Nothing," he said at last. "I ain't got nothing to give."

She stopped and looked at him, surveyed him head to toe with a weary satisfaction. "No, I guess you ain't," she said. "You ain't got a thing."

"Well then, what you got? Nothing but a poor little dead baby's foot which I don't believe you've got anyhow."

Slowly she reached into her pocket and produced it, held it toward him in her open palm, and he leaned forward, breathless, peering. He shivered, almost imperceptibly. Then his face darkened and his eyes grew brighter and he slapped her hand. The foot jumped out of her hand and fell among the grasses.

"That ain't nothing. It's a doll, it's just a doll-baby's foot."

She could tell that he was disappointed but feeling smug too because, after all, he had caught her in the expectable lie. "I never told you it was real." She stooped and retrieved it. It lay pink and soiled in her soiled palm. Bulbous foot and ankle, little toes like beads of water. It looked too small and too separate from the rest of the world to be anything at all

He took it from her. "I knowed it wasn't no real baby." Became thoughtful, turning it in his fingers. "Hey, look at this."

"I don't see nothing."

He held the tubular stub of it toward her. "Look how smooth it's cut off. It's been cut with a knife."

She touched it and the amputation was as smooth as the mouth of a soft drink bottle. "What's that got to do with anything?"

It had got darker now, drawing on toward the supper hour. Fiberville grew gloomier behind them, though most of the lights were on in the kitchens of the houses.

"Means that somebody went and cut it on purpose. . ." Another flushed fantasy overcame him. "Say, what if it was a Crazy Man? What if it was a man practicing up before he went and kilt a real baby?"

"It's just some little kid messing around," she said.

"Ain't no kid would have a knife like that." He ran his thumb over the edge of the cut. "Had to be a real *sharp* knife. Or an axe. Maybe it was a meat chopper!"

"Kid might get a knife anywhere."

He shook his head firmly. "No. Look how even it is and ain't hacked up. Kid would rag it up. A man went and done it, being real careful."

At last she nodded assent. Now at the same moment they turned and looked up the riverbank into Fiberville, the squat darkening houses where the fathers and mothers and older sons now wore strained strange faces. The men didn't shave everyday now and the women cried sometimes. They had all turned into strangers, and among them at night in the houses were real strangers from far-off places saying hard wild sentences and often shouting and banging tabletops. In the overheated rooms both the light and the shadows loomed with an unguessable violence.

Blue Dive

*H*is name that was ever used was Stovebolt Johnson and he was a short black man, heavily muscled, a chunk of a man. In the middle of nowhere he clambered gingerly down the steps of the Greyhound. As he stepped onto the ground the round bottom of his guitar clipped the bus door, twanged softly. The guitar was tied over his shoulder with seagrass twine and was enveloped in a washed and faded flour sack. He grunted involuntarily when he heard the knock of it against the metal. When at last he was all the way down he kept his back to the bus as it hissed and shivered and roared, then plowed away into the gray east wind. Stovebolt wasn't studying any bus; he was looking at the horizon, staring away as far as his eyesight would reach.

There was nothing anybody else would have remarked. The two-lane asphalt highway stretched from one end of his vision to the other, narrowing to a pencil mark as it went on in this flat country. On both sides of the road newly turned dark brown fields rolled on endlessly. In the gray late morning sky to the north six blackbirds pursued a hawk, skimming and swooping. When the bus had gone, there was no other sound and no other sight but the fields and the sky and the birds and telephone poles and a few lines of bushes and this man, Stovebolt Johnson. Still he stood for a minute or two, gazing toward the edge of the world, and then he unslung the guitar from his heavy torso and pulled away the flour sack and examined the guitar until he was satisfied there was no damage. "Mm hmm," he murmured, "that's all right."

Testing, he struck three chords on the strings and out here in the wind and the flatness they sounded as lonesome as starlight. Then he tied the guitar back in its sack and thumbed it over his shoulder.

He reached into the breast pocket of his khaki wool jacket and took out a mint bar of Red Coon. From his pants he produced a pocket knife and cut away a rounded corner with the hawkbill blade and slipped the tobacco into the right side of his mouth and commenced chewing very slowly. Even now he was still looking at the horizon and he turned softly on his heel to take the whole of it in. He breathed deeply; his ripply shoulders rose and fell. Something there in the dirt by the edge of the highway caught his attention and he squatted and eyed the ground for a moment, but it was nothing more than a scrap of tin foil from a cigarette package. He grunted again. He had thought he'd found him a dime.

Now he began walking. A little puddly car lane divided two fields and he crossed the highway and began to follow it. He took short but leisurely strides, making good steady time going along, and the rhythm of his walking brought words into his mind and an old tune.

> Going down this road feeling bad,
>
> > O Lord,
> I'm going down this road feeling bad.
> Down this road feeling bad,
>
> > Lord Lord,
> I ain't going to be treated this way.

But when he thought about it he decided he wasn't feeling bad at all; he felt open and free and truly pleasured by the quiet country about him and he brushed his thighs with his fingertips as he walked. Still that song persisted in his head.

He went about a quarter of a mile before he came to another car lane branching left. He turned and went down this way. The ground was softer here and the ruts were sharper and the puddles wider and deeper. Now and again he hitched at the weight of the guitar and now and again he snapped his fingers to the tune in his mind. There was no doubt in him how good he felt; maybe he had never felt better than right now.

After another thousand yards or so this road straggled into the front yard of a house. It was a shackly little house, smudged white asbestos shingles and a tin roof and a short front porch with narrow splintery pine planks eaten away at the outer edges by weather. There were two trees, a spindly little pecan and a grandly spreading water oak with a rubber tire swing hanging down by a frayed cotton rope. There was an outbuilding, a little shed open on this side to the sky, but there was no car under it. He hadn't expected the car to be gone and he halted at the indefinable border of the yard. He spat a dollop of juice and considered.

But there was no place else to go. So he walked on up and stepped to the door and knocked smartly. For a moment there was no sound, and then children's voices chirruped inside. "Mama, Mama, there's a man here now." "Mama, Mama." And then silence again, but he could feel in his shoe soles the slight quiver of someone walking from the back of the house, from the kitchen, he guessed.

She opened the glass-paned door and stood inside the shadow of the room, and it was hard to make her out through the bulging rusty screen door.

"What is it you want?" Her voice was soft and carefully matter-of-fact.

"Excuse me," Stovebolt said. He tried to peer. "Donna? Is that you, Donna?"

"I suppose you've got the wrong house," she said, as if there were dozens of them scattered up and down these broad empty fields.

"Excuse me," he said again. "I'm Stovebolt Johnson here, and I'm looking for the man name of Franklin Childress. Pointy, some folks call him."

"I don't know that man."

"Well now, wait a minute. This here is his house, or leastways it used to be his house. And it's urgent to me to find Pointy Childress because he can give me a job. He promised he could give me a job."

"I don't know any of that," she said. "We took this house from

Charlie James after he went to work for the furniture factory up in High Point."

"That's him, that's one," Stovebolt said. "He was an old buddy of Pointy's. I recall I've met him before. He must have took this house from Pointy, whatever happened to Pointy. And I've got an awful need to see Pointy because I have to have that job."

"I don't know."

"Look now," he said. "Maybe you've heard of Pointy Childress and forgot about it. He was a big tall bald man with two gold teeth right in front. He was running a little roadhouse up the highway here. It was a little concrete block place, sky-blue painted, and it was called the Blue Dive and folks used to come in there and drink beer and all."

"I know the Blue Dive," she said. "Everybody knows that place a long time. But I never heard of that man you name."

"This is a puzzler, ain't it?" He tried to smile as friendly as he could, though he couldn't tell what she could see through the screen. "I've come a long way on the hopes of that job."

"Well, come in the house," she said. "Maybe we can find out something." She held the screen door open a few inches and he opened it all the way and entered.

As his eyes were adjusting to the dimness of the room it seemed for a moment that this comely young woman was dividing into three. But it was two children who separated themselves from her skirt to stand apart regarding him, their eyes big and bright in their dark faces.

"Hello there, young'uns," Stovebolt said.

The little boy stepped back a few steps and stood watching him gravely, his finger hooked in the corner of his mouth. His sister, who looked to be about a year older, clapped her hand to her forehead and turned twice about on her toes; she was trying hard not to giggle.

The handsome young woman was talking again. "My husband ought to be home for dinner in a few minutes," she said. "He might can help you with what you want to find out."

"I'm thanking you," he said. "Looks like I've kind of got in a bind here."

The living room was small and no lights were on. There was a sagging reddish sofa and an upholstered rocking chair and two straight chairs, and here and there over the patchy linoleum lay soiled and broken toys. On the screen of a little television set in the corner a gray animated cartoon fluttered frenziedly, cat and mouse.

"Can I give you a cup of coffee?" she asked. "Always I keep some heating on the stove."

"I could use a cupful if it ain't no trouble. I been walking in the cool wind."

"What do you take?"

"Whole lot of sugar, is all."

The little boy popped his finger out of his mouth and pointed it, gleaming wet, at Stovebolt's shoulder. "Can you play that thing?" he asked. His manner of inquiring was sharp and belligerent, a dare.

"Yes I can."

"What can you play?"

"I can play anything," Stovebolt said. "I can play the best music there is in the world. I can play happy and sad and in-between."

"Like what?"

"I can play," he said, "to beat anything you'll ever hear off of *that*." He nodded his head at a giant box of cornflakes glimmering on the television screen.

"I want to see you play it."

The mother came in with a steaming white coffee mug which she held cradled at the bottom as well as by the handle. "I hope I've got it sweet enough for you."

"Oh it's fine," Stovebolt said. "And I sure do appreciate it." He turned back to the little boy. "If you want to hear me play you'll have to come out here on the porch. I've got to have me some working room when I play my guitar."

He pushed through the door to go and sit on the edge of the porch. He had been reflecting that if he was a woman's husband driving up from work at noontime he might not be overcome with joy to find a strange man and a guitar in his house. He spat out his chew of tobacco and worked up all the juice he could and spat that out too. The first sip of coffee he wallowed about in his mouth, rinsing, and then got rid of. He'd known any number of men who could chew and drink at the same time, but he'd never got the hang of it. He took a swallow. It was strong and sweet as molasses. "You mama makes a fine cup of coffee," he said to the boy. "What kind of music do you like to listen?" He took the guitar out and fingered a few aimless notes.

" 'Knock Three Times,' " the boy said.

Stovebolt grinned, thinking he might have guessed that would be it or something pretty near. "I never heard of that one," he said. "I'm going to play you a song called 'One Dime Blues.' You ever hear that one?"

The boy shook his head.

"Well, you listen now and see if you don't think it's a mighty fine song." He got down another swallow of coffee and launched out with a startling bright chromatic run, playing quite loudly.

The little boy's mouth slackened to a red astonished O and he clasped his hands behind his neck. His sister standing behind him waited until she could bear it no longer and then she began to dance. She pirouetted, the five white-cotton-ribboned braids of hair spinning like the horses on a toy carousel; her bony knees jerked upward and her heels in her worn red tennis shoes slapped sounding on the porch boards. Stovebolt could feel without turning the presence of the young mother behind him in the doorway. He kept playing for maybe five minutes and as he played he felt happier and happier. He finished and damped the strings quickly with the heel of his palm.

"There you go now," Stovebolt said. "How you like that one?"

The little girl stood stockstill and looked at him and giggled, bubbled over with giggles like a flowing fountain. The little boy was grave and his voice still belligerent. "Now play 'Knock Three Times,' " he said. "Or play any damn thing, I don't care."

Stovebolt threw his head back and laughed. "That's the way to talk," he said. "When the music is good, there ain't no reason to be too choicy about what songs." He drank half the coffee left in the mug.

The girl had stopped giggling and was looking out down the road. "Daddy's coming," she said in a placid dreamy voice.

It was a rust-pitted yellow Dodge pickup bobbing and floundering through the ruts and puddles. It veered from side to side in the lane as the driver tried to escape the larger holes.

"Is that your daddy's truck?" Stovebolt asked.

"I don't know," the little boy said.

The truck stopped in front of the shed and a man got out. He was a shorter man than Stovebolt had expected—he couldn't be much taller than his wife—but there was no mistaking the loosely flowing strength in him. He came toward the porch, glancing questioningly at each of the group gathered there.

The mother stepped out onto the porch. "Hello, honey," she said.

"Darlene," the man said. But his eyes rested steadily on Stovebolt and he didn't appear to be thinking about anything else.

She came to the porch edge. "Honey, this here is Stovebolt Johnson and he's looking for a man and we was hoping maybe you could help him."

He halted directly in front of him and Stovebolt stood up and put out his hand. "Howdy. I'm Stovebolt, like she says."

The other man hesitated, then shook hands. "I'm B.J., like I guess she's told *you*."

"No," he said. "I hadn't been here long enough to get acquainted. Except maybe a little bit with him." With his head he indicated the man's son.

B.J. glanced at the boy, then back at Stovebolt. "Are you some kind of music man?"

"Yes," he said, "it's the truth I am."

The little boy shouted. "Daddy, he can play the *blue pee* out of that thing!"

B.J. smiled, and seemed at last to relax. "That right?" he murmured. He took a Camel out of his shirt pocket and turned out of the wind to light it.

"What was the name of that song? Play that song one time for him." Stovebolt reached over and squeezed the boy at the back of his neck. "Ooh," he squeaked.

The mother said, "Mr. Stovebolt has come looking for a man that promised him a job. And I didn't know who it was."

"Who was that, then?" B.J. asked.

"Pointy Childress he was called," Stovebolt said. "He offered me a job playing music at a little roadhouse beer joint he had around here. I mean to say, he downright promised me."

"I've heard of him," B.J. said. "When would this be that he promised you?"

"This is going back three years now."

"You a little late showing up. That man has been gone from here a good year and a half, anyhow. He was gone after the first week we moved into the house here. I didn't know him myself but just to nod at."

"Uh oh, that don't sound so fine. Kind of hard to find a job sometimes in my line of business."

"Is that right?" said B.J. "Seems to me most people kind of like Rafer here, they just crazy about hearing music." He grinned at his son.

"Well, but these days now, mostly it's the TV they got turned on in the places. Or they've got them a record box where the customers have to pay for the music. But what I play, the way I play it, you can't get out of no machine."

Rafer shouted again. "Daddy, make him play that guitar for you. You ought to hear the way he does."

"What happened to the man you want I don't have no impression. It's another man entirely running the Blue Dive. It might be he'd want to hire him some music and he might not. Hard to say about him."

"Where would he be that I could talk to him?"

"Right now he wouldn't be nowhere. But he'll show up at his place about two o'clock and you can talk to him then, I expect."

"I reckon I'll do it," Stovebolt said. "What's he called by?"

"His name is Locklear Hawkins," B.J. said. "I can't tell you much about him to help you out, because I ain't been able to figure him all that close. He's a new kind of man, Hawk is."

"Folks name him Hawk, do they?"

B.J. smiled. "Yeah, he kind of likes that. He's younger than you and me."

"B.J.," the mother said, "ain't you going to ask Mr. Stovebolt to come in and have dinner with us?"

"Sure I am. I was just fixing to."

"I'll go in and set it then. It's already on the stove and waiting." She went into the house.

Stovebolt was wrapping his guitar again. "I thank you awful kindly," he said, "but I can't stay. If I want to be meeting this here Hawk-man, I got to be prowling on. The way you mention him, I better meet him early and talk till late if I want to haul me down a job."

B.J. smiled shrewdly. "That might be the hardest part of it, sure enough. But there ain't no sense you walking up to the Blue Dive. I got to go right by there on my way back to the cotton gin and I can give you a ride, drop you off right at the door."

"It wouldn't be out of your way, you sure?"

"Go right past it," B.J. said. "And it's dinnertime and you got to eat anyhow, so you'll just have to come on in and sit down with us."

"I couldn't put you out," Stovebolt said. "Your wife wasn't figuring on no stranger coming to her table, descending down on her like a turkey buzzard to eat up her food."

"Well, I know Darlene and you don't. She'd purely skin my head, you didn't sit down and eat a bite." He touched Stovebolt's elbow, steering him toward the screen door.

"Daddy," Rafer shrieked, "ain't you going to make him play? I want you to hear it, what he does."

Halfway back to the highway where the car lane smoothed out a bit, B.J. slowed the truck and looked across the seat admiringly at Stovebolt, who sat with his guitar resting on the floorboard between his knees. "Lord a mercy," he said. "I never seen anything like that."

"What you mean?" Stovebolt asked. His voice was thick and drowsy.

"How much you eat, what I'm talking I never seen a man put it down like that. Is that the way you eat normal?"

"First home-cooked rations I've had since I don't know when. Man, I hope Darlene ain't excited against me. I guess I ate about everything in the house."

B.J. grinned and punched him lightly on the shoulder. "Don't you worry none," he said. "That just warmed her heart to you."

*   *   *

Three miles farther up the highway they came to the Blue Dive. B.J. swerved the truck across the road into the parking lot, spraying up dust and noisy gravel. "This is it," he said. "I hope you a lot of luck here."

Stovebolt shook hands with him once more. "Don't know how to properly thank you," he said. "You've been so awful kindhearted to me. It was nothing I ever expected."

"Nothing to it," B.J. said. "We're happy to see you."

When the truck pulled away, Stovebolt stood in the parking lot observing, taking his time. The Blue Dive was something like he'd expected from what had been described to him, but there were differences too. For one thing, it was larger than he'd thought. It was a rectangular concrete block building, sure enough painted a mild blue, but there were yellow lights at every edge and he supposed that at night the place would look greenish. No big plate glass windows in front, but a row of six slotted windows high up, as if the occupants were readying to fight off an Indian attack. And no neon lights but just a painted sign, black on white, over the door, fixed into the blocks with mortar nails. BLUE DIVE.

"Mm hmm," Stovebolt murmured, though as yet he really didn't know what he thought.

Carrying the guitar at the base of the neck he walked to the door and entered. Inside, it was more familiar-seeming. A concrete floor, damp in places, and patched here and there with new pourings of cement; a long bar a little taller than waist high with no rail and with wooden stools lined before; a streaky mirror with scraps of paper taped up in various spots, surrounded with red and white bulbs enclosd in a plywood frame painted probably blue. It was a good-sized place, sixty feet long maybe; lots of room for dancing—and fighting too, if it was that kind of joint. Stovebolt searched the bar ends and the ceiling corners for a television set without finding one. There was, however, a jukebox against the right-hand wall, emitting fluorescent light like a hospital corridor.

He advanced to the bar. Behind the cash register in the center of the bar, a middle-aged man wearing gold-rimmed spectacles sat reading a newspaper. He didn't look up, asking, "What can I get you?"

"Excuse me," Stovebolt said, "but I'm looking for the man name of Mr. Locklear Hawkins."

The man raised his head, and with the light behind him, Stovebolt couldn't see his eyes behind his glasses. "Who you say now?" he asked.

"A Mr. Locklear Hawkins, I believe."

"He ain't here." He didn't return to reading but kept his hardly discernible face motionless, waiting.

"Well, is he ever here, or is he at some other part of the world?"

"This here is his place. He'll be coming in after while."

"About when would that be?"

"Hard to tell about him. Might be a little while, might be a mighty long while."

He ought to be here right now, Stovebolt thought, studying the good manners of his help. "Well, I think I'll wait on him, if it's all right with you."

"Ever what you like," the man said. "Wouldn't you want a beer while you're waiting?"

"Maybe so," Stovebolt said, "maybe so." He patted his right-hand pants pocket automatically, though he knew he had twenty-seven cents there. "How much will it run these days?"

"Fifty cents."

"All right. I'll take a cold Blue Ribbon."

From his left pocket he produced a small tight roll of bills secured with a grimy cotton string. He untied the string carefully and unsheaved a five-dollar bill and tied the roll back just as it had been.

The dripping can was before him and the man stood there, his face still unreadable; but Stovebolt could sense the amusement in him. He tendered the bill slowly and the man opened the cash register and smacked his change down in front of him.

Now Stovebolt felt himself growing nettled, and he thought he had better make what overture he could. The way things smelled here it would be a long roll uphill. "If you don't mind telling me something," he said, "why do they call this here place the Blue Dive?"

"Because it was painted blue from the start."

"But what I mean to say, why not a little more high-class name? Like The Top Hat maybe, or The High Society? I recall a place in Mobile called The Duke that the people seemed to appreciate."

The barman leaned forward, melting a bit. "That was the name of it before the present management," he said. "The people around here used to it. You ain't landed in Detroit city, you know."

"I was just speculating," Stovebolt said.

"Well, I believe Hawk did have some ideas along that line and then went and decided that folks was too familiar to it to change."

"Let me ask you something. The people that come in here, what kind of music do they like?"

"They like it all. On a good hard night they'll play every last song on that jukebox."

"Mm hmm," Stovebolt said.

"But what ain't on it, I don't know whether they're going to care for or not. I see you're a musician, you hauling that guitar, but why ain't you hauling it in a case? That old totesack."

"Used to have a case. Red leather."

"Where's it at?"

"Huh," Stovebolt said. "If I know where that case is at, I know where there's three hundred and fifty dollars of my good money. But that particular nighttime is long gone away, and I ain't never going to know what direction it took."

"That right?" the barman said. "Well, I can understand that. I been there myself."

The door opened; an oblong of gray light fell across the room. A slight soft-looking man seated himself on a stool. When the barman went to him he ordered a Schlitz.

Stovebolt lifted his beer and sucked down about half of it. "Mm hmm." He couldn't precisely recall the last time he had drunk a beer, but it had been a few years, of course. I want to be careful, he thought. I could start gobbling this stuff and wind up here no better off than a stray dog. He carried the can across to the jukebox and noted the selections. Dionne Warwick. James Brown. The O'Kaysions. Major Lance. It was to a T what he'd expected. He used a dime to punch up

"Dancing in the Streets," by Martha and the Vandellas, and then returned to his stool. He knew the song he had paid for. That's an old-time song, he thought, old fast blues. They've just silvered it over with a big shiny arrangement. He sat listening, mentally picking out the changes, until the record ended.

With the music gone the Blue Dive seemed hushed, sunk at the bottom of an ocean of daze, and no one moved except to take a short reflective sip of beer.

Finally the slight man who had lately come in spoke to Stovebolt. "You play that guitar?"

"Yes I do," Stovebolt said, but he was in a spell, and his voice came out thoughtless and dreamy.

"What kind is it, a Gibson?"

"No sir. This one is a Ginger." He unshucked the instrument and dropped the floursack on the bar beside his beer can. He extended the bottom of it, where the name Ginger was burned in a thin spidery hand.

"I never heard of no Ginger."

Stovebolt roused himself, shook off his momentary lethargy. "It was an old-time man made me this guitar," he said, "an old-time banjo-maker. He asked me did I want him to write *Gibson* or *Martin* on the front of it when he was finished. Says, a lot of folks want them a storebought name on it if they going to play in front of people. I told him, Hell, you making it, put your own name on it. Ginger Parham, and he put Ginger. Tickled him to do it. He was a redheaded white man, a mountain man."

"You don't tell me," said the other. "What kinds of things you play, what kinds of songs?"

"I play whatever there is," Stovebolt said. "I play the best music in the world."

"That right?"

"It surely is." He laid it across his lap and jimmied with the tuning. No tuning needed, but he wanted to cancel out some of the effect of the jukebox. "What you want to hear?"

"How about 'My Girl'?" the man said.

Mm hmm, Stovebolt thought, now I know who you are. "Don't

recollect that one right off," he said. "Play you a little old song called 'Yellow Gal.' "

He started it off as fast as he could make it go, playing as many notes as he could stick in anywhere. He played three choruses before he even thought of singing, and when he sang it was with a metallic low-tenor timbre quite unlike his natural baritone talking voice.

"O yellow gal, come see me tonight
Yellow gal, when the moon is bright
Yellow gal, we gonna do up right
Yellow O yellow O yellow gal

Yellow O yellow O yellow gal
Yellow O yellow O yellow gal
O yellow O yellow O yellow gal
Yellow O yellow O yellow gal."

He whacked the side of his heel against the bar stool leg, driving it along. Now pay me some mind, Stovebolt thought, because I'm going to do me something right here. His hand slipped like water up the neck to the high registers. Mm hmm. And now get yourself ready, because I'm going to drop it off short right . . . *here*. The strings trembled buzzing for a moment and then he laid his finger across them.

Again the Blue Dive was suspended in a ghostly deep silence. The other two men didn't move and seemed not even to breathe until Stovebolt picked up his beer and drank down the last of it. He placed the empty on the bar and said, "I'll have me another if you don't mind. That one kind of parched my throat."

"Jim," said the slight man, "I'm going to buy him that beer, and I don't care if he wants to drink the whole coolerful if I got the money."

Stovebolt chuckled. "I oughtn't to do that. It don't suit me when I drink too much."

"Well then," the other told the barman, "what is it he wants let him have."

"I'm thanking you. I believe I'll have me just one more Blue Ribbon."

"Where did you ever learn to play like that?"

"Well," Stovebolt said, "for the most part I figured it and worked it out myself. But back when I was starting off, I used to go anywhere I heard of that somebody good was making music. Back then it wasn't nothing to me to travel anyway I could two, three hundred miles to pick up on somebody I admired. You ever hear Big Bill Broonzy?"

"Can't say so."

"He was one. I went all the way to Jacksonville, Florida, one time he was playing. He was a famous man and wound up in Paris, France. It ain't a style like mine, but I surely did admire to hear that man. He was a hard-drinking man too, and always had a bottle by him. Folks that don't like this stuff is crazy, he used to say."

"Well now, how you think of B.B. King?" the slight man asked.

"He's all right," said Stovebolt, "he does fine. But I don't know what I agree with the electric guitar. A man can make it do a lot of different things, but that ain't hard, and the sound of it comes funny the way I listen. Best man on electric I ever hear is John Lee Hooker."

"Don't believe I've heard him either."

"He's a good one. He's rough and tough."

"Um," the man said. "I guess you know a lot of musicians I never heard, it being your business and all. What are you doing in these parts here?"

"I'm trying to pull me down a job. I'm waiting in this bar to see a Mr. Hawkins to see couldn't he use some live music, some hard-driving guitar like I can play for him and the people like to hear."

"Now that would be all right, if you was to play here. I'd be willing to sit a good long time to hear it."

Stovebolt turned to the barman. "You hear what this man says?"

"I hear him."

Stovebolt went on. "And there's a man name of B.J. and his wife Darlene, and they said they'd be willing to come and listen."

"I know B.J. a long time," the barman said.

"They mighty fine folks," Stovebolt said. "Mighty fine."

Three others came in, two young men and a girl, shy-eyed and silent. When they saw Stovebolt, a stranger, sitting at the bar with his guitar in his lap, they showed surprise. They went to a table near the end of the bar and sat, sneaking glances at Stovebolt and whispering to one another. When the barman had brought their beer they bent their heads over the table and murmured.

Stovebolt fingered the strings, jotting up riffs and disjointed phrases. He had no notion of playing a whole tune just yet; he was simply preventing the newcomers from playing the jukebox.

In a while one of the young men rose and approached him. "Hello," he said. "What's your name?"

"I'm Stovebolt Johnson."

"Oh yeah," he said, but he seemed disappointed. "I thought maybe I heard of you, but I guess I ain't."

"Don't let it trouble you," Stovebolt said. "There's a whole raft of people never have heard of me."

"Do you play that guitar?"

"Yes he plays it," said the slight man. "He plays it, Billy, so as you'd never want to hear nobody else."

"Well, Mandy over there was wishing you might play us something on it."

Stovebolt looked across at the girl and she dropped her eyes to the table. "What you say her name was?"

"Mandy. Mandy Owens is her name."

He had a tune which in his mind he called "Stovebolt's Blues," with innumerable verses he could shift about to fit almost any occasion. "Seems like I know a song called 'Mandy,' " he said. "Maybe she'd like to hear the one about her own name."

"For a fact she would," the young man said. "I'll go and tell her."

Stovebolt closed his eyes and sidled into the song, soft and lilting. Mm hmm, he thought, not too slow now, and let it hang over the edges like that. But not too slow . . . He played along until the words came strong into his mind.

"Now Mandy, Mandy, where was you last night?
Mandy, Mandy, Mandy, where was you last night?
The stars was all a-shining and the moon was big and bright."

Now, he thought, I might better be careful what words I'm singing. I could get them down on me, stirring up bad feelings. Stovebolt thought the words were important, and you never knew when somebody might take these old-time words personally.

> "O Mandy now, you the apple of my eye.
> Listen, pretty Mandy, you the apple of my eye.
> You know I'm the man that loves you till the day I die."

While he was singing the door opened and someone entered, but Stovebolt didn't open his eyes. He kept caressing the blues song, to make it sweet and enticing. Playing for these young people, he thought, it's almost like courting a skittish woman. He sang three more verses and played one chorus and stopped.

He opened his eyes and looked at them. They smiled, still embarrassed, and then applauded softly and timidly. "We thank you a lot," the young man said.

"Glad to play for you," Stovebolt said. "That's my business, to be amusing folks."

"It was real good," the young man said. "We intending to buy you some beer."

"Awful good of you, but I'm a little bit ahead already."

The barman came and touched him on the arm. "Hawk came in while you doing that last piece. I mentioned you want to talk to him and he says to sit down and wait at the table yonder and he'll be out in just a minute." He indicated a table in the dim far corner.

"All right," Stovebolt said. He picked up one of the three full cans of beer that sat in front of him and carried that and his guitar over and sat. He drank almost half the beer before a man pushed through a doorway strung with beaded curtains and came toward him.

Uh huh, Stovebolt thought, this is him, all right.

He was a tall thin man, very light-skinned, with an aquiline nose and a large but well-groomed Afro haircut. He was dressed like no one else in the room, perhaps like no other man in the county. He wore a green velvet shirt and tight-fitting maroon pants secured by a wide black patent leather belt. On each hand were two rings and on his left wrist three thin silver bracelets. The green shirt was open halfway down his chest.

Stovebolt thought, This here is Mr. Brains, if ever I see him. I had better watch where I'm walking.

Mr. Hawkins slid into the chair on the other side of the table. His movements were easy, cool and silky, and he had about him an air of calm control. His voice too was cool but firm at the edges when he said, "I understand you've been looking for me, Mr. Johnson."

"It didn't start that way," Stovebolt said. "I begun looking for Pointy Childress, but I been told he's long gone away from these parts here."

"That's so. Mr. Childress now owns an establishment in Norfolk, Virginia."

"Well, I might be needing to get the location of that, but I hope not. Pointy offered me a job here at the Blue Dive, it was—oh three years back, maybe. In fact, he right-out promised me a job when I would come by here."

"Mm." Mr. Hawkins leaned back in his chair and crossed his hands on the table. "I'm sure you realize, Mr. Johnson, that the present management can't be responsible for the business arrangements of past managements. It's a whole new setup entirely."

"Sure-now," Stovebolt said quickly. "I wouldn't be coming to you on what Pointy said." I see you before, he thought. Talk like a bank president till it suits your pocketbook to talk like a black man. "I'd be coming to you as my own man every time."

Mr. Hawkins smiled. "What is it you want then, Mr. Johnson, with me?"

"I'm still looking for that job. I take notice here, and I see that there ain't no live music. And I was thinking, Pointy or not, you could step up your business some, especially when word gets around as I'm playing, and I was playing here regular."

"Well, I don't know, Mr. Johnson." His eyes were half-closed, and Stovebolt saw in them a dark sharp light. "It might be more complicated than you think. What kind of music do you offer?"

"I play whatever music there is," Stovebolt said. "I play the best music in the world."

"You mean you play the blues."

"I can play you some *blues*."

"You mean you play those old-time nigger whining songs about how you're mean and broke and dog-ass miserable."

Stovebolt managed to stop off his rage in his throat, but his free hand under the table clenched and trembled. When he spoke at last his voice was turgid and congealed. "I don't know how you listen the blues, but there's all different kinds of blues songs. There's one kind and then there's another."

Mr. Hawkins touched his fingertips together in front of his face, resting his elbows against his chest. "But that's the kind of music you play, though."

"Wait a minute," Stovebolt said. He pushed his empty aside with the back of his wrist and rose and walked very deliberately to the bar. He picked up another can and drank from it, feeling all the eyes in the room on him. Then he walked back to the table, carrying the beer in his right hand, the guitar dangling limply in the other. He sat down heavily. "Wait a minute," he said, "I play any kind of music. You name it, and if I ever hear it I can play it for you right off."

Mr. Hawkins was aloofly amused. He seemed to be growing thinner and sharper before Stovebolt's eyes. "But why would I need you? I've got a jukebox right over there, and it seems to do well enough. No one complains to me about it."

"Machine music," Stovebolt said. "It's purely hateful to me."

"But it does well enough. And then there's the revenue it brings in. Quarters and dimes add up, you know."

"That might be, but it ain't bringing you in any *new* business. Ain't nobody going to drive fifteen, twenty miles to listen to it. They'll just go to another place that's closer by and plug into another machine just exactly like it."

The thin man nodded slightly. "Could be that you have a point there, Mr. Johnson. But it could be too that there are other complications you haven't thought about. You see, there's a law in this state that if I offer live music here in the Blue Dive I have to buy a cabaret license. That would cost me something a little over three hundred dollars."

"I know about that law. I been playing in different places maybe

more years than you've been born. And I know the white law don't
bother messing with a black man's little old concrete block roadhouse
for such a reason as that. And anyway, you would be making up for
that too if I stayed here a good fair while."

"It may be that you're right again, Mr. Johnson. It may be that
they wouldn't bother to enforce that particular law, or it may be that I
have a way of sliding by it. But they'd hear about you, and then they'd
be asking about you." He leaned forward and pressed his hands flat on
the table. "So I'll ask you beforehand: *How long is it since you've been
out of prison?*"

Then it seemed to Stovebolt that he had gone blind for a moment,
not angry blind or blind from sickness, but that a wall had risen all
round him, soft and black and deafening, a hopeless wall of darkness
he could never scale nor tear through. He felt the strength leaking from
his body and his will, so that he wanted to lay his head back and howl
like an animal in pain. . . . He ought to have known that it must come
to this, and perhaps he had known, but had managed to thrust it away
while gripped by the wide hallucinatory fever of once more being free
for a while. But when this Hawk-man asked him that question the
whole sense of his gray destiny washed over him.

But still he fought back. His willpower flickered, then flamed up
again. Where did this storebought dude get off, anyhow? What belonged
to Stovebolt was his own, and that included most certainly every day
he had lived fretting behind the concrete walls. This Hawk-man here
was nobody he ever had to account to, and the main thing was that he
could pick up and go. Hadn't been any promises made here.

"This-now last time they gave me three years in, four years off,"
Stovebolt said. "What you minding it for, anyhow? I pulled it and have
come away clean and I ain't never going back. I'm making clear to you
that that is my business and not another soul's."

"All right," the thin man said. "Calm down. But you must have
known that if I was going to hire you I would have to find out anyway."

"Well then," he said, "but that's the meat of the question, whether
or not you going to hire me."

"I'll have to think about it," he said. "Say you can play other kinds
of music besides the slow blues?"

"Sure I can." He began immediately a fast dance tune, sloppily and a bit crazily, not even getting some of the notes right.

Hawkins held up his hand. "Wait," he said. "Don't play at me. Play for the people. They'll be the ones making the judgment."

Stovebolt looked back past the bar and saw that the room was almost half-filled with people. He was surprised, not having noticed that anyone had come in. He had been concentrating on the man across the table. Mr. Brains here, he reflected, he sure will take it out of you. "Sure-now I will," he said, "and you can listen in and make up your mind."

"Don't worry about that. I'll be keeping an eye out."

And what do you mean by that? Stovebolt thought. The Hawkman can't stop making threats the way some dogs can't help chasing cars. "All right," he said. "I appreciate you taking the time and consideration." He got up and went back to the bar.

The slight man was still sitting next to his stool and he peered at him brightly as he came up. "What did Hawkins say?" he asked. "Is he going to take you on?"

"Couldn't tell you a thing," Stovebolt said. "We still negotiating on it."

"Man, I hope he does. This place could stand to have some good live music."

"That was the way I put it to him."

"Well, here's hoping." He lifted his beer and saluted Stovebolt.

Stovebolt grinned. "Right." There were now four full cans of beer waiting on the bar and he took one and drank it down, the whole can, with one deep breath.

"How about playing us another tune?"

Stovebolt belched silently. The gas bubble went like needles through his palate. "Right," he said. "What you wanting to hear?" But now he didn't want to play; he simply didn't feel like it, tired and irritated. "First off, though, where is the john in this place?"

"Over there."

He laid the guitar carefully across the bar and walked through and found the dark green door and went in. After he had urinated, he washed his hands and rubbed water on his face. Then he leaned with his back against the wall and pondered, his eyes hooded. He was feeling down now, and it seemed to him that no matter where he walked or how carefully he was always stepping into a hole full of snakes. There had been a bad luck over his life like a dark tent roof, and he could travel a thousand miles any direction the wind blew and he would still be underneath. This man Hawkins, where could he have come from, to be so uptown and tightass? What kind of people did he think he had out front every night drinking beer? It was nothing but field workers here, and Stovebolt knew them and they knew Stovebolt. But this sharp man had another kind of idea, sure enough. Hell with him, Stovebolt thought. The blues is the blues. When I'm in for playing the blues, I'm going to play it.

He went back to the bar and resumed his seat.

The slight man was waiting. "You look different now someway," he observed.

"Washed my face," Stovebolt said. "Feel like a new man." He took up his guitar. "There's a real old-time song name of 'John Henry.' You ever hear that?"

"Oh yeah." He smiled without enthusiasm. "It's old enough for sure."

"Well, I ain't going to play it, but while I was back there washing up it come into my mind. You know why?"

He shook his head.

Stovebolt nodded at the jukebox. "Because it's a song about a down-home nigger just like me that's got to beat the machine. That's what it's about. . . . You get to studying on it sometimes, you see the men that made up some of these old songs, they had them a notion. It's the truth they did."

"Never thought about it like that."

He wagged his head solemnly. "Every time, when you think about it, the old folks way ahead of us."

Now he started playing. He played and sang like a man fighting off droves of devils. No sooner would somebody name a song than he would ply into it and sing with such resonance that his voice could be felt humming in the wood of the bar. Fast dance tunes and slow ballads and blues. Sometimes the people would dance frenziedly, or on the slow songs they would move in slow circles, languidly linked together. When they ran short of tunes to suggest, Stovebolt kept right on going, picking up the first one that entered his mind, and laying it out for them, precise and easy and thunderous. His voice began to get hoarse and raspy at the edges, but that didn't harm anything, and only gave the lyrics piquancy.

They kept putting beers on the bar for him and he kept gulping them down, drinking hard and steady, but feeling no effect except for a calm sweet uplifting of his spirits. While he was draining another one, B.J. came up with Darlene on his arm. She smiled shyly and nodded, and B.J. slapped him on the shoulder. "Stovebolt, man," he said, "what my boy Rafer said about you, he was *right*. I maybe wouldn't have believed anybody could do it like you do. There ain't no way in the world you ain't got this job sewed up in a toe sack."

He grinned and shook B.J.'s hand. "I'm still remembering that fine dinner you gave me," he said to Darlene.

She looked at her feet.

"You got to come by again tomorrow or when you can," B.J. said. "My kids like to driving me crazy, asking about you, when you be back."

"Handsome young'uns," Stovebolt said. "But I don't expect I'll be here tomorrow to meet them. I'll be someplace down the road."

"What you talking?" B.J. said. "He got to hire you. There ain't been nothing like this around here, never."

"This Mr. Hawkins don't have to do *nothing*. I done figured it out that he ain't got no use for me. That is clear as daylight. But I thought one time before I got gone I would give the people a taste of what they be missing. That's a private arrangement I got in my mind for Mr. Hawkins."

B.J. shook his head. "I can't understand it at all. I'm telling you the people would flock in here like bees to clover."

Stovebolt smiled. "Yes," he said. "I can play you some music. But the Hawk-man has got another purpose about things."

"I don't understand it nohow."

"What I'll do now is, I know a song that's got Darlene's name in it, and if she would like it, I'll sing it for her."

"It would tickle her to death," B.J. said. "Just look at her."

She was still gazing at the floor and smiling.

"That's what I'll do then. Here." He reached behind him to the bar and held out two cans of beer. "See if you can't take care of these for me while I'm singing."

"Well, thank you now," B.J. said.

He gave a different version of 'Stovebolt's Blues,' singing pretty things about Darlene. He sang five more songs, slowly and softly now, winding himself down gently. It was twelve-thirty and the people began to drift away awkwardly and unwillingly, sometimes lingering by the door to hear the end of a chorus or the last notes of a tune.

Finally everyone was gone but three or four young men, and Jim the barman wiped his face on his sleeve and flicked on the harsh white ceiling lights. "Man, I tell you," he said, "if you keep on here, we going to have to take on more help. I never seen people put down so much and come up so happy from it."

The thin sharp Mr. Hawkins pushed through the beaded curtains at the back and came in behind the bar. He stood there waiting for Stovebolt to make his move.

"I guess it's good evening, Mr. Hawkins, and good-bye, Mr. Hawkins," Stovebolt said. "I don't believe I'm going to give you the satisfaction of asking just in order to be turned down."

He nodded carefully. "Mr. Johnson, I think you must have known already what my judgment was going to be."

"Indeed I did. But I thought you might have a few words about it."

The thin man in his velvet shirt took a deep breath. He looked the squat powerful singer up and down, measuring the whole man. "Mr. Johnson, this is my place bought with my money and what I borrowed from the bank. I have certain plans in mind. And in my plans there is no room in this nightclub for any Rastuses or any Sambos." His hands moved behind the bar, and it was obvious that he had some sort of weapon there. "And there's no room for anybody named *Stovebolt*."

Some other time, he thought, and I would lay this dude flat out on the floor with a busted something. But the instant of anger flickered away. He was still happy, though washed out, and he still felt free and easy. So he grinned. "I think I do understand you, Mr. Hawkins, and maybe I would even agree. You're right that one of us is behind the times. I'm just not so simple-certain which one of us it is." As he got the sack and wrapped the guitar, he kept his eyes fixed on the man. Then he turned his back on him and went out the door into the chilly night.

Stovebolt Johnson was walking again, under the midnight sky, under the stars. The highway shone a dim grainy gray in the starlight, before and behind him stretching away forever. He didn't have to walk; he was planning to flag down and board the first bus that came either way. But he liked the motion of it, the easy rocking forward that set up a rhythm in his head. He hummed aimlessly, his body still warm even in the cold wind.

In a little while new words to 'Stovebolt's Blues' came to him, and he tried them out as he walked along, not singing but murmuring almost tonelessly.

Now I been down to the place call Hawk's Blue Dive.
Yes I been down now, place call Hawk's Blue Dive.
I got to tell you, baby, I didn't know if I'd come back alive.

He thought about the words and then decided that they would do all right. Yes indeed, they would do just fine.

There was one clear yellow star that stood in the sky directly behind the twiggy tip of a wild cherry tree. As the wind moved, the tip kept brushing through the light of it. But, Stovebolt knew, it was never going to brush that light away. He reached into his shirt pocket and took out the bar of chewing tobacco and began to unwrap it.

Uncollected Stories

Linnaeus Forgets

The year 1758 was a comparatively happy one in the life of Carl Linnaeus. For although his second son, Johannes, had died the year before at the age of three, in that same year his daughter Sophia, the last child he was to have, was born. And in 1758 he purchased three small bordering estates in the country near Uppsala and on one of these, Hammarby, he established a retreat, to which he thereafter retired during the summer months, away from the town and its deadly fever. He was content in his family, his wife and five children living; and having recently been made a Knight of the Polar Star, he now received certain intelligence that at the opportune hour he would be ennobled by King Adolf Fredrik.

The landscape about Hammarby was pleasant and interesting, though of course Linnaeus had long ago observed and classified every botanical specimen this region had to offer. Even so, he went almost daily on long walks into the countryside, usually accompanied by students. The students could not deny themselves his presence even during vacation periods; they were attracted to him as hummingbirds to trumpet vines by his geniality and humor and by his encyclopedic knowledge of every plant springing from the earth.

And he was happy too in overseeing the renovations of the buildings in Hammarby and the construction of the new Orangery, in which he hoped to bring to fruition certain exotic plants which had never before flowered on Swedish soil. Linnaeus had at last become a famous man, a world figure in the same fashion that Samuel Johnson and Voltaire and Albrecht von Haller were world figures, and every post brought him sheaves of adulatory verse and requests for permission to dedicate books to him and inquiries about the details of his system of sexual classification and plant specimens of every sort. Most of the specimens were flowers quite commonly known, but dried and pressed and sent to him by young ladies who sometimes hoped that they had discovered a new species, or who hoped merely to secure a token of the man's notice, an autograph letter. But he also received botanical samples from persons with quite reputable knowledge, from scientists persuaded that they had discovered some anomaly or exception which might cause him to think over again some part of his method. (For the ghost of Siegesbeck was even yet not completely laid.) Occasionally other specimens arrived which were indeed unfamiliar to him. These came from scientists and missionaries traveling in remote parts of the world, or the plants were sent by knowledgeable ship captains or now and then by some common sailor who had come to know, however vaguely and confusedly, something of Linnaeus' reputation.

His renown had come to him so belatedly and so tendentiously that the great botanist took a child's delight in all this attention. He read all the verses and all the letters and often would answer his unknown correspondents pretty much in their own manner; letters still remain to us in which he addressed one or another of his admirers in a silly and exaggerated prose style, admiring especially the charms of these young ladies he had never set eyes on. Sweden was in those days regarded as a backward country, having only a few warriors and enlightened despots to offer as important cultural figures, and part of Linnaeus' pride in his own achievements evinced itself in nationalist terms, a habit which Frenchmen and Englishmen found endearing.

On June 12, 1758, a large box was delivered to Linnaeus, along with a brief letter, and both these objects were battered from much travel. He opened first the box and found inside it a plant in a wicker basket which had been lined with oilskin. The plant was rooted in a black sandy loam, now dry and crumbly, and Linnaeus immediately watered it from a sprinkling can, though he entertained little hope of saving—actually, resuscitating—the plant. The plant was so wonderfully woebegone in appearance, so tattered by rough handling, that the scientist could not immediately say whether it was shrub, flower, or a tall grass. It seemed to have collapsed in upon itself, and its tough leaves and stems were the color of parchment and crackled like parchment when he tried to examine them. He desisted, hoping that the accompanying letter would answer some of his questions.

The letter bore no postmark. It was signed with a Dutch name, Gerhaert Oorts, though it was written in French. As he read the letter, it became clear to Linnaeus that the man who had signed it had not written it out himself, but had dictated it to someone else who had translated his words as he spoke. The man who wrote the letter was a Dutch sailor, a common seaman, and it was probably one of his superior officers who had served him as amanuensis and translator. The letter was undated and began: "*Cher maître Charles Linné, père de la science botanique; je ne sçay si . . .*"

"To the great Carl Linnaeus, Father of Botany: I know not whether the breadth of your interests still includes a wondering curiosity about strange plants which grow in many different parts of the world, or whether your ever-agile Spirit has undertaken to possess new kingdoms of science entirely. But in case you are continuing in your botanical endeavors, I am taking liberty to send you a remarkable flower [*une fleur merveilleuse*] that my fellows and I have observed to have strange properties and characteristics. This flower grows in no great abundance on the small islands east of Guiana in the South Seas. With all worshipful respect, I am your obedient servant, Gerhaert Oorts."

Linnaeus smiled on reading this letter, amused by the odd wording, but then frowned slightly. He still had no useful information. The fact that Mynheer Oorts called the plant a flower was no guarantee that it was indeed a flower. Few people in the world were truly interested in botany, and it was not to be expected that a sailor could have leisure for even the most rudimentary study of the subject. The most he could profitably surmise was that it bore blooms, which the sailor had seen.

He looked at it again, but it was so crumpled in upon itself that he was fearful of damaging it if he undertook a hasty inspection. It was good to know that it was a tropical plant. Linnaeus lifted the basket out of the box and set the plant on the corner of a long table where the sunlight fell strongest. He noticed that the soil was already thirsty again so he watered it liberally, still not having any expectation that his ministrations would take the least effect.

It was now quarter till two, and as he had arranged a two o'clock appointment with a troublesome student, Linnaeus hurried out of his museum—which he called "my little back room"—and went into the main house to prepare himself. His student arrived promptly, but was so talkative and contentious and so involved in a number of personal problems that the rest of the afternoon was dissipated in conference with him. After this, it was time for dinner, over which Linnaeus and his family habitually sat for more than two hours, gossiping and teasing and laughing. And then there was music on the clavier in the small rough dining room; the botanist was partial to Telemann, and sat beaming in a corner of a sofa, nodding in time to a sonata.

And so it was eight o'clock before he found opportunity to return to his little back room. He had decided to defer thorough investigation of his new specimen until next day, preferring to examine his plants by natural sunlight rather than by lamplight. For though the undying summer twilight still held the western sky, in the museum it was gray and shadowy. But he wanted to take a final look at the plant before retiring and he needed also to draw up an account of the day's activities for his journal.

He entered the little house and lit two oil lamps. The light they shed mingled with the twilight, giving a strange orange tint to the walls and furnishings.

Linnaeus was immediately aware that changes had taken place in the plant. It was no trick of the light; the plant had acquired more color. The leaves and stems were suffused with a bright lemonish yellow, a color much more alive than the dim brown the plant had shown at two o'clock. And in the room hung a pervasive scent, unmistakable but not oppressive, which could be accounted for only by the presence of the plant. This was a pleasant perfume and full of reminiscence—but he could not remember what the scent reminded him of. So many associations crowded into his mind that he could sort none of them out; but there was nothing unhappy in these confused sensations. He wagged his head in dreamy wonder.

He looked at it more closely and saw that the plant had lost its dry parchmentlike texture, that its surfaces had become pliable and lifelike in appearance. Truly it was a remarkable specimen, with its warm perfume and marvelous recuperative powers. He began to speculate that this plant had the power of simply becoming dormant, and not dying, when deprived of proper moisture and nourishment. He took up a bucket of well water, replenishing the watering can, and watered it again, resolving that he would give up all his other projects now until he had properly examined this stranger and classified it.

He snuffed the lamps and went out again into the vast whitish-yellow twilight. A huge full moon loomed in the east, just brushing the tree tips of a grove, and from within the grove sounded the harsh trills and staccato accents of a song sparrow and the calmly flowing recital of a thrush. The air was already cool enough that he could feel the warmth of the earth rising about his ankles. Now the botanist was entirely happy, and he felt within him the excitement he had often felt before when he came to know that he had found a new species and could enter another name and description into his grand catalogue.

He must have spent more time in his little back room than he had supposed, for when he reentered his dwelling house all was silent and only enough lamps were burning for him to see to make his way about. Everyone had retired, even the two servants. Linnaeus reflected that his household had become accustomed to his arduous hours and took it for granted that he could look after his own desires at bedtime. He took a lamp and went quietly up the stairs to the bedroom. He dressed himself for bed and got in beside Fru Linnaea, who had gathered herself into a warm huddle on the left-hand side. As he arranged the bedclothes she murmured some sleep-blurred words which he could not quite hear, and he stroked her shoulder and then turned on his right side to go to sleep.

But sleep did not come. Instead, bad memories rose, memories of old academic quarrels, and memories especially of the attacks upon him by Johann Siegesbeck. For when Siegesbeck first attacked his system of sexual classification in that detestable book called *Short Outline of True Botanic Wisdom*, Linnaeus had almost no reputation to speak of and Siegesbeck represented—to Sweden, at least—the authority of the academy. And what, Linnaeus asked, was the basis of this ignorant pedant's objections? Why, that his system of classifying plants was morally dissolute. In his book Siegesbeck had asked, "Who would have thought that bluebells, lilies, and onions could be up to such immorality?" He went on for pages in this vein, not failing to point out that Sir Thomas Browne had listed the notion of the sexuality of plants as one of the vulgar errors. Finally Siegesbeck had asked—anticipating an objection Goethe would voice eighty-three years later—how such a licentious method of classification could be taught to young students without corruption of minds and morals?

Linnaeus groaned involuntarily, helpless under the force of memory.

These attacks had not let up, had cost him a position at the university, so that he was forced to support himself as a medical practitioner and for two barren years had been exiled from his botanical studies. In truth, Linnaeus never understood the nature of these attacks; they seemed foolish and irrelevant, and that is why he remembered them so bitterly. He could never understand how a man could write: "To tell you that nothing could equal the gross prurience of Linnaeus' mind is perfectly needless. A literal translation of the first principles of Linnaean botany is enough to shock female modesty. It is possible that many virtuous students might not be able to make out the similitude of *Clitoria*."

It seemed to Linnaeus that to describe his system of classification as immoral was to describe Nature as immoral, and Nature could not be immoral. It seemed to him that the plants inhabited a different world than the fallen world of mankind, and that they lived in a sphere of perfect freedom and ease, unvexed by momentary and perverse jealousies. Any man with eyes could see that the stamens were masculine and the pistils feminine, and that if there was only one stamen to the female part (*Monandria*) this approximation of the Christian European family was only charmingly coincidental. It was more likely that the female would be attended by four husbands (*Tetrandria*) or by five (*Pentandria*) or by twelve or more (*Dodecandria*). When he placed the poppy in the class *Polyandria* and described its arrangement as "Twenty males or more in the same bed with the female," he meant to say of the flower no more than God had said when He created it. How had it happened that mere literal description had caused him such unwarrantable hardship?

These thoughts and others toiled in his mind for an hour or so. When at last they subsided, Linnaeus had turned on his left side toward his wife and fallen asleep, breathing unevenly.

He rose later than was his custom. His sleep had been shaken by garish dreams which he could not now remember, and he wished he had awakened earlier. Now he got out of bed with uncertain movements and stiffly made his toilet and dressed himself. His head buzzed. He hurried downstairs as soon as he could.

It was much later than he had supposed. None of the family was about; everyone had already breakfasted and set out in pursuit of the new day. Only Nils, the elderly bachelor manservant, waited to serve him in the dining room. He informed his master that Fru Linnaea had taken all the children, except the baby asleep in the nursery, on an excursion into town. Linnaeus nodded, and wondered briefly if the state of his accounts this quarter could support the good Fru's passion for shopping. Then he forgot about it.

It was almost nine o'clock.

He ate a large breakfast of bread and cheese and butter and fruit, together with four cups of strong black tea. After eating, he felt both refreshed and dilatory and he thought for a long moment of taking advantage of the morning and the unnaturally quiet house to read in some of the new volumes of botanical studies which had arrived during the past few weeks.

But when he remembered the new specimen awaiting him in the museum, these impulses evaporated and he left the house quickly. It was another fine day. The sky was cloudless, a mild, mild blue. Where the east grove cast its shadow on the lawn, dew still remained and he smelled its freshness as he passed. He fumbled the latch excitedly, and then he swung the museum door open.

His swift first impression was that something had caught fire and burned, the odor in the room was so strong. It wasn't an acrid smell, a smell of destruction, but it was overpowering and in a moment he identified it as having an organic source. He closed the door and walked to the center of the room. It was not only the heavy damp odor which attacked his senses, but also a high-pitched musical chirping, or twittering, scattered on the room's laden air. And the two sensations, smell and sound, were indistinguishably mixed; here was an example of that sensory confusion of which M. Diderot had written so engagingly. At first he could not discover the source of all this sensual hurly-burly. The morning sun entered the windows to shine aslant the north wall, so that between Linnaeus and his strange new plant there fell a tall rectangular corridor of sunshine his gaze couldn't clearly pierce through.

He stood stock-still, for what he could see of the plant beyond the light astonished him. It had opened out and grown monstrously; it was enormous, tier on tier of dark green reaching to a height of three feet or more above the table. No blooms that he could see, but differentiated levels of broad green leaves spread out in orderly fashion from bottom to top, so that the plant had the appearance of a flourishing green pyramid. And there was movement among and about the leaves, a shifting in the air all around it, and he supposed that an extensive tropical insect life had been transported into his little museum. Linnaeus smiled nervously, hardly able to contain his excitement, and stepped into the passage of sunlight.

As he advanced toward the plant, the twittering sound grew louder. The foliage, he thought, must be rife with living creatures. He came to the edge of the table but could not yet see clearly, his sight still dazzled from stepping into and out of the swath of sunshine.

Even when his eyes grew more accustomed to shadow, he still could not make out exactly what he was looking at. There was a general confused movement about and within the plant, a continual settling and unsettling as around a beehive, but the small creatures that flitted there were so shining and iridescent, so gossamerlike, that he could fix no proper impression of them. Now, though, he heard them quite clearly, and realized that what had at first seemed a confused melange of twittering was in fact an orderly progression of sounds, a music as of flutes and piccolos in polyphony.

He could account for this impression in no way but to think of it as a product of his imagination. He had become aware that his senses were not so acute as they ordinarily were. Or rather, that they were acute enough, but that he was having some difficulty in interpreting what his senses told him. It occurred to him that the perfume of the plant—which now cloaked him heavily, an invisible smoke—possessed perhaps some narcotic quality. When he reached past the corner of the table to a wall shelf for a magnifying glass he noticed that his movements were sluggish and that an odd feeling of remoteness took power over his mind.

He leaned over the plant, training his glass and trying to breathe less deeply. The creature that swam into his sight, flitting through the magnification, so startled him that he dropped the glass to the floor and began to rub his eyes and temples and forehead. He wasn't sure what he had seen—that is, he could not believe what he thought he had seen—because it was no form of insect life at all.

He retrieved the glass and looked again, moving from one area of the plant to another, like a man examining a map.

These were no insects, though many of the creatures here inhabiting were winged. They were of flesh, however diminutive they were in size. The whole animal family was represented here in little: horses, cows, dogs, serpents, lions and tigers and leopards, elephants, opossums, and otters. . . . All the animals Linnaeus had seen or heard of here surfaced for a moment in his horn-handled glass and then sped away on their ordinary amazing errands. . . . And not only the animals he might have seen in the world, but the fabulous animals too: unicorns and dragons and gryphons and basilisks and the Arabian flying serpents of which Herodotus had written.

Tears streamed on the botanist's face, and he straightened and wiped his eyes with his palm. He looked all about him in the long room, but nothing else had changed. The floor was littered with potting soil and broken and empty pots, and on the shelves were the jars of chemicals and dried leaves, and on the small round table by the window his journal lay open, with two quill pens beside it and the inkpot and his pewter snuffbox. If he had indeed become insane all in a moment, the distortion of his perceptions did not extend to the daily objects of his existence but was confined to this one strange plant.

He stepped to the little table and took two pinches of snuff, hoping that the tobacco might clear his head and that the dust in his nostrils might prevent to some degree the narcotic effect of the plant's perfume, if that was what caused the appearance of these visions. He sneezed in the sunlight and dust motes rose golden around him. He bent to his journal and dipped his pen and thought, but finally wrote nothing. What could he write down that he would believe in a week's time?

He returned to the plant, determined to subject it to the most minute examination. He decided to limit his observation to the plant itself, disregarding the fantastic animal life. With the plant his senses would be less likely to deceive him. But his resolve melted away when once again he employed the magnifying glass. There was too much movement; the distraction was too violent.

Now he observed that there were not only miniature animals, real and fabulous, but there was also a widespread colony, or nation, of homunculi. Here were little men and women, perfectly formed, and —like the other animals—sometimes having wings. He felt the mingled fear and astonishment that Mr. Swift's hapless Gulliver felt when he first encountered the Lilliputians. But he also felt an admiration, as he might feel upon seeing some particularly well-fashioned example of the Swiss watchmaker's art. To see large animals in small, with their customary motions so accelerated, did indeed give the impression of a mechanical exhibition.

Yet there was really nothing mechanical about them, if he put himself in their situation. They were self-determining; most of their actions had motives intelligible to him, however exotic were the means of carrying out these motives. Here, for example, a tiny rotund man in a green jerkin and saffron trousers talked—sang, rather—to a tiny slender man dressed all in brown. At the conclusion of this recitative, the man in brown raced away and leaped onto the back of a tiny winged camel which bore him from this lower level of the plant to an upper one where he dismounted and began singing to a young lady in a bright blue gown. Perfectly obvious that a message had been delivered . . . Here in another place a party of men and women mounted on unwinged great cats, lions and leopards and tigers, pursued over the otherwise deserted broad plain of a leaf a fearful hydra, its nine heads snapping and spitting. At last they impaled it to the white leaf vein with the sharp black thorns they carried for lances and then they set the monster afire, writhing and shrieking, and they rode away together. A grayish waxy blister formed on the leaf where the hydra had burned. . . . And here in another area a formal ball was taking place, the tiny gentlemen leading out the ladies in time to the music of an orchestra sawing and pounding at the instruments. . . .

This plant, then, enfolded a little world, a miniature society in which the mundane and the fanciful commingled in matter-of-fact fashion but at a feverish rate of speed.

Linnaeus became aware that his legs were trembling from tiredness and that his back ached. He straightened, feeling a grateful release of muscle tension. He went round to the little table and sat, dipped his pen again, and began writing hurriedly, hardly stopping to think. He wrote until his hand almost cramped and then he flexed it several times and wrote more, covering page after page with his neat sharp script. Finally he laid the pen aside and leaned back in his chair and thought. Many different suppositions formed in his mind, but none of them made clear sense. He was still befuddled and he felt that he might be confused for years to come, that he had fallen victim to a dream or vision from which he might never recover.

In a while he felt rested and he returned again to look at the plant.

By now a whole season, or a generation or more, had passed. The plant itself was a darker green than before, its shape had changed, and even more creatures now lived within it. The midpart of the plant had opened out into a large boxlike space thickly walled with hand-sized kidney-shaped leaves. This section formed a miniature theater or court-yard. Something was taking place here, but Linnaeus could not readily figure out what it was.

Much elaborate construction had been undertaken. The smaller leaves of the plant had in this space been clipped and arranged into a grand formal garden. There were walls and arches of greenery and greenery shaped into obelisks topped with globes, and Greek columns and balconies and level paths. Wooden statues and busts were placed at intervals within this garden, and it seemed to Linnaeus that on some of the subjects he could make out the lineaments of the great classical botanists. Here, for example, was Pliny, and there was Theophrastus. Many of the persons so honored were unfamiliar to him, but then he found on one of the busts, occupying a position of great prominence, his own rounded cheerful features.—Could this be true? He stared and stared, but his little glass lacked enough magnification for him to be finally certain.

Music was everywhere; chamber orchestras were stationed at various points along the outer walls of the garden and two large orchestras were set up at either end of the wide main path. There were a number of people calmly walking about, twittering to one another, but there were fewer than he had at first supposed. The air above them was dotted with cherubs flying about playfully, and much of the foliage was decorated with artfully hung tapestries. . . . There was about the scene an attitude of expectancy, of waiting.

At this point the various orchestras began to sound in concert and gathered the music into recognizable shape. The sound was still thin and high-pitched, but Linnaeus discerned in it a long reiterative fanfare, which was followed by a slow, grave processional march. All the little people turned from their casual attitudes and gave their attention to the wall of leaves standing at the end of the main wide pathway. There was a clipped narrow corridor in front of the wall and from it emerged a happy band of naked children. They advanced slowly and disorderly, strewing the path with tiny pink petals that they lifted out in dripping handfuls from woven baskets slung over their shoulders. They were singing in unison, but Linnaeus could not make out the melody, their soprano voices pitched beyond his range of hearing. Following the children came another group of musicians, blowing and thumping, and then a train of comely maidens, dressed in airy long white dresses tied about the waists with broad ribbons, green and yellow. The maidens too were singing, and the botanist now began to hear the vocal music, a measured but joyous choral hymn. Linnaeus was smiling to himself, buoyed up on an ocean of happy fullness; his face and eyes were bright. . . .

The beautiful maidens were followed by another troop of petal-scattering children, and after them came a large orderly group of animals of all sorts, domestic animals and wild animals and fantastic animals, stalking forward with their fine innate dignities, though not of course in step. The animals were unattended, moving in the procession as if conscious of their places and duties. There were more of these animals, male and female of each kind, than Linnaeus had expected to live within the plant. He attempted vainly to count the number of different species, but gave over as they kept pouring forward smoothly, like sand grains twinkling into the bottom of an hourglass.

The spectators had gathered to the sides of the pathway and stood cheering and applauding.

The animals passed by, and now a train of carriages ranked in twos took their place. These carriages were each drawn by teams of four little horses, and both the horses and carriages were loaded down with great garlands of bring flowers, hung with blooms from end to end. Powdered ladies fluttered their fans in the windows. And after the carriages, another band of musicians marched.

Slowly now, little by little, a large company of strong young men appeared, scores of them. Each wore a stout leather harness from which long reins of leather were attached behind to an enormous wheeled platform. The young men, their bodies shining, drew this platform down the pathway. The platform itself supported another formal garden, within which was an interior arrangement suggestive of a royal court. There was a throne on its dais, and numerous attendants before and behind the throne. Flaming braziers in each corner gave off thick grayish-purple clouds of smoke, and around these braziers small children exhibited various instruments and implements connected with the science of botany: shovels, thermometers, barometers, potting spades, and so forth. Below the dais on the left-hand side a savage, a New World Indian adorned with feathers and gold, knelt in homage, and in front of him a beautiful woman in Turkish dress proffered to the throne a tea shrub in a silver pot. Farther to the left, at the edge of the tableau, a sable Ethiopian stood, he too carrying a plant indigenous to his mysterious continent.

The throne itself was a living creature, a great tawny lion with sherry-colored eyes. The power and wildness of the creature were unmistakable in him, but now he lay placid and willing, with a sleepy smile on his face. And on this throne of the living lion, over whose back a covering of deep plush green satin had been thrown, sat the goddess Flora. This was she indeed, wearing a golden crown and holding in her left hand a gathering of peonies (*Paeonia officinalis*) and in her right hand a heavy golden key. Flora sat in ease, the goddess gowned in a carmine silk that shone silver where the light fell on it in broad planes, the gown tied over her right shoulder and arm to form a sleeve, and gathered lower on her left side to leave the breast bare. An expression of sublime dreaminess was on her face and she gazed off into a far distance, thinking thoughts unknowable even to her most intimate initiates. . . . She was attended on her right hand side by Apollo, splendidly naked except for the laurel bays round his forehead and his bow and quiver crossed on his chest. Behind her Diana disposed herself, half reclining, half supporting herself on her bow, and wearing in her hair her crescent-moon fillet. Apollo devoted his attention to Flora, holding aloft a blazing torch, and looking down upon her with an expression of mingled tenderness and admiration. He stood astride the carcass of a loathsome slain dragon, signifying the demise of ignorance and superstitious unbelief.

The music rolled forth in loud hosannas, and the spectators on every side knelt in reverence to the goddess as she passed.

Linnaeus became dizzy. He closed his eyes for a moment and felt the floor twirling beneath his feet. He stumbled across the room to his chair by the writing table and sat. His chin dropped down on his chest; he fell into a deep swoon.

When he regained consciousness the shaft of sunlight had reached the west wall. At least an hour had passed. When he stirred himself there was an unaccustomed stiffness in his limbs and it seemed to him that over the past twenty-four hours or so his body had aged several years.

His first clear thoughts were of the plant, and he rose and went to his work table to find out what changes had occurred. But the plant was no more; it had disappeared. Here was the wicker container lined with oilcloth, here was the earth inside it, now returned to its dry and crumbly condition, but the wonderful plant no longer existed. All that remained was a greasy gray-green powder sifted over the soil. Linnaeus took up a pinch of it in his fingers and sniffed at it and even tasted it, but it had no sensory qualities at all except a neutral oiliness. Absentmindedly he wiped his fingers on his coat sleeve.

A deep melancholy descended upon the man and he locked his hands behind his back and began walking about the room, striding up and down beside his work table. A harsh welter of thoughts and impulses overcame his mind. At one point he halted in midstride, turned and crossed to his writing table and snatched up his journal, anxious to determine what account he had written of his strange adventure.

His journal was no help at all, for he could not read it. He looked at the unfinished last page and then thumbed backward for seven pages and turned them all over again, staring and staring. He had written in a script unintelligible to him, a writing that seemed to bear some distant resemblance to Arabic perhaps, but which bore no resemblance at all to his usual exuberant mixture of Latin and Swedish. Not a word or a syllable on any page conveyed the least meaning to him.

As he gazed at these dots and squiggles he had scratched on the page Linnaeus began to forget. He waved his hand before his face like a man brushing away cobwebs. The more he looked at his pages the more he forgot, until finally he had forgotten the whole episode, the letter from the Dutch sailor, the receiving of the plant, the discovery of the little world the plant contained—everything.

Like a man in a trance, and with entranced movements, he returned to his work table and swept some scattered crumbs of soil into it and carried it away and deposited it in the dustbin.

It has been said that some great minds have the ability *to forget deeply*. That is what happened to Linnaeus; he forgot the plant and the bright vision that had been vouchsafed to him. But the profoundest levels of his life had been stirred, and some of the details of his thinking had changed.

His love for metaphor sharpened, for one thing. Writing in his *Deliciae Naturae*, which appeared fourteen years after his encounter with the plant, he described a small pink-flowered ericaceous plant of Lapland growing on a rock by a pool with a newt as "the blushing naked princess Andromeda, lovable and beautiful, chained to a sea rock and exposed to a horrible dragon." These kinds of conceits intrigued him, and more than ever metaphor began to inform the way he perceived and outlined the facts of his science.

Another happy change in his life was the cessation of his bad nights of sleeplessness and uneasy dreams. No longer was he troubled by memories of the attacks of Siegesbeck or any other of his old opponents.

Linnaeus had acquired a new and resistless faith in his observations. He was finally certain that the plants of this earth carry on their love affairs in uncaring merry freedom, making whatever sexual arrangements best suit them, and that they go to replenish the globe guiltlessly, in high and winsome delight.

Notes Toward a
Theory of Flight

*D*rummond woke. There was a gray-black smoke all before his eyes. Help help, oh Lord, the house is on fire. . . . No, it was merely his tail; he was sleeping with his fine bushy tail wreathed round his face. He peered through with his fierce yellow eyes, but nothing was happening. The living room was quiet as grass; not even dust motes stirred in the slant sunbeams shooting through the south windows.

So he went back to sleep and began to dream of, of— . . . He could never quite tell what it was he dreamed of. But now he was awake again, prodded to alertness by a certain odor. The cool, faintly metallic smell of an equation had needled by. "Equation" wasn't exact, of course; Drummond had no mathematics, knowing only the One and the Many. But since all his physics was bent toward the severely practical, the personal, the nifty precision of numbers was not necessary. If he thought that a certain theory might work, he tried it out. Success or failure, that was all; he had no need to keep records.

He stood, stretched, arched his back, and lowered himself from the sofa to the carpet like a towel dropping off a rack. He strolled gently to the open door that led into the dining room. Here he paused for long moments, his right front paw raised. What was beyond the door, round the corner? Was it Madame Crone waiting poised to pounce? He began to hope that it was. He had forgotten the equation he had dreamed, and it made him feel very much like whipping somebody's ass.

He peeked, but there was no one there.

Disappointed, he walked on through the silent dining room. The slat-shadows of the louvers passed over his fur like the bar lines of a violin concerto.

The kitchen was cooler, uncarpeted. Drummond detested this slick cold linoleum which gave no grip for pad or claw. Too many times in thoughtless pursuit he had tried to halt himself and had skated into wall or shelf corner. Not really painful, but it made a man feel such an idiot. Next to eating, fighting, and his too slowly progressing theory of flight Drummond thought most about his *bella figura*, about keeping his cool. Linoleum, glass-topped tables, and catnip: these were the enemies of Cool.

There was no one in the kitchen and no fresh smell of food, but he checked the blue porcelain bowls, his and Madame's, anyhow. Phooey. He lapped a bit of water and found it stalish. How long till suppertime? He couldn't say; nobody could. It was Drummond's conviction that they put out food whenever they goddamn felt like it and called it Suppertime. It was exasperating. Having no mathematics, Drummond had learned to be quite precise about other things.

But he had forgotten his dreamed equation, and he needed to ponder. Now where was the best place in the house to think? He walked on through the kitchen and down the hall, toward the dim bedroom.

The bedroom rested in curtained stillness and the plump bed quilt was as inviting as cream. That's what it looked like, yards of clotted cream with a frilly border. And it was redolent always with the warm smell of Susan-his-mistress. He gathered his haunches and leaped.

His heart jolted and his skin went all electric. Great-God-Almighty-Damn! Here Madame had been sleeping, right in the middle of the bed where he couldn't have seen her.

Immediately she was awake, alert as a jazz solo. She sat upright in defensive posture, jabbing the air.

"Zfiss-sizz and skin/slash, I'll settle your hash!"

She had caught him totally unaware, since he had been thinking about how to think about the theory of flying.

"Miseries and claw/cut, I'll slice your butt!"

Drummond felt disheartened. That was it, he had no heart to

fight. Why couldn't he have come across her a while ago when he'd had that bit of an itch to scrap? Now he only wanted the bed, that was all. He needed it in order to—what? He had forgotten what he needed the bed for. That's the way Madame was, every moment driving a fellow to distraction.

He sat back and waited. He was confident that he could get the bed and he wouldn't have to fight for it. But he'd remember how she was treating him. Oh yes, there were lots of things she was storing up for herself, and she not knowing.

He sat waiting. Wide barrages of hostile message came from Madame, from her fur, her ears, her tail, her eyes. But this was mostly static, Drummond knew; he wasn't afraid of this sleek black old female.

He waited, and she grew calmer, bemused, and finally bored. She gave a faintly derisive shrug and hopped off onto the floor. Drummond went to the edge and watched her closely and she went round the bed and out the door, into the hall. He had to make certain she wasn't faking, planning to sneak back upon him.

In a few moments he heard her tag clang against metal as she investigated the empty porcelain bowls.

He settled himself into a curl, draping his tail over his nose. He grew sleepy. From outside came the harsh yammer of a blue jay.

Wait a minute, hold on . . . He hadn't come here to sleep, he'd come to think about flying. What was it he had dreamed before? Something about air resistance, wasn't it? Why was it that birds could fly, dumb goddamn birds with not a brain among a flock of them could fly in the air, while cats—the truly intelligent creatures—were condemned to creep earthbound?

So far as Drummond could see it was feathers and feathers alone which made the difference. It was because feathers presented so much surface area to air currents. It wasn't that the stupid birds actually had to *do* anything in order to fly. They merely spread themselves out, flattened themselves, and the breeze did most of the work. Birds presented a lot of surface area to the wind; it was all in those disgustingly bad-tasting feathers.

Cats didn't have feathers. Cats had only fur, which was usually too short to be of any use in flying.

A cool, faintly metallic, odor came into his head. That was it, the equation that had waked him up. Fur equals feathers.

For Drummond did not have short, slick, puny fur like Madame Crone had. (She, by God, was going to get hers; Drummond had plans in mind for that ugly female.) Drummond had long handsome fur, fine as silk fringe, finer. Fine as woolen lint, fine as intuition.

But that was the trouble. It was too fine, too soft, to offer air resistance. The wind would go through it as through a sieve. . . . But if it could be made stiffer. Glue, maybe. Or starch. He'd have to think of a way to stiffen his fur, make it air-worthy.

And there was also the problem of weight and surface proportion. Birds could spread out so much surface in proportion to their weights. . . .

For a moment Drummond allowed himself to daydream. He thought about flying, skimming the clear air and picking off bird after bird. It would be like knocking ornaments off a Christmas tree. The blue jays would be the first to go, the whole goddamn race of them. All sorts of things he could do. Those tiny, high-flying, noisy things—what-you-call-ems? . . . Airplanes. He wasn't interested in eating one. He'd just bat one down, see what made it go.

Meanwhile, the problem of surface area . . . What was the maximum surface he could present to the wind?

He decided to try an experiment. He stretched his neck out and laid his chin flat on the quilt. He stretched all four legs out as far as they would go and laid his paws flat. He looked for all the world, he thought, like a miniature bearskin rug attached to a handsome bushy tail. Could he glide in this posture, sleighlike, kitelike?

The bedroom light snapped on and Susan-his-mistress stood by the door, looking at him. She giggled. "Drummond, what in the world are you doing?" she said.

Then she began to laugh. Loudly and unmannerly.

He rose to his feet, rueful and abashed. His feelings were injured. He didn't see what was so goddamn funny. He had seen *her* do plenty of uncool things, things undignified. He had seen her when she was downright vulgar.

It was no secret about her. Drummond had told everybody; every cat on the block knew.

III

Poetry

The World Between the Eyes

February

Wouldn't drive and wouldn't be led,
So they tied cotton line around its neck and it backed,
Clipped steps, as the rope stretched.
Whereat,
They shot it clean through the shrieking brain.
And it dropped in a lump.

                         The boy, dismayed
With delight, watches the hog-killing,
Sharply alive in its tangle. Recoils,
Tries to hold it sensible; fails;
All the meaning in a brutal hour.

They bring the sledge down, and difficult
With the horse plunging white-eyed, hoofs
Askitter in the slick steep bank; the blood-smell's
Frightful and he snorts, head clatters back.
The pig's still gently quivering,
                  he's got a blue and human eye.
Lug it over and tumble it on, and the horse
Goes straining. The men swear
And grin, their teeth show hard in piercing air.

Frost gauzy on leaf and stone,
    The sky but faintly blue, wiped white.

  . . . And into the yard. The fire popping and licking,
They roll the big black cauldron to it. Saturday,
The neighbor women and men and kids, the faces
Broad with excitement. Wow wow across the gravel,
The cast iron pot; settles on the flame,
Black egg in its scarlet nest. Dark speech of the men,
Women waiting silent, hands under the blue aprons.

Long spike rammed through the heels
And up he goes against the big-armed oak
And dipped down in, dipped again, so
His hair falls off. (Swims in the filmed water
Like giant eyelashes.) Like a silver gourd
His belly shines and bulges. He's opened
And his steam goes up white,
The ghost of hog in the glassy morning.
They catch his guts.

                    The child, elated-drunk
With the horror, as they undo joint
And joint, stands with the men, watches
Their arms. They yank and slash, stammer
Of blood on the denim, eyelets of blood
On arm and fabric. They laugh like scythes,
Setting the head aside to see the dismantling
With its own blue eyes—still smiles
A thin smug smile!

                    And they cleave it
And cleave it. Loins. Ham.
                    Shoulder. Feet. Chops.
Even the tail's an obscure prize.
Goes into buckets; the child hauls
From hand to hand the pail all dripping.
Top of the heap, tremulous as water, lies

The big maroon liver.

               And the women receive it.
Gravely waiting as for supper grace.

The kitchen is glossy with heat, surcharged
With the smell of hog. Every surface
Is raddled with the fat. He slides
His finger on the jamb, it feels like flesh.
The whole lower house juicy with hog,
A bit of it in every cranny.
Where does it all come from?
               (A most unlikely prodigious pig.)
And now the women, busy, talk
Within the great clouds of oil and steam, bared
Elbows, heads nodding like breezy jonquils.
Clash of kettles, spoons
Yammering in the bowls, the windows opaque gray
With pig.

The sun reaches under the tree. They're gleaning
The last of him and the slippery whiskey jar
Goes handily among them. Wipe their mouths
With greasy wrists. And the smug head
Burst and its offerings distributed. Brain.
Ears. And the tail handed off with a clap of laughter.
They lick the white whiskey and laugh.

And his bladder and his stomach sack! puffed
Up and tied off and flung to the kids,
Game balls, they bat them about,
Running full tilt head down across the scattered yard.
And then on a startled breeze
The bladder's hoist, vaults high and gleams in the sunlight
And reflects on its shiny globe
The sky a white square
And the figures beneath, earnest figures
Gazing straight up.

Tiros II

(August 1960)

From where I watched the shiny satellite
Almost occluded summer Sirius.
I might have sworn they'd touch and set the night
Afire, transforming to a furious
Match. They did not. The new light went on by
Like a silver zipper zipping up the sky.

This is how we will climb the stars you say.
I perfectly agree. Some blinking
Bullet shot past the moon, shot past day
And night, will flounder on through the winking
System, a man aboard—not you or I,
Of course, but some young sir who likes to fly.

And this is not some queer extreme we think
Of, idling, but iron fact. Space is real,
Near and cold, black as India ink,
Frightening as falling down a well.
Those stubborn codes the stars are sending—why
Not assess some newer history?

For all I know there are orchids, birds,
Bats, rats, Siberians out there; perhaps, far back,
A titantic spacefish, too huge for words,
Which gobbles up the worlds, a shape of black.
Its length is measurable in light-years.
It has five tails and thirteen pairs of ears.

Death of W. H. Auden

He fumbles in his mind for the correct passport,
And steps idly back, looking
Precisely upon his watch. He jingles
His business suit. Is there anything
He has forgotten? He regrets only landscapes
That now he'll never greet friendly again.

He would like a drink. He'd like to have brought
A crossword. The boredom of another border
Looms huger than dying. His face
Is grave and waiting. He pats all his pockets,

And notices his doing it
And begins to muse and stands bemused
While his body drifts forward to departure.

In the wind the ashen crowd has gathered
To watch his leaving, but no one waves,
Or thinks to wave.

Seated Figure

Immense blind wind marching the grove,
Mauling the still house, and thrusting
Its paw in the torn flue. The stove
Roared, fierce, stuffed with flame to bursting.

The darkened mother crouched to her needle.
Rocking chair tipped back and forth.
Slowly, the house began to sidle
In the bare wind scouring the scoured earth.

Even when blue snow swarmed fast
On the pane and the light went glassy gray
She gave no sign. Time was past
She took notice of wind-fray.

All things hurtled in the night.
The roof groaned; arose. Then gone,
Like an owl, tumbling the thick light.
She drove her needle under the bone moon.

FROM

Midquest

The River Awakening in the Sea

Deep morning. Before the trees take silhouettes.

My forehead suckles your shoulder, straining to hear
In you the headlong ocean, your blood, island-saying sea now.
Wild stretches, bound to every water, of seas in you,
Uttering foam islands like broad flotillas of cabbage butterflies.
Gray tall clouds vaguely scribbling the pages of sea-top.
Your small breathing gently whetted in your nostrils, suffusing
The blood-warm pillowslip. Bedroom curls and uncurls with breath.
And all houses dark and nothing astir, though no one
Is truly asleep, everyone begins slowly to reach toward another,
Entering to each other with hands and arms impalpable, shadowless.
Slowly they turn dreaming as waves above roll deeper waves beneath.
Now they murmur amorphous words,
Words far away, no more guessable than the currents
Beginning to shudder and tremble as the hour enlarges.
Strands of current nudge into arpeggios the wide keyboards of
 whitebait.

                              Perhaps now in you my body
Seeks limits, now contoured horizons
Deliver to self accustomed bitter edges.
Deliver to the man, plunging narrow in the sea, curb and margin.

Or wind diving out of the sky and raising
In the waters falling towers of lace and spittle,
Oaring underneath with strong legs so tides pile and gasp.
So corded surf comes forward half-circle,
Spreading and cataracting.

                        We are fitful in the sheets,
We clutch. My forearm digging your breast,
I am swimming your salt skin.
Early light, stringent, has opened the bedroom, searches
Crease between wall and ceiling and molds itself on the dresser
In domestic shapes: brush and comb, deodorant can, cologne bottles,
Black clots of hairpins like barbwire.
Torn sheet of light sizzles in the mirror.

Sea coming apart now, green fingers
Shaking and shredding like cobweb. The sky
Punishes the waves, in-thrusts glassy caves,
Caves growing mouthlike round spindles of wind.

Do you dream of falling?
I dream your mouth gasps numbly open, your breath caught back
     pulsing,
Arms outflung, protesting reckless deeps you do not escape.

How the world was formed,
The dead dropped down brick by brick to sea bottom,
The dead and the sleeping, layer upon
Layer, they hug each other forever, their bones
Grin in the fathomless dark, wary as eyes.
Here is the bedrock: the dead, fold upon fold.
Lamprotoxu, Chiasmodon,
Dragonfish, Sea Viper, Black Gulper,
Burning like comets over choked bones.

While I am wishing never to wake, the oily bull-muscle
Of sea water shoves us landward, straining and warping like kites.
Yellow ring of earth rises above burned eyes.

My senses touch daylight and recoil, the furious net
Of daylight plumbs the bed.

Continent or momentary island,
Midlife, this land too known, too much unknown, 28 May 1971,
First day of my thirty-fifth year.
Sleeping sleeping I cannot halt the faithless instinct to be born.

The trees glow with raucous birds.
I rise and yawn,
Begin to scratch for clothing.

My naked foot upon this alien floor.

My Grandmother Washes Her Feet

I see her still, unsteadily riding the edge
Of the clawfoot tub, mumbling to her feet,
Musing bloodrust water about her ankles.
Cotton skirt pulled up, displaying bony
Bruised patchy calves that would make you weep.

Rinds of her soles had darkened, crust-colored—
Not yellow now—like the tough outer belly
Of an adder. In fourteen hours the most refreshment
She'd given herself was dabbling her feet in the water.

"You mightn't've liked John-Giles. Everybody knew
He was a mean one, galloping whiskey and bad women
All night. Tried to testify dead drunk
In church one time. That was a ruckus. Later
Came back a War Hero, and all the young men
Took to doing the things he did. And failed.
Finally one of his women's men shot him."

"What for?"

       "Stealing milk through fences. . . . That part
Of Family nobody wants to speak of.
They'd rather talk about fine men, brick houses,
Money. Maybe you ought to know, teach you
Something."

       "What *do* they talk about?"

             "Generals,
And the damn Civil War, and marriages.
Things you brag about in the front of Bibles.
You'd think there was arms and legs of Family

On every battlefield from Chickamauga
To Atlanta."

      "That's not the way it is?"

"Don't matter how it is. No proper way
To talk, is all. It was nothing they ever did.
And plenty they *won't* talk about . . . John-Giles!"

Her cracked toes thumped the tub wall, spreading
Shocklets. Amber toenails curled like shavings.
She twisted the worn knob to pour in coolness
I felt suffuse her body like a whiskey.

"Bubba Martin, he was another, and no
Kind of man. Jackleg preacher with the brains
Of a toad. Read the Bible upsidedown and crazy
Till it drove him crazy, making crazy marks
On doorsills, windows, sides of Luther's barn.
He killed hisself at last with a shotgun.
No gratitude for Luther putting him up
All those years. Shot so he'd fall down the well."

"I never heard."

           "They never mention him.
Nor Aunt Annie, that everybody called
Paregoric Annie, that roamed the highways
Thumbing cars and begging change to keep
Even with her craving. She claimed she was saving up
To buy a glass eye. It finally shamed them
Enough, they went together and got her one.
That didn't stop her. She lugged it around
In a velvet-lined case, asking strangers
Please to drop it in the socket for her.
They had her put away. And that was that.
There's places Family ties just won't stretch to."

Born then in my mind a race of beings
Unknown and monstrous. I named them Shadow-Cousins,
A linked long dark line of them,
Peering from mirrors and gleaming in closets, agog
To manifest themselves inside myself.
Like discovering a father's cancer.
I wanted to search my body for telltale streaks.

"Sounds like a bunch of cow thieves."

                      "Those too, I reckon,
But they're forgotten or covered over so well
Not even I can make them out. Gets foggy
When folks decide they're coming on respectable.
First think you know, you'll have a Family Tree."

(I imagined a wind-stunted horse-apple.)

She raised her face. The moons of the naked bulb
Flared in her spectacles, painting out her eyes.
In dirty water light bobbed like round soap.
A countenance matter-of-fact, age-engraved,
Mulling in peaceful wonder petty annals
Of embarrassment. Gray but edged with brown
Like an old photograph, her hair shone yellow.
A tiredness mantled her fine energy.
She shifted, sluicing water under instep.

"O what's the use," she said. "Water seeks
Its level. If your daddy thinks that teaching school
In a white shirt makes him a likelier man,
What's to blame? Leastways, he won't smother
Of mule-farts or have to starve for a pinch of rainfall.
Nothing new gets started without the old's
Plowed under, or halfway under. We sprouted from dirt,
Though, and it's with you, and dirt you'll never forget."

"No Mam."

"Don't you say me No Mam yet.
Wait till you get your chance to deny it."

Once she giggled, a sound like stroking muslin.

"You're bookish. I can see you easy a lawyer
Or a county clerk in a big white suit and tie,
Feeding the preacher and bribing the sheriff and the judge.
Second-generation-respectable
Don't come to any better destiny.
But it's dirt you rose from, dirt you'll bury in.
Just about the time you'll think your blood
Is clean, here will come dirt in a natural shape
You never dreamed. It'll rise up saying, Fred,
Where's that mule you're supposed to march behind?
Where's your overalls and roll-your owns?
Where's your Blue Tick hounds and Domineckers?
Not all the money in this world can wash true-poor
True rich. Fatback just won't change to artichokes."

"What's artichokes?"

                    "Pray Jesus you'll never know.
For if you do it'll be a sign you've grown
Away from what you are, can fly to flinders
Like a touch-me-not. . . . I may have errored
When I said *true-poor*. It ain't the same
As dirt-poor. When you got true dirt you got
Everything you need. . . . And don't you say me
Yes Mam again. You just wait."

                    She leaned
And pulled the plug. The water circled gagging
To a bloody eye and poured in the hole like a rat.
I thought maybe their spirits had gathered there,
All my Shadow-Cousins clouding the water,
And now they ran to earth and would cloud the earth.

Effigies of soil, I could seek them out
By clasping soil, forcing warm rude fingers
Into ancestral jelly my father wouldn't plow.
I strained to follow them, and never did.
I never had the grit to stir those guts.
I never had the guts to stir that earth.

Cleaning the Well

Two worlds there are. One you think
You know; the Other is the Well.
In hard December down I went.
"Now clean it out good." Lord, I sank
Like an anchor. My grand-dad leant
Above. His face blazed bright as steel.

Two worlds, I tell you. Swallowed by stones
Adrip with sweat, I spun on the ache
Of the rope; the pulley shrieked like bones
Scraped merciless on violins.
Plunging an eye. Plunging a lake
Of corkscrew vertigo and silence.

I halfway knew the rope would break.

Two suns I entered. At exact noon
The white sun narrowly hung above;
Below, like an acid floating moon,
The sun of water shone.
And what beneath that? A monster trove

Of blinding treasure I imagined:
Ribcage of drowned warlock gleaming,
Rust-chewed chain mail, or a plangent
Sunken bell tolling to the heart
Of earth. (They'd surely chosen an art-
less child to sound this soundless dreaming

O.) Dropping like a meteor,
I cried aloud—"Whoo! It's *God
Damn* cold!"—dancing the skin of the star.
"You watch your mouth, young man," he said.

I jerked and cursed in a silver fire
Of cold. My left leg thrummed like a wire.

Then, numb. Well water rose to my waist
And I became a figure of glass,
A naked explorer of outer space.
Felt I'd fricasseed my ass.
Felt I could stalk through earth and stone,
Nerveless creature without a bone.

Water-sun shattered, jelly-
bright wavelets lapped the walls.
Whatever was here to find, I stood
In the lonesome icy belly
Of the darkest vowel, lacking breath and balls,
Brain gummed mud.

"Say, Fred, how's it going down there?"
His words like gunshots roared; re-roared.
I answered, "Well—" (*Well well well . . .*)
And gave it up. It goes like Hell,
I thought. Precise accord
Of pain, disgust, and fear.

"Clean it out good." He drifted pan
And dipper down. I knelt and dredged
The well floor. Ice-razors edged
My eyes, the blackness flamed like fever,
Tin became nerve in my hand
Bodiless. *I shall arise never.*

What did I find under this black sun?
Twelve plastic pearls, Monopoly
Money, a greenish rotten cat,
Rubber knife, toy gun,
Clock guts, wish book, door key,
An indescribable female hat.

Was it worth the trip, was it true Descent?
Plumbing my childhood, to fall
Through the hole in the world and become . . .
What? *He told me to go. I went.*
(Recalling something beyond recall.
Cold cock on the nether roof of Home.)

Slouch sun swayed like a drunk
As up he hauled me, up, up,
Most willing fish that was ever caught.
I quivered galvanic in the taut
Loop, wobbled on the solid lip
Of earth, scarcely believing my luck.

His ordinary world too rich
For me, too sudden. Frozen blue,
Dead to armpit, I could not keep
My feet. I shut my eyes to fetch
Back holy dark. Now I knew
All my life uneasy sleep.

Jonah, Joseph, Lazarus,
Were you delivered so? Ript untimely
From black wellspring of death, unseemly
Haste of flesh dragged forth?
Artemis of waters, succor us,
Oversurfeit with our earth.

My vision of light trembled like steam.
I could not think. My senses drowned
In Arctic Ocean, the Pleiades
Streaked in my head like silver fleas.
I could not say what I had found.
I cannot say my dream.

When life began re-tickling my skin
My bones shuddered me. Sun now stood

At one o'clock. Yellow. Thin.
I had not found death good.
"Down there I kept thinking I was dead."

"Aw, you're all right," he said.

Dead Soldiers

I remember seven floods, the worst
In 1946 when the sluice-gates burst
And logs came blundering from the paper mill,
Choking Pigeon River below Smathers Hill,
Clanging culvert pipes and headfirst fast
Into Fiberville Bridge. It wouldn't last,
Old latticework of peeling paint and rust.
Everyone gathered at Campbell's store just
To see how long before it broke.
                              Old man
Campbell was unabashedly drunk again.
(Not that he hadn't good cause—this time, at least.)
His house and store stood the floodbank, yellow yeast
And black poison water already chewing
Off his lower lawn. Five big logs slewing
Down kidnapped his pumphouse. He swore in angry
Disbelief when he saw it strewn in the hungry
Acids. "Sweet Jesus Christamighty Gawd,"
He said, and spat whiskey spittle at the broad
And broadening river. "Somebody ought to by Christ
Do something. A man could stance it oncet . . . but *twicet*—"

No one offering to halt the flood, he took
A drink and held his pint to the light to look
How much. Three-quarters gone. He swigged it off
One gulp, turned purple, and began to cough.
"Somebody by God ought—"

                    The only help
He got was thumping on his back for a gulp
Of desperate breath. He dropped the empty, staring
Morose at piebald pine and oak logs boring

Chopped butts a moment up into drizzly day
Light, dipping like porpoises, swooping away
Toward Tennessee. "Guy works and slaves and where's
It get you," he said. "A limp dick, gray hairs,
A pile of debt is all I know. You'd think
The goddam Mill would've thought—"

                              Midnight ink
Resistless, the flood kept swelling, blacking the rose
Garden laid back out of elm-reach where snows
Could quilt it warm. "If Elsie was alive she'd die
To see it." Dime-sized rain from the sagging sky
Dropped and he raised his startled face. "*Son*
Of a bitch." The farmers gaping him for fun
Began to mumble, thinking how more rain
Would ruin them too. If it happened again—
Having been flooded two years before—they'd have
Bank notes so deep only a Peace Valley grave
Could free them.
                  Suddenly Campbell departed the hill,
Dashed into his house, and returned ready to kill
Somebody or maybe only something, bearing
New whiskey, a .22 rifle, shells; and swearing
Rare enough to shame a rattlesnake.
Instantly he gained respect.

                        "Chrisake,
Virgil, what you doing?"

                        "I ain't going to stand
Here and not fight back what's taking my land
And house," he said.

                    "You can't goddamnit shoot
A river."

              He spat. "I'd like to know why not."
And so he did. Loaded, and started pumping

Slug after slug at the water rising and thumping
His house like a big bass drum. All at once
The basement doors burst open and out floated tons,
Or what seemed tons, of emptied whiskey jars.

"Lord, Virgil, did you drink all that?"

                                        "Sure's
You're damned I did." He grinned. "But the goddamn dead
Soldiers won't stay dead. Must be," he said,
"The goddamn Day of Resurrection." And started in
Picking them off. Insensible husks of gin,
Bourbon, scotch, and moonshine sank as once more
He killed them certain. How many? At least a score
Of each, though nobody counted, struck dumb no doubt
At load on load of bottles rumbling out.
He never missed. He must have known by heart
Where each one sat on the shelf. Maybe a part
Of his crazy pride was knowing to a decimal point
How much he drank, having little to flaunt
Himself with else. Or maybe this unguessed cache
Of glassware was to him not splendid trash
But secret treasure he alone knew how
To value, now bobbing away in the fearful flow.
Anyway, he shot them to splinters, accurate
As cancer, muttering no one could quite hear what.
At last he busted them all. At last they'd never
Rise again, bright jewels in pitch river.

And now we heard a great inanimate groan,
A scream of something dying that stretched bone
And muscle in electric spasm. Enormous shriek
Of shearing iron made our knees go weak.
The bridge was falling. Drooping in curlicues
Like licorice, and shrugging up torn spews
Of shouting metal, and widening outward like a mouth
Slowly grinning to show each snagged-off tooth,

It plunged the water with a noise like the fall of Rome.
Everyone hollered at once. Gray boil of foam
And halved girders jumped cloudward between the piers,
Subsiding in a hail of bolts.

                    No cheers
Then, no laughing, but a silence solemn and deep
As church spread in the crowd like opiate half-sleep.
The great event was over; they'd finally seen
It all. A postcoital calm flushed clean
Their senses as they turned bright-glazed eyes
Toward mired roads home under purpling pink-streaked skies.

That's what I think *they* saw. But what *I* saw
Was Virgil Campbell with a meaningful slow
Smile lift his gun, and just when the bridge tumbled
He fired upon it a single shot, and grumbled,
"Better put it out of its misery."

After twenty-five murky years I still see
Him there, crazed Minuteman at river edge
With a .22 Marlin bringing down a bridge.

                    *   *   *

"Well, here you are at last," my father said.
"I've been looking for you." I turned my head
To find him suddenly solid in sudden dusk
Behind me, shape looming lightless, and gravid musk
Of cigarettes and wet wool standing like smoke
About him, an imminent immuring cloak
Formless. But awesome as God to a child of ten.
"Don't tell me you've got so dumb you don't know when
It's milking time." I followed him to the truck
And we went wallowing home through rutted muck.
"Virgil Campbell took a .22
And shot the iron bridge down," I said.
                    "That's true,"

He said presently, "if you think so. I can
Swear to it he's an independent man."

And nothing else for a while. At the barn he
Added, "That must have been something to see."

Rimbaud Fire Letter
to Jim Applewhite

That decade with Rimbaud I don't regret.
But could not live again. Man, that was *hard*.
Nursing the artificial fevers, wet
With Falstaff beer, I walked the railyard,
Stumbled the moon-streaked tracks, reciting line
After burning line I couldn't understand.
In the long twilight I waited for a sign
The world its symbols would mount at my command.

My folks thought I was crazy, maybe I was.
Drinking behind the garbage back of Maxine's Grill,
I formulated esoteric laws
That nothing ever obeyed, or ever will.
Les brasiers, pleuvant aux rafales de givre.—Douceurs!
I must have dreamed those words a hundred times,
But what they meant, or even what they *were*,
I never knew. They glowed in my head like flames.

Four things I knew: Rimbaud was genius pure;
The colors of the vowels and verb tenses;
That civilization was going up in fire;
And how to derange every last one of my senses:
Kind of a handbook on how to be weird and silly.
It might have helped if I had known some French,
But like any other Haywood County hillbilly
The simple thought of the language made me flinch.

So passed my high school years. The senior prom
I missed, and the girls, and all the thrilling sports.
My teachers asked me, "Boy, where you *from?*"
"From deep in a savage forest of unknown words."

The dialogue went downhill after that,
But our positions were clear respectively:
They stood up for health and truth and light,
I stood up for Baudelaire and me.

The subject gets more and more embarrassing.
Should I mention the clumsy shrine I built
In the maple tree behind old Plemmons' spring?
Or how I played the young Artur to the hilt
In beer joints where the acrid farmers drank?
Or how I tried to make my eyes look *through?*
—I'd better not. Enough, that I stayed drunk
For eight hot years, and came up black and blue.

One trouble was that time was running out.
Rimbaud had finished "all that shit" before
He reached his nineteenth year. I had about
Nineteen short months to get down to the core.
I never did, of course. I wrote a bunch
Of junk I'm grateful to have burned; I read
Some books. But my courage was totally out to lunch.
Oh, Fred Fred Fred Fred Fred . . .

Remember when we met our freshman year?
Not something you'd want to repeat, I guess, for still
R. worked his will in me, a blue blear
Smoke poured forth. (That, and alcohol.)
(And an army of cranky opinions about whatever
Topic was brought up.) (And a hateful pose
Of expertise.) Jesus, was I clever!
And smelt myself as smelling like a rose.

I had a wish, *Mourir aux fleuves barbares,*
And to fulfill it could have stayed at home.
But down at Duke in 1954
(*I like Ike*) it carried weight with some
Few wild men and true who wanted to write
And even tried to write—God bless them

Everyone!—and who scheduled the night
For BEER and the explication of a POEM.

Well, you recall: Mayola's Chili House,
Annamaria's Pizza, Maitland's Top Hat,
The Pickwick, and that truly squalid place,
The Duchess, where the local whores stayed fat
On college boys, and the Blue Star, the I.
P. D. But the joint that really made us flip
Sat sunsoaked on Broad St., where we walked by
Rambeau's Barber Shop.

Those were the days! . . . —But they went on and on and on.
The failure I saw myself grew darker and darker.
And hearing the hard new myths from Bob Mirandon,
I got Rimbaud confused with Charlie Parker.
It was a mess, mon vieux. Finally
They kicked me out, and back to the hills I went.
But not before they'd taught me how to see
Myself as halfway halved and halfway blent.

Jim, we talked our heads off. What didn't we say?
We didn't say what it cost our women to prop
Our psyches up, we couldn't admit *the day*
And age belonged still to our fathers. One drop
Distillate of Carolina reality
Might have cured much, but they couldn't make us drink.
We kept on terribly seeing how to see,
We kept on terribly thinking how to think.

They turned me down for the army. I wanted it raw,
I wanted to find a wound my mother could love.
(*Il a deux trous rouges au côté droit.*)
I wanted Uncle Sugar to call my bluff. . . .
No soap. I wound up hauling fertilizer,
Collecting bills, and trying to read Rimbaud
At night, and preaching those poems to David Deas or
Anyone else I thought might care to know.

The only good thing was that I got married.
And I watched the mountains until the mountains touched
My mind and partly tore away my fire-red
Vision of a universe besmirched.
I started my Concordance to Samuel Johnson,
And learned to list a proper footnote, got down
To reading folks like Pope and Bertrand Bronson,
And turned my back on the ashes of Paree-town.

But as my father said, "Fire's in the bloodstream."
The groaning it cost my muse to take off my edge
Still sounds in my sleep, rasps my furious dream.
—Tell you what, Jim: let's grow old and sage;
Let's don't wind up brilliant, young, and dead.
Let's just remember
                —Give my love to Jan.
Yours for terror and symbolism,

              ole Fred.

28 May 1971

My Grandfather's Church Goes Up

(Acts 2:1-47)

God is a fire in the head.
      —Nijinsky

Holocaust, pentecost: what heaped heartbreak:

The tendrils of fire   forthrightly tasting
foundation to rooftree   flesh of that edifice . . .
Why was sear sent   to sunder those jointures,
the wheat-hued wood   wasted to heaven?
Both altar and apse   the air ascended
in sullen smoke.

         (It was surely no sign
of God's salt grievance   but grizzled *Weird* grimly
and widely wandering.)

         The dutiful worshipers
stood afar ghast-struck   as the green cedar shingles
burst outward like birds   disturbed in their birling.
Choir stall crushed inward   flayed planking in curlicues
back on it bending,   broad beams of chestnut
oak poplar and pine   gasht open paint-pockets.
And the organ uttered   an unholy *Omega*
as gilt pipes and pedals   pulsed into rubble.

How it all took tongue!   A total hosannah
this building burgeoned,   the black hymnals whispering
leaves lisping in agony   leaping alight,
sopranos' white scapulars   each singly singeing
robes of the baritones   roaring like rivers
the balcony bellowing   and buckling. In the basement
where the M.Y.F.   had mumbled for mercies

the cane-bottomed chairs   chirruped Chinese.
What a glare   of garish glottals
rose from the nave   what knar-mouthed natter!
And the transept tottered   intoning like tympani
as the harsh heat   held hold there.
The whole church resounded   reared its rare anthem
crying out Christ-mercy   to the cloud-cloven sky.

Those portents Saint Paul   foretold to us peoples
fresh now appeared: bifurcate fire-tongues,
and as of wild winds   a swart mighty wrestling,
blood fire and vapor   of smoke vastly vaulting,
the sun into darkness   deadened and dimmed,
wonders in heaven   signs wrought in the world:
the Spirit poured out   on souls of us sinners.
In this din as of drunkenness   the old men dreamed dreams,
the daughters and sons   supernal sights saw.
God's gaudy grace   grasped them up groaning.
Doubt parched within them   pure power overtaking
their senses. Sobbing   like sweethearts bereft
the brothers and sisters   burst into singing.
Truly the Holy   Ghost here now halted,
held sway in their hearts   healed there the hurt.

Now over the narthex   the neat little steeple
force of the fire   felt furiously.
Bruit of black smoke   borne skyward
shadowed its shutters   swam forth in swelter.
It stood as stone   for onstreaming moments
then carefully crumpled   closed inward in char.
The brass bell within it   broke loose, bountifully
pealing, plunged   plangent to the pavement
and a glamour of clangor   gored cloudward gaily.

That was the ringing that wrung   remorse out of us clean,
the elemental echo   the elect would hear always;
in peace or in peril   that peal would pull them.

Seventeen seasons   have since parted
the killing by fire   of my grandfather's kirk.
Moving of our Maker   on this middle earth
is not to be mind-gripped   by any men.

Here Susan and I   saw it, come
to this wood, wicker   basket and wool blanket
swung between us,   in sweet June
on picnic. Prattling   like parakeets
we smoothed for our meal-place   the mild meadow grasses
and spread our sandwiches   in the sunlit greensward.
Then amorously ate.   And afterward
lay languorous and   looking lazily.
Green grass and pokeweed   gooseberry bushes
pink rambling rose   and raspberry vine
sassafras and thistle   and serrate sawbriar
clover and columbine   clung to the remnants,
grew in that ground   once granted to God.
Blackbirds and thrushes   built blithely there
the ferret and kingsnake   fed in the footing.
The wilderness rawly   had walked over those walls
and the deep-drinking forest   driven them down.

Now silence sang: swoon of wind
ambled the oak trees   and arching aspens.

In happy half-sleep   I heard or half-heard
in the bliss of breeze   breath of my grandfather,
vaunt of his voice   advance us vaward.
No fears fretted me   and a freedom followed
this vision vouchsafed,   victory of spirit.
He in the wind   wept not, but wonderfully
spoke softly   soothing to peace.
What matter he murmured   I never remembered,
words melted in wisps   washed whitely away;
but calm came into me   and cool repose.
Where Fate had fixed   no fervor formed;
he had accepted   wholeness of his handiwork.

Again it was given   to the Grace-grain that grew it,
had gone again   gleaming to Genesis
to the stark beginning   where the first stars burned.
Touchless and tristless   Time took it anew
and changed that church-plot   to an enchanted chrisom
of leaf and flower   of lithe light and shade.

Pilgrim, the past   becomes prayer
becomes remembrance rock-real   of Resurrection
when the Willer so willeth   works his wild wonders.

Burning the Frankenstein Monster:
Elegiac Letter to Richard Dillard

It is Henry, as everyone knows, who's really the monster,
  Not the innocent wistful crazy-quilt of dead flesh
We remember as being in love with flowers and children like
    flowers.
  It's the will made totally single which frightens us,
Monstrum horrendum, informe, ingens, cui lumen ademptum:
  Virgil's misshapen eyeless one-eye gone mad
And disturbing the fabric of ongoing time. —You were right,
    Richard,
  What I mostly ripped off from Rimbaud was the notion of fire
As symbolic of tortured, transcendent-striving will.

(But *The Inkling* is long out of print, bemuses not even my mother.
  Let it smolder to ash on whatever forgotten shelf.)

Why must poor Karloff be born out of fire, and die, fire-fearing,
  In the fire? Is he truly our dream of Promethean man?
Does he warn us of terrible births from atomic furnaces, atomic
  Centuries, shambling in pain from the rose-scented past?
Having been burned and then drowned, reversing the fate of Shelley,
  The lame monster brings back upon us the inverted weight
Of the romantic period. Whose children we are, but disinherit,
  Stranded in decades when all is flame and nothing but flame.

And my vividest memory: light first seen by the monster, pouring
  Through the roof peeled back little by little, at last
Bathing in splendor the seamed unlovable face with its stricken
  Eyes; and the creature in agony uplifting his hands,
Whimpering gutturally, hoping to be drawn up like water vapor
  Into the full forgiving embrace of the progenitor Sun.
What wouldn't *we* give to undergo in our latter years the virgin

Onslaught of light? To be born again into light,
To be raised from the grave, rudimentary senses unfolding like
    flowers
  In a warm April rainfall . . . But then they reseal the roof;
Little by little his hands drop again to his sides and the brightness
  Lapses in stone-colored eyes, his mind huddles forlorn.

Henry is watching in barely controlled hysteria, thinking
  Thoughts inarticulate, biting his raglike hands.
He is a child of the lightning also, of the flash unrepeated
  Revelation which blasts and creates in an instant, all.
Flash he must follow to destruction, before us melting whitely
  To madness. Let him then marry, let the wine be fetched
Out of the family cellars, the servants giggling like tipsy chickens
  When the baron proposes his toast: "A son to the House
Of Frankenstein!" —Has he forgotten that Henry already has
    fathered
  A son given over to the care of Fritz, dark spirit of Earth?

Fritz is unbearable. Crazy perhaps and certainly turned evil
  By reason of fear, it's he who teaches the monster to fear,
Perverting the light to a means of torture. This troll always scurrying
  Upstairs and down with a torch in his hand is reduced
Finally to shadow, to shadow hanged and splayed on the prison
  Wall. This is justice, of course, but it horrifies the mad
Doctor, the sane doctor, and every one of those whose consciences
  Whisper: *The fault is yours, for the dead must bury the dead.*

Return to the lake where the two abandoned children are playing:
  Here is no murder, no trial of death upon life.
Entrancement of naked simplicity washes both the bright faces;
  Pastoral daisies, the currency of joy between two,
Float in the water; the monster is struggling to utter first laughter.
  Now the sweet daisies are gone, and the hands that had held them
    ache,
Tremble with joylessness. Suddenly metaphor is born to the injured
  Criminal brain, and he plucks a final white bloom,

Launches it silvery drifting. The death of all flowers forever
  Is accomplished. From moist green ground he has plucked his
    own death.

Nuptials broken . . . The father in silent dry-eyed accusation
  Brings to the wedding the single drowned flower of death. . . .
(Notice in horror films, Richard, how weddings impendent on
    science,
  Knowledge unborn, recur. In *Dracula, Curse*
Of the Demon, in Freund's *The Mummy*, in Hillyer's *Dracula's
Daughter*, in *Dr. Jekyll and Mr. Hyde*.
Hearing "the loud bassoon," but prevented—until we listen
  To Salvation's full passion—the church, we stand aghast.
Faith calls to faith, but our faith must be earned from terror,
    consummate
  Love must be thirsted for, light must be wholly desired.)

White-gowned Elizabeth sees in the mirror the wayward monster
  (Calendar girl who confronts a medieval death's-head);
Hears the low growl, a deep rasp as if earth were tearing in tatters;
  Obligingly faints. And the monster her bridegroom lifts
Her over the threshold, through door after door, but the ritual is
    empty.
  Only one union is Karloff permitted: to wed
Terribly the flames, to return to the trauma of being fathered
  Once again, conceived in the raging delirium of fire.

    Father and son, they are bound to a wheel of crazed fire.

Father and son, with one instant of recognition between them:
  Jagged and hungry the gears that ponderously chew
The circle, and father and son for a moment pause to examine.
  "You who brought me into this world what have you done?"
"No. Never you I sired but a healthy longed-for imago."
  "I am but I and I come now to claim my birthright."
"Born of my will from the grave, for you this world holds nothing."
  "Maker and monster we shall not die apart."

Richard, this world is ever the world the fathers fashioned.
  Right and the right to be right belong to dreams
Not as yet come into flesh. The courageous monsters perish
  Always alone, and yet always in a final light
Glorious and stark. As the hilltop mill is always burning,
  Raising its arms of clean blaze against the stars.

Second Wind

The day they laid your Grandfather away
Was as hot and still as any I recall.
Not the least little breath of air in hall
Or parlor. A glossy shimmering July day,
And I was tired, so tired I wanted to say,
"Move over, Frank-my-husband, don't hog all
The space there where you are that looks so cool";
But it's a sin to want yourself to die.

And anyhow there was plenty enough to do
To help me fend off thoughts I'd be ashamed
Of later. (Not that ever I'd be blamed.)
The house was full of people who all knew
Us from way back when. Lord knows how
They'd even heard he died. And so it seemed
I owed them to stand firm. I hadn't dreamed
There'd be so terribly many with me now.

I'd fancied, don't you see, we'd be alone.
A couple growing old, until at last
There's one of them who has to go on first,
And then the other's not entirely *one*.
Somehow I'd got it in my mind that none
Of the rest of the world would know. Whichever passed
Away would have the other to keep fast
By, and the final hours would be our own.

It wasn't like that. I suppose it never is.
Dying's just as public as signing a deed.
They've got to testify you're really dead
And haven't merely changed an old address;
And maybe someone marks it down: *One less.*

422

Because it doesn't matter what you did
Or didn't do, just so they put the lid
On top of someone they think they recognize.

All those people . . . So many faces strained
With the proper strain of trying to look sad.
What did they feel truly? I thought, what could
They feel, wearing their Sunday clothes and fresh-shined
Prayer-meeting shoes? . . . Completely drained,
For thoughts like that to come into my head,
And knowing I'd thought them made me feel twice bad . . .
Ninety degrees. And three weeks since it rained.

I went into the kitchen where your mother
And your aunts were frying chicken for the crowd.
I guess I had in mind to help them out,
But then I couldn't. The disheartening weather
Had got into my heart; and not another
Thing on earth seemed worth the doing. The cloud
Of greasy steam in there all sticky glued
My clothes flat to my skin. I feared I'd smother.

I wandered through the house to the bedroom
And sat down on the bed. And then lay back
And closed my eyes. And then sat up. A black
And burning thing shaped like a tomb
Rose up in my mind and spoke in flame
And told me I would never find the pluck
To go on with my life, would come down weak
And crazed and sickly, waiting for my time.

I couldn't bear that. . . . Would I ever close
My eyes again? I heard the out-of-tune
Piano in the parlor and knew that soon
Aunt Tildy would crank up singing "Lo, How a Rose
E'er Blooming." —Now I'll admit Aunt Tildy tries,
But hadn't I been tried enough for one

Heartbreaking day? And then the Reverend Dunn
Would speak. . . . A *Baptist preacher in my house!*

That was the final straw. I washed my face
And took off all my mourning clothes and dressed
Up in my everyday's, then tiptoed past
The parlor, sneaking like a scaredey mouse
From my own home that seemed no more a place
I'd ever feel at home in. I turned east
And walked out toward the barns. I put my trust
In common things to be more serious.

Barely got out in time. Aunt Tildy's voice
("Rough as a turkey's leg," Frank used to say)
Ran through the walls and through the oily day
Light and followed me. Lord, what a noise!
I walked a little faster toward where the rose
Vine climbed the cowlot fence and looked away
Toward Chambers Cove, out over the corn and hay,
All as still as in a picture pose.

What was I thinking? Nothing nothing nothing.
Nothing I could nicely put a name to.
There's a point in feeling bad that we come to
Where everything is hard as flint: breathing,
Walking, crying even. It's a heathen
Sorrow over us. Whatever we do,
It's nothing nothing nothing. We want to die,
And that's the bitter end of all our loving.

But then I thought I saw at the far end
Of the far cornfield a tiny stir of blade.
I held my breath; then, sure enough, a wade
Of breeze came row to row. One stalk would bend
A little, then another. It was the wind
Came tipping there, swaying the green sad
Leaves so fragile-easy it hardly made
A dimpling I could see in the bottom land.

I waited it seemed like hours. Already I
Felt better, just knowing the wind was free once more,
That something fresh rose out of those fields where
We'd worn off half our lives under the sky
That pressed us to the furrows day by day.
And I knew too the wind was headed here
Where I was standing, a cooling wind as clear
As anything that I might ever know.

It was the breath of life to me, it was
Renewal of spirit such as I could never
Deny and still name myself a believer.
The way a thing is is the way it is
Because it gets reborn; because, *because*
A breath gets in its veins strong as a river
And inches up toward light forever and ever.
As long as wind is, there's no such thing as *Was*.

The wind that turned the fields had reached the rose
Vine now and crossed the lot and brushed my face.
So fresh I couldn't hear Aunt Tildy's voice.
So strong it poured on me the weight of grace.

My Father's Hurricane

Like dust cloud over a bombed-out city, my father's
Homemade cigarette smoke above the ruins
Of an April supper. His face, red-weathered, shone through.
When he spoke an edge of gold tooth-cap burned
In his mouth like a star, winking at half his words.

At the little end of the table, my sister and I
Sat alert, as he set down his streaky glass
Of buttermilk. My mother picked her teeth.

"I bet you think that's something," he said, "the wind
That tore the tin roof on the barn. I bet
You think that was some kind of wind."

"Yes sir," I said (with the whole certainty
Of my eleven years), "a pretty hard wind."

"Well, that was nothing. Not much more than a breath
Of fresh air. You should have seen the winds
That came when I was your age, or near about.
They've taken to naming them female names these days, ·
But this one I remember best they called
Bad Egg. A woman's name just wouldn't name it."

"Bad Egg?"

                    He nodded profoundly as a funeral
Home director. "That's right. Bad Egg was what
I think of as a right smart blow,
No slight ruffling of tacked-down tin.
The sky was filled with flocks of roofs, dozens
Of them like squadrons of pilotless airplanes,
Sometimes so many you couldn't even see between.
Little outhouse roofs and roofs of sheds

426

And great long roofs of tobacco warehouses,
Church steeples plunging along like V-2 rockets,
And hats, toupees, lampshades, and greenhouse roofs.
It even blew your aunt's glass eyeball out.
It blew the lid off a jar of pickles we'd
Been trying to unscrew for fifteen years."

"Aw," I said.

       "Don't interrupt me, boy,
I am coming to that. Because the roofs
Were only the top layer. Underneath
The roofs the trees came hurtling by, root-ends
First. They looked like flying octopuses
Glued onto frazzly toilet brushes. Oaks
And elms and cedars, peach trees dropping
Peaches—splat!—like big sweet mushy hailstones.
Apples and walnuts coming down like snow.
Below this layer of trees came a fleet of cars:
T-models, Oldsmobiles, and big Mack trucks;
And mixed in with the cars were horses tumbling
And neighing, spread-legged, and foaming at the mouth;
Cows too, churning to solid butter inside.
Beneath the layer of cars a layer of . . . everything.
What Madison County had clutched to its surface
It lost hold of. And here came bales of barbwire,
Water pumps, tobacco setters, cookstoves,
Girdles shucked off squealing ladies, statues
Of Confederate heroes, shotguns, big bunches
Of local politicians still talking of raising
Taxes. You name it, and here it came.
There was a visiting symphony orchestra
At Hot Springs School and they went flashing by,
Fiddling the 'Storm' movement of Beethoven's Sixth.
Following that—infielders prancing like black gnats—
A baseball game about five innings old.
The strangest thing adrift was a Tom Mix movie,

All wrinkled and out of order. Bad Egg
Had ripped the picture off the screen, along
With a greasy cloud of buttered popcorn."

                              "Wait,"
I said. "I don't understand how you
Could see the other layers with all this stuff
On the bottom."

                    "*I was coming to that,*" he said.
"If it was only a horizontal stream
It wouldn't have been so bad. But inside the main
Were other winds turning every whichway,
Crosswise and cockeyed, and up and down
Like corkscrews. Counterwinds—and mighty powerful.
It was a corkscrew caught me, and up I went;
I thought I'd pull in two. First man I met
Was Reverend Johnson, too busy ducking candlesticks
And hymnals to greet me, though he might have nodded.
And then Miz White, who taught geometry,
Washing by in a gang of obtuse triangles.
And then Bob Brendan, the Republican banker, flailing
Along with his hand in a safety deposit box.
Before I could holler I zipped up to Layer Two,
Bobbing about with Chevrolets and Fords
And Holsteins. . . . I'm not bragging, but I'll bet you
I'm the only man who ever rode
An upside-down Buick a hundred miles,
If you call holding on and praying 'riding.'
That was scary, boy, to have a car wreck
Way up in the middle of the air. I shut my eyes. . . .
But when I squirted up to Layer Three
I was no better off. This sideways forest
Skimming along looked mighty dark and deep.
For all I knew there could be bears in here,
Or windblown hunters to shoot me by mistake.
Mostly it was the trees—to see come clawing

At me those big root-arms—Ough! I shivered
And shuddered, I'll tell you. Worse than crocodiles:
After I dodged the ripping roots, the tails,
The heavy limbs, came sworping and clattering at me.
I was awfully glad to be leaving Layer Three."

"Wait," I said. "How come the heavy stuff's
On top? Wouldn't the lightest things go highest?"

"Hold your horses," he said, *"I was coming to that.*
Seems like it depended on the amount of surface
An object would present. A rooftop long
And flat would rise and rise, and trees with trunks
And branches. But a bar of soap would tumble
At the bottom, like a pebble in a creek.
Anyhow . . . The Layer of Roofs was worst. Sharp edges
Everywhere, a hundred miles an hour.
Some folks claim to talk about close shaves.
Let them wait till they've been through a tempest
Of giant razor blades. *Soo-wish, sheee-oosh!*
I stretched out still on the floor of air, thinking
I'd stand a better chance. Blind luck is all
It was, though, pure blind luck. And when I rose
To the Fifth Layer—"

　　　　　　　"Wait," I said. "What Fifth?
At first you only mentioned four. What Fifth?"

"I was coming to that," he said. "The only man
Who ever knew about the Fifth was me.
I never told a soul till now. It seems
That when the hotel roofs blew off, Bad Egg
Sucked a slew of people out of bed.
The whole fifth layer of debris was lovebirds."

"Lovebirds?"

　　　　　　　"Lovebirds, honeypies, sweethearts—whatever
You want to call them."

                    "J.T., you watch yourself,"
My mother interjected.

                    "I'm just saying
What I saw," he said. "The boy will want
The truth, and that's the way it was. . . . Fifty
Or sixty couples, at least. Some of them
I recognized: Paolo and Francesca,
And Frankie and Johnny, Napoleon
And Josephine; but most I didn't know.
Rolling and sporting in the wind like face cards
From a stag poker deck—"

                    "J.T.!" she said.

"(All right.) But what an amazing sight it was!
I started to think all kinds of thoughts. . . ."

                          "Okay,"
I said. "But how did you get down without
Getting killed?"

                    "I was coming to that," he said.
"It was the queerest thing—"

Three Sheets in the Wind:
Virgil Campbell Confesses

Tell you, J.T., the way you see me now,
A solid by God citizen, ain't how
I've been always thought of. There was a time
I lived as raunchy as any wild boy come
Down off the mountaintop, guzzling jar
On jar of whiskey, and zooming a souped-up car,
And chasing after women dawn to dawn.
It never came to mind I might slow down,
Or might as well, since there's no way I'd ever
Have it all, that there's a drowning river
Of moon out there and a river of women too.
I wasn't taking good advice, you know—
Not that plenty didn't come my way.
My woman Elsie made sure to have her say
And she'd leagued up with a hardshell Baptist preacher.
Lordy, how I hated to hear that creature
Stand up and witness at my busting head.
Then Elsie'd say again just what he said
Just one more time. It was no sweet cure
For a thirsty flintrock flaming hangover.
I never paid them any serious mind;
You know how it is, there's a kind
Of crazy gets in the blood and nothing but
The worst that can happen will ever get it out.
The worst that can happen never happened to me,
But there was something that came mighty nigh.

This frolic girl that lived up Smathers Hill—
I won't say her name, because she still
Lives there—appeared to be the country sort

Of willing gal you always hear about
And generally never meet. But we'd fall in
Together now and then, and now and then
She'd take a snort if it was offered nice.
And so we horsed around, more or less
Like kids, had us a drink or two and a laugh.
I'd make a pass, and she was hanging tough.
But finally we found ourselves in bed
Together, and I don't think that that's so bad
And awful Jesus will lock the door on you.
Nothing but an itch for something new
And curious, nothing but a sport we giggled
Over when I laid hold of something that jiggled.
Where by God's the harm? You got a friend
Who right-now needs some help, you lend a hand,
Don't you? And never think about it after.
Well, if a woman's lost the man who loved her
And is feeling low, why not pitch in
And give? Every preacher's brimstone bitching
Won't turn my mind on that. —But looky-here,
I might be trying to make myself seem square
And open. To tell the truth, we sneaked around.
That's what was so unpeaceable in my mind.—
We sneaked and thought we were secret as mice;
But Pigeon Forks is a mighty little place,
And two Saturdays hadn't passed before
Elsie found out what we were doing, and more,
A whole lot more, besides. You'd think the tale
Would talk about our diddling, but that wasn't all
By any means. These snuffbrush gossips hear
A story, they fix it up till it's as queer
And messy as the wiring in radios
And sinful as Nevada. Say adios
To anything you know's the truth when those
Old ladies start to twist it by the nose.

But she got enough of the truth to smell
Us out. And planned with that durn preacher they'd tail
Us around until they saw the living sight
Of us having some fun while they were not.
I'll make it short. They caught us plain as day
Light in her bedroom. Before you could say
Jack Robinson they flung the door wide open
And there we were. Halfway between hoping,
Wishing, farting and fainting, I leapt out
The window and ran like a rabbit showing my scut,
Scared enough to run to Cherokee,
And praying that the shooting wouldn't hit me.
Feet don't fail me now. But it wasn't feet
That done me in. The wind lifted a sheet,
A great big white bedsheet, on the backyard
Clothesline into my eyes. I went down hard.
The clothesline caught me under the chin and down
I went, out cold and nekkid on the ground.

From here on in it's awful mortifying
To talk about. In fact, I'd still be lying
If Elsie was still alive to hear. . . . When I
Woke up all I could see was a kind of sky,
A wet-white sky that covered me from head
To toe. It came to me that I was dead—
She'd shot my vitals out—and here's the shroud
They buried me in like a cold and clammy cloud.
I fought against it like an animal,
Kicking and clawing, and got nowheres at all.
I hollered till I damn near deefed myself
And thought how I'd do it all different if
I could only live my earthly life again:
I'd be a sweet and silent religious man.

What had happened was, they'd sewed me in,
In one of those wet bedsheets off the line,

Elsie and the preacher. What they'd done
I didn't know then. But that was *their* good fun.

Then: *pow!* Pow pow pow. I took
Some knocks so hard my suffering eyeballs shook.
Pow pow pow. *So this is hell,*
I thought, *and I've deserved it about as well*
As *anybody ever.* But still it seemed
Unfair, and came on quicker than I'd dreamed.
You think a sinner would get some reprieve,
If only lying a half-hour in his grave.
But no. Immediately they'd hauled me down
And made a marching drum out of my skin.
I was squealing like a little piggy, not
So much from pain as out of fear of what
Was coming next. I dreaded the boiling oil
And the forty hotted pitchforks up my tail.
Go on and laugh, but I am here to tell
You that if there really is a Hell,
Elsie helped plan it. —Because it wasn't God,
But Elsie laying on with a curtain rod.

There's not much left to say. Finally
Her strength gave out, and there she let me lie,
And went off home. And after the awfullest struggle
I got myself unwrapped and crawled, like a bug will
Crawl, out of that wet sheet. There wasn't a scrap
To wear. I went home dressed like a drowned Arab.

I was a sobered feller. Every time
I'd think of another woman there'd come a flame
Rash all over my skin and I'd remember
Having my ass dressed out like sawmill timber.
And the sight of a hanging bedsheet has reminded
Me, and my dick shrunk up till a flea couldn't find it.

"Virgil, your Elsie did you a sight of good,

Made you respectable," my father said.
"Too bad I can't drink with a man on Reform."

"A drink, you say?" he said. "Well, where's the harm?"

Remembering Wind Mountain at Sunset

Off Hurricane Creek where
the heady rattlers even the loggers
abash, out of Sandy
Mush and Big Laurel and
Greasy Branch, off the hacksaw edge of Freeze Land,
those winds huddle in the notch
atop Wind Mountain, where counties Madison
and Buncombe meet but never join.
Hardscrabble Aeolus,
that stir of zephyrs is the sigh of poor
folk screwed in between the rocks up
Meadow Fork and Sugar Camp and Trust, Luck,
Sliding Knob, and Bluff.
A lean wind and a meat-snatcher. Wind
full of hopeless bones.

High on Wind Mountain I heard
from the valley below
the wearied-to-silence lamentation of busted hands,
busted spines, galled mules and horses, last breeze
rubbing the raw board-edge of the corncrib,
whimper of cold green beans in a cube of fat,
the breathing of clay-colored feet unhooked
from iron brogans.
A glinty small miasma
rises off the rocks in the cornfield.
The cowbell dwindles
toward dusk.

I went walking up Chunky Gal
To watch the blackbird whup the owl.

Friend, you who sit where some money is,
I tell you, Sometimes the poor are
poor in spirit, the wind is robbing
them of breath
of life, wind from always Somewhere Else,
directionless unfocused desire,
but driving the young ones like thistle seed
toward Pontiac, Detroit, Cincinnati,
Somewhere, wherever is money,
out of the hills.
Can't make a go
in bloody Madison, too much the rocks
and thickety briars suck the breath of the hand.
Suck the womenfolk to twig-and-twine
limberjacks, suck the puckered houses sad,
tumbly shack by blackberry wilderness
fills to the ridgepole with copperhead
and sawbriar. The abandoned smokehouse
droops, a springhouse hoards dead leaves.

I see blackbird fighting the crow
But I know something he don't know.

Over Hunger Cove
the rain-crow keeps conjuring rain
till Shitbritches Creek is flooded, tobacco
drowned this year one more year,
the township of Marshall bets half its poke
and the French Broad takes it
with a murmur of thunder.
Lord, let these sawtooth tops
let me breathe, give me one good stand
of anything but elderbush and milkweed,
I'll keep Mama's Bible dusted off,
I'll try not to murder
for spite nor even for money,

just let that wind hush
its bones a little and not fly so hard
at the barn roof and the
half-built haystack, I'll go to the Singing
on the Mountain with Luramae this
time I swear I will.

Fished up Bear Creek till I was half-dead.
Caught a pound of weeds and a hornyhead.

Where you're from's
Hanging Dog, ain't it, boy I knowed
your daddy years back, that was your Uncle
Lige wasn't it lost his arm at
the old Caldwell sawmill, they called him Sawmill
after, took to hunting sang
and medicine root, heard old Lige had died,
is that the truth, I disremember, he
was how old? Hundred and forty-nine
counting nights and hard knocks,
that's what he told me, I'll never forget.
Standing right there by that stove he said it.

If you could eat the wind,
if you could chew it and swallow
it for strength like a windmill.
If anything could be made of this wind in
winter with its scythes of ice when it comes dragging
blue snow over the ridgetops and down
the mountainside here to the house, finds any
little cranny, wind squirms through the holes
like an army of squirrels.
Go over and sit by the fire, won't
be long till your fingers turn blue again
anyhow. Somehow
I don't have my proper strength
a-winters, been to the doc how many times,

it's a poser to him says he, I told him
Doc I just get down weak as rag soup and
he says, Maybe you need a rest, By God
rest I says, reckon maybe I do,
why don't I lay up here for a while.

I saw blackbird fighting the hawk,
He whupped his hiney with a pokeweed stalk.

And then he says, Now how you
going to pay me? I says, Pay you Doc, you'll just
have to garnisheer them Rest Wages.

Two women fighting over a box of snuff,
Lost three tits before they had enough.

First snow like a sulphate powder, bluish,
and up-top the trees like frozen lace, crystal white
against the crystal blue of morning north,
look fragile as tinsel, no wind yet much,
only down the back of your neck now and again to
remind you how long about milking
time it'll come on.
It'll come, everything hurtful will come on.
Here is the place where pain is born.
No salve or balm.
Ever you notice how deep cold the rocks get?
No I mean it, you hoeing round in the field
summertime, hit rocks, sparks
jumping every whichway, come winter
you can beat all day on a rock with a crowbar,
never see spark one, rocks
get froze up deep in the heart is why, told
my oldest boy, No wonder our raggedy
ass is cold, even the goddam rocks
have done give up.

        And if you was to get

a little warm, go in by the cookstove there,
just makes it worse, wind when
you go out peels the feeling-warm right
off, you'll think you've fell
in Spring Creek River, way it goes over you
ice water, but the funny part is, come summer
same wind out of the same place,
feels like it's pouring out of a coalstove,
ain't a breath of soothe in it. Now that's funny.

Maybe the wind like that gets me so low.
Hateful to think of it stepping on my grave
when I'm took off, and then still clawing
you know the apple tree
and the hayfield and the roof of this house,
still clawing
at my young ones after I'm laid safe
out of it. What's the relief in that?
Under the sod you know here'll
come that Freeze Land wind crawling my joints.

Turkey buzzard took old blackbird flying
Like a piss-ant riding on a dandelion.

Youngish preacherman, heard him
say they ain't no bad without some good
in it somewhere, wanted
to ask him, What's the good in poison oak,
tell me because I can raise twenty solid acres
right in a jiffy, sawbriar too, didn't think
what was the good of this Freeze Land wind, you
know it gets so much inside you, never think
about it being anything, I mean
nothing, just there is all, not anything.
Something you can't see like that you never think.
Like that War in Europe, what'd I know
back here in the stump roots, but they stuck

me over there in the mud
till wild rose and ragweed took my bottom land.

For fighting niggers and hauling loads,
Pulled fifteen months on the county roads.

Friend, you who sit
in the vale of comfort,
consider if you will that there are corners
in this flab land where shale edge
of hunger is chipping out
hearts for weapons, man don't
look from year to year but day by day
alone, suffering of flesh
is whetting the knife edge of spirit in
lower Appalachia, margins
where no one thinks you're his buddy,
don't come driving that big-ass Lincoln
up Hogback Ridge if you like your paint job,
they's some old
bushy boys in here kill a man for
a quarter, eyegod, you seen about that feller
in the papers? I'm not saying
what I've heard about them Henson brothers,
you knowed old man Henson or your daddy did,
him that burned the sheriff
out, had two boys nigh
as lowdown as ever he was, I
don't know what-all I've heard tell.

Up on Wind Mountain there ain't no help.
Blackbird went and killed hisself.

Friend, sit tight on your money,
what you've got, there's a man
on a mountain thinks he needs it worse.

All this I heard in the stir
of wind-quarrel in Wind Mountain notch,

rich tatters of speech
of poor folk drifting like bright Monarchs.
And then on the breeze a cowbell,
and the kitchen lights went on in the valley below,
and a lonesome churchbell
calling
home, home, home, home
till I could bear it no more.
Turned my back.
Walked down the mountain's other side.

They hauled old blackbird's carcass away,
Buried him head-down-deep in red clay.

Here comes the preacher to say the last word:
"It's a fitten end for old blackbird."

My Mother's Hard Row to Hoe

Hard, I say. Mostly I can't think how
To make it clear, the times have changed so much.
Maybe it's not possible to know
Now how we lived back then, it was such
A different life.
                    "Did you like it?"
                                         I
Felt that I had to get away or die
Trying. I felt it wasn't *me* from dawn
To dawn, "slaving my fingers to the bone,"
As Mother used to say; and yet so bored
It was a numbing torture to carry on
Because that world was just plain hard.

Mother was always up a five o'clock,
Winter and summer, and jarred us out of bed
With her clanging milkcans and the knock
Of water in the pipes. Out to the shed
I went, and milked five cows and poured the milk
Into the cans—so rich it looked like silk
And smelled like fresh-cut grass. Then after that
The proper workday started. I did what
She told me to, no never-mind how tired
I was, and never once did she run out,
Because that world was just plain hard.

Because from May through August we put up hay
And worked tobacco and, sure as you were born,
We'd find the hottest stillest July day
To start off in the bottom hoeing corn.
From the pear orchard to the creek's big bend,
Corn rows so long you couldn't see the end;

443

And never a breeze sprang up, never a breath
Of fresh, but all as still and close as death.
We hoed till dark. I was hoeing toward
A plan that would preserve my mental health,
Because that world was so almighty hard.

I'd get myself more schooling, and I'd quit
These fields forever where the hoe clanged stone
Wherever you struck, and the smell of chickenshit
Stayed always with you just like it was your own.
I felt I wasn't *me*, but some hired hand
Who was being underpaid to work the land,
Or maybe just a fancy farm machine
That had no soul and barely a jot of brain
And no more feelings than any cat in the yard
And not good sense to come out of the rain.
That world, I say, was just too grinding hard.

But I'd learn Latin and Spanish and French and math
And English literature. Geography.
I wouldn't care if I learned myself to death
At the University in Tennessee
So long as I could tell those fields good-bye
Forever, for good and all and finally.
—"You really hated it then?"
                              No, that's not true.
 . . . Well, maybe I did. It's hard to know
Just how you feel about a place; a blurred
Mist-memory comes over it all blue,
No matter if that place was flintrock hard.

There were some things I liked, of course there were:
I walked out in the morning with the air
All sweet and clean and promiseful and heard
A mourning dove— . . . *No! I couldn't care.*
You've got to understand how it was *hard*.

My Father Washes His Hands

I pumped the iron handle and watched the water
Cough his knuckles clean. Still he kept rubbing,
Left hand in his right like hefting a baseball;
The freckles might have scaled off with the clay.
But didn't. They too were clay, he said, that mud
The best part maybe of apparent spirit.

"What spirit?" I asked.
                              He grinned and got the soap
Again and sloshed. A bubble moment I saw
Our two faces little in his palm.
"The Spirit of Farming," he said, "or the Soul of Damnfool."
Our faces went away and showed his lifeline.
"Damnfool why?"
                              "A man's a fool in this age
Of money to turn the soil. Never a dime
To call his own, and wearing himself away
Like a kid's pencil eraser on a math lesson.
I've got a mind to quit these fields and sell
Cheap furniture to poor folks. I've got a mind
Not to die in the traces like poor Honey."
(Our jenny mule had died two weeks before.)
"A man's not the same as a mule," I said.

He said, "You're right. A man doesn't have the heart. . . .
We buried Honey, me and Uncle Joe,
While you were away at school. I didn't tell you.
Two feet down we hit pipe clay as blue
And sticky as Buick paint. Octopus-rassling,
Uncle Joe called it. Spade would go down
Maybe two inches with my whole weight behind
And come up empty. Blue glue with a spoon.

445

I soon decided to scale down the grave.
I told him straight. *I'm going to bust her legs*
And fold them under. His face flashed red at once.
My God, J.T., poor Honey that's worked these fields
For thirteen years, you'd bust her legs? I nodded.
She can't feel a thing, I said. He says,
By God I do. I told him to stand behind
The truck and stop his ears. I busted her legs.
I busted her legs with the mattock, her eyes all open
And watching me crack her bones and bulging out
Farther slightly with every blow. These fields
Were in her eyes, and a picture of me against
The sky blood-raw savage with my mattock.
I leaned and thumbed her eye shut and it was like
Closing a book on an unsatisfactory
Last chapter not pathetic and not tragic,
But angrifying mortifying sad.
The harder down I dug the bluer I got,
And empty as my shovel. It's not in me
To blubber, don't have Uncle Joe's boatload
Of whiskey in my blood yet. Heavy is how
I felt, empty-heavy and blue as poison.
So maybe it's time to quit. The green poison
Of money has leached into the ground
And turned it blue. . . . That grave is mighty shallow
That I dug, but I felt so out of heart I couldn't
Make myself go farther and farther down.
I stopped waist-high and we built up a mound
That will soak away by springtime and be level."

"Are you really going to quit the farm?" I asked.
"I wouldn't quit if I could get ahead,
But busting my behind to stay behind
Has got to be the foolishest treadmill a man
Could worsen on. The farm can wait; there's money
To be made these days, and why not me?

Better me than some cheap crooks I know of,
And that's a fact."

        "Whatever you say," I said,
"It's kind of sad, though. . . . And now old Honey's gone."
"*Gone?* Six nights in a row I'd close my eyes
And see her pawing up on her broken legs
Out of that blue mud, her suffering hindquarters
Still swallowed in, and in her eyes the picture
Of me coming toward her with my mattock;
And talking in a woman's pitiful voice:
Don't do it, J.T., you're breaking promises. . . .
And wake up in a sweat. Honey's not gone,
She's in my head for good and all and ever."
"Even if you quit the farm?"
                    "Even if."

I handed him the towel. He'd washed his hands
For maybe seven minutes by the clock,
But when he gave it back there was his handprint,
Earth-colored, indelible, on the linen.

Susan's Morning Dream of Her Garden

The way a tree climbs down into the earth,
and earth to keep it from drifting like a bed
seizes the cloudmass roots;

and into ground lean the lonely
and elaborate dead as soft as sleet,
burbling one to another always,

a full Four Hundred of juicy talkers; the way
the headstrong sunflower, and boxwood, Harpwoof
Spragglewort, moondime and Dusty Miller, the pansies

with their Pekinese faces, and grimbleweed lift
out and up in light their informal forms,
pistil and petal half-shadow;

is the way my hand goes into the dirt.
Or is it flesh I enter?
My own, or lubberhubby's lying this plot with me?

Haho. He. He is loose in sleep
and musical as a horse, goeth as a zinnia
brave to daybreak and casts a watershaped snore.

Why are men so toady, tell me, touching
the moss and root? I'll tend me well my contrary garden.
Now my rows of queenly corn erupt to cadenza;

and the cabbages unfurl
outward and inward like sentences of Proust,
the sweet rose invites her oriental suitors all

iridescent in green and oil, and yonder my neat row
of bones blooms out mouths of marrow,
yet I am not replete or reconciled.

448

Garden, garden, will you not grow for me
a salon full of billets-doux and turtledoves?
Garden, garden, green tureen,

will you not put me forth the olden ladies upside-down
in their hooped skirts like the bells of lilies,
their clapper legs chiming sentimental songs?

I long to belong to
the chipper elegance, those centuries where
the hand of man has never said an ugly word.

I own an antique plate in which I see
a little garden with a swing, a young girl in
the swing, tra-la, and flush with birds of every hue,

troo-loo.
The swing-girl's face is a mint of pale pink roses.
In the garden I grow I'm the girl in the swing, ting-a-ling.

And I rise and rise in my swing through the globe
of green leaves giddy till I become
a rose-pink butterfly with arms of eyes.

We whirl, my garden and I, until
the minuet boils, the sun
and moon and ground and tree become a waltzing sea,

a jiggy river of green green
green. Hurl-whorl green in which we roll
as down a well of hay.

I sing as high and clear-O as a finch
in a yellow-green willow tree,
transparent and vivid as dragonflies.

I'd be a fool, a woman's a fool, to be drawn back
into the waking world,
all dinky clutter and dirty bathtub.

You don't catch me yet, New Day, I'm snugging

deeper in the larder of dream,
I'm burrowing like a lovely whistlepig

into the green earthflesh of sleep, keep
your tarnished-silver fingers, Sun, off my bright hair,
off my pillow, my mellow wallow.

I'm diving to a door I sense below,
a door as yellow with catlight as an owl's eye,
that opens truly into the garden

on my antique plate and can draw
my waking body in and there no one
can draw me out again. No use, you-all,

I'm gone beyond your smirch, you can't
get in, I'm the slattern in the pattern,
admire, admire!

   . . . But sunlight now comes licking at my dream-door,
boohoo. *Day day go away*,
come again some other sleep.

Yet there's no help for it, and up I go
to breast the unendearing morning,
eject, usurpt, and half-awake.

I lie like cool meat on the bed like a
dimestore plate which has no picture on it,
no pattern at all.

My Grandmother's Dream of Plowing

I never saw him plowing, but Frank was well
And whole and plowing in the field behind
Jackson and Maude whose heads went up and down
Like they agreed on what they were talking over.
There was a light around him, light he was blind
To, light tolling steady like a bell.
The dirt peeled back from the share like meal, brown
Loam all water-smelling. What he'd uncover
With his plowing I felt I already knew:
He'd turn up that bell from the church the Klan
Burned down because of the Negro organist.
That bell they couldn't find had washed in the tide
Of earth and finally had come to rest
In our own bottom land that used to grow
Tobacco. . . .
          I was wrong; for when the sun
Gleamed on something in the furrow-side
I went to look, and it wasn't a bell at all.
It was a big and shining lump of gold.
It was a Mystery gold, and just the tip
Of it stuck out. With my bare hands I brushed
Away the crumbs and dug it out of the soil.
I got up on my knees and tried to wrestle it up,
And after a while I did, aching, and rolled
It out and stood looking at it all hushed.
About as big as a twenty-five-pound sack
Of flour. And burning burning like the flame
Of Moses' bush. It lay there in the furrow
Like, like . . . Oh, I can't say what like.
I picked it up and cradled it to my breast,
Thinking how it was a Gold made out of dream

And now we'd never fear about tomorrow
And give our frets and cares a well-earned rest.

"Is that your baby that was never mine?"
Behind me Frank had stopped the plow. His voice
Came up against me like another person,
Like a stranger maybe intending harm.
His voice was dressed in black and laid a curse on
All the fancies I'd thought up for us.
I turned around to tell him Hush, but then
I knew it *was* a baby in my arm,
The strangest baby. As fat and dimpled as
The Baby Jesus in the pictures on
The Upper Room. And this golden child was
Speaking to me, not just baby-talk,
But real words that I ought to understand.
Except I couldn't hear. Bent my head down
But couldn't hear, no more than you hear the dark.
"It's not my baby, and just never you mind,"
I said to Frank. "This baby I've found will bring
Us luck," I said, "because it turned from gold
To flesh. That means—it has to mean—something
To us, something to help us when we're old."
"We're old," Frank said, "we're old already, Anne.
And, see, the baby's changed to something else.
It's turned into an ugly little man."
I looked, and felt the beating of my pulse
Grow harder in my throat, knowing it was true.

I held to me an evil little goblin
With an evil smile. And, must-be, astray in its mind,
The way its eyes were loose, and its head bobbling
Up and down like corn tassel in the wind.
All over I went water then and trembled
Like a flame of fire. I turned my face away
From Frank. I'd never felt so ashen-humbled.

What had I brought upon us? *Oh what, what?*
Something terrible the field had birthed,
And now I'd gathered it up, and who could say
It wouldn't haunt us forever from this day
Onward? I'd never thought such ugly thought
As standing there with what the plow unearthed
And wishing it would go away. Or die.
That's what I wished: *Please die, and let us be.*

Now here's the awfullest part. What I said
To do, it did. It rolled its eyes glass-white
Back in its head, and kicked and shivered like
A newborn calf, and murmured in white froth
A tiny whimper, and opened on its mouth
A glassy bubble and sucked it gagging back
Into its throat, and opened and closed its throat,
And sighed a sigh, and lay in my arms stone dead.

It was my fault. It turned into a stone,
And it was all my fault, wishing that way.
Whatever harm had the little goblin done?
And now I'd killed it. I began to cry,
And cried so hard I felt my eyes dissolve
To dust, to water, fire, and then to smoke.

"And then you woke," I said, "to the world you love."

"And now I know," she said, "I never woke."

Earthsleep

It is the bottomless swoon of never forgetting.

It is the foul well of salvation.

It is the skin of eternity like a coverlet.

It is a tree of fire with tongues of wind.

It is the grandfather lying in earth and the father digging,
The mother aloft in the air, the grandmother sighing.

It is the fire that eats the tree of fire.

It is Susan in the hand of sleep a new creature.

I am a new creature born thirty-five years to this earth
Of jarring elements, its fractuous hold
On the man and woman brings
Earth to bloodmouth.
                    Here where I find

I am I founder.
                    Lord Lord
Let this lost dark not.

Who's used?
Who's not scrawled upon
By the wilderness hand of
Earth and fire and water and air?

How simple simple blessèd simple.

It is the fathomless noon that blossoms after midnight,
And daybreak at the margin of the oaks
Begins to sculpt our sleeping bodies
In the wimpled bed.

What shapes may we take now
Where destiny uncurls its roots of fire?

Let it then be flesh that we take on
That I may see you
Cool in time and blonde as this fresh daybreak.

No one no one sleeps apart
Or rises separate
In the burning river of this morning
That earth and wind overtake.

The way the light rubs upon this planet
So do I press to you,

Susan   Susan

The love that moves the sun and other stars
The love that moves itself in light to loving
Flames up like dew

Here in the earliest morning of the world.

Castle Tzingal

The book-length sequence of poems, Castle Tzingal, offers a story of tragic horror set in a mythical middle European castle in the fifteenth century. To this castle a spy, Petrus, has been sent to discover what may have happened to the musician-poet, Marco, nephew of neighboring King Reynal. The castle is a dark and suspicious place, rotten with intrigue and painfully under the cruelty of its mad ruler, King Tzingal. The principal speakers include a tiny artificial man, the Homunculus, the long-suffering Queen Frynna, the aged and ineffectual Admiral, the coldly evil Astrologer and his catamite Page, and the mad king himself. The spy finds out that the object of his quest, Marco, has been murdered and beheaded, that his head has been kept alive by alchemical means, and that it still retains the power of song and poetry. In fact, it is the dead poet's song which brings about, after a number of sad events, the downfall of King Tzingal and the destruction of his castle.

456

The Homunculus

I'm hardly the first man to live in a bottle
And see the world through a different size.
I'm the King's most privy counselor,
And know the secrets lisped at midnight
By love-performing ministers
And cunning courtesans. I spy the spies
Who never seek beneath their beds
Or in the arras-folds hard by the banisters
Of the shadowed gallery. Wiser heads
Than yours are indiscreet when all intent
On easing the vexed blood-itch. I tell
No one but the King the things I hear,
Who poisoned whom, and where the florins went.

A dirty trade, you say. Well,
What's a bit of a fellow to do?
In high-heeled boots I'm eighteen inches tall,
A whole intelligence force in minuscule.

My father was a mage, my mother a pour
Of mystery chemicals. I was born
On a table bright with flame and glassware,
And had no childhood except an ignorance
Of politics and gossip. And what a boring year
My childhood was. No company
But the pottering alchemist, his cat
Who wanted to gobble me up, and three
Disgusting nodules of melting flesh
That were earlier attempts at being me.
I was happy to be set to work,
To know who knows, and how he knows, and why.
I'm useful to the State, usefuller

Maybe than a general or diplomat.
I may find out a secret to forestall a war
Or hear a plan that threatens our defeat.
Oh, I could tell you stories—but I won't—
That would blanch your face salt-white.

My name is Flyting, but they call me Tweak.
I'm cousin-german to the mouse and hare
By means of my father Astrologer
Who draws our futures, and some kin to the Admiral.
Because I am, you see, half-man half-mineral.
I'm silent in a dusty nook,
But in the Council Chamber I speak
My mind straight out and am respected.
No one can trust me but the King
Who caused me to be made.
That's my safety from the murderous boot
And poison marmalade.
I have no love of being loved; a minim man
Prefers to flourish by means of fear,
To cast beyond his stature giant shade.

What things might I say if I so inclined!
The Astrologer's passion for a comely page
Is news; Queen Frynna has no peace of mind
Since a nimble harpist sojourned here
Last twelvemonth; there's a wealthy vein of silver
Runs beneath our Castle Tzingal; the magpie
Singing in the courtyard wicker cage
Is a transformed enemy sorcerer.
This sort of information finds its flowering
In time; all knowledge becomes of use,
And when it does I bear it to the King.

—Ah no, I can't be bribed to speak. Whatever
Could you bribe me with?
The things I dream of are forever

Beyond my reach, sunk deep in earth
Or at a human height. Unlike all others born,
I was conceived with purpose, drawn up to plan,
And have a surer measure than a man.
It's a rarefied temptation
Could smudge my honesty,
And as for what *you* offer . . .
                Well, we'll see.

The Admiral

Here the soughing along the black wall
And turret of Castle Tzingal!
I foresee an icy winter this time out,
Deep snow and tempest and heavy seas.
God's mercy on all poor sailors who
Climb aloft in the bitter squall.
I remember how in the rigging we'd freeze
To stone amid the biting snow
Until the bosun warmed us with the cat.

None of that now for me.
All seasons now I lie in drydock
And count my medals and clean my braid,
Come down to luncheon mark
At eight bells, set my boots out for the maid.
I pull my final duty: to bore
The queen and court and visiting ambassador
With tales of seafights long forgotten.
I distract at table while the King
Observes, and deliberates on war.
An old man whom the smell of sea
Nevermore reaches, for whom the sting
Of saltspray is a darkening memory.

Young sailors, take warning.
The certainty of your hand deserts,
Your fresh blue eye grows blear,
And the snows of heavy winter
Lie less lightly every year.

Sleepless midnight, and the knobble bones
Keep revel down with ray and shark.

This North-whelped wind is a chorus
Of far-drowned sailors; groans,
Tears, and prayers flying in the dark.

I cannot sleep for all the tears,
For all the cries, of my drowned men.
I picture the foamsprent wave, how it receives
The tumbling snow and drives,
Drives against a lonesome reef
Its full freight of grief.
And I cannot sleep.
And the wind cannot stop.

I pull the foamy counterpane
Tight beneath my chin
And stare at the coffered ceiling
Until the dawn leaks in.

I would now put to sea once more,
Up anchor and away to the world's swift edge;
And over, sailing to the farthest star
That shines on the western verge.

But cannot.
Cannot even sleep, except to dream
Or half-dream the whirling eye of maelstrom
That sucks the ship, even the stars,
Into its sudden gullet.
And down I go, pulled splay against
The force invisible and unvanquished
That wrinkles the fabric of the world
And takes me steady as a bullet.

Heave, heave away, my lads.
We tack and turn into the wind,
And we sail blind
Without commission, chart, or polestar,
Into the world we leave behind.

Song for Disembodied Voice

There is a music sings without a voice.
There is a beauty has no body.
There is a light informs the sunlight.
There is a cold and secret place.

Not even the frore and darkened walls of Tzingal can keep in
Music that silvers the wind with shadow.
I am a hidden singer without a throat;
The songs I sing may cause the chambermaids to weep in
Their sleep in the restless fulgurant night.
I have a song that sings of death as a meadow
Of polished daisies; another song
Of a waterfall the tears of youthful lovers;
A song to be plucked on the spider's lambent string;
A song that says the destinies of rivers.
I have five songs of penitent devotion,
I have a song as salt and lacy as the ocean.

But I have no blood or flesh or bone;
Am become the purity
Of breeze-tressed long-lined melody
As silken-whispery as a lady's veil
And as transparent to the sun and moon.

A melody as changing as cloud-seam.
A story as dark and tangled
As the shoal of storm-cloud the north wind mangled.
A music that ends in leaping flame.

Who could have thought that it would end or begin
This way, the singer dissolved in song?
That a murdering hand could lengthen the line
Of the lay, a sorcery hand make strong

Even past my death
The story I am compelled
To tell, and must sing on till it is told
In one unstopping suprahuman breath?

If there's a mercy in either of our lives,
In the one we count or that arrives
When our accounted days shut down,
It is that memory
Can broider the ode and elegy
With freshest pictures of the dawn;
Or turning sidewise upon itself indite
A wistful intimation of approaching night.

I have a sorrow that no tear can cool.
I know the ghostly bird sings out of tune.
I find the parts that never make a whole,
The broken halves that never join as one.

I'd make my song like the wind-tossed willow tree,
Promiseful-green and all a-lilt,
Its lissome strands interweaving light
As when the silver withes entwine as if spilt
From the corona of a fountain bright
With sun-spangle from a pleachy sky.

I'd make a song of maidens bathing in a stream,
Their flanks and shoulders white
And gleaming as new-starched lace,
A song of a garland of children fat
And dimpled spiraling toward heaven's dome,
A song about a lovesick shepherdess,
If I were free to choose my theme.

But Arcady is fled and gone
Until I rend the guilty sleep
Of Castle Tzingal and, like the sun,
Wither this black scheming up.

I am no more alive,
And all my murderers thrive.

I have a truth to say, no tongue to tell.
I know a heartsick prison without a wall.
A star lies silent in a silent well.
Not feeling cold, I live in coldest hell.

The Queen

The poppy's silver dust spills in the claret
Like snow in a moonlight sea;
This is the dust of endless bitter hours,
This the draught of a prayerful timely
Death mossy silence underscores.
Voile cloud dims the opium moon. Near it,
A lonely star
Glows cool and fitfully
Declines, seeming to rise then droop again,
Toward the unabidable dawn.

Hereafter's unyielding doors fly open with this cup.
If I but take a sip
I shall have taken a queenly step
Within the burning threshold. There I halt and wait
Until my eyes accustom the huge light.

. . . It's none so bitter as I imagined.
A dainty taste of it suffuses my blood
Momently and makes my mind a drowsy flower.
If now my courage thinned
And I could bring myself to drink no more,
Might I not live wise, age-lined,
And content? . . . No.
I should become stark mad.

Better to drink the sleep I have prepared
And lay my wasting body down,
My ravaged soul,
And close my eyes to see my gentle mother again
And faithfully become Eternity's ward.

Shall I find Marco? I desire
To hear a last sweet ballad.

Sing to the blue mountain, my dear one,
*   Where do you wander?*
The skies muffle over with cloud
*   And the seas founder.*

The lone long wind embroiders
*   Her delicate empearlèd shroud,*
The azure butterfly shall kiss my mouth
*   Now I am dead.*

Now I am dead
Shall I find Marco singing in the vast cool fire?

No drop remains within
The cup. I have taken
My death solitary and polite
A little at a time.
And I embrace the night
I have longed to become.
And I am not the same
Though still I clasp my dream.

*   Sing sing the flowing willow*
*   That shadows the flecked stream*
*   Sing sing the pink mallow*
*   Like a vanishing flame*

Epilogue: Song for Disembodied Voice

The starry frost returns, the hapless flower
Withdraws like a frightened deer
Into its woodland deep and dark.
The happy season of the world has left no mark.

The tapestry itself unweaves and weaves.
The swallows cross against the sun,
Light and wind take force as one.
The snow dances the spiraling-down of lives.

The stars hang over the plot of death
Like souls that burn and quaveringly wing
Toward a sphere of utter darkness swirling
Slow and silent above a withered heath.

A history as changing as cloud-seam,
A story as dark and tangled
As the shoal of stormcloud the north wind mangled.
A music that ends in leaping flame.

Source

Child in the Fog

Did the ghosts watch my prayers when the strange
Fat hats of everything attacked?
Or was it the fearful Nobody?
From the silent creek, glories of wet gauze.
The pigeons curled up in fists and mourned to me.

I began to know how
The Hour Without Eyes is gathering in the world.

The barn's hard lines went soft; rafters
Dissolved to spirit; the mice in the loft
Mumbled warm dreams.
The gray tin roof wept an old woman's tears.

This was the rapture of humility which kept saying,
You are a child, you are suitable to be awed.
I heard the whole silence.
My heart went white.

It was the first day of school and Mama
Had betrayed me to the white fog leopard,
Tree-croucher to eat my bones.
I crept to first grade like an opossum.
Afterward, the fog was my comforting cool sleep;
I could walk unseeable.
Not even the ghosts could be sure where I'd been.

Today I will build a fire the fog will clasp.
Childhood will burn in the grate and the white smoke
Will go out friendly to the white world.
All that I feared will attenuate in air,
Muffling in hush the dripping hills,
And the other lost children, and the one lost child.

Humility

In the necessary field among the round
Warm stones we bend to our gleaning.
The brown earth gives in to our hands, and straw
By straw burns red aslant the vesper light.

The village behind the graveyard tolls softly, begins
To glow with new-laid fires. The children
Quiet their shouting, and the martins slide
Above the cows at the warped pasture gate.

They set the tinware out on checkered oilcloth
And the thick-mouthed tumblers on the right-hand side.
The youngest boy whistles the collie to his dish
And lifts down the dented milk pail:

This is the country we return to when
For a moment we forget ourselves,
When we watch the sleeping kitten quiver
After long play, or rain comes down warm.

Here we might choose to live always, here where
Ugly rumors of ourselves do not reach,
Where in the whisper-light of the kerosene lamp
The deep Bible lies open like a turned-down bed.

Awakening to Music

I don't forget head down
striding the raw ridges, snow-bit,
knuckles red burning knots of ice
in my pockets, wind turning funnels of snow-snuff,
and cursing as I bulled along
a whiteface heifer who must have daintily
tiptoed through
the curlicues of busted barbwire
and loped excited away in sparkling cold
to skirmish my father's neighbors' fields
or maybe the whole wide silly world
in a sharp wind getting sharper always
at the awkward hour, dawn
bleaching to ash or dark coming on with
no one abroad to ask of
about stray cows.

    Till finally we met.
This coquette, tossing her rag-curled
forehead, tossing the silky string
of lucid snot pearly from chin to knees
like a Charleston necklace.
           "Come home now,
Daisy"; and she'd ballhoot
the rocky road with a racket like a marble
rolling down a washboard, leaving
a breath-white ghost I blinked at.

I'd curse to melt the snow in air.

Sometimes:
        with hands frost-grained

from the bucket bail I'd clutch the brood-warm
teats and God help us how she'd kick a shapely
leg as sudden as a door blown shut.
Or just as quick in August when
thistle-thorns embedded in the udders.
                    Sickness worst of all.
The little Jersey down in the smelly straw,
eyes back, brown eyes enfolding flame-blue
eggs in the light of a Coleman fizzing
like seltzer, and Doc McGreavy lying down
in warm embrace, ear
to guttering lungs, choosing without having to look
the iron and glass in the lumpy black bag.
The terrible births: my throat wire-taut,
hands stiff, while Doc plunged shoulder-deep
in flesh-muck, a one-armed swimmer.

                    Yet even so the main thing:
was every morning the cuddling when my head
went into her toasty flank, the grandest magic helmet
breathing and her red belly
rubbing my intimate right shoulder,
and milk-squirt slicing through the foam
like yard on yard of brocade piling up.

That was how I came from sleep to another sleep,
came into a warm swamp-broad sleep,
warm rain on heart-shaped leaves and dozing orchids,
came to the pulsing green fountain where music is born.

And all those years I went clothed in this sleep,
odor and warmth
of cows blanketed about my head.

How would I get it back? Go to blood
again, sleep the light green sleep?
How can I wake, not waking to music?

Narcissus and Echo

Shall the water not remember   *Ember*
my hand's slow gesture, tracing above   *of*
its mirror my half-imaginary   *airy*
portrait? My only belonging   *longing;*
is my beauty, which I take   *ache*
away and then return, as love   *of*
teasing playfully the one being   *unbeing.*
whose gratitude I treasure   *Is your*
moves me. I live apart   *heart*
from myself, yet cannot   *not*
live apart. In the water's tone,   *stone?*
that brilliant silence, a flower   *Hour,*
whispers my name with such slight   *light:*
moment, it seems filament of air,   *fare*
the world become cloudswell.   *well.*

Recovery of Sexual Desire
After a Bad Cold

Toward morning I dreamed of the Ace of Spades reversed
And woke up giggling.
New presence in the bedroom, as if it had snowed;
And an obdurate stranger come to visit my body.

This is how it all renews itself, floating down
Mothy on the shallow end of sleep;
How Easter gets here, and the hard-bitten dogwood
Flowers, and waters run clean again.

I am a new old man.
As morning sweetens the forsythia and the cats
Bristle with impudent hungers, I learn to smile.
I am a new baby.

What woman could turn from me now?
Shining like a butter knife, and the fever burned off,
My whole skin alert as radar, I can think
Of nothing at all but love and fresh coffee.

Rib

I have taken the rib of a woman
and fashioned a hazelnut.
Inside it lives an elfin
cobbler whose delight
is carving tiny women from bone.

In April the shell breaks open
and the women all fly out
in a swarm of breathless shine
to infest the sleepy roses
of the temperate zone.

The Virtues

The vices are always hungry for my hands,
But the virtues stay inside their houses like shy brown thrushes.

I feel their presences
Behind the white clapboard walls with all the ugly gingerbread.

They are walking about the dim cool rooms
In hand-sewn linen dresses.

Is it empty to wish they will come out
To sweep the walks when I stand under the oak across the street?

The virtues are widowed sisters.
No man has been with them for many years.

I believe they are waiting for cataclysm.
They will open their doors.

When perfect ruin has taken down this city,
Will wander forth and sift thoughtfully in the hot rubble.

Message

For David Slavitt

True.
     The first messenger angel may arrive
purely clothed in terror, the form he takes
a swordblade of unbearable energies, making
the air he entered a spice of ozone.

And then, the mad inventories. Each force
of nature, each animal and pretty bird,
is guilty with persistence. The tear of sorrow,
huge as an alien star, invades
our sun's little system.
               Irrelevant,
such enormity: because the man is alone
and naked. Even the tenuous radiations
of the marauding star crush him like falling timbers.
The worst is, he must choose among sorrows
the one that destroys him most.
               But see how all
changes in that hour. He ascends
a finer dimension of event, he feels with senses
newly evolved the wide horizons unknown till now.
He is transformed head to foot, taproot to polestar.
He breathes a new universe, the blinding whirlpool
galaxies drift round him and begin to converse.

Forever Mountain

J. T. Chappell, 1912–1978

Now a lofty smoke has cleansed my vision.

I see my father has gone to climb
Easily the Pisgah slope, taking the time
He's got a world of, making spry headway
In the fresh green mornings, stretching out
Noontimes in the groves of beech and oak.
He has cut a walking stick of second-growth hickory
And through the amber afternoon he measures
Its shadow and his own shadow on a sunny rock.
        Not marking the hour, but observing
The quality of light come over him.
He is alone, except what voices out of time
Come to his head like bees to the bee-tree crown,
The voices of former life as indistinct as heat.

By the clear trout pool he builds his fire at twilight,
And in the night a granary of stars
Rises in the water and spreads from edge to edge.
He sleeps, to dream the tossing dream
Of the horses of pine trees, their shoulders
Twisting like silk ribbon in the breeze.

He rises glad and early and goes his way,
Taking by plateaus the mountain that possesses him.

My vision blurs blue with distance,
I see no more.
Forever Mountain has become a cloud
That light turns gold, that wind dislimns.

        This is a prayer.

AFTERWORD
A Pact with Faustus

Now I read through the dense pages of Thomas Mann's *Doctor Faustus* with a practiced and fairly sophisticated eye. Much escapes me still, no doubt of that; and I confess that I find occasional boring stretches where I used to find continual excitement. But the novel holds its power; I am mostly fascinated, entranced.

Yet it is a strange, crabbed, difficult, and often obscure book in purpose and in manner, and how it could ever come to be the favorite novel of an adolescent boy in a little Appalachian mill town is hard to figure. *Doctor Faustus* still may be my favorite twentieth-century fiction; I have read only *Don Quixote* and *Huckleberry Finn* as many times, *The Sound and the Fury* and *The Sun Also Rises* maybe not half as often.

For one thing, Mann's novel is the story of a modern artist, the tragic composer Adrian Leverkühn, and already at the age of fifteen I had long determined to pursue a career as a writer. Leverkühn's story —for all its pathos and its heartbreaking conclusion—had to serve as the only description I found of what such an unimaginable life might be like.

I was not alone in my outlandish ambition. In the grimy little town of Canton, North Carolina (pop. eternally 5,000; tucked away in the folds of the far western mountains of the state), it happened that one of my two best friends, Harry Fincher, had decided to become a composer. It must have been Fuzz—that was his nickname—who suggested the book to me. My resolve to read every word of it was strengthened when the gray gentle lady who was our librarian told me I might draw the book out, but that I would never finish it.

479

I read it avidly, then turned back immediately to read over certain favorite passages again and again. Fuzz and I discussed it at length on the two-mile walk home from high school. That is, it was two miles for him; I would walk an extra mile out of my way in order to talk. We walked from the school grounds north to the elderly iron bridge that crossed the slow Pigeon, down the main street of the town with its three blocks of shops and farm supply stores, up the steep hill to cross another bridge over the railroad tracks, then around the road that curved by Champion Paper and Fiber Company—loud, smoky, noisome—until we parted company at a third bridge. This one crossed the river below the paper mill, and the water had been turned inky and was flecked with ugly patches of chemical foam. Fuzz turned left and climbed to his house perched halfway up the ridge, overlooking the dingy mill settlement called Fiberville; I turned right and pursued Beaverdam Street to its end, to where our farm edged into the hills and piny woods.

We talked about the novel endlessly and absorbed its language and some of its thought so thoroughly that it served as a kind of code between us, a shorthand by which we communicated whole areas of attitude and judgment merely by dropping a phrase or even a word from its close pages. "Schildknapp," we would say of someone; or of certain kinds of music, "cow warmth." We knew what we meant, and of course we were delighted that the others in our company did not. We made up a Secret Society of two, just as boys are always doing, but I think that ours really must have been different from most. It was a cabal of the intellect, however callow and confused our intellectual tendencies were.

Two young men of ordinary mountain background, with distinctly limited opportunities at High Culture, who have decided to pursue artistic careers—it is inevitable that they would become close, given the time and place. Fuzz and I were close friends, but we were not dear friends, and our relationship was so mutually protective that it was not entirely healthy. We felt that we were in a conspiracy against the placid town and against our perfectly nice parents. We felt—God forgive us!—superior in some way that we could not articulate, and much put-upon, despised for our interests and aspirations.

These can be dangerous feelings for adolescents to entertain, and in our case they were released in one painful episode in which we went through Canton one night, breaking random store windows and wreaking other damage. There is no reasonable explanation for these crimes except our general consciousness of being trapped, held back. The incident made the two wonderful geniuses indistinguishable from garden-variety delinquents. I think it was the later realization of that fact which caused us such thorough shame, though the punishments we received from our parents were severe and, in my case, unforgettable. There were the physical ordeals, and then for an interminable period of time I was forbidden to read.

I would not ascribe this silly rebelliousness to the influence of Mann's novel, but there were qualities in the book that aggravated our feelings of hopelessness. *Doctor Faustus* made it clear that as artists Fuzz and I were never going to catch up with the twentieth century; we knew already that we were starting from too far behind. There was that picture of artistic society that Mann drew. We could never imagine knowing a group of people who discussed art, literature, music, and philosophy with such serious but easy familiarity, who thought of these as necessary and inevitable parts of daily existence. And then there was the problem of making a living. This was the bugbear that our parents and teachers and everyone else always held up as the direst threat. "Can't nobody make a living tooting a damn horn." That was the way it was put to us, without let or surcease.

"Tooting a horn," Fuzz said. "They don't know what it means, *to compose*. What do they think? That I sit around playing the trumpet and then write down whatever happens to come out of the bell?"

I nodded my disgusted agreement, though in fact that was the procedure he sometimes employed.

"These people are philistines," he said. "People with red noses are philistines." He loved pronouncements of this sort. "People with long narrow heads are narrow-minded," "women with soft biceps are self-indulgent," and so forth.

In some important respects we failed to recognize, our own backgrounds were much like that of Mann's hero, Adrian Leverkühn. Canton was actually a smaller and newer Kaisersaschern. Mann's humorous accounts of Kretschmar's lectures about music to an audience which had never heard that music strikes home. The one piece of classical music we had any intimacy with was Handel's *Messiah* in its annual performance at Central Methodist Church. We sang in the choir there (a good place to meet girls) and knew large parts of the score.

Handel was all right; we agreed that *The Messiah* was *good herbs*. But of the modern composers mentioned by Mann—Debussy, Stravinsky, Mahler, Schoenberg—we had heard not so much as a note. We read what accounts of these composers we could find in books and had to imagine how the music described might sound. Fuzz played the scraps of harmonic illustration on the piano, but these were so fragmentary as to be merely puzzling—and frustrating.

But the age of recordings was about to dawn. My parents gave me a record player as a Christmas present, and one summer I saved up my allowance until it amounted to thirty-two dollars, hitchhiked the twenty miles into Asheville, and returned with a record set, four 12-inch 78 rpm records in an album, an Artur Rodzinski version of Sibelius' Fourth Symphony. This was the closest thing to modern music I could find, and it served well enough. Full of dissonance and drama, flashing with inchoate phrase, the Fourth still seems to me a lovely and surprisingly sturdy piece of work. We played it until we knew every note we could hear by heart. Fuzz transcribed some sections by ear for piano—a difficult task, considering Sibelius' reliance on orchestral color—and began to analyze the harmonies.

Sibelius' Fourth Symphony must stand at the farthest pole from the kind of music Mann describes Leverkühn as writing. We were aware of this fact as soon as we heard the first bars, but it was *modern*, it was not Handel; and it was all we had. I was not able to hear any of the work of Schoenberg, Berg, or Webern until I went to Duke University. Berg's Violin Concerto, when I first played a recording, sounded just as I thought it ought to; it was a fine and recognizable shock to the nervous system.

I have said that though Fuzz and I were close we were not warm friends. It is surprising that we were able to remain friends at all. In the first place I was jealous of his art; I envied the inaccessibility of the discipline. Anybody can write down sentences and phrases and lines of whatever they may choose to regard as poetry, but in order to write music you must be able to read the notation easily and you must have facility at the piano. You must study harmony, theory, counterpoint, and the rest of it. (With what was left of my thirty-two dollars after buying the recording, I bought a present for Fuzz, Walter Piston's textbook on counterpoint.) I envied him the vocabulary of music. How satisfying to speak of roots, progressions, intervals, tritones, passing notes! These words implied logic and system, they were part of a secret language, they had magical aura which the vocabulary of literary composition lacks. There was an expressive stringency about them that I most thirstily desired. (In my senior year in high school I found what I was looking for in the work of Baudelaire and Rimbaud, but I never told Fuzz, or anyone else in Canton, of these researches.)

Where there was envy on my side there was inescapably an attitude of superiority on his. He had about him something of Leverkühn's famous "coldness." I see that in writing this account I still call my friend Fuzz, but he never spoke of me or addressed me otherwise than as "Chappell." When he showed me his compositions he would point out certain harmonic progressions that had given him anxiety. "See here. You see that, don't you?" But I didn't see, and when he played the passage on the piano I couldn't hear what difficulties he had overcome. I was a rotten music student. At age eleven I told my teacher that I was giving up piano lessons for baseball. When she said that I was making a grave mistake, I couldn't help wondering if she'd seen me play baseball. Compared to the way I performed at shortstop, I was a Paderewski at the keyboard. I knew, however, that I had no talent for the instrument.

Our friendship was more harshly distressed by the fact that we fell in love with the same girls. This happened twice, and the second time was important. Her name was Doris; she was a slender blonde with hopes of becoming a concert pianist. She had a friendly manner and, as many musicians do, a keen appreciation of the ridiculous. I met her at Duke, where I had gone in order to study writing with Dr. William

Blackburn and to continue my friendship with Fuzz. But he had transferred to Boston Conservatory, carrying on his relationship with Doris at what must have been exasperating long distance.

So I met Doris and, as I say, fell in love. There is no point in detailing the adolescent agonies this situation led to, the heated and fugal conversations, the awkward tears, the nocturnal soul-searchings —all that lush rhodomontade of the emotions that matures young people even as it shows them in the most embarrassing light. Enough to say that it eventually led to the final break between Fuzz and me. Fuzz and Doris married and moved to Boston, and over the next two decades we had almost no contact. I married Susan, and the kind of happiness I found in marriage did not make me anxious to resume the relationship. And I had more luck with my writing than Fuzz had with his music, so that his accustomed sense of superiority might have been strenuously tried. Equality would have made the old arrangement impossible to carry on.

Fuzz and Doris were not so happy, I think. They broke up. A few years after the break Doris died of cancer. Three years later Fuzz dropped dead on a Boston street from the result, as I understand, of an earlier household accident. The details have never been given me.

Now this is a sad story, inconclusive, and maybe without clear meaning. But time and memory are assiduous searchers of meaning, and the long history still carves various shapes upon my life. Fuzz lives in my memory not as the later figure of bitterness but as I knew him at the beginning, as the earnest student and dedicated artist and faithful friend. He stands as a sort of Leverkühn, and the latter years that I know nothing about, the years of absence, underscore the resemblance for me.

It is all very odd. Reading the novel again, I can see that Mann has rather lightly characterized his composer, giving him a limited and strictly adhered to set of traits and a smallish number of leitmotif phrases. Leverkühn is often only Nietzsche in disguise, a fact I was but dimly aware of in my high school years, and the novel is more concerned with his intellectual stance than with his personality; a description of his artistic career takes the place of character development. It is surprising that Leverkühn comes alive for any reader; yet if a reader is predisposed, if he already possess certain longings and tendencies, then the doomed composer is a formidably living figure. Leverkühn is attractive, and not least of his attractions is his fatal illness. Mann is at some pains to undercut the inevitably romantic situation with his cosmopolitan irony (which sometimes become a bit wearisome) and with his clinical detachment. Syphilis is not shown to be desirable. . . . And yet Leverkühn's plight has its Byronic aspects; Mann's composer acquires—it is presented as a deliberate act—a *destiny*. The term of twenty-four years is prescribed to his striving and I liked the notion of mortality as taskmaster; it seemed to me that one might accomplish a great deal if he was certain that he had but a short time to do it in.

We hear that art is long and life is short, but that is not exactly the way things are. Even an adolescent artist discovers that art is *infinitely* long and that a human life burns all its candescence in what seems a millisecond. The undertaking is vast, the tools flimsy and minuscule, and it takes a lifetime to acquire even these makeshift tools. If an artist could acquire all the resources and techniques that had ever been devised, these would still not be enough; and he has time to acquire only a pitiful few of them. Perhaps that is why so many artists set out so early to establish a distinctive manner; manner is an adroit way of covering up those shocking deficiencies that sometimes only an artist is aware of.

So that a modern artist throws his whole personal life into the breach, hoping to make up with the intense qualities of that raw material what time does not allow him to master in the way of more objective technique and stratagem. It is not a matter of autobiography or confession; it is the using of one's very marrow and soul as a means of expression. It is not a matter of hapless suffering for the work but of a disciplined suffering inside the work; it is a matter of careful self-destruction in order that destruction may lead to absorption. It is perhaps heroic in a minor and foolishly quixotic way, and it is not healthy, but it is more common than most of us ordinarily imagine.

Leverkühn's dilemma may lead a young artist to the conclusion that what probably cannot be done in a leisurely and well-considered lifetime may be done under duress of terrifying pressure. One must, however, choose his disease; syphilis is uncertain in its effects, and anyway has become curable. Like a great many others, I chose alcohol—it was only partly a conscious decision—and found it unsatisfactory.

In fact, I lived to find the whole notion unsatisfactory. In order to become a Leverkühn, a Rimbaud, a Hart Crane, one has not only to cultivate a certain range of proclivities but also to possess at the outset a certain set of talents and an unshakable sense of self-importance. The self-importance is not so hard to come by, but the talents may be entirely alien. Without these, the self-importance leads merely to a crass boorishness. It is impossible to destroy yourself without painfully damaging other people. Has anyone remarked what a boor Leverkühn is? Mann gives him such aristocratic airs, such a romantic aura, that we are likely to overlook this unwholesome fact about him—just as his biographer, Serenus Zeitblom, is careful to do. Yet a boor is what he is, and often in the most embarrassing ways.

There came a time when I had to distance myself from the figure of Adrian Leverkühn, and I have to say that there was some sense of despair in doing so. For this decision—and again, it was only partly a conscious decision—had to be based on a recognition of the deficiencies and limitations of my talent. It is clear that I am no figure of literary "importance," that I have not the means and no longer any desire to transform the outer contours of the art. In my case adventurous experimentation with form seems to lead to overintellectualization, to desiccation, of content. I have got to where I should like for my work to be humane, and I do not much care if it even becomes sentimental. Perhaps it would be nice if a few artists in our time decided to rejoin the human race, and I think that I would be glad to do so, however much I disagree with its politics.

New heroes come to me, figures I wish I had known how to long to emulate as a lad. Spinoza is a lovely and brilliant man; there is more worth for me in Robert Browning than in a platoon of John Berrymans; I don't see how Carl Ruggles can be much less a composer than Mann's imaginary figure; Chaucer is a supreme artist, full of grace and light and wisdom and humanity. Is he really so much less a poet than Dante? Is consistent System so much greater a good than superabundant spirit?

As soon as I set these rhetorical questions down, they no longer look rhetorical. There are probably sufficient critical reasons to prefer Dante over Chaucer and maybe even Berryman over Browning. . . . But I have been through that, and it has seemed important to me to set, however regretfully, strict critical necessity aside. It is only my temperament that makes me say so, of course, but sooner or later an artist must take account of his temperament as one of his basic materials. There are already so many artists whom one admires more than he likes. Am I the only reader who finds in the achievement of James Joyce something that is—well, a little *obtuse?* Who sees Chekhov as being in some intimate way not only better, but greater?

Probably not.

Probably I do not always think so myself. I may distance myself from Leverkühn, but I cannot cut loose from him entirely; and never would I abjure him. Mann, by means of his hero, succeeded in making the hard discipline desirable and exciting. Leverkühn's disdain of easy popularity is a trait worth emulation, though it may lead to a lack of proper sympathy on the part of the artist. Mann thought of himself as actually "composing" Leverkühn's music with his lyrical, analytic, and critical descriptions, and the complexity and gravity he ascribes to these imaginary works might serve well as models for every serious artist. (I would almost be willing to bet that these descriptions actually did influence later composers like Penderecki and Stockhausen.) Of course, the final descent into madness would be attractive to adolescents; it is striking, melodramatic, and to the unwary young it looks like destiny with a capital D. It wouldn't be fun, but it would give one's life importance. Wouldn't it? Somehow?

It may seem from my confused and truncated account that Mann's ceaseless irony was lost upon Fuzz and me. Richard Winston has complained that the English translations reduce Mann's humorous and glittering style to a monotonous level of coyness. With my extremely poor German, I cannot answer to that objection. But I can attest to the fact that his larger ironies and even some of his smaller jokes were effective. We could not hear in that prose the multitudinous allusions to Goethe, Spengler, Schiller, but we did know—I can't say how—that Leverkühn was modeled on Nietzsche and our thorough mountain Protestant heritage allowed us to identify the character Ehrenfried Kumpf with Martin Luther. We had no doubt that Mann drew the sad members of his "Kridwiss circle" from people he had known personally and we recognized that the ideas promulgated by "Unruhe," "Vogler," "Breisacher," "Daniel zur Höhe," and the others were proto-Nazi ideas, although we had never heard of, for example, Stefan George. These were the first years of McCarthyism, after all, the early 1950s, when a distant and pallid version of Nazi ideology was establishing its first public and undeniably permanent foothold in American political folkways.

But politics did not much engage the two high school boys; we were after the novel's high-flown talk of artistic aims and methods. On the technical side, Fuzz was much taken—only intellectually, because he couldn't hear any—with the idea of atonal music. The notion of the twelve-tone system he rejected because it appeared in principle boring and mechanical. Leverkühn's practice of tying his compositions to literary and artistic works seemed enticing, and we decided, naturally, that I would supply the literary matter for the music of Fincher—just as Zeitblom supplied Leverkühn. I could look forward to a lifetime of writing mocking philosophic operettas and mystic oratorios.

As a would-be writer, I was overwhelmed by the richness of thought and technique in Mann. I admired unstintingly his proliferation of theme, his seriousness of purpose, his ability to widen to the farthest horizons the implications of his narrative. I envied his ability to draw a whole stratum of society, to people the book with eccentrics and caricatures who were still believable as characters. I envied most of all the profound reservoir of cultural history he was able to utilize.

The latter resource of the great German convinced me, though, that I must never never try directly to write like Thomas Mann. It was obvious that he possessed a wealth of background that one cannot attain to merely by reading books. (Now it is obvious too that he likes to parade this irritating fact before his readers.) Neither was his manner appealing for me to attempt to imitate. An aspiring American writer may have a talent for sarcasm, and even for humor, but it is rare that he will have one for irony. I had not the patience for his slow and excruciating drama; I desired more immediate and more striking effects. Mann's richness combined with the economy and brilliance of lyric poetry: that was what I wanted.

It goes without saying that I was never able to achieve these contradictory aspirations. Ten years later I formulated a temporarily workable evasion of the problem, though it was hardly satisfactory. I decided that the intellectual structure of a novel, its larger themes and purposes, could be drawn up outside the literal narrative, could be determined in the preliminary working stages and then abandoned except as a large system of reference. No need to talk directly about theme; since it was the motive force for the story, the Ur-impulse, it would necessarily *seep through* into the narrative, which could then maintain as clean and irresistible a line as a novel by Dashiell Hammett. That was what I aimed at in my books, *The Inkling* and *Dagon*.

I did not foresee some of the unfortunate consequences of this method: that I would be producing works which even for the most forbearing and well-intentioned readers might seem unmercifully brief, puzzling, hermetic, unpleasantly singleminded, humorless and inhumane. To enclose a story to this strict extent is to give it something of the atmosphere of a cruel scientific experiment whose purposes are largely unguessable. *The Inkling* is a story about a boy who represents pure Will and his sister who is Appetite; I had to keep telling my friends that the last thing in my mind when I wrote the book was Faulkner (that is certainly true!), and that the story is something in the nature of an allegory about Rimbaud and Verlaine. I can hardly blame them for deciding to go on thinking that I had simply ripped off Faulkner; I would probably have made a better book by doing so. Yet at that time I felt that I saw the largest conflicts of our western societies as determined by the antagonistic forces of will and appetite, and it seemed to me that the two unhappy poets embodied this antagonism. I was heartened to find, some years after the publication of *The Inkling*, an essay by Wallace Fowlie in which ideas identical with mine were iterated.

Composing *Dagon*, however, I could find no way to avoid exposition of the ideas behind the story. In the interest of economy, however, I put all these in one place, in an indigestible lump of a sermon given by the minister-protagonist, Peter Leland. This awkward decision was no solution. Any reader who skipped that one chapter, intimidated by its strident boredom, would have no opportunity of seeing what the story was about. It seems that many readers had the good sense to leap over that passage but not quite enough to forego reading the rest of the book, with the result that they came out baffled and irritated. The logical solution would be to infuse the premises into the narrative in dramatic fashion, little by little. But I didn't have enough confidence to allow my characters to talk about ideas. I was afraid that they would all sound confused and overbearing, the way I sound toward the end of a long evening party.

But I do not disown these two stories, nor anything else I have written. Their failures proceed from honest personal deficiencies on my part, and not from lack of care or toil; and there have been—and it now seems that there may continue to be—readers better qualified than I to point out their shortcomings. We are speaking, after all, of books that were published some twenty years ago, and when I think of them I think of Adrian Leverkühn and the kind of goals I was able to derive from that mythical figure.

I think of my friend Fuzz Fincher too. He lives on in me as a not-very-ghostly confidant, and I am likely to refer certain compositional problems to his skepticism and highmindedness and thorough sense of the ridiculous. I think about the music he must have written during the decades when we had lost touch and wonder if any of it might be preserved. I have not heard so much as a note. Yet I believe that it must be good music, serious and well made, full of interest and surprise, and even if it has not been preserved it exists in my imagination as pure in its ideas as Leverkühn's *Apocalypsis* or his *Lamentations of Doctor Faustus*.

BIBLIOGRAPHY

It Is Time, Lord. New York: Atheneum, 1963.

The Inkling. New York: Harcourt, Brace & World, 1965.

Dagon. New York: Harcourt, Brace & World, 1968.

The World Between the Eyes. Baton Rouge: Louisiana State University Press, 1971.

The Gaudy Place. New York: Harcourt Brace Jovanovich, 1972.

River. Baton Rouge: Louisiana State University Press, 1975.

The Man Twice Married to Fire. Greensboro, North Carolina: Unicorn Press, 1977.

Bloodfire. Baton Rouge: Louisiana State University Press, 1978.

Awakening to Music. Davidson, North Carolina: Briarpatch Press, 1979.

Wind Mountain. Baton Rouge: Louisiana State University Press, 1979.

Earthsleep. Baton Rouge: Louisiana State University Press, 1980.

Moments of Light. Los Angeles: The New South Company, 1980.

Driftlake: A Lieder Cycle. Emory, Virginia: Iron Mountain Press, 1981.

Midquest. Baton Rouge: Louisiana State University Press, 1981.

Castle Tzingal. Baton Rouge: Louisiana State University Press, 1984.

I Am One of You Forever. Baton Rouge: Louisiana State University Press, 1985.

Source. Baton Rouge: Louisiana State University Press, 1985.